ADVANCE PRAISE

"In an important book about the events of the 2008 financial crisis, Øygard writes prose that is as clear and economical as that found in an Icelandic saga – and the story he tells is no less dramatic."

EVA JOLY

Member of the European Parliament, former French magistrate, former advisor to the Ministry of Justice and Ecclesiastical Affairs, Icelandic government and former French presidential candidate

"This is the amazing story of a radical break with previous established international practice on how financial crises should be addressed which proved amazingly successful and altered financial crisis management practice. It's told by an insider with an outsider's perspective; it's frank, colourful, very personal and it even manages to be a fun read. I just regret that I didn't have the opportunity to read it before the Swedish financial crises of 1992 and 2008."

LEIF PAGROTSKY

Former Swedish Minister for Industry and Trade, and former Swedish Minister for Culture and Education

"*In the Combat Zone of Finance* tells a story with two parts: the first part is the classic story of a bubble. Here, nothing is new; it is just more extreme. The other is the story of the first European banking crisis of the single market. As this market is gigantic, the impact was immense, both politically and economically."

MÁR GUÐMUNDSSON

Former Governor, Central Bank of Iceland

"There is no better way to study and try to understand the dynamics of the largest financial crisis since 1929 than by reading the accounts of the key leaders that had to manage, mitigate and ultimately resolve the crisis. Svein Harald Øygard's book on how he handled the crisis in Iceland – the country most affected by the 2008 financial crisis – is an immensely important story. This book serves, in part, to remind us all what to do to avoid such catastrophes in the future."

DR CHRISTIAN CASAL

Director, McKinsey & Company and former Leader of EMEA Banking Practice, McKinsey & Company

"A thorough and analytical book which also has a free narrative form characterized by the author's own encounter with the financial industry, the people and the politics in Iceland. It gives economists a rare opportunity to look into the financial world."

BJORN SKOGSTAD AAMO

Former Director, the Financial Supervisory Agency of Norway

"The story is incredible (no dry economics!), with sharp observations and exceptionally precise sarcasm. It's simply fun reading and, of course, important with lots of lessons to learn from!"

HARALD MAGNUS ANDREASSEN

Chief Economist, Sparebank1 Markets and Norway's highest-ranking chief economist

“This is a book that cannot easily be placed in a single genre. In part it is Øygard’s memoirs, in part it is an analysis of financial and economic crises and in part it is an account of the historical crisis of Iceland. The book is interesting, educational and entertaining.”

TERJE ERIKSTAD

Journalist, *Nordic Business Daily*

“Imagine if, out of the blue, you were asked to be the Governor of the Central Bank of Iceland. Many would consider this strange, especially at a time when the country was bankrupt, the people had taken to the streets and everything appeared hopeless. Even stranger would be to accept the job. That is precisely what Svein Harald Øygard did, and he has written an exceptionally good book about this experience.”

TOM STAAVI

Head of Information, Finans Norge and
former Editor, *Dine Penger*

DRAUMALANDIÐ

Ó, leyf mér þig að leiða
til landsins fjalla heiða
með sælu sumrin löng,
þar angar blóma breiða,
við blíðan fuglasöng.

Þar aðeins yndi fann ég,
þar aðeins við mig kann ég,
þar batt mig tryggðaband;
því þar er allt sem ann ég,
það er mitt draumaland.

THE LAND OF DREAMS

O, let me you lead
to the high moors of that land
where endless summer reigns.
The air with flowers fragrant
and filled with birdsong sweet.

There only I find delight,
there only I belong.
With steadfast bands it binds me,
for there is all I cherish
There is the land of my dreams.

(*Guðmundur Magnússon/Jón Trausti*)

Published by
LID Publishing Limited
The Record Hall, Studio 204,
16-16a Baldwins Gardens,
London EC1N 7RJ, UK

info@lidpublishing.com
www.lidpublishing.com

A member of:
BPR
Business Publishers Roundtable

www.businesspublishersroundtable.com

Published in co-operation with Hegnar Media and in agreement with Stilton Literary Agency.

Printed in Great Britain by TJ International
ISBN: 978-1-912555-65-9

Cover and page design: Matthew Renaudin

SVEIN HARALD ØYGARD

IN THE COMBAT ZONE OF FINANCE

AN INSIDER'S ACCOUNT OF THE FINANCIAL CRISIS

LID

MADRID | MEXICO CITY | LONDON
NEW YORK | BUENOS AIRES
BOGOTA | SHANGHAI | NEW DELHI

CONTENTS

FOREWORD

A UNIQUE OPPORTUNITY

Everything came crashing down: the banks, the currency, the companies, the number of jobs, the economy, the values of most, the government and the Central Bank. Beautiful Iceland, a wealthy country with a proud thousand-year history, became the tattered symbol of the 2008 global financial crisis – a combat zone of global finance in a world of debt.

However, amazingly, as the dust settled, the post-crisis debt level of the country's households, its companies and of the state itself ended up far, far below pre-crisis levels. In a sample of 30 countries, Iceland in 2007 had the highest overall debt level to GDP ratio of all. From 2007 to 2019, Iceland's debt ratio fell more than in any other country. Other countries hit by the financial crisis sank deeper in a sea of debt. Iceland didn't.

Imagine a medical experiment. A hundred patients are offered different treatments. One recovers quicker and becomes healthier than any, the patient that by some measures initially suffered the most. The only one that took the completely opposite cure. The initial condition, the cure, the outcome and the relevance of the lessons must be understood. The case clearly warrants a closer look.

Of the 47 bankers who saw a jail from the inside due to their actions in the global crisis, 25 were Icelanders. The US, the birthplace of the crisis, jailed one. The UK none. Most countries desperately aimed for calmness and an illusion of reliability, while in Iceland there was nothing left to lose. Iceland provided us all with an opportunity to see what had been going on behind the shiny facades and to see how our global institutions really behaved. In contrast to other countries, in which the inner secrets remained shrouded, Iceland lifted bank secrecy laws and made a real attempt to unearth the crimes and the wrongdoings. And there were many. One scheme, though, stands out.

What's more, Iceland defied the perceived rules of finance and became the only country where all systemic banks collapsed and no bailout was even attempted, where the currency adjusted freely, where money got locked in with capital control and the creditors were forced to shoulder the burden, hence where the state did what it had to and the private sector was forced to adapt.

Few, if any, cases offer as many insights about the nature of financial catastrophes, from their origin through the inevitable crash, into the recovery, and until the last crisis measures are abolished – in this case more than ten years later – as the Iceland saga. In no other place could the inner workings of global finance be seen more clearly. And as long as some countries, companies, households and banks rely on large accumulations of debt, this is knowledge that unfortunately one day will become relevant to your country, your savings, your job and your life.

I was appointed interim Governor of the Central Bank of Iceland, Seðlabanki Íslands, after everything had collapsed. I was parachuted into the crisis-ridden country, becoming possibly the first, and surely one of only a handful, of noncitizens ever to head an independent Central Bank.

At the press conference on my first day in office, I said that our joint ambition should be to change Iceland from a symbol of the financial crisis to a symbol of recovery. As Iceland did.

My role gave me a unique vantage point from which to observe Iceland, its people and its institutions, as well as the forces of global banking, finance and economics. I saw how institutions and leaders behaved, from inside the system, during one of its worst crises. I could review what had previously happened and what happened in the midst of the crisis, and I had a base to observe the amazing events that followed.

When I arrived in Iceland in February 2009, I found a financial crash site. The entrance to the Central Bank had for some time been guarded by riot police, even in peaceful Iceland. I stayed until the fall of 2009 and later contributed to a 2012 study on growth strategies for Iceland. To be clear, I made only a small contribution to Iceland's recovery. But for a short while, I was immersed.

In this book, I tell the story of Iceland's remarkable journey and place it in contrast to the journeys of other crisis-hit countries. The first third of the book covers the run-up to the crisis and illustrates how hard it is to see that a crisis is looming, but also shows what to look for. The second part covers the time of desperation after the crash and shows the importance of decisive action, the breadth of tools available, the importance of mobilization and the amazing capacity for change that can be unleashed. The last third covers the years of recovery and shows the importance of creativity and persistence. It also shows how one may free oneself from debt built through four decades. If one can write the law, that is. In many ways the most remarkable part of the saga.

I interviewed some 90 people as I researched this book: Icelandic and non-Icelandic government ministers; governors and Central Bankers; top level employees of the International Monetary Fund (IMF); bankers and traders, some active, some prosecuted or jailed; investigators; grass-roots activists; hedge fund managers; debt dealers; and negotiators. Many are leading global players in their fields. Many have never spoken out before. Some told me too much. Most are referred to in present tense, as the interviews reflect their current views.

My focus is on the systemic issues, less so on individuals and their actions. I tell this story through the voices of the people who were engaged, on all sides, through those difficult times. I don't name most of them, but the list of interviewees can be found in the appendix. The book is written as narrative nonfiction. The appendix summarizes the references and sources of data.

The three leading banks in Iceland had grown to an enormous size over the course of half a decade. They defaulted in three days. The third-largest bankruptcy in the history of mankind occurred in a city with 150,000 inhabitants. How such growth could occur is in itself a mystery and is surely a story that provides many lessons.

After the collapse, Iceland tore apart its biggest banks. It applied a US model for bank restructuring that put the interests of depositors first, leaving creditors and investors to fight for the remains. The model was vigorously opposed by many, but later inspired the rules that now govern Western banks.

Different countries and institutions responded in very different ways. The British and the Dutch, backed by the EU, behaved like a pack of wolves. The UK put Icelandic institutions on its official list of terrorist organizations when Iceland was on its knees. The Netherlands and the UK took Iceland to court to force draconian terms, but Iceland won. As systemic interests were threatened, American and European institutions took massive executive action, with interventionism at the speed and precision of a military operation, as formulated by Professor Adam Tooze in his book *Crashed*. But the US placed Iceland and all but 12 other currency areas *outside* the perimeters of its defendable fortress of money.

Russia's Vladimir Putin was launched as a would-be saviour. China earned itself a stepping-stone into the Western financial system. Sweden, Denmark, Norway, Finland and Poland graciously provided support for Iceland – and booked a profit in the end. The IMF eagerly built a showcase, paradoxically with delayed fiscal austerity and without bank bailouts or structural reforms. But, with capital controls that were formalized and made part of the IMF programme. Hence, the rubble left behind from the disaster was available as Iceland was rebuilt.

Equally amazing, the tools tested in Iceland were eventually included in the IMF toolbox for ailing nations. Indeed, little Iceland changed the mighty IMF more than the IMF changed Iceland.

The European Central Bank (ECB) and Seðlabanki had become the banks' main sources of cash in their final days. The ECB got its money back. Seðlabanki suffered losses, the Republic's largest direct loss from the crisis.

The three leading banks had sold the Icelandic currency, the kronas, from Seðlabanki as they desperately chased foreign currency. Thus, after the crisis, a vast amount of kronas floated around in the global financial system. Seven years later, however, the kronas were clawed back – by the Republic. From formidable opponents.

Twenty of the 50 largest US hedge funds came to Iceland in search of profit as the country's banks imploded and the economy crashed. Some made billions. Others got burned. Quite remarkably, they made concessions, zeroing out the losses of the Republic and turning them into a net gain. Even the superpowers of finance had to give in. Their behaviour, contributions, strengths and weaknesses were revealed.

This saga will take you to the frontiers of finance, where financial instruments that were first celebrated later turned into weapons of economic mass destruction, and then, once again, came in handy. The crisis was extraordinary. And so were many of the tools used in the recovery.

Iceland is a small, open, market-oriented economy with its own currency and economic policy institutions. The identities of most players who were active in Iceland have by now been revealed. Furthermore, in a country like this, it is easy to see the connections between the fortunes of households and companies and the workings of the economy and the impact of the global forces that swept over Iceland. No other country in the world offers better access to economic data and modelling on debt, income and living conditions. Economists can perform studies in Iceland that cannot be done anywhere else. The public debate is lively and the political processes transparent.

A Norwegian version of this book was published in May 2019 and an Icelandic version in September 2019, both with some tailoring to local readers. This English version is adapted for international readers and includes multiple updates.

Two editors have provided invaluable support: Mary Kuntz and Anna Herzog. I have called on many to provide input, test ideas and to read through the manuscripts. A big thank you to all of you.

I also want to thank the staff of Seðlabanki for the openness with which they received me, despite some initial reservations. They put in a tremendous effort throughout the long journey to recovery, working long hours, often during periods when forward progress was hard to see. These men and women and their counterparts at the institutions that supported their efforts are truly the ones who deserve the credit for making Iceland a symbol of recovery and, yes, for saving Iceland.

However, the sacrifices and the efforts of Gudmundur Þór and his likes were what mattered the most in the end.

Svein Harald
sveinharaldoygard@gmail.com
September 2019

CHAPTER 1

IN THE YEAR 1262, THE CHIEFTAINS OF ICELAND MET

Thingvellir is one of my favourite places.

It lies east of Reykjavik and is surrounded by layers and layers of black volcanic rock. Some sections have been spared from recent eruptions, and these grass-covered meadows seem even greener in contrast to the barren rock.

Europe and North America rest on separate tectonic plates, the Eurasian and the North American. The plates are drifting apart, by up to 25 millimetres on average per year on the Reykjanes Ridge. Thingvellir is located right at the spot where the plates are separating. In the gap, where Thingvellir lies, Iceland emerges and grows, fuelled by new eruptions.

Somewhat symbolically, a small canyon crosses through Thingvellir, as though demarcating the rift created by the continued separation of Eurasia and North America. Here you can sense our common history.

Starting in the year 930, the Icelandic chieftains made their way each year, many by horseback, from all corners of Iceland to convene in Thingvellir. They met friends. They fought. They showed off their daughters as they came of age for marriage. They set up court, settled their disputes and made joint decisions. In this way, they formed the world's first parliament.

This was an impressive feat at a time when most societies settled disputes in far cruder ways. The chieftains agreed on legislation and formed an effective legal system. The executive branch of the government, though, was lagging already then. A strong clan and strong alliances were needed to ensure your rights.

The 'Age of the Sturlungs', among the bloodiest and most violent periods in the history of Iceland, began around 1220. Powerful chieftains, *Goðis*, amassed followers and clashed in battles. They protected everyone in their clans, fighting off all threats and avenging wrongdoing against their clans, or *ætt*, as they are called in the Norse language. Many were the feuds. The country was hard to rule.

In 1262, the chieftains negotiated a treaty that would steer Iceland's fortunes for the next 600 years: the *Gamli sáttmáli*, or *Old Covenant*. It was an agreement with King Haakon IV Haakonsson of Norway and his son and successor, Magnus VI, the Lawgiver. It gave the Norwegian king the right to tax the Icelanders. In exchange, the Icelanders received a code of laws. They also retained the right to make their own laws. In Iceland's 19th century fight for independence, history became the sharpest weapon, as in no other fight for freedom. The right from 1262 to decide their laws had never been ceded, the Icelanders proclaimed.

The agreement of 1262 also guaranteed peace, ensuring that the Icelanders' Viking ships could sail freely between Norway and Iceland. Haakon IV also promised shipments to Iceland. Critical supplies, such as barley. To brew beer. Forever. These shipments, however, often did not arrive. Some say that this Norwegian debt was the first debt in Iceland not honoured, unmentionably large if calculated up until today with compounded interest rates.

With the settlement of 1262, Norwegians and Icelanders were to have equal rights in each other's countries. However, one paragraph of the covenant read: "*... að íslenskir séu lögmenn og sýslumenn á landi voru.*"

Loosely translated, all senior civil servant positions in Iceland were to be held by Icelanders, who had to be members of the powerful clans, by now reduced from about 40 to just a handful. The paragraph had been negotiated to retain the power of their *Goðis*.

And, being part of an agreement with the King of Norway, it definitely meant "no Norwegians."

Seven hundred and forty-seven years passed by.

Then, in the dark, late evening of 26 February 2009, the Icelandic Parliament, Althing, passed a new law relating to the Central Bank of Iceland. A paragraph was added to the legislation between the second and third readings. It ensured that the restriction of 1262 would not apply to the temporary appointment of a Central Bank governor. In the even later hours of the night, the Icelandic President, Ólafur Ragnar Grímsson, approved the law. Early the next morning, on 27 February, the new interim governor was appointed.

He was Norwegian.

He was me.

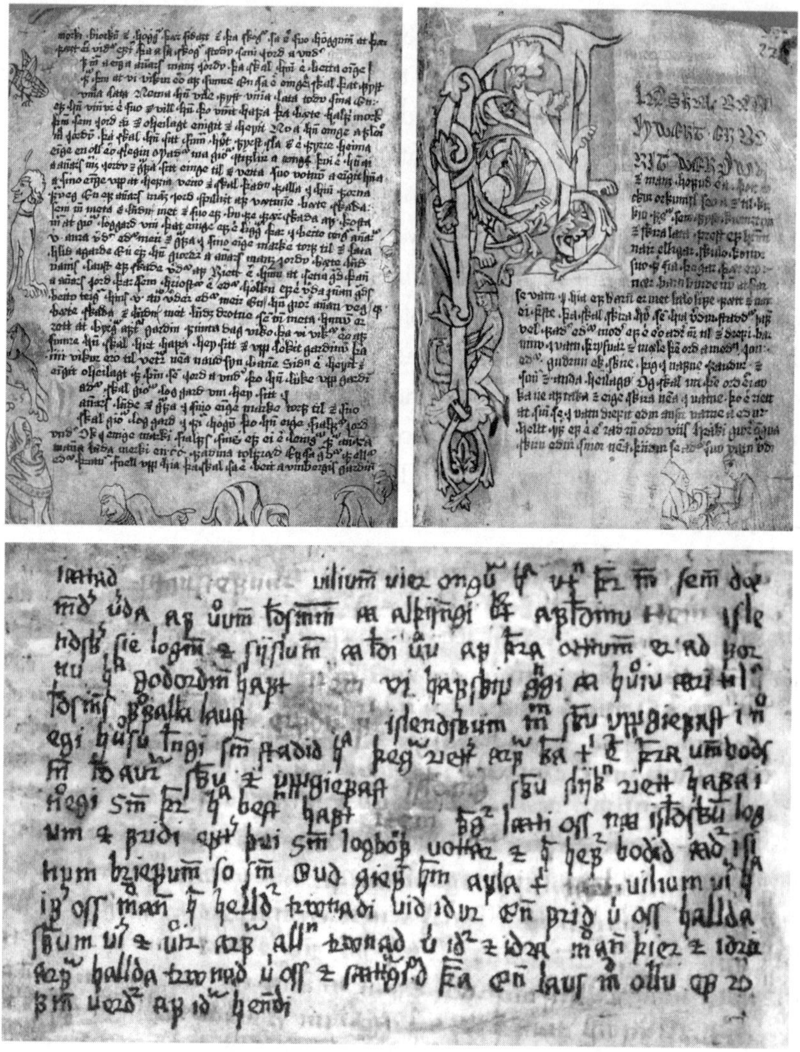

↳ **Examples of Norse handwritten manuscripts from Árni Magnússon's collection.** At the bottom is one of the oldest known records of the Old Covenant. From the end of the second line on it reads; *"Item isle- ndskir ... Item islendskir sie logmenn ok syslumenn a landi voru af þeirra ættum er ad fornu hafa godordin haft,"* which means, "In addition, laymen and civil servants in our country must be Icelandic, of the families as in old times that have had the role of *goðorðene*," referring to the heads of the clans who had a permanent seat on the Althing.

PARACHUTED INTO THE EPICENTRE OF THE FINANCIAL CRISIS

If you count the defaults of the three largest Icelandic banks in three days as one, you get the *third-largest* default in the history of mankind. All in just one small city, in one small country.

Even taken one at a time, the defaults were notable. On Tuesday and Thursday in one week in October 2008, the two largest, Glitnir and Kaupthing, defaulted on their debts, immediately ranking among the top ten collapses ever recorded. Both were ahead of infamous Enron. Kaupthing even outranked Washington Mutual.

Add in the third bank, Landsbanki, which collapsed in between the other two, and you have *three of the seven largest* debt defaults by financial institutions globally in 2008, the peak year of the financial crisis.

I was in Oslo in early February 2009, standing at the intersection of the streets named after the Norwegian kings Haakon VII and Olav V, when my phone beeped. The text asked me to call the secretary general of the Ministry of Finance of Norway, Tore Eriksen.

He had a small question: "Can we propose you to become the new Central Bank Governor of Iceland?"

Like most Norwegians, I have a deep admiration for Iceland and the Icelanders. They are famously hardworking. We romantically think of them as our siblings. With their Viking ships, they embarked on a rough journey 1,000 years ago in search of new opportunities. They were the tough ones. We were the ones who stayed behind.

Tore remembers that I first went quiet.

But then he got my answer: "Life is too short to not say yes to such an ask."

I went on to ask advice after the fact from two colleagues at McKinsey & Company, the consultancy where I was a senior partner. One colleague quickly affirmed my yes. The other advised against.

He only saw risks.

In my old, dusty notebook from 2009, with pages beginning to yellow, I can still read my notes from our conversation. One page is marked 10 February 2009. Three points are written on the top of the next page: "Jester on a scene," "Substitute role" and, most seriously, "Mission impossible."

Next, I called an Icelandic colleague living in Denmark. Here the notes read: "Can have impact," "Can help" and "Is a huge opportunity."

But, also a word of warning: "Can create noise." And some advice: "Don't be affiliated with the transition."

As an Icelander, he knew what awaited me.

A thousand thoughts went through my head. On risks. On what might happen. On the role. On the life I was leaving behind. On the impact I could have. I held on to one: the excitement of being at the helm, making a difference in a neighbouring country facing its most serious crisis.

I decided to uphold my yes.

I then called the Global Managing Director of McKinsey at the time, Ian Davis, a man of high principle.

His response was unequivocal. "To such calls of duty, the answer ought to be yes," he said. "As partners in McKinsey, such assignments are among those we should take on."

"I support you – 110%," he added enthusiastically.

And then he paused.

And went silent.

"There will be some nervousness," he continued.

Silence. Again.

"You now need to leave McKinsey.

"You must sell out your shares and terminate all connections. All conflicts of interest, real or perceived, must be avoided.

"And we will immediately assign you a risk team. To manage the risk of the transition and the assignment."

Rightly so, I guess.

Over the coming months, a total of 27 international banks with loans to Icelandic banks would go to court, partly blaming me, requesting compensation for their losses. Most of the 27 were from Austria and Germany, but the list also included banks from Egypt, Japan, Luxembourg, Norway, Switzerland, Taiwan and the UK.

And yes, my priorities had to be clear. My task was to help resolve the challenges of Iceland. At any cost. Nothing else.

The Icelandic government that had been in office since May 2007 had resigned on 1 February 2009, after months of protests following the October 2008 crash. The Central Bank Governor who had served since 2005 stayed on despite around-the-clock protests and with demonstrators hammering on the steel door of the bank. Bodyguards, otherwise totally unheard of in now peaceful Iceland, had to be mobilized.

On its first full day in office, the incoming government requested the bank governor's resignation. He refused twice, claiming the independence of the governorship.

The incoming government had one more tool at hand. It could propose a change to the law governing the Central Bank, which it did. The prior law said the bank should have three governors, of which one was chairman. The new law said the bank would have only one governor.

Who had to be an economist. The then lead governor was a lawyer.

He left the building the day the new law was passed.

Iceland has many highly competent economists. The interim governor, however, would have to be appointed overnight, like a rabbit out of a hat. A foreigner was needed. That way, the government could choose a permanent governor later, through an orderly process with no incumbent again claiming the chair.

In the search for a candidate, the Icelandic Minister of Finance called his Norwegian counterpart.

"Can you suggest a new interim governor for us?" was the ask of the Icelandic minister.

"We thought they were just testing the idea," says Tore Eriksen as he looks back on the events.

"But then the request was repeated."

I met the requirement of being an economist. Furthermore, as a former deputy minister of finance of Norway, I had been one of a handful of people in the top team that worked to resolve the Norwegian macro, currency and banking crisis in the early 1990s.

Apparently, I was on a list in a drawer somewhere in the Ministry of Finance. Maybe I was also considered dispensable, a person with no official role or ties within the government. Someone who would not create any liabilities for Norway.

If all failed.

Someone who would not be seen to be pitting Norway alongside Iceland against the EU in the battle that was then raging. The worst ever since Iceland, Norway and Lichtenstein established their cooperative agreement with the EU in 1993.

Except for a summer job while at university, I had never worked in a Central Bank. And now I was to become Central Bank governor of the country most severely hit by the largest financial crisis since the Great Depression.

The Norwegian Central Bank Governor at the time, Svein Gjedrem, offered me a crash course on how to run a Central Bank. He and Audun Grønn, from the international department, managed my training.

Lesson one was on the details of actually conducting monetary policy; in other words, how to run the process for setting the interest rate. I was impressed, but also a bit overwhelmed. With everything we had on our plate in Iceland, we would have no room for 26 meetings on every interest rate decision, as was customary in Norway. Lesson two was on liquidity management. This meant figuring out the right amount of money to pump into the economy, and how to do it. Next came discussions on macroeconomics, government debt, currency and the banks.

I asked for a deployable SWAT team of economists, a team I could call in case I got stuck. The team was established. Audun was to be the SWAT team leader. An unusual role for an economist.

Fortunately, I never had to dial '911-crisis.' In fact, I found an impressive array of competencies when I entered Seðlabanki.

I only called Gjedrem once. To ask if I had gone crazy.

After my lessons at the Central Bank, I dusted off my old textbooks on monetary theory, my favourite class and highest grade at university 25 years earlier.

A lesson for students in economics: follow your classes closely. One day you may get a call from a faraway country.

Passing the legislative changes through parliament to enable my appointment would likely take some time. But it could also happen at any minute. Hence, I had to be available. I jumped on a plane to Reykjavik.

Some later said I was hidden away in a hotel awaiting my appointment.

Which is not true. Why would I need to hide? No one knew me, and I knew no one.

I walked the streets.

Every Saturday, protesters met in front of Althing in downtown Reykjavik, even on those harsh, cold winter days. Among the crowd was Gudmundur Þór, a farmer and innkeeper who had finally had enough. Enough of what he saw as greedy bankers and poorly disclosed risks. Enough of half-told stories and cover-ups. Enough of no one admitting any responsibility. Himself bankrupt and with fear for what more was to come.

Fed up, Þór had gathered his pots and pans and gone to Reykjavik to protest. It was the first time he had ever taken to the streets.

↳ **From a demonstration in front of the Althing in Reykjavik.**
Source: Halldór Kolbeins / AFP / NTB scanpix

Like many others throughout the country, Þór was swept up in a crisis that was not of his own making. The consequences were both painful and of long duration. He was strong, tall and persistent; but against the powers he now faced, even his Icelandic steadfastness, hardened through thousand years in the North Atlantic, was of little help.

I went to watch the protests against the bankers, the politicians and the governor, and to ask questions. The protestors I met were friendly despite the tensions. No wonder. No one knew that the curious Norwegian asking all the questions was the governor-to-be.

I also invaded the library at the University of Reykjavik, grabbing all the books I could find on macroeconomics and monetary policy and sitting silently in a corner rereading them all. I wondered if the librarian would find the sudden intense interest in monetary policy a bit peculiar, but she showed no reaction.

Unfortunately, most of the challenges I was to face were not described in any textbook. Much less any solution.

A HIRED GUN OF FINANCE

"Øygard Is a Bag of Shit," read the headline of the Norwegian financial news site, E24.

About two months after I started in Seðlabanki, exhausted after a long and wearying work week, I sat all alone in my apartment in rainy Reykjavik one Sunday afternoon, already feeling sorry for myself. Working on my laptop, I opened E24. What stared back at me was to become the site's eighth most-read article in 2009.

In a speech, my predecessor had claimed: "Øygard is so unknown that even Google hasn't heard of him."

This accusation I can live with, I thought. Back then, as today, words like 'volatility', 'collapse', 'conflict' and the rantings of critics were earning more Google hits than 'stability', 'growth', 'cooperation' and words of praise and support.

"Maðurinn kom af fjöllum. Hann vissi ekki hvað þetta var," said one of my predecessor's allies. "The man came from the mountains. He doesn't know what's going on."

I was about to get some cultural enlightenment. In Norway, one heads into the mountains to refresh one's mind, to get an overview of the world and to reflect. It is something that is honoured and celebrated.

In Iceland, to be in the desolate and inhospitable mountains is to be cut off. Historically, all the action happened on the farmland and, more recently, on the sea and in the coffee bars of Reykjavik.

And yes, I had been somewhat naive.

I was surprised that a pre-crisis leader in his party convention speech would spend even a minute on me, rather than focusing on the way forward. After all, the country was in a crisis of historic proportions. And I had no other agenda than to answer a call for help.

The party leadership had hoped to use the convention to set a new direction and to carefully apologize to the people of Iceland. Not to belittle me and the new government. But now, those plans had been blown apart by the recently deposed governor.

I knew that I would be parachuted into a country in the depths of a financial crisis. I didn't know that the drop point selected for me was in a political minefield. My predecessor, a modern chieftain, had been taken out, something the new government later listed among its greatest achievements.

My predecessor had also been prime minister of Iceland for 13 years, up to 2004, after which he took on the position of governor. In his years as leader,

Iceland moved from the top ten to the top five of all countries, measured by GDP per capita. As prime minister, he had supposedly met more US presidents, five in total, than any other head of government. The US presidents came and went, one after the other, while he stayed.

One of the protesters' main demands, though, had been for his removal. Some blamed him for the policy choices that led to the crisis. But he also had many followers and was respected and adored by many. A fighter. A chieftain. Now, he had been forced out through the legal manoeuvres of the minority government.

I had been its instrument. A hired gun of finance, some might say. This was not to be forgotten.

No wonder a foreigner was needed. Little had I known.

But then, I had been warned.

When leaving Norway, Tore Eriksen, the well-read secretary general, had asked me, "Are you ready?"

I answered, "Yes, I have read all the available analyses and reports and prepared a plan."

He repeated his question, "But, are you ready?"

I said, "Yes, as ready as I can be."

He repeated yet again, "But, are you really ready?"

I looked at him in confusion.

He continued, "Have you read the old Norse sagas? Have you read how the tribesmen have their heads chopped off or cleaved down to their molars with an axe?"

He knew the history. He knew what was awaiting me. I had thought his question was a joke.

Now, after two months in my new position, I knew better.

CHAPTER 2

THE TALLEST TOWER IN THE SMALLEST SQUARE

THE FIVE STAGES OF A FINANCIAL CRISIS

"Every banking crisis starts out as a party at which someone has spiked the punch in the crystal bowl."

A banker from London explained the evolution of a crisis to me, building on the punch bowl analogy first used in 1952 by William McChesney Martin Jr, then the US Federal Reserve Governor.

"The full punch bowl is like the banks' access to new money," said Glenn Kim as I meet him in London for our interview. He worked at Lehman Brothers until 15 September 2008, and later helped resolve the crisis in Iceland and Greece.

"It all starts well, with everyone in a good mood. Then the drinks get stiffer because the punch is more concentrated. Partygoers like the sensation, but it is really a sign that there is less in the bowl."

"Suddenly, the punch runs out. Some of the partiers chase around to find more. The party gets wilder."

"And no one has the sense to call the police. To end it."

"But, really, all should long since have gone home."

A financial crisis typically has five stages.

First, a sector or sectors gain altitude through debt-financed growth. A high altitude is needed for a large fall. Exactly who takes on that debt varies. It could be banks. It could be companies, households or governments.

Why they take on debt also varies. It could be the result of government policy or, more typically, a combination of actions by banks, the government, Central Banks, households and companies. Left alone, loosely regulated, a financial system's natural response is to surge. At first, this debt expansion may bolster consumption, investments, growth and asset values. Policymakers, businesses, even ordinary people applaud.

Often, the policymakers even take credit for the expansion. Few mention that the whole wobbly structure may rest on a foundation of debt. Few see or act on the signs of excessive debt accumulation and the first blinking lights, warning that the economy is overheated.

The reality is, with excessive debt and debt-service costs, the groundwork for a financial crisis has been put in place.

The second stage starts when markets change, and euphoria turns to mistrust. A liquidity crisis kicks in. New money is no longer available to keep the party going. Borrowers hoping to refinance maturing loans instead find themselves in despair. Money that was in ample supply when times were good cannot be found when it is needed the most. Markets slam shut. Companies, banks, households, even governments find themselves without a chair when the music stops.

Liquidity, cash, is the lifeblood of the financial system. If it stops circulating, the body begins to struggle. Especially the outer extremities. If one part gets an infection or a wound, other body parts suffer.

In the third stage, more and more sellers appear, of shares, bonds and properties. But buyers can't be found. In a distressed market, asset values tumble.

In the fourth stage, plunging asset prices and the overall fear in the markets have a cascading effect, setting off defaults, distressed situations and business closures, adding to the broader drop in consumption and investment. The crisis now spreads. What had been a purely financial crisis now works its way into the real economy, the world of bricks-and-mortar stores and businesses. Companies close or scale down. Jobs are lost. Households and companies hold back on spending. Unemployment grows while GDP shrinks.

In the fifth stage, the contagion spreads to state finances. Governments spend money to save the banks. The tax base shrinks. The crisis-related spending increases.

This sequence repeats itself, in country after country and crisis after crisis. Mankind never seems to learn. But now you know what to look for. Sometimes it takes an economy years to move through all five phases, sometimes only months.

The 2008 global financial crisis started with excessive lending to the US housing sector. Gradually, loans of questionable quality with unclear probability of repayment assumed a larger proportion of the market. Banks began packaging these loans into bundles that were passed on to other financial institutions, sometimes in other countries. When defaults started to rise, it was hard to know who was exposed and who to trust. Meanwhile, access to new money dried up. Liquidity disappeared. Values dropped, and companies and banks began to default, most notably the fourth-largest investment bank in the US, Lehman Brothers. Increased uncertainty and less access to money led to even lower investment levels.

As if on a delayed fuse, the lower investment levels in Europe led to lower economic activity and falling tax revenue, just as governments were forced to increase spending to deal with their sputtering economies. Government finances suffered. The problems escalated through 2011, leading to a euro crisis, after what had already been three years of pain.

In Iceland, in contrast, the entire sequence took a couple of weeks. Some might say days.

However, the warning signs had been there. For almost half a decade.

But, mixed with a vast array of immediate good news and short-term gratification, the signs were easily ignored. From this we can all learn how hard it is to see a looming crisis and to focus on the fundamentals in the midst of all the noise.

Here, policymakers had a choice of riding the wave or being seen as naysayers. They chose to ride the wave. The biggest wave ever.

SOME GOOD YEARS

The ancestors of Gudmundur Þór settled in Iceland in the year 880. He knows this because their history was written down in *Landnámabók*, the book of settlers. It recorded when they came and where they settled.

His ancestors claimed land on a plain on the south side of Iceland, even farther north than Anchorage, Alaska. On a clear day, they could see the snow-covered top of the volcano Hekla. With 20 eruptions in recorded history, it did not take a lot of Viking fantasy to name it 'the portal to hell.'

The villages nearby, Selfoss, Stokkseyri and Eyrarbakki, are all built on the lava field *Þjórsárhraun*. The field consists of 26 cubic kilometres of lava covering 1,000 square kilometres.

Þór's family have made the most of their land through centuries of hard work. Some plots of land, sheltered from lava flows, have been turned into grassland. A farm, 80 heavy-coated horses, a greenhouse heated by geothermal steam, a job on the side and a small hotel made for long days and a good living.

Þór even has a salmon creek. Small, but its salmon are among the largest.

After a long day of work, Þór likes to sit with his friends in his *heitur pottur*, a hot spring tucked away between mounds of black volcanic rock. In some countries, life and politics are discussed on piazzas and in pubs. In Iceland, discussions are more heated and forceful. To drown the gusts and howls.

The years went by on a steady course. Þór had little reason to fear the future.

In 1993, I was in Þór's neighbourhood for the first time, when as Deputy Minister of Finance of Norway, I joined a meeting of all Nordic ministers of finance. Nature in Iceland is impressive. Horseback riding on the green fields fighting against the volcanic rocks left a lasting impression. Luckily, my grandmother had often taken me to riding school when I visited her in my childhood. None from any other Nordic ministry of finance dared to keep up with the pace set by the Icelandic officials when they set off on a ride.

When an Icelandic village grows, it first gets a church, then a hot water pool and then a bank. Or, rather, a few banks. Perhaps all three national banks, later to be named Glitnir, Kaupthing and Landsbanki, maybe even a local savings bank or two. Þór opened an account at his village's bank, carefully depositing his paychecks.

In addition to his personal savings, Þór and his employer made payments into his pension fund every year, Iceland being one of a few countries in the world aiming for a fully funded pension system.

Þór and his family had also borrowed for his house, receiving a mortgage from a separate housing fund. It was a small and circular system. The housing fund (HFF) was financed by the pension funds, which neatly bought bonds issued by HFF, with a state guarantee.

But, as often happens in finance, well-intentioned schemes can trigger unforeseen consequences. HFF, with its state guarantee, was able to outcompete the banks. To stay in the market and build their business, the banks started engaging in riskier business.

It used to be that every seventh year, the Icelandic economy got a boost. The economic cycles were almost biblical. Right on schedule, the all-important fishing industry would peak. The catch of fish hit a new high. Earnings and export revenues soared. Everyone brought home a fatter paycheck. The inland industries followed by raising prices and salaries. But as the value of the catch inevitably declined again, salaries and prices stayed up. At this point, competitiveness was ensured by a weakened currency, which continued to get weaker still.

Indexing, to raise mortgages, salaries and prices in line with inflation, was introduced in the 1970s. With this automation, there were few mechanisms available for dampening inflation.

A natural response was to spend all the money you earned as soon possible. If you wanted to build a house, you would cash your paycheck, buy cement and start on the foundations. Even before the rest of the house was fully financed. Real estate and property were what mattered.

Even Volvo sold its cars as *fasteígn á hjólum*, real estate on wheels.

In 1981, the Icelandic government revalued the króna: 100 old krónur, ISJ, were turned into one new króna, ISK. From 1939 to 2009, the Icelandic króna lost 99.95% of its value vis-à-vis the Danish krone.

Gradually policymakers became serious about fighting inflation. Seðlabanki became independent. And it was given one clear target: to combat inflation. To do this, it kept interest rates high.

Along the way, the fishing companies expanded their catch to new species and pursued new markets. The Icelanders were good salespeople and willing to take risks. In addition, tourism expanded and manufacturing companies grew. Iceland's economic base became surprisingly broad, with many companies bringing in technology from abroad and adapting and refining it for use in Iceland.

The Icelanders became masters at making the most of what they had, even the country's small size. International companies ceased seeking patents in Iceland. The country was too small and the process for filing, all in Icelandic, too complex for them to bother. Hence, the Icelanders could produce anything they wanted for their own use and land air cargoes straight into foreign markets on the day the patents expired. While their international competitors had to wait.

In 1996, I was back in Iceland, working for a company with a dozen manufacturing plants globally, including one in Iceland. The latter was doing well. Many of its specialists had degrees, including PhDs, from the world's top universities. They developed new products and production processes and were not shy about questioning old practices.

For us, Iceland was the place to go to be challenged. And to learn.

All seemed quite well.

Few knew even then that the stage was set for an economic disaster.

LIKE BEES TO HONEY

"It was easy to be a good banker between 2001 and 2007."
– Icelandic pre-crisis bank executive in interview

To mitigate volatility, the Icelandic state and the banks built buffers, or reserve funds, that could be drawn on to see them through a shortfall. The state budgets showed a surplus, and state borrowing was modest.

The international credit rating agencies, Moody's, Standard & Poor's and Fitch, score each country or sovereign, to use their terminology, based on its creditworthiness. With this, they guide the actions of lenders around the world. In the early 2000s, the troika ranked the Republic of Iceland, with its robust state finances, among the strongest.

Banks are also ranked. Being headquartered in a country with a highly rated sovereign is the first hurdle for a top ranking. As a rule, a bank cannot have a better rating than its homeland state. That's because a country in distress may tax or even confiscate its banks.

On the other hand, a strong government can provide support if a bank gets itself in trouble. The state can inject new capital or step in to buy deteriorating assets. And, yes, republics, kingdoms and sultanates with strong state finances usually do back their banks and thus protect the banks' depositors and lenders from loss.

From 2000 onward, all three leading Icelandic banks were seen as low risk and received top grades. The rating agencies expressed complete confidence that the banks would repay their debts. Furthermore, the Icelandic banks were used to working with high interest rates. They simply paid a little bit more to the international banks and investors that lent them money. Not a lot, just an extra quarter or even a full percentage point of interest per year. Still, it proved to be a potent combination.

Low risk and high rates attracted capital, as bees to honey.

"There was a wall of money out there," recalled a banker of the pre-crisis years. "Many investors were seeking higher returns as international interest rates fell."

And while others might have reduced interest rates to moderate the inflow, the Icelandic banks continued to offer a slightly higher rate to their lenders. The money poured in.

Next, the investors and international banks bought ISK to get money into Iceland. The price of the króna went up. Now, every ISK could buy more foreign currency, FX. This lowered inflation and pleased Seðlabanki.

With interest rates still high and perceived risk still low, the stronger currency made investments in Iceland even sweeter.

As the flow of capital into Iceland increased, many assets rose in value. Those with ever more capital wanted to buy the same pool of properties and companies. Asset values were bid up. At the same time, eager bankers, flush with funds, allowed their borrowers to take on more debt. Part of it was used to buy shares and whole companies. The Icelandic stock market index, OMX Iceland All-Share, rose from a level of about 1,000 in 2003 to almost 8,000 in 2008.

At this point, the banks' losses were remarkably modest. Any customer in trouble, it seemed, could just sell his assets and repay his loans. The banks could also write up their asset values and show strong profits and solid financials.

In March 2007, the banks made up 55% of the value of the Icelandic exchange. Holding companies, whose holdings consisted largely of the banks, accounted for another 15%. The top seven companies on the Reykjavik exchange, based on market value, included four banks and two bank-owning holding companies. The first industrial company was in seventh position.

Bank shares continued to grow and grow in value. Along with real estate, bank shares were considered the best possible collateral for a loan!

Thus, the banks' value was what guaranteed a large part of the banks' value.

With the increased capital inflows and the increase in transactions and loans, the fee income of the banks also grew. Most transactions yielded at least a small payment for the bank. Sometimes there were huge one-time fees.

Now the banks could show an even larger profit. Especially as the banks themselves took direct ownership positions in some of the transactions they were financing. Trading income, profits from the bank's own risk-taking, represented 30% of Kaupthing's income in the period from 2003 to 2006. That was a remarkably high figure, almost triple the level of the leading banks in the other Nordic countries, Nordea, DnB, Danske Bank, SEB and Handelsbanken.

The three Icelandic banks posted better key ratios than their reputed peers. They reported a higher level of equity capital, technically measured by their Tier 1 Capital Ratios, than the group of five leading Nordic banks. They also reported extraordinary profitability. The average Icelandic bank's return on equity exceeded the group of five's, often by a wide margin. That was despite the Icelandic banks having a larger equity base to serve and a higher cost of funding.

The good returns made the honey even sweeter. Money flowed to the Icelandic banks, enabling their growth.

Investing in Icelandic bank bonds turned out to be a brilliant move in 2003, 2004, 2005, partly also in 2006 and again in 2007.

But not in 2008.

In April 2010, a Special Investigative Committee (SIC) appointed by the Icelandic Parliament delivered its report on the causes of the Icelandic crash. The report consisted of nine volumes, about 2,400 pages in all.

At Reykjavik City Theatre, the full text was read out by actors to an audience of amazed and outraged citizens. Each took their turn, word by word, in a 146-hour nonstop reading.

In retrospect, the excesses were glaring. In 2005, Glitnir, Kaupthing and Landsbanki got hold of around €14 billion by tapping European debt securities markets, wrote the SIC. This amount was higher than Iceland's gross domestic product that year and double the amount in debt securities issued the previous year.

"The three banks had an incredible network into the treasury departments of the international banks," says a former Glitnir employee as he looks back on the wild years. "The banks knew exactly who to call to get money."

According to the SIC, the banks were at first able to issue the debt securities on very favourable terms, paying just 20 basis points (0.20 percentage points) over the benchmark interest rate. When funding in the European markets became more difficult, right on cue the debt securities market in the US opened.

That opening was largely due to the growth of Collateralized Debt Obligations (CDOs), said the SIC report.

With this, most normal restrictions ceased to exist.

BANKS HERD CATTLE OVER THE MOUNTAIN AND ACROSS THE DESERT

"In Europe a lot of banks issue mortgages to homeowners and then hold them in their own portfolios, content to collect the payments and interest," says a former New York banker.

"In the US, banks package those mortgages into bonds, which are then sold into the market.

"The market for debt is gigantic," says the banker.

At first, the bankers focused on smaller, pre-arranged loans, called prime mortgages. Also, in the early days, the loans were passed straight through.

Some time later, the bankers started to combine them into fixed packages, the Collateralized Debt Obligations, CDOs. These packages could consist of car loans, credit card debt, mortgages and corporate debt. They were taken on by separate entities, Special Purpose Vehicles (SPVs). The SPVs combined the loans and sold them off in tranches, some with secure payments and low interest rates, some with less secure payments and higher interest rates.

"CDOs are complicated," says a banker. He should know. He worked for some years from 2003 in the 'complex risk and options trading unit' of a large Nordic bank.

Think of the old wild west cowboy movies.

A rancher collects a large herd of longhorn cattle, 100 in total. To get the herd to the nearest railroad where the market is, the cowboys must drive all 100 head of cattle through the desert, over a steep mountain range and through hostile territory, with coyotes and thieves around every bend.

At the ranch, the cattle are worth $100 dollars each. At the market, $120. Adding it all up, the cattle have a base value of $10,000. In addition, there is a value uplift, a profit pool from the cattle drive, of $2,000. One trader wants to buy from the rancher the rights to the first 80 that arrive, another the next eight, yet another the next nine and the largest risk-taker buys the right to take the last three, which he will receive only if all 100 and thereby also his three last ones actually make it through the wasteland.

A broker suggests a split of the profits. The risk-taker gets 50 from the pool for each of the three longhorns. The others get less extra per head. But then the risk-taker has a greater chance of losing a large part of the initial value of his cattle.

The one taking the 80 receives a small profit on each but is likely to get all 80 cattle to sell at the railroad.

This is how the CDOs worked.

Substitute cattle with mortgages and you have the construct that laid the ground for the largest financial crisis since the Great Depression, which later triggered the euro crisis and years of despair across Europe.

In the CDOs, the bonds included weren't categorized up front, but after the results were already logged. The 3% that showed the worst performance ended in the lowest category, called the equity piece. The following 3% to 12% went into the next tranche, then the next 12% to 20% and, finally, the remaining 80% of the loans. The interest on the bonds was, however, allocated in advance. Here, the most, relatively, went to the holders of the equity piece, the ones who might have bought the rights to the last three longhorns at a discount. If all went well, the risk-takers could earn back their money ten to twenty times. But if things went south, they could also lose it all.

Hence, the CDOs were packages that were changed continuously.

"They were almost like managed funds, with tranches based on risk and returns," explains a then strategist of the structured debt department of Bank of America.

The big international banks made money on fees from the debtors, fees from the investors and management fees on the CDOs. But even more money was made if they could move loans up into lower-risk tranches, for example, by moving a basket of medium-risk loans into a tranche with perceived lower risk. This way, more cattle were assumed to make it through the desert.

Here, the Icelandic bank bonds helped, as they were thought to be low risk.

The high-return, supposedly low-risk Icelandic bank bonds were snapped up for the CDO packages. It worked like this: the Icelandic banks issued bonds. US CDO issuers bought the bonds and put them into an SPV that packaged them into the CDOs. They then sold the CDO parts to investors. In this circuitous way, the CDO investors' money indirectly financed the Icelandic banks. And, thereby also the ever-higher lending levels of the Icelandic banks to both countrymen and foreigners.

The Icelandic banks, with their high ratings, were counted among the healthy cattle. The rating agencies expected them to make it to the railway station. But the Icelandic banks also paid a high interest rate. They made a large contribution to the profit pool.

In 2006 and 2007, the Icelandic bonds became even more sought after. By then, the CDO market had grown to hundreds of billions of dollars.

The market got ever more bustling. "To handle all the traffic, Standard & Poor's in 2006 launched a CDO evaluator on its website," recalls a banker. Basically, it was an automated rating model. Now CDO packagers could just plug in their data and see exactly what they needed to do to get a top rating. By adding Icelandic bank bonds, with their high interest rates and high credit rating, modelers would see the positive impact. Even if those bonds were possibly faulty. Human judgment was now decoupled from the decision making. Artificial intelligence steered it all.

Furthermore, to meet demand, existing CDOs were packaged into super CDOs, called CDO-Squared. Here, CDOs were put into other CDOs.

As demand rose, the CDOs got filled with lower and lower quality loans. These included subprime mortgages, code for loans with less certainty of repayment.

A nice topping, in the form of an Icelandic bond or two or even three, became ever more important.

WHEN REALITY DEVIATES FROM THEORY

Foreign currency investors look for currencies whose exchange rate is expected to strengthen and that are located in countries where interest rates are comparatively high. They swarm to such opportunities, which in itself makes the exchange rate strengthen further.

In theory, such currencies should not exist. Markets are supposed to create an equilibrium. Meaning the sum of the interest rate and expected change in the exchange rate should be equal in all free-market countries. High interest rates should come with an expectation that the currency will weaken. Low interest rates should come with an expected strengthening of the currency.

That's what the theory, known as the 'interest rate parity theory', asserts.

Investors and lenders scour the globe, looking for places and situations where reality defies theory. And in some cases, the theory may indeed not apply for years.

As was the case in Iceland.

Here, investors could get high rates *and* a strengthening currency.

At least for a while.

Borrowers also seek to defy the theory. They look for a comparatively low interest rate and a weakening currency.

This is what the Icelanders got by borrowing in euro, Swiss franc and Japanese yen.

At least for a while.

In Iceland, in the years leading up to 2008, the basic rules of finance did not seem to apply. The cost of capital was low, at least for those who took out loans in foreign currency. Earnings rose, as did economic activity.

A paradox, some may say, as the high interest rates were put in place to dampen economic activity and lower inflation, Here, however, the so-called transmission mechanism had been partly decoupled.

The higher interest rates helped strengthen the krona and thus dampen inflation. But, the impact on the economy as such was modest. Icelandic companies and households turned to FX lending, mainly provided by the three banks.

Consumption and imports grew, with imports vastly exceeding exports. The construction industry boomed, with the construction of houses, offices, a large aluminum plant and an associated power project in east Iceland.

Iceland's current account deficit became the highest in the world, north of 25% of GDP. A quarter of this was related to the aluminum project. The inflow of capital, routed through the Icelandic banks, seemed able to cover it all.

Armed with funds, the Icelandic banks also embarked on an international buying spree. They bought numerous banks.

When FIH, a Danish bank, was put up for sale in 2004, the seller's advisor, Morgan Stanley, hadn't included any of the Icelandic banks on the list of possible buyers. The advisor believed that FIH was just too big a bite for little Iceland's banks to swallow.

"To us, as always, this seeming impossibility was irresistible," wrote Armann Þorvaldsson, the Kaupthing executive in charge of deals, in his book *Frozen Assets.*

"In the beginning, we struggled to get them (Morgan Stanley) to take us seriously, but they soon realized we were dead serious."

He described the sequence of events in his book about life in Kaupthing.

Kaupthing bid £730 million – quite a big bite for a bank then valued at slightly above £1 billion. The bid was then raised to £750 million after a discussion with Morgan Stanley. Now the bank is ours, Kaupthing thought.

But over the weekend, Morgan Stanley called. The advisor had unexpectedly received a higher offer. Substantially higher. £900 million.

A representative from Kaupthing flew to Stockholm on Sunday morning to be closer to the seller. On the plane from Reykjavik, he saw some fellow passengers engrossed in a sheaf of papers with the code name of the FIH deal, 'Davos', on the cover.

Once on the ground in Stockholm, the readers from the plane jumped into a taxi.

"Follow that car," shouted the Kaupthing representative as he jumped into his own taxi to follow the readers, heart thumping.

The taxis wound through the streets of Stockholm, finally coming to a halt in front of a building at Norrmalms. It was the office of the law firm of the sellers. Now Kaupthing knew that another even more aggressive party was chasing the deal.

Another fellow Icelandic bank, Landsbanki.

Kaupthing raised its bid and was able to fight off its countrymen. It got FIH, an asset that would play a key role in the tragic events that followed.

The Icelandic banks also bought BN Bank in Norway and Singer & Friedlander in the UK. Armed with cash, Icelandic companies bought fashion brands, airlines and even a part of Hamleys, Saks Fifth Avenue and American Airlines. Just to name a few. One bank owner bought West Ham United Football Club. Another aimed to buy Newcastle United.

All looked well in the Icelandic economy.

State finances benefited from the growth as tax revenue soared. The state ran a surplus. The government promised tax cuts.

Þór liked what he saw, even though these days he had fewer visitors from abroad. The strong krona scared foreign tourists away. In addition, he had trouble hiring locals, since banks and construction companies were sucking up every worker. He had heard there were more graduates in Iceland in financial engineering than in 'normal' engineering.

On the plus side, his Polish assistant, Kacper, had agreed to be paid in an ever-weaker euro. And Þór's costs had declined because he shifted some of his loans to a foreign currency. He had resisted at first, but his bank had called again and again, finally convincing him to convert the loans to Japanese yen.

"What are your thoughts about the foreign exchange risks?" the cautious Þór had asked his banker.

"Good question," his friendly banker replied. "Frankly, I'm not sure whether Swiss franc or yen is best.

"Probably you should manage the risk by having both."

Þór financed both his new car and a loan to expand his hotel in yen. Counted in ISK, his loan shrank year by year, even without repayments. His loan in yen, measured in ISK, declined by 17% from January 2003 to January 2007 as the value of the Icelandic currency soared. No wonder close to 84% of all car loans in Iceland were denominated in foreign currency at the end of 2008.

Every now and then, the bankers came from Reykjavik to fish in Þór's salmon stream. Often by helicopter. Sometimes accompanied by their lenders.

Þór found it all a bit strange, but if this was the new economy, it was not all bad. Nobody from the bank warned him what would happen if the ISK stopped rising or even dropped. Meanwhile, most politicians cheered the financial manoeuvring. The bankers vigorously fought any naysayers, even acquiring leading media companies to make sure the right message got out.

West Ham United was, however, still not Þór's team. He really could not understand how the bankers could spread money around without reflecting on the price and quality of what they bought. He felt the first inklings of the unrest to come.

NOT THAT UNFAMILIAR

"Overall, the internationalization of the Icelandic financial sector is a remarkable success story that the markets should better acknowledge."
– November 2007 report of Professors Fridrik Mar Baldursson and Richard Portes in a report prepared for the Icelandic Chamber of Commerce

The Icelandic state had a long record of supporting its banks when they got into trouble. The rating agencies possibly took that history of support into account in the years before the financial crisis, as they conferred high grades on Iceland's banks. They might also have assumed that Icelandic bankers, regulators and politicians had learned something about the risks of banking, especially the perils of concentrated exposures, connected party lending and dubious accounting practices. But, no.

Islandsbanki was established in 1904 as a privately owned bank to help finance the fisheries. From 1904 to 1921, it served as the mint for Iceland's currency. Gradually another bank, Landsbanki, operated as the country's Central Bank up until Seðlabanki was established in 1961.

In 1930, Islandsbanki collapsed due to losses on loans it made to, among others, the fisheries. It suffered a lack of liquidity and shut down after parliament, in a late-night meeting, rejected a proposal for a state guarantee. Two months later, a new bank was established by the state from the wreckage, *Útvegsbanki Íslands.* The Fisheries Bank of Iceland.

Fifty years later, the three largest banks in Iceland were Landsbanki Íslands, Útvegsbanki Íslands and Búnaðarbanki Íslands, the latter meaning the Agricultural Bank of Iceland. All were state-owned. The board members were chosen by parliament. Their CEOs, three in each bank, were usually each approved by one of the three largest political parties.

In 1985, Útvegsbanki Íslands collapsed. It had made a loan to Hafskip, a shipping company. The loan was equal to 100% of the bank's equity capital. When Hafskip went down, Útvegsbanki went down with it. But this time, Seðlabanki, after consulting the Minister of Finance and the Minister of Commerce, sent out a letter of support and rescued Útvegsbanki.

The chairman of the board of Hafskip had also been chairman of Útvegsbanki.

The Hafskip CEO was, along with others related to the shipping company, prosecuted for breaching various laws. After a trial that lasted for years, he received a 12 month suspended jail sentence.

In February 2003, the former, prosecuted Hafskip CEO became chairman of Landsbanki. Apparently, he was considered the candidate best suited. And, yes, he and his son were the largest owners. He held the role until 7 October 2008, when Landsbanki too went down.

On 7 July 2019, the French state prosecutor requested that the same Landsbanki chairman should receive a new jail sentence. Five years.

Concentrated lending also caused problems for Landsbanki in 1991, in the aftermath of the implosion of the Soviet Union. After the political upheaval, the former USSR was no longer able to afford imports. An Icelandic wool manufacturer, Álafoss, lost half its business. Álafoss was established in 1896, next to a waterfall that drove the mill. By the middle of the next century, it had turned Icelandic sweaters into high fashion. Now, in 1991, it went into receivership. Landsbanki was its bank. The bank took a severe hit.

Sambandid also featured on Landsbanki's list of large exposures. In the late 1980s, it was the largest conglomerate in Iceland. It was owned by the Icelandic cooperatives. Operating losses, from its fish and fur farming businesses, among others, led to financial difficulties.

At the end of 1992, Landsbanki's capital ratio fell below the minimum legal requirement. In March 1993, the state injected half and half new capital and a subordinated loan equalling 1% of GDP. The legislation was passed in two days. Samvinnubanki Íslands, the bank owned by the Icelandic cooperatives, also ran into difficulties. It was rolled into Landsbanki.

Útvegsbanki, the third state-owned bank, was privatized when it was merged with three small, privately owned banks into Íslandsbanki in 1990. In 2006, Islandsbanki rebranded itself and turned into Glitnir.

A process to privatize Landsbanki and Búnaðarbanki started in 1997.

There were rules in place to distribute ownership and to restrict the buyers of a privatized bank from financing the purchase through loans from the bank itself. Called by some the anti-Gordon Gekko rules, named after the lead character of the *Wall Street* movie. But for a class of young Icelanders, Gekko was a hero and not a villain.

And, yes, the rules didn't stop the banks from providing financing to one another. A loan from Kaupthing financed 70% of the purchase price of Landsbanki, while loans from Landsbanki funded 35% of the purchase price of Búnaðarbanki, soon to be merged into Kaupthing.

This was the start of a banking system built on a web of interlinkages, dependencies and related vulnerabilities.

"There were doubts about how the purchases of the two banks had been financed in 2003," says a then FME employee. "Later, it was clear that the purchase of one bank had been financed by loans from the other, and vice versa."

"It was my impression that the Icelandic financial market regulator, FME, tried to hold things back," says Bjørn Skogstad Aamo, a Nordic FSA leader at that time.

"But from what I heard, it was overruled on a political level. The FME had a very limited ability to push back."

There was a level of pure deceit that made the regulator's job even harder. In 2003, Hauck & Aufhäuser, a German bank, was listed as a 15% shareholder in Búnaðarbanki.

"Búnaðarbanki ... sent one of its managers to Germany to meet with H&A to discuss the possibility of cooperation between the two banks," reported the SIC.

"Much to their surprise, nobody at H&A knew anything about the deal. Furthermore, they had never even heard of Búnaðarbanki."

No wonder.

"There were contracts we didn't see," says a then FME employee.

A 2017 SIC investigation revealed that H&A was never a real owner in Búnaðarbanki or in Kaupthing after the two merged.

The SIC concluded that the Icelandic government had been systematically duped by a later main owner of Kaupthing, let's call him Mr. OO. An offshore company, Welling & Partners, registered in Tortola in the British Virgin Islands was the vehicle. H&A just provided services, for a fee.

The service of appearing to be a 'fit and proper' owner.

Mr. OO was the real owner and later became one of the two largest borrowers from the giant Kaupthing bank.

"It surprised us how meticulously this was planned," said a SIC member.

For decades, the board members of the banks were chosen by parliament, with the composition of the board reflecting the strength of the political parties.

And politics and business continued to be intertwined in Iceland, in a way I found strange.

I worked in the Central Bank of Norway, Norges Bank, as a student assistant in 1982. I left my last political position, as Deputy Minister of Finance of Norway, selected by the Norwegian Labour party, in 1994. Since then, I had been working in business as a strategist and turn-around expert for almost 15 years. However, the press release from the Icelandic Prime Minister's office on my appointment in February 2009 did not start by listing my last position, but my first.

Which was technically correct, but when the press, in its normal eagerness to simplify, cut everything except the first paragraph of the statement, I turned into a Central Banker with a Labour party affiliation. Possibly as intended by the author of the press release.

That did not make my work easier. I did not see my role as political. For me, professionalism, independence and cooperation were the chief qualifications of a Central Banker.

Especially in a period of crisis.

BOYS, DON'T YOU SEE THE PARTY?

"Nobody wanted to entertain the idea that the good times would not last, not to mention that they may come to a sudden and painful end ... In Iceland, the problem was further exacerbated by the fact that policymakers were simply not willing to listen to warnings while the economy was experiencing an illusion of prosperity. On the contrary, Icelandic policymakers were very active in speeding up the train."
– *Bringing Down the Banking System*, Gudrun Johnsen

Beware when a government brags about the performance of the economy. It just may be that it is surfing on a wave of debt.

When consumption, construction, investments, GDP, employment, tax revenue and asset values are all growing, it is hard to argue that the government shouldn't celebrate a strong economy. In fact, most governments will try to take credit for such growth, attributing it to their own policies and strategies. Few will take measures to slow the economy down. Few will take a hard look at what lies beneath those high-flying numbers.

Research summarized in the book *Bringing Down the Banking System* shows that 17% is a figure to watch. That is the average annual real growth of credit in economies where unsustainable growth is followed by a collapse.

Similarly, an unsustainable credit boom generally exists if bank credit to the private sector rises by more than 50% in a three-year period.

In Iceland, the cumulative three-year credit growth rate peaked at 97% in 2006.

"There was no way to avoid a crisis. There would have had to be a correction anyway. As a country, we were running the highest deficit ever observed," says a Seðlabanki economist.

"The story has two parts: the first part is the classic story of a bubble. Here nothing is new; it is just more extreme. The other is the story of the first European banking crisis since the single market was established," says the Icelandic Central Bank Governor from August 2009 to August 2019, Már Guðmundsson.

Not everyone was complacent. Some were shouting out warnings, loud and clear.

The front page of an analyst's report from 14 June 2005 shows a woman blowing air into a bubble. It was a report on the three Icelandic banks prepared by one of the highest-ranked credit analysts in the Nordics, Pål Ringholm.

Most people on the inside, however, were having a grand time, even as things started spinning out of control.

Even the then Minister of Finance of Iceland, who is expected to be a sober voice of reason, chastised the sceptics in an exchange in the Icelandic Parliament on 17 March 2007.

He said, "These people do not see what has been happening here in recent years. They just do not see, probably because they do not want to see what they see."

He added: *"Drengir, sjáiði ekki veisluna?"* – "Boys, don't you see there is a party?"

He was urging the sceptics to set aside their doubts and join the fun.

The Central Bank of Iceland made a study in 2015 comparing the 2008 crisis to other Icelandic crises, going back to 1875.

"The extent of financial imbalances in the run-up to the 2008-2010 crisis was unprecedented and red warning lights were flashing across the board well before the crisis hit," said the report. "All financial variables examined ... exceeded their long-term trend levels by multiple standard deviations and many did so starting four or five years before the crisis."

By 2007, the numbers were stunning. Housing prices and noncore bank funding were beyond a 40-year high, relative to trend. The ratio of credit to GDP was beyond a 1,000-year high. The ratio of bank assets to GDP was beyond a 10,000-year high.

Assuming that *homo sapiens* had made statistics for that long.

Macro imbalances were also evident, with output and demand well above trend; a very large trade deficit and an overvalued currency, according to the study.

I was back in Iceland on multiple occasions from 2000 onward, as I was working with companies active both in Europe and the US, making Iceland a convenient halfway point for meetings. To stay informed, we often invited Icelandic industry organizations to present, including in August 2005 and October 2006.

Those organizations were ever more optimistic and answered our probing questions ever more smoothly.

THE BEST BUY

"It was no surprise. It was for all to see. But no one wanted to hear. The sentiment was all in favour of the banks."

– Central Bank employee in interview

There was a 'Discover Iceland' event for bankers in the summer of 2007. The top bonus earners, the double-digit GBP-million elite, from the financial capitals of Europe attended.

"At first, I found it strange that they had all come to Iceland," says one senior Icelandic banker. "But then one of them told me that the Icelandic banks were a top ten debt issuer in Europe."

Starting in 2005, Icelandic banks in search of loans began tapping the European market, where banks eager to borrow could find willing investors. The loans were in the form of medium-term notes, MTNs.

Such notes have a set duration and the investor cannot request repayment ahead of time. No security or collateral is assigned to the notes. However, the issuers of MTNs normally have an investment-grade rating. The MTNs are unsecured senior debt securities with a pre-set interest rate that are sold directly to investors. Generally, the notes are not listed.

The Icelandic government also issued such bonds from time to time, although strong state finances limited its borrowing needs. It had deliberately been cautious, with issuances normally in the $200-250 million range.

Iceland was underrepresented in the market. But not for long.

The banks did not show similar caution and seized every bit of capital that was available. They borrowed a billion in a single go. In 2005, the three biggest banks moved in and sucked up €5 billion. Then lenders started getting cold feet.

"Yes, there were problems at the end of 2005," says Seðlabanki's Jón Sigurgeirsson.

One JPMorgan banker sent an email on 14 November 2005, the first of many warnings to the Central Bank.

She referred to the high overnight interest rates in Iceland, then at 11.75%. These rates kept money in Iceland. Then she warned about Iceland's vulnerability in the event of a currency depreciation. The risk in that case would be that bank customers in Iceland who took out loans in foreign currencies would not be able to repay if the Icelandic currency weakened.

The senior staff in Iceland's Central Bank did start to worry and voiced their concern.

In the streets of Reykjavik, right outside the Central Bank, however, this was when the foreign currency lending really took off.

"All the calls on my fixed line telephone are taped," says Sturla Pálsson, who worked in the bank's market department at the time. "In December 2005, I asked IT to stop overwriting or deleting any recordings. I wanted to have it all documented. I had a sense we were seeing history being made."

"We saw the first warning signs late 2005," confirms a senior banker, later to be found in the *Financial Times*' list of jailed Icelandic bankers.

"That's when we should have started to manage for a soft landing," says the banker. "But no one was willing. We all had big stock options, meaning we had a big upside if everything went well."

When European investors were no longer willing to buy MTNs to fund further growth, the three banks turned to the American and Asian markets.

They found willing buyers for their securities in the US. According to the SIC, Icelandic bank securities were sought after for CDOs because the banks carried a high credit rating while also paying relatively high interest rates.

That made Icelandic bank bonds a 'best buy'. Low perceived risk and high rates. To the extent anyone saw risks, they were spread out across the broader portfolios.

Now the US and European funding ran in parallel.

SOMETHING TO CELEBRATE

"The government wanted the banks to expand, and the general attitude toward financial regulation in Iceland was that the best people to regulate the banks were the bankers themselves."
– *The Rise, the Fall and the Resurrection of Iceland,* Sigríður Benediktsdóttir, Gauti BerÞórusin Eggertsson and Eggert Þórarinsson

It took the orderly Swiss 300 years to build a banking sector eight times the size of GDP.

It took Iceland five years to get to nine times GDP.

Beyond domestic services and industries, the Icelandic economy had historically been supported by three industries.

For most of Iceland's history, the fisheries were its most important export sector, but in recent decades, limited stocks of accessible wild catch had constrained growth. Tourism was important, but seasonal. Renewable energy, allowing for growth in aluminum smelting and ferroalloys, had become a third leg. But a massive new power plant, Kárahnjúkar, and the aluminum plant it supported, were controversial. The project and the prospect of similar projects to come mobilized environmentalists of all stripes. Rarely had the country been more divided.

Then, along came another industry, banking, which most people cheered. Modern. International. Clean. With well-paid, professional jobs.

And Iceland needed a new source of growth. In 2006, it was about to post the largest trade deficit of any western European OECD country in the last 20 years, even after adjusting for imports for the new power and aluminum plants. The deficit was enabled by, and partly caused by, a vast inflow of borrowed money brought in through the banks. An inflow that was partially passed on to Icelandic companies and households as they increased their borrowing.

Something to celebrate, many thought.

FIX UP YOUR HOUSE! WHY SHOULD I? YOURS IS WORSE

"We looked at early warning indicators for financial crises and concluded that Iceland looked worse on almost all measures than Thailand did before its crisis in 1997, and only moderately more healthy than Turkey before its 2001 crisis."
– Danske Bank analyst report, March 2006

It was hard to be a banking sceptic in the period leading up to 2006. It was even harder after early 2006. That's when Iceland suffered a difficult series of events known as the Geyser crisis. A crisis that the banks managed to avert. Once they came through this challenge, their self-confidence and sense of invincibility became absolute.

"Now they really believed they could fly and walk on water," says Sígrún Daviðsdóttir, a journalist who covered the crisis.

In March 2006, Denmark's Danske Bank issued a crushing report on the Icelandic economy, calling it the most overheated in the OECD area. That was just for starters.

"On top of the macro boom, there has been a stunning expansion of debt, leverage and risk taking that is almost without precedent anywhere in the world," wrote Danske. "External debt is now nearly 300% of GDP, while short-term external debt is just short of 55% of GDP. This is 133% of annual Icelandic export revenues."

The chief economists in Kaupthing, Landsbanki and Glitnir all denounced the report's findings.

"The Danske Bank report looks written with the intent of putting the Icelandic economy in the least favourable light possible," wrote the Glitnir researchers, clearly outraged. "What sets it apart from previous reports is that rather than just voicing concerns, it actually predicts a coming financial crisis followed by a severe recession in the next couple of years."

Apparently, they said this to criticize the report.

The Icelandic authorities joined the chorus of critics. Danske Bank was dismissed as the voice of a past Danish colonial power. Arguing the case of the Icelandic banks became a matter of national pride.

"Criticism from many of the foreign banks is simply the act of competitors who want to crush the Icelandic competition," said the Icelandic Prime Minister in March 2006.

"The Danske Bank analysts more or less spoke the truth," says a person now who was involved in overseeing the banks back then.

"By late 2005, we could see all the imbalances," says Fitch Ratings' lead analyst. "We had introduced a flagging system. All the Icelandic indicators were red."

In February 2006, 31 months before the disaster, Fitch added a 'negative' after its AA minus rating of the sovereign, the Republic of Iceland. Its 22 February report was titled 'Macro Imbalances Trigger Negative Outlook'.

"This was a time of international prosperity," the Fitch analyst recalls. "Many people expected AA-minus-rated countries to be flawless. Our move, which the market saw as a downgrade, was unusual."

"'Are you guys sure you know what you're doing?' was a question we heard a lot."

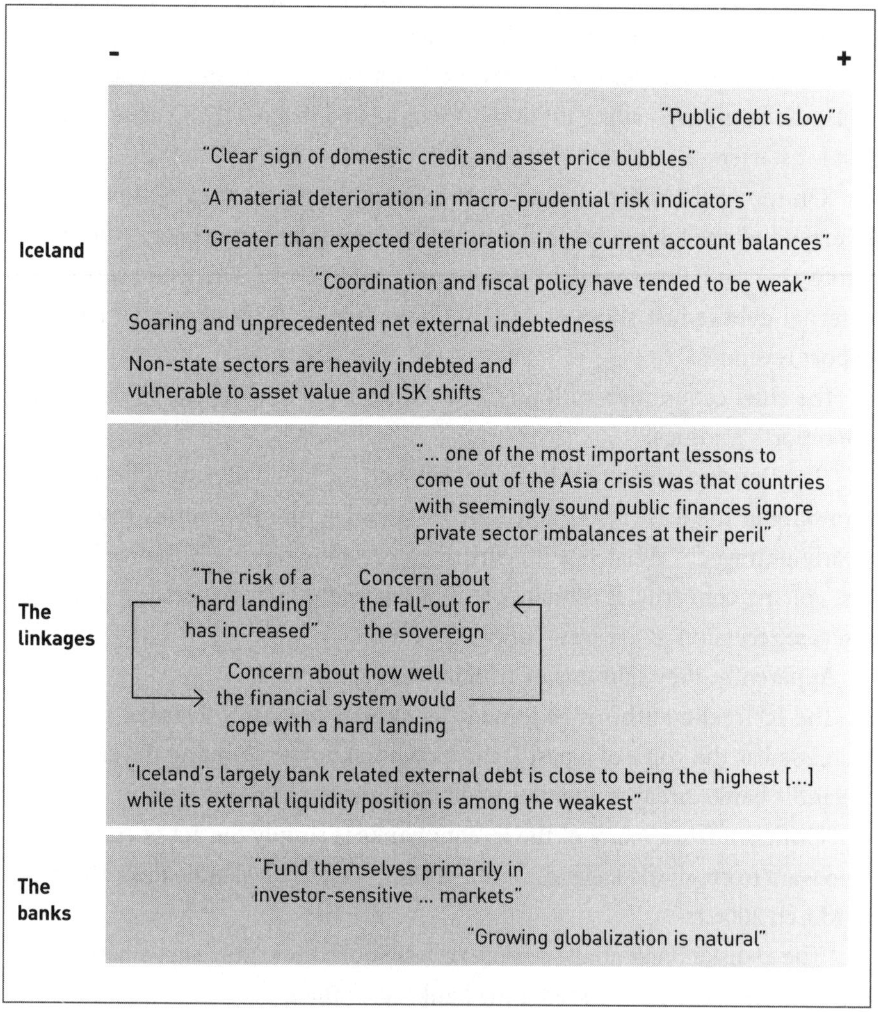

↳ **Summary of the 2006 Fitch Ratings diagnostic.**
Source: Fitch Ratings Republic of Iceland rating 22 February 2006.
Summary and placement made by the author.

Interestingly, as can be seen in the Fitch summary, the report painted the macro imbalances as the main risk. The report, though, concluded that those risks could come to harm the financial sector as a knock-on effect. And then roll back and hit the state.

No other OECD state had anywhere near the external imbalances of Iceland, Fitch said.

No wonder it was hard for the authorities to ask the banks to get their house in order. Their own house was in just as much disarray.

"The banking analysts were largely focused on the individual banks and their performance," says a former rating analyst. "That was where the rating business originated. That was the core." That was where the big money was made.

"Bank analysts often gave little thought to the systemic issues."

They applied a two-year horizon.

All bank ratings were reviewed by a committee that included the sovereign-rating analyst.

"Sovereign ratings were no cash cow," says a former ratings analyst.

However, sovereign ratings were needed, as they normally served as a ceiling. A domestic bank cannot be rated higher than the sovereign. With one exception: subsidiaries backed by a foreign-parent bank.

"I was out giving presentations and having lunches and dinners all the time after we issued the negative outlook," says the analyst. "Everybody wanted to hear the story. And yes, we did get some powerful emails from Iceland."

"But I don't remember having to look over my shoulder."

The market valuation of the banks fell markedly, and the ISK depreciated.

The Icelandic banks reacted swiftly. They broadened their reach, with Kaupthing issuing bonds in Japan, Canada, Mexico, Australia and the US. The banks also began to raise direct funding through deposits. The intention was to solidify their funding and reduce the risk of failure. But, as will be seen, this also dramatically increased the impact of the failure.

"What eventually got us out of the situation was the fact that the world was still drowning in liquidity," wrote Armann Þorvaldsson, a former Kaupthing executive. "Although the European bond market had had its fill of Icelandic bank exposures, money was available from other markets at a price."

The Icelandic banks paid more than other banks, almost 1% over the market reference rate, the LIBOR rates, but it did the trick, he wrote.

"Although there were other things that contributed to the end of the crisis, it was the access to liquidity that was of primary importance," wrote the former Kaupthing executive.

The crisis was over – or so it seemed.

As the fears about Iceland's banks faded, the price of insuring loans given to the three banks declined all the way up to mid-2007. At this point, $5,000 could insure $1 million of bank bonds for two years.

In early 2007, one of the rating agencies, Moody's, gave the Icelandic banks its highest rating. This was a certificate of health that was hard to argue with.

Especially with the banks' accounts looking great and for government representatives who themselves were under fire.

THREE BANKS SCORE THE HIGHEST MARKS

In the early 2000s, all three of the big banks in Iceland were considered 'safe' borrowers. Starting in 2000, Kaupthing, for example, was given an A3 rating by Moody's. In 2003, this was raised to A2 and in 2004 to A1. Moody's gave the rating yet another uptick in 2007, to Aa3.

On 24 February 2007, 19 small months before the disaster, it took all three banks up into the highest category, 'triple A'. No banks carried lower risks than the Icelandic ones, was Moody's message.

The rating agency said the higher ratings resulted from a change in methodology. Moody's now attached more weight to the strength of the broader economy and the hosting state, through what it branded the Joint Default Analysis.

Quite ironically, Moody's gave an uptick of the rating as it attached more weight to one factor among the weakest parts of the chain, the country's ability to support the banks.

"The new ratings of the Icelandic banks reflect the strength of the Icelandic economy and the Icelandic banking sector," quickly commented the Glitnir CFO. "This should strengthen the funding operations of the bank, as it should give access to a wider group of investors. Therefore, this should generally improve the operating environment."

Others were more nervous.

"We were amazed when the methodology was changed," says the former head of the financial stability department in the Central Bank. "We were very surprised. It was totally unrealistic."

Jón Sigurgeirsson had long been responsible for the Seðlabanki relationship with the sovereign rating agencies, though working at the IMF at the time. He called the Moody's sovereign analyst and asked: "What the hell are you thinking?"

The one responsible for the country analysis at Moody's was clear in the response. The sovereign team hated the decision. There had been a debate. It was clearly a corporate decision.

"We spent a lot of time preparing for discussions with the rating agencies," says a former bank employee. "We had full-day meetings. We also had regular analyst calls. All were fine. There was only one guy from Merrill Lynch whom we always found to be difficult."

Fitch downgraded Iceland only three short weeks later, 15 March 2007.

"The 2006 data came out much worse than expected," says the lead analyst, Paul Rawkins.

"The current account deficit was expected at a negative 21% of GDP. It ended at negative 27. The external debt was expected at about 160% of GDP and came in at 200. External debt was expected at 3.2 times external income but came in at 4.3."

" ... it is becoming increasingly hard to conceive of a smooth unwinding of Iceland's macroeconomic imbalances," wrote Fitch.

"We tried to say that risk was increasing," says a Seðlabanki employee. "But carefully. We were afraid that we ourselves would trigger a crisis. Who wants to carry the blame for the inevitable?"

And a similar dilemma arose for policymakers: should you step on the brakes when the very act of doing so might trigger the crash you're trying to avoid? Should politicians massively tighten policies when the budget shows a surplus and when the banks still say all is fine? And, even if you consider it to be the right action, how can you actually get popular support for spoiling the party?

A COUNTRY THAT BUILT A FUND FROM SHIT

"The buccaneer of the olden times relied on his prowess as a fighter. There was no nonsense about it, he was an avowed robber. The modern buccaneer is a very different type of individual, who may be seen in public life in silk hat and frock coat and has often not set eyes on the place he is looting."

– "The New Age", 5 June 1913, article on *Kiribati*

Kiribati is a small nation that lies in the South Pacific, exactly where the world map is cut in two. Actually, four. Both hemispheres and also the 180-degree meridian! Kiribati is the only country in the world to achieve this, making it almost unfindable on many maps.

Its population of 110,000 is spread over 33 reefs and atolls. They are always the first in the world to celebrate the new year.

"Remember, it is pronounced Kiribas," I was told by Kiribati's honorary consul to the UK.

When the first European missionary made the voyage to Kiribati, to translate the bible into the local language, which meant inventing a written version and codifying it, it is said that all the lead shapes for printing the letter 's' were lost just before arrival, due to the roughness of the waves breaking over the reef. So, the letter 's' never became part of the written language.

Kiribati has for years held a prominent spot on the list of the world's least-developed countries. GDP per capita is about $1,500, roughly one-fortieth of Iceland's. About 20% of the 'I Kiribati', as the people from Kiribati are called, cannot meet their basic needs.

Physically, Iceland grows year after year as volcanic activity increases the size of the country. In Kiribati, the situation is exactly the opposite. Most of its islands peak at six feet above sea level. With climate change, rising waters are threatening to engulf the proud nation.

But before that happens, the country may die of thirst. Salt-water intrusion from rising seawater is spoiling the groundwater by contaminating the fresh water reservoir on top that Kiribati depends on.

It is probably the only country in the world that has bought land in another country, 6,000 acres in Fiji, to grow its food and possibly relocate parts of its people as its islands disappear. Kiribati can no longer grow enough food at home owing to salination. The generous Fiji government has also offered to provide space for the whole I Kiribati nation if needed.

Kiribati originally did have a hilltop, on the island of Banaba. It was created from petrified guano. Over hundreds of thousands of years, seabirds had left their excrement on Banaba as they flew over the Pacific. Chemically, guano is high-grade phosphate, one of three key nutrients in plant fertilizers.

Under British colonial rule, the priority was to bring phosphate to New Zealand and Australia as cheaply as possible, says the honorary Kiribati consul who is now writing the history of his nation.

From 1900 to 1979, phosphate mining stripped away 90% of Banaba's surface, says the consul as he talks me through the Kiribati history. The British sold phosphate from Kiribati at £6 per ton. The locals got 6 pence per ton, less than 3% of its true value. And even that little bit had to be used in the pricey trade stores of the colonialists.

Gradually, the price of phosphate increased, especially through the 1970s. And Kiribati's dependency on it remained. In 1973, phosphate accounted for 89.8% of Kiribati's exports, shows my read of Kiribati's 1973 economic plan. The rest consisted of nuts.

Coconuts.

But, with foresight, in 1956 Kiribati started to build what was possibly the world's first sovereign wealth fund: The Revenue Equalization Reserve Fund of the Gilbert and Ellice Islands Colony. In 1956, the colony was officially classified by the British as a place that would never be able to achieve independence, a policy only to be changed as late as 1975!

The fund was created as a store for the phosphate mining wealth. And a cover for the colonialists.

In 1956, the phosphate reserves were expected to last 30 years. But they only lasted for 23. They were exhausted in 1979. Exactly the same year Britain granted Kiribati independence.

"Hardly a coincidence," says the historian.

The plan was for Kiribati to tap its wealth fund as the country now had lost half its GDP and half its government revenue. But the country's first president decided otherwise. The current generation was to adapt to leaner times and the fund was to be saved for the future.

Other Pacific guano nations set up similar funds. The fund managers were approached by every con man in the world. Nauru bought planes. Tuvalu went into Texan properties.

Again, Kiribati was fortunate in having politicians who were both honest and cautious. It established a policy of having two fund managers, James Capel, later acquired by HSBC, and Nikko Asset Management. Both were among the largest in Asia.

A sizeable part of Kiribati's reserves was invested into bonds of top-rated banks. In one of the world's wealthiest, most developed and regulated countries, in Kaupthing and Glitnir of Iceland.

After Kaupthing went under, the claims of creditors were made public in 2012. They show a claim from the Kiribati Reserve Fund of ISK 1,470,744,442. Kiribati's Glitnir position was a bond with a nominal value of ISK 2,856,652,910.

In sum, about 20% of Kiribati's GDP was held in the Icelandic banks. In relation to its GDP, Kiribati had become the single largest non-Icelandic investor in Icelandic banks.

ON THE BLACKLIST

"In 2006, I met with a group from Barclays Bank," said a former chief economist in the Central Bank. "They were extremely concerned about Iceland."

A meeting with the Icelandic financial market regulator, FME, had done nothing to tamp down their fears.

"We learned that the FME does not understand risk," the Barclays' bankers said.

Barclays halted all further lending.

In late 2007, the UK-based bank Standard Chartered put Landsbanki on its blacklist.

"We in Landsbanki were squeezed out of a loan consortium," said a former Landsbanki employee. "Standard Chartered would not participate unless Landsbanki was excluded."

BANKS THAT CHASE BORROWERS

"If someone is offering to lend you money you haven't asked for, then you are in a credit bubble."
– Icelandic pre-2008 bank executive

"Two thirds of Icelandic companies ended up in distress after the crash," says a former loan portfolio manager in one of the Icelandic banks. "About 40% of them, however, already had insufficient cash as far back as a year earlier."

He continues: "In 2009, everyone blamed the crash for the severe recession that gripped Iceland, but the numbers had been there to see for at least two years before the crash occurred."

"For many companies, buying and selling other companies had become more exciting than simply operating their businesses."

A special report prepared for the SIC looked at the ratio of loans held by customers that had at least one late payment. Among the larger loans, this ratio increased from 10% in late 2007 to 20% in the spring of 2008.

"There just was a lack of focus on operations," says a former portfolio manager.

"The banks were offering us loans for everything," says a former executive of a fishing company. "'Take on more debt and use it to buy shares,' they said. 'Borrow on the value of your fishing quotas.' They were chasing us in 2005, 2006 and 2007.

"The Scotch they gave me for Christmas got older and older, while the bankers who called on me got younger and younger.

"Soon, the whisky was older than the bankers."

The executive got invitations to grand gala events, but he stopped going. "The value of our debt was already 60-65% of the value of our shares. And it was all in FX."

He watched as the króna got stronger and stronger. "Something is wrong," he thought, "when our company, which was supposed to be one of the strongest, is struggling for survival."

By April 2008, the banks had changed their behaviour.

"We were ready to expand our plant. The drawings were done. We were good to go," says the executive.

But suddenly, the three banks started dragging their feet. They said everything was in order, but they never quite signed the loan. A Danish bank also turned the company down. "They thought we were an Icelandic bank," says the executive. "Then they realized we were a fishing company and said yes."

"I cancelled the project anyway. I just sensed something was wrong."

13 REASONS FOR SUCCESS

"Business deals are my fix. I have been addicted to them for most of my life and as I became increasingly hooked, the temptation to borrow way over my head to fund them became too much to resist."

– Thor Björgólfsson, the largest owner, and second-largest borrower,
after his father, of Landsbanki

In 2007, an Icelandic company, Nordic Partners, bought a landmark high-end hotel at Copenhagen's best address, Kongens Nytorv. The purchase was, naturally, financed with a loan from Landsbanki.

The hotel d'Angleterre dates back to 1755. It has been in its current building since 1795.

In 1602, the Danish government, which then ruled Iceland, imposed a strict trade monopoly, cutting off Iceland's direct market access. In 1787, the monopoly was abolished, but only Danes could trade in Iceland. Trading posts were auctioned off, with prices on sales and purchases of goods set by the Danish king.

No wonder free trade, liberalism, Icelandic pride and the absence of regulations and foreign intrusion became a part of Iceland's ideology of independence.

The d'Angleterre came to be the favourite meeting place for the Danes. From 1872 onward, it was de facto owned by a Danish industrialist whose bank, Privatbanken, was a centre of gravity for the Danish business community. Many in Iceland looked on with joy when d'Angleterre passed into Icelandic hands in 2007. Finally.

Útrásarvíkingar is a term coined in Iceland in the years leading up to the crash. Its literal meaning is 'viking who conquers new lands.' It was applied to Icelandic financiers who bought American and European companies. Like the d'Angleterre. Many were national heroes, living testaments to the 'Viking spirit'. They put Iceland 'on the map' once and for all, with individuals and companies that were among the richest and most powerful in the world.

"'How is it that these financial Vikings are so much smarter than everyone else? Or are they just paying more?' That was the question I got when I was in Denmark," says a journalist.

"We have a different mentality," says an executive who has led companies in Iceland and in other Nordic countries. "*Þetta reddast* is the Icelandic mentality. It means 'Things will work out. We will find a solution.'"

"This epitomizes the Icelandic attitude. That, and a willingness to keep going, stamina and a positive attitude. Less so, plans and risk analysis."

The former Icelandic President, Ólafur Ragnar Grimsson, gave his take on what made Iceland different in a speech at the Walbrook Club in the City of London on 3 May 2005. He started by saying that he had recently been asked to explain how daring Icelandic entrepreneurs were able to succeed where others failed.

He said it was tempting to leave the British business world perplexed. "This mystery would give my Icelandic friends a clear advantage, a fascinating competitive edge," he said.

Then he got down to business. Grimsson pointed to globalization and information technology as enablers. "Obstacles to the growth of small states have largely been abolished and replaced by a wide-open field where talent, imagination and creativity determine who reaps the rewards."

Next, he listed six examples of successful Icelandic companies: the holding company Baugur, the airline Avion, pharma company Actavis, prosthetics company Össur, Kaupthing and Bakkavör, a manufacturer of fresh foods.

Of these six companies, two later went bust, two were restructured, and one is hard to trace. Only one, Össur, is still a consistently high-performing, innovative industrial company.

Grimsson cited no fewer than 13 reasons for the Icelandic success: a strong work ethic, a focus on results rather than process, a willingness to take risks, an absence of bureaucracy, strong personal trust, the formation of small groups of operators working closely and strategically together, entrepreneurship, a tradition of honouring those who dare to venture into foreign fields, the importance of personal reputation, a competitive domestic market, the smallness of the country and the absence of ulterior political motives, an ability to establish cooperative ventures and, lastly, creativity.

Interestingly, many of these virtues were later cited as weaknesses that contributed to the collapse. But to Grimsson in 2005, they were sources of competitive strength. Almost a new ideology.

In such an atmosphere, no wonder it was hard to be a conventional, by-the-book risk manager in a bank or in the FME.

And yes, if you visit Iceland's tourist attractions, like the steaming geysers, the deep canyons or the wild waterfalls, you will rarely see any warning signs. There are few, if any, ropes or barriers to protect you from taking a wrong step.

When surrounded by nature at her wildest, attempting to protect the tourists with laws, signs and safety ropes may seem pointless.

"The business tycoons made us feel like we were playing in the big leagues. We shouldn't underestimate that effect," said one banker.

"And then, with an increasing sense of financial wellbeing, what happens is that you undergo a detachment from your basic values."

The president ended his address by referring to a promise he had given in a recent speech: "You ain't seen nothing yet."

So very true.

Unfortunately, the real answer to what was different in Iceland was much simpler.

Debt.

More debt.

Ever more debt.

Here's why debt can be so effective. Imagine that you buy a company for $100. Thirty dollars of that is equity. Seventy dollars is debt. Some time later, if the markets are strong or you make some improvements, you sell the company for $130, an increase of 30%. Thanks to all the debt, your equity will have grown much faster, in this case doubling. If you get an even higher price, your equity will have increased even further; for example, if you sell to a countryman who also can raise debt. Or if you yourself have taken on even more debt.

As you may do if you are well connected with a bank.

Or if you own it.

Even if you bought the bank with borrowed money.

With debt. Ever more debt.

FINANCIAL WEAPONS OF MASS DESTRUCTION

If you invest in the debt of a company and you want insurance against a default, you can buy what is called a CDS.

CDS is an acronym for Credit Default Swap; in short, an instrument you can buy that insures against the default of country X or bank Y. The entity that issued the CDS will now pay you if the debtor defaults on his debt. It's like fire insurance. In the worst-case scenario, you still get paid.

At first glance, this all looks quite innocent and useful. Look again. Renowned investor Warren Buffett called CDSs "financial weapons of mass destruction."

If you as an investor believe a bank, for example, will increase in value, you can buy its shares. If you believe it will fail, you can go short. In that case, you borrow shares that you sell, then buy them back later, hopefully for you at a lower price. You then return to your lender the new, cheaper shares, allowing you to pocket the difference. Or you buy CDSs if you believe the situation of the bank may deteriorate further, leading to a higher value for the CDSs. The insurance policies.

And, yes, you can buy CDSs even if you haven't lent money to the country or the bank in question. If you do so, it is almost as if you are buying an insurance policy on your neighbour's house because you know it's built of wood and the wiring is a little faulty – even if you live next door in a well-built house of brick and mortar. With this strategy, you score a win if anything in your neighbour's house goes wrong; for example, if it's struck by lightning or if the neighbourhood is hit by a firestorm.

Similarly, if you manage a large portfolio of shares and bonds, you may be looking for a way to hedge your risks. One option would be to buy a CDS on the bank or company that you expect to collapse first if the broader market weakens.

Naturally, the more risk overall in an economy, the more demand there is for CDSs relative to supply, and the higher their price. Analysts take advantage of this fact by using the CDS price as a measure of perceived risk.

You can also turn this calculation around. Start with the general market interest rate and add the price of the CDS covering the debtor. Theoretically, you should get the level of interest the debtor should pay, a rate that takes into account all risks.

With all this, CDSs become immensely important. Suddenly, the small, often nontransparent and unregulated CDS market steers the often much larger debt market. The tail wags the dog. For banks dependent on market loans, as the three Icelandic ones were, there was not much that mattered more than the price of the CDS.

The first CDSs were issued on Kaupthing in the autumn of 2005.

Kaupthing cheered. "We thought it was prestigious; we thought we were now a significant player in the capital markets," wrote a Kaupthing executive.

The cheering stopped. Quickly.

"I don't think anything caused us as much damage in as many ways as the CDS market," he wrote.

"It eventually played a prime role in the collapse of the Icelandic banking system."

On 24 March 2006, JPMorgan wrote a report on the Icelandic banks. "The banks have grown to a size where their funding needs dictate a much bigger presence in the international debt markets, and they have consequently attracted more attention," JPMorgan wrote.

"More importantly, an active CDS market has developed. This has allowed people with strong negative opinions to exercise their views."

When you look at who issues CDSs, the picture gets even more complex. One part of the answer is easy. In the US, an insurance group, AIG, became an active issuer of CDSs. AIG assumed that few of the firms its CDSs covered would default and require them to make a payment. To simplify, CDSs are often compared to fire insurance policies. AIG acted as if this simplified comparison was literally valid. AIG thought their claims would be scattered more or less evenly across time and locations. All faulty assumptions.

And, yes, AIG was present when the payout from the default of the Icelandic banks was settled in the first week of November 2008.

And, yes, AIG was itself bailed out by US taxpayers.

Making the situation more complicated, some Wall Street firms started to issue and sell CDSs in new ways. These would yield a pool of insurance premiums to the issuers, but also require them to pay if a default were to occur.

These pools of premiums, and latent payments, were put together in broad portfolios of securities, often including CDSs for as many as 100 banks, companies and countries. Investors could now buy different tranches, depending on the level of risk and return they wished to target.

These constructs were called synthetic CDOs.

Let's return to the searing heat of our old wild west ranch.

Assume the traders at the ranch don't actually take possession of the cattle. The rancher retains the ownership. Assume the traders only get to share the profit pool from moving the herd, and then promise to pay the rancher only for the longhorns that don't make it.

In simple terms, instead of buying all the cattle up front, they only pay for the ones that die from sickness, thirst or the coyotes. They don't pay for all the cattle, just for the deceased. The don't pay up front, but afterwards. Really not that mysterious.

It could still be seen as an investment product, and not an insurance policy. The profit pool is just as attractive. Instead of buying all the cattle, investors just buy a few. The loss is the same on the cattle that don't make it, whether you buy the herd outright or just pay for the ones left for the vultures. A periodization difference is the expression an economist would use. And, better yet, the investors don't have to lock in any funds to pay for the sturdy cattle, whose value is stable the whole way along the journey. This structure is more capital efficient, in economist-speak. The profit opportunity is only in the move anyway, with its risks and upsides.

Combine it across 100 herds, so that no individual herd particularly matters, and you have a synthetic CDO.

This explains a mystery. We now know who it was that was willing to issue CDSs that would compensate other investors if the Icelandic banks failed. It was nobody and everyone, all stacked into big portfolios.

Some buyers of synthetic CDOs, however, are known. Eight Norwegian municipalities ended up being large CDS buyers, buying products structured by Citigroup and a Norwegian brokerage, Terra Securities. The municipalities had sold their hydropower plants. They now considered how to invest for the future. They were advised to buy an innovative product, collateralized synthetic CDOs. Also, here they made a commitment to pay for the dead cattle. But, here they only had to pay up a small part of the latent, unsized payment up front. The buffer. But, as the cattle died, more funds were called upon. And then more. And more. Soon the lion's share of the value created through generations as the power plants had been built and the local water resources utilized, was gone.

To sum up, financial engineers from the world's banking capitals created ever more complex concoctions, from CDOs to CDO-squared, synthetic CDOs and collateralized synthetic CDOs. They all became part of the witches' brew that first overheated the Icelandic economy and then froze it in its tracks.

In total, 3,771 of these so-called synthetic CDOs globally were rated by Standard & Poor's. Of these, 9% included one Icelandic bank, another 9% had two and 14% had all three. In total, 32%.

The appetite for issuing CDSs on the part of the three Icelandic banks was vast for some time. The logic was the same. Here the CDS payments were high and the rated risk low. If synthetic CDSs were made by robots, the robots would have automatically recommended adding Icelandic CDSs. Just as the human bankers did.

A total of around $71 billion of CDS exposure to the three Icelandic banks was open when the dust settled in November 2008, after the collapse a month earlier. Many players, however, were on both sides. They had both bought and sold CDSs. The net positions were $7.6 billion.

At first, the cost of the Icelandic-bank CDSs was around 0.2-0.3%, meaning that an annual payment of $2,000-3,000 would yield $1 million in case of default. And opposite, a premium of $2,000-3,000 would oblige the issuers to make a payment of up to $1 million if a default were to occur.

Through late 2005, and especially early 2006, Kaupthing's CDS price escalated as the perceived risk of default grew. The increase fed into the interest rate on its debt. Market observers, analysts and academics all commented on the change.

In early 2006, the Norwegian Oil Fund went short in Iceland. It bought CDS positions, seeing default protection as the most profitable investment in Iceland. This was the judgment of the fund's fixed income trading desk, says the current head of the Oil Fund. Iceland was not happy.

The Icelandic Prime Minister did call the Norwegian Prime Minister, who again called the Norwegian Central Bank Governor, who was responsible for the Oil Fund. "What are you guys doing?" the Governor was asked.

"I never got a call from my superiors saying I should buy or sell this or that," says the former CEO of the Oil Fund. "There was no political element in our decision making. A government cannot favour open markets and then stop market players from acting on what they see."

The Prime Minister of Iceland at the time, Halldór Ásgrímsson, said the move violated a Nordic mutual defence pact against financial destabilization, and besides, it simply seemed unneighbourly.

"Our analysts had looked at all the numbers. Their work was very thorough. We thought we would be invited to meet Icelandic authorities to share our findings," says an executive who was at the Oil Fund at the time. "Instead they attacked us in speeches and statements."

Early in 2019, I got a call from a broker. He wanted to sell me a new financial instrument. "Wow, that's a CDS structure," I responded. "Do you really sell CDSs?"

He couldn't answer. They went under a new name in 2019. He didn't know the history of CDSs.

Old mistakes need to be remade by the new generation.

THE ALARM BELL GOES ON AND OFF, THEN ON AND ON AND ON

In April 2007, investment bankers started having trouble finding buyers for nonsecured US mortgages, says Michael Ridley, who worked for JPMorgan at the time.

His group at JPMorgan looked at who the previous buyers were to see who could get beaten up if the market crashed. They also looked to see which issuers across markets were most dependent on these instruments to secure funding.

"What we found was a bit of a surprise," Ridley recalls.

The next day he found himself on a plane to Reykjavik.

The business of herding cattle across the desert had grown at a rapid pace. It had become enormous. But now investors were starting to get nervous. Some of the longhorns had grown weak with thirst and were staggering. Others had diseases that could spread from herd to herd. Meanwhile, way out on the horizon, a sandstorm was forming that could wipe out multiple herds in one go. Even the investor with rights to the safest 80 cattle wasn't on firm ground. Especially as he, like many others, had borrowed money to engage in the trade. And no one knew who sat on which positions.

The first alarm bell went off on Thursday, 9 August 2007, says a US Fed historian. That was when panicked investors stampeded out of a fund run by a French bank, BNP Paribas. The fund had invested in US subprime loans. BNP quickly shut the stable door, forbidding further transactions in the fund. BNP said it was unable to assess the value of the fund's shares.

The European Central Bank, the ECB, however, opened the vault, lending banks unlimited funds overnight.

"For the ECB, this was a big decision," says a former ECB official.

The next morning, the market desk of the US Fed joined in. At 9.10am, it made $19 billion available. At 10.30am, it added a further 16 billion. In the afternoon, another 3 billion.

Then things calmed down. For a while.

In September 2007, a British bank, Northern Rock, collapsed. Depositors again lined up to get their funds. The Bank of England stepped in with liquidity support. In February 2008, the bank was nationalized.

"This is not good at all," was the comment a banker recalls. Seven or so traders of the largest investment banks met at a pub in London. They started to discuss the latest events.

"All, though, thought they were safe. They had taken steps to secure themselves."

But as they went around the table, they understood that they all had traded with the others at the table. And their seven Wall Street friends."

"We really started to get worried in mid-2007," says Timothy Geithner, who was President of the Federal Reserve Bank of New York and later Secretary of the US Treasury. "We started taking action."

"In the US, banks only make up about a third of the financial system."

Investment banks and finance companies like GE Capital and the insurance group AIG make up the rest.

"In some sense," says Geithner, "the banks were too small compared to the total financial system. Our tools were best suited to serve banks. We in the Federal Reserve could support the banks. We could provide liquidity against collateral. We wanted the banks to increase their liquidity buffers. We lowered the rates and increased the quotas."

The US banks were slow to draw on that liquidity from the Fed. European banks, however, turned up en masse. They had a currency mismatch. They had been financed by money from US money market funds, but now that market had dried up. Toward year end, a worry emerged that the banks would halt their business.

The ECB watched what was happening with growing concern. "We saw a lot of stress on the dollar and we realized something was going on," said a former ECB official. "Banks were starting to fear the weaknesses of other banks. They slowed their lending. They built buffers. And they all asked for dollars."

"There are two dollar systems in the world," explains Geithner. "One domestic and one foreign. The US needs to support both. As the crisis emerged, the US dollars wanted to go home. But the US monetary authorities sent them back out in the world."

The IMF was also getting worried. It convened a crisis task force in the fall of 2007, chaired by John Lipsky, the first Deputy Managing Director. Its focus was on the US. There was no mention of Iceland.

On 12 December 2007, the Fed opened another valve. It offered to take securities from banks, allowing the banks to get 'money' in return. This transaction was then to be reversed at some point in the future.

The Fed provided $20 billion for 28 days. Another $20 billion for 45 days. The mechanism was called TAF, the Term Auction Facility. Here banks could bid to access a defined volume, as opposed to asking for money at the Fed's 'discount window'.

One reason for this was the fear that banks might be reluctant to access the discount window because it might stigmatize them. Approaching the Fed and asking for money could be seen as a sign of weakness. Winning an auction, on the other hand, was a sign of savvy business judgment.

But, money is money.

Next, the Fed, the ECB and the Swiss National Bank established a swap agreement. The latter two could pull dollars from the Fed by placing a comparable amount of local currency on the Fed's account.

Then things calmed down again. For a while.

The IMF task force had hit on a plan for buying debt as a possible mitigation measure, $700 billion worth. Some IMF policymakers even wanted to go public and voice their concerns. The US was their largest worry.

But then, who wants to call "wolf, wolf"?

Everyone stayed quiet.

At the end of February 2008, another fund, Peloton, was liquidated. In March came the crisis at Bear Stearns. For the first time since the Great Depression, the US Fed provided liquidity to a nonbank entity, an investment bank.

Next the ECB asked the US Fed for $60 billion.

"We knew there were problems," says a Seðlabanki employee. "In January 2008, we started to drink a toast every Friday after work: 'Salud, we have survived another week.'"

In early 2008, Seðlabanki started to talk to other countries and Central Banks, he continues. Not to bail out the banks, but as a way to build market confidence that they could avoid or at least survive disaster.

"We said yes, we are small, but saveable. That is the way to avoid Iceland becoming a trigger."

Meanwhile, the governors of the Central Bank of Iceland were becoming increasingly curious about what a banking crisis looked like, says a former employee of Lehman Brothers.

"I explained how the crises of Korea, Thailand, Indonesia and Sweden had evolved.

"I strongly encouraged them to make the three Icelandic banks someone else's problem."

A SPIDERWEB OF LINKAGES

"... holding companies ... were essentially used as a vehicle to transform leverage into equity."
– The Icelandic Financial Crisis

The lead owners of Iceland's three largest banks had each borrowed money, either from their own bank or from the other two banks, to buy their shares. All three banks had loaned money to the same companies. All were linked in a complex set of relationships. Anything that hurt one of the banks was likely to hurt the other two.

In one bank, two owners had invested €35 million when the bank was privatized. At the time of the bank's failure, they had borrowed €1.5 billion from the same bank. Essentially, for some, a tiny sliver of their own money invested in the banks served as a fee giving the 'owners' the ability to insert a straw and suck out cash. From the top. Rules, regulations, regulatory supervision, international auditing houses, rating agencies, market and self-control did not contain the sheer greed and the owners' apparent desire to rape and pillage.

Glitnir's lending to its main owner, the holding company Baugur, and companies owned by Baugur, was among the largest. This lending rose rapidly after Baugur became a shareholder in Glitnir, from about 40% of Glitnir's capital base in early September 2007 to close to 90% in early 2008.

Baugur owned stakes in a variety of companies, largely in the UK: Big Foot Group, Goldsmiths, Hamleys, House of Fraser, Julian Graves, Karen Millen, Oasis and Somerfield.

"It was a question of how to 'group' Baugur. Which holdings should be counted as part of Baugur and which as independent companies?" says a former FME employee. Hence, which companies' debt should be linked to the holding company, from a risk and integrity point of view? "The rules required 50% ownership for us to group them as part of Baugur."

"We had to follow the rules."

The group of firms that Baugur either owned or had stakes in also borrowed from the two other banks. That meant that all three banks were exposed to Baugur, well beyond the regulatory maximum of 25%. At the peak in December 2007, the combined loans from the three banks to Baugur equalled almost half the regulatory capital of the three banks combined. Any problems in just one company – Baugur – could wipe out half the foundation of Iceland's three giant banks. And as Baugur was also a major owner of Glitnir, a problem in Glitnir would undermine the two other large banks.

The regulators showed little concern at these developments. The FME even allowed Landsbanki to categorize its two largest owners as 'not related', even though they had bought the bank together. And were father and son.

Kaupthing also had its adventures. Robert and Vincent Tchenguiz in the UK had borrowed what amounted to 55% of Kaupthing's capital base. Their UK real estate structure was Kaupthing financed. And one of the brothers was on the board of Kaupthing's largest owner, hence also in a position to influence Kaupthing's lending policies.

A holding company called Stodir Hf. owned 32% of Glitnir. Stodir's principal lenders were Kaupthing and Landsbanki. Just as with Baugur, all three banks would be exposed if the value of Glitnir declined.

This intricate web of cross ownership was not a secret. Many maps had been drawn showing the systemic linkages, including an overview from 2006.

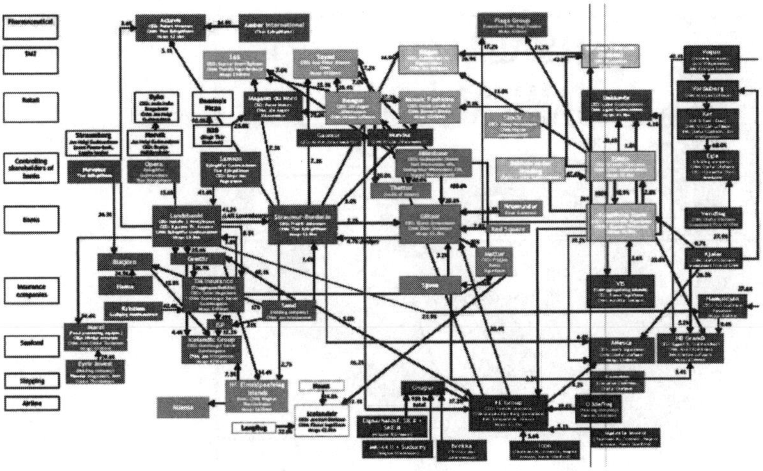

↳ **Icelandic ownership landscape.**
Source: JP Morgan, 2006

But, prior to the SIC report in 2010, few if any knew how bad it really was. Seðlabanki had always had a representative on the FME Board. In keeping with the letter of the law, there was, however, no tradition of him sharing what he learned from the FME in discussions with the broader Central Bank leadership. Since I arrived in the midst of the crisis, I agreed with our representative that he should keep me informed. I started to get the news from the FME board. On the web of linkages. On the connected party lending and on other matters. When I saw the report on Landsbanki, I had to leave the room. I was about to vomit.

Remember the former Icelandic President as he celebrated the "strong groups of operators who work closely and strategically together" and strong interactions "without difficulties and major bureaucratic hindrances?"

Starting in 2007, the 'small groups' really got going. One reason being that the funding from international banks to Icelandic-owned companies dried up.

Around 1720, an Icelander named Árni Magnússon amassed a stunning collection of Icelandic manuscripts covering Icelandic and Nordic history. After his death, his manuscripts were sent to Denmark. For years, Iceland struggled to get them back.

"We used to say, 'Let's get the scripts home,'" says a former high-ranking bank executive.

"Now we were saying, 'Let's bring the bank loans back home.'"

↳ Icelandic artist Halldór Baldursson interpreting the events: "Bank loans!! Bank loans!!", the banker shouts.

The international banks were about to scale back their lending to the Icelandic holding companies, many of which were owned by the owners of the Icelandic banks. Now the three banks stepped in and provided new loans, effectively moving the risk to Iceland.

"We wanted to avoid an Icelandic crash, so we brought the loans back home."

"That was our mistake."

From mid-2007 to mid-2008, loans from the Icelandic banks to foreign entities doubled. A lot of those foreign entities were owned by the people who also owned the Icelandic banks.

The SIC identified the ten people who had borrowed the most from the three banks, either in their own name or through their companies. The Landsbanki borrowers who made the list included the chairman of the board himself and his son. Glitnir's group included its chairman, his father, mother and his spouse. Two of the owners in Kaupthing also joined the top ten, one being Mr. OO. The largest borrower of all was the British-Iranian property developer Robert Tchenguiz, himself a board member of Exista, Kaupthing's largest owner. Hence, eight out of the ten largest borrowers of the three giant banks had direct connections to their lenders.

Again, remember the list of 13 virtues, including 'small groups working together' to create opportunities. For some.

Just before I took up my new post, I received an urgent command from the McKinsey risk team. They insisted that I should prepare a complete list of all my investments and roles, and that I should put it under the nose of the civil servant at the prime minister's office who oversaw my assignment, which I did.

As far as I could see, there were no latent conflicts.

But, I did notice that no one even glanced at the list. At least not while I was there. No questions were asked. They obviously had many other concerns on their minds.

Possible conflicts of interest were not high on the list of priorities.

THE CASH MACHINE AND THE LETTERS OF ETERNAL LOVE

"'When there's so much money available, you should take it while it lasts,' was the prevailing sentiment at the time. It was another land-grab situation."
– Thor Björgólfsson, the largest owner of and second-largest borrower from Landsbanki, in his memoirs comparing pre-crisis Iceland to his time in Russia

One of the most important tasks of a Central Bank is to manage the money flow of the banking system, and to ensure that the right amount of money is always available. It does this in large part through repo facilities.

Greatly simplified, repo facilities allow banks to borrow cash short-term from the Central Bank by offering securities as collateral. For each daily or weekly loan, the bank puts up a basket of collateral specific to each kind of loan or facility. The transaction is then reversed some time later, a day or a week for example, when the bank pays back the loan, with interest.

Usually, any highly rated bond can be used as collateral. A bank can thus submit a bond from another bank as security and get cash. With this method, cash can be made from thin air.

Individuals cannot get loans from a Central Bank. We can only get loans from a regular bank by giving the bank some security in return – for example, a right to our house.

The Icelandic banks found ways around such limits. Here, bank A issued bonds to bank B, which in turn issued bonds that were bought by bank C, which issued bonds to bank A. Quite aptly, the bonds became known as 'love letters', letters of eternal love.

Now, watch what happens. The banks could then submit those love letters to the ECB and Seðlabanki as collateral, allowing them to receive 'fresh money' in return.

Through this arrangement, the banks could borrow without putting up meaningful collateral. In addition, only a fifth of the value of bank bonds had to be included when calculating the associated level of equity each bank needed to maintain. Regulators believed that loans to banks were not risky.

Hence, if bank A sells a bond to bank B that sells it to C, which then again sells it to A, and each bank uses this as collateral in a Central Bank, all the banks get funding. And the associated equity needed is only 1.6% from each bank, one fifth of the standard 8% equity hurdle. The owners of the banks, who provide the equity, can then borrow that fresh money with only the thinnest sliver of equity. Voila, a money machine has been created.

No wonder owning a bank was attractive. Who wouldn't want to own a licence to print money?

In sum, the banks' tab with the Icelandic Central Bank and the ECB reached about €9 billion just ahead of the crash.

The 'love letter' borrowing grew particularly fast from March to May 2008. In April 2008, the then ECB Governor, Jean Claude Trichet, contacted the Central Bank of Iceland because of concern over 'abnormal artificial bonds' being submitted as collateral from the Icelandic banks. The ECB hit the brakes and banned love letter-based lending. Seðlabanki acted more slowly. The consequences became clear a short year later. One of the two Central Banks completely avoided losses. The other had to be recapitalized.

The main source of funds for the three banks in 2007 was deposit taking. Central Bank financing started in 2006, grew in 2007, and by 2008 had grown to be the most important source of new funds.

Hence, deposits, which the Central Bank partly guarantees, and state financing through Central Banks were the funding sources that grew the most from the first mini-crisis onward.

These were the sources of funds that allowed the banks to increase the lending to their owners.

PHONY EQUITY

It was important for the three banks to keep their share prices high. Kaupthing did this by actively buying its own shares. Its ownership stake would again and again approach the 5% limit, where the law demanded that it would have to be flagged. Such publicity was not desirable.

Therefore, Kaupthing found buyers to whom it could offload the shares. Again, and again. A portion of the shares were passed on through covert operations. Many of these deals were financed through loans from Kaupthing, the SIC reports.

Kaupthing traded both in Stockholm and Reykjavik, says the special prosecutor, who was appointed in 2009 to investigate economic crimes related to the crisis. For part of the year, the market in Stockholm opened two hours ahead of Reykjavik. A trader at Kaupthing Reykjavik managed the Stockholm market.

But one day the trader overslept. The share price fell 4% in the absence of the caretaker.

He had a stressful day when he finally turned up at work. He had to get the share price backup.

Management at Kaupthing also owned large stakes in the bank. Partly, they built those stakes through incentive schemes, which are common at many companies. What is not common is that Kaupthing lent them the money to buy the shares. Mostly with just a personal guarantee. On 25 September 2008, however, the Kaupthing Board met and decided to release their employees from such personal liabilities. A release that was cancelled later.

A couple weeks before its collapse in October 2008, Kaupthing announced that a sheikh from the Middle East had bought 5.01% of the bank.

Kaupthing had been careful not to reveal earlier share purchases. Now, however, it wanted everyone to know. Hence, a 5.01% stake this time and not 4.99 as previously.

The news of the purchase briefly boosted market confidence in Kaupthing.

At the trading desk in one of the other banks, all cheered in admiration when they heard of the sale of Kaupthing shares to the Middle Eastern investor.

"These guys at Kaupthing are so good," one commented.

"They're always on top of things."

What market participants did not know was that Kaupthing had illegally financed the deal, as determined later by the Icelandic Supreme Court. The deal was without risk to the alleged buyer. And, supposedly, $50 million was deposited into the sheikh's bank account.

When the scheme was revealed, four former top bankers at Kaupthing, including the CEO and the Chairman of the Board, received prison sentences of three to five-and-a-half years for fraud and for abusing and misleading markets.

But before the crash, apparently neither the Icelandic exchange nor the Icelandic Financial Services Authority investigated the extent to which the banks conducted transactions to support the value of their own shares.

"The bankers were stuck," says a legal expert, making the best case for the banks. "Keeping the shares would expose the bank to losses as the stock price dropped in value. Selling shares in the market while having knowledge of its troubles would clearly have been illegal."

Another possibility was to establish companies that could buy the shares. But they would require financing from the bank. Putting the shares into such Special Purpose Vehicles, SPVs, might have seemed the least of evils. Even though the bank retained the risk. Another tough dilemma.

"We tolerated poor practices in the sense that banks had always traded actively in their own shares," says a pre-2008 banker.

It was not illegal.

"But leveraged holding companies with no access to funds are not the right owners of banks," says the banker.

The loans given by the banks to finance purchases of their own shares were counted as regular loans.

"This is, in fact, utterly disconnected from reality, as the shares have not been paid for at all," wrote two accounting experts, Jón Þ. Hilmarsson and Stefán Svavarsson, in an article from 2018. The so-called loans were, in fact, uncollected claims after the bank's sale of its own shares.

The two experts wrote that as a result, recorded owners' equity was overstated by 50%. And, similarly, the interest income on the loans was included as normal income, even though it was never collected.

Here, no one was held responsible, neither the CEOs nor the board of directors.

The two accounting specialists also noted that the auditors involved, KPMG and PwC, also got off without ever having to explain their auditing work or unqualified opinions.

One of the international giants, however, was sued. Compensation was demanded: ISK 100,000,000,000.

ON PAGE 46 OUT OF 98

Seðlabanki Islands publishes an annual 'Financial Stability' report.

The title of the summary in the July 2007 edition reads: "The commercial banks are more resilient."

On page 46 of the 98-page report, the Central Bank though had a different message.

A clarification was hidden toward the bottom of the page:

> *It is clear that the Central Bank's role as a provider of liquidity for the financial sector is confined to local currency, i.e., the Icelandic króna, and that it may only lend to financial institutions against adequate collateral.*
>
> *Rating agencies and others assume that the government will assist systemically important institutions that encounter difficulties, on the grounds that this would cost the economy less than the financial crisis that might otherwise result.*

And then it continued:

> *However, neither the treasury nor the Central Bank issues financial companies with such formal guarantees and they have never made declarations to this effect to agencies responsible for Iceland's sovereign and banking sector ratings.*

Quite a response to Moody's 2007 upgrade.

"One of the governors wanted to include this," says the person who edited the report. "The position was not new, however. It was not a piece of news."

"Why then highlight it?" he asks rhetorically. "Especially as doing so could have created tension."

Hence, placing it at the bottom of page 46 seemed like the right choice.

"It is the one who claims that someone has issued a guarantee who needs to prove it. You can't just say a guarantee has been made and then expect it to be honoured."

Truly a piece of wisdom worth noting, dear reader.

Perhaps Seðlabanki was just too subtle. As late as May 2008, Fitch, the rating agency, wrote: "The authorities have stated that they will support the banks if necessary."

"We wouldn't have written that unless someone told us so," says a Fitch analyst today. "The authorities read through all our reports. We assumed they could have borrowed $5-10 billion."

No one can confirm whether Moody's ever read page 46. The firm's Iceland analyst at the time declined a request for an interview for this book.

And, surely, no one working for Kiribati read it.

THREE BANKS PREPARE THREE LIFEBOATS

"The Icelandic banks did not buy toxic securities – but together, they administered their own potent mix of systemic poison."
– Fridrik Mar Baldursson and Richard Portes in *Gambling for Resurrection in Iceland: The Rise and Fall of the Banks*

"The three banks deeply feared a depreciation of the ISK," says a former bank employee.

The banks' accounts were in ISK. The equity was counted in ISK. But a vast portion of the banks' loans and liabilities – for Kaupthing, 70% – were in FX.

"If the ISK weakened, both the loans and liabilities would increase as measured in ISK. But the equity would remain unchanged. Suddenly, the equity ratio could become insufficient. The banks saw a need to safeguard themselves, to hedge their equity."

" ... the Board of Kaupthing had concluded that one of the biggest risks to the bank was the possible and inevitable deterioration of the currency," wrote a former Kaupthing executive in his recollection of the events.

Note the use of the word 'inevitable'.

And here, some calculations may be of interest. With 70% in FX and an equity buffer of about 3 percentage points, the 'inevitable' depreciation would have to be beyond 30-40% to take Kaupthing down below the regulatory limits.

"By early 2008, all the banks had covered their positions," says Ásgeir Jónsson, the former chief economist in Kaupthing, who was appointed Central Bank Governor of Iceland from August 2019. "From 2005, we were absolutely sure it would tank."

"Kaupthing had started in 2005, Landsbanki in the fall of 2007 and Glitnir at the end of 2007. By 2008, all were covered."

All had bought FX forward, meaning they had access to FX at a predefined price some time in the future.

Now they would make money if the ISK weakened.

"The weakening króna resulted in very high inflation, which further added to the bank's profit," wrote the former Kaupthing executive on the first weakening of the krona and the Kaupthing results in the first half year of 2008.

Hence the banks had hedged themselves against the Iceland country risk.

In their core banking business, however, risk increased.

"Icelandic Banks Defy Credit Squeeze," read a headline in the *Financial Times* from 10 October 2007.

"Icelandic banks should be lying low in the current credit market, given that they took a battering last year when the country suddenly turned," read the article, referring to the 2006 liquidity squeeze.

"Yet Kaupthing, Glitnir, Landsbanki and Straumur-Burdaras are still on the acquisition trail," the article noted, adding the fourth-largest Icelandic bank to the usual group of three.

The newspaper then listed, for the period February to September 2007, no less than $4.7 billion worth of completed and planned acquisitions.

The *Financial Times* quotes the Chief Economist at the Chamber of Commerce: "The funding of the Icelandic banks is now better than many international banks."

"It's in our mentality not to do something we don't understand," the Glitnir CEO was quoted as saying. "Being basic has been one of the strengths of Icelandic banks."

In November 2007, two months after the collapse of Northern Rock, the management team of Glitnir consisting of 50 people met at the Turnberry Golf Course in Scotland, now owned by Donald Trump. Here, they announced a plan to double Glitnir's balance sheet. Supposedly, some members of the team left the bank shortly thereafter. This was just too much.

Keflavik Savings Bank, a local bank serving a town of 16,000 inhabitants, decided on a medium-term strategy that included a plan to open a New York branch office.

With their currency hedging in place, lifeboats had been prepared for an escape should the ISK sink. But, contrary to their beliefs, the banks themselves had even larger weaknesses than the mother ship.

INSIDE KAUPTHING

"Everyone wanted to work at Kaupthing," says an employee from just before the crash. "Everyone there had top grades."

"I really wanted to work there," says the former Kaupthing economist.

"I really focused on the trades I was asked to make. To deliver as well as I could," says a former Kaupthing trader.

"It was hard work and long days. I hoped to be paid through the share programme. We got loans to buy shares. There were no drugs and strip clubs, only hard work. And then my shares went to zero," says the economist.

"Four people made the decisions. We got quite angry when we saw the schemes they had been running. Desperate actions in desperate times can be understood, but not structures like the loans to the board members of the bank's largest owner."

The largest owner was an entity called Exista. Robert Tchenguiz was among its board members. He had borrowed at peak $2 billion from the bank and its Luxembourg subsidiary, revealed the SIC. This added up to 45% of the bank's capital base. A large part was overdraft financing with no collateral, on which he paid an interest rate spread of 2.75, compared to Kaupthing's rate of beyond 4. Kaupthing lost on every dime loaned to its owner.

WORRIED NEIGHBOURS

As early as 2004, the Norwegian Financial Supervisory Authority, Finanstilsynet, requested a report on the status of the Icelandic banks. A Professor in Finance, Thore Johnsen, was mobilized.

"An equity crisis is likely to mark all three banks, and there is good reason to fear a house-of-cards effect through the combination of these factors and the overall contagion between the banks," read the translation of his report summary, finalized way back in January 2005.

After this, the three banks were closely monitored. The Norwegian FSA notified the Norwegian banks that it had doubts when the Icelandic subsidiaries applied for membership in the joint deposit insurance fund of the Norwegian banks.

"Such a report was unusual. But we needed to do it, as all three Icelandic banks were making inroads and trying to place themselves under the Norwegian deposit guarantee scheme," says the former Norwegian FSA director, Bjørn Skogstad Aamo.

"We also invited ourselves to meet the Deposit Insurance Fund to express our concern," says Aamo. "This was even rarer."

He continues "Other Nordic banks had entered the market, but only with these three did we have serious concerns. Glitnir was asked to report monthly on its liquidity. It was the only one."

"We learned from the Nordic banking crisis to only engage in businesses we understand," says Trygve Young, the credit risk manager in one of the top five Nordic banks, DnB. "All engagements outside our credit strategy required approval by the Credit Committee. That included any transactions with one of the three Icelandic banks. We set a 'zero-exposure limit' on all facilities. Nothing was allowed, unless specifically approved. The rule even applied to our investment bank, DnB Markets."

The Finnish chose a subtler tactic. They simply sat on all applications from Icelandic banks that wanted to enter Finland. "Pending." "Pending." "Pending," was the reply the banks got when they complained. "Remember, this is real money," the Finnish governor, Erkki Liikanen, responded when confronted with the banks' complaints.

"I worked in the European Central Bank's monetary policy unit in 2006," says another source. "February 2006 was when we first flagged the Icelandic risk."

"We started to get worried in 2006 and 2007," says the Swedish Central Bank Governor Stefan Ingves.

"This will not end well. I started to send more and more specialists to Iceland. They reviewed the capital base and ownership structures of the banks, but they could not explain from where the banks were raising the capital to keep growing."

"We had prepared ourselves," says the former Swedish Minister of Finance, Anders Borg. "We made a list at the end of 2006 and early 2007 of the main risks.

"Iceland, Latvia and Ireland were on the top.

"We checked the risks faced by the Swedish banks. We were worried about their exposure to Iceland. But, to our surprise, no large Swedish banks had material exposure."

In 2006, the Swedish governor came to Iceland by invitation of the Icelandic governor. A pleasant visit. Everyone went salmon fishing. Ingves recalls that as he was leaving, he pulled the Icelandic governor aside and said: "You have a problem with your banks. We have some experience in dealing with this. We have had our crisis. Call me anytime if you want to discuss."

"He never called to ask for help," says Ingves.

In early 2005, a company I led in Oslo was about to sublease an office in Olav Vs Gate to Kaupthing. To us, the rent was attractive. Kaupthing was willing to pay whatever was needed to get what it wanted. The lease was to last from 1 July 2005 to 7 November 2008.

I brought the proposal up for discussion in the management team. Our financial sector specialist, Simen Vier Simensen, said we should demand a prepayment for the whole lease period.

He was certain that the bank would not survive the lease.

A COUNTRY THAT HURTLED DOWN THE TRAIN TRACK

"The country really came hurtling down the track," recalls a Fitch macro analyst.

The government put more wood on the fire, even though the economy was already overheated.

The Housing Financing Fund (HFF) was allowed to finance a larger portion of the mortgages, up to 90%. A popular sweetener for the electorate. The private banks, especially Kaupthing, competed aggressively. The authorities reduced the buffer or reserve requirements for the banks. Housing prices skyrocketed. In Iceland, contrary to most other countries, housing costs are included in the core inflation measure. Hence, the reported inflation rate increased. Since the Central Bank had an inflation target, it was now obliged to raise interest rates. "We made a comparison with New Zealand," says a former rating agency analyst. "They are used to ups and downs. There, however, the government restrained itself and ran with a much larger budget surplus. In Iceland, the government cut taxes."

The task of cooling down the system was given to Seðlabanki, leaving it to them to increase interest rates. But that only made things worse.

The number of new FX car loans peaked in the fall of 2007, only one year before the crash. About 70% of the total outstanding balance of FX mortgages were debt issued in 2007 and early 2008, when there were already clear signs the ISK was overvalued. Eighty per cent of the FX car loans were in particularly strong currencies, like yen and Swiss francs.

The banks, which saw a depreciation of the ISK as inevitable, hedged their own currency exposure. They feared a depreciation of more than 30%. But they still sold FX loans at full speed in the narrow streets of Reykjavik. The policymakers did not forcefully intervene. Among the long list of Iceland's policy mistakes, this one, as will be seen later, ranks among the ones that harmed Icelanders the most.

For this there is no excuse.

THE 0.6% IMPACT OF A QUADRUPLE ECONOMIC SHOCK

"With the benefit of hindsight, we should have shouted from the rooftops that a system had been built in which banks were too important to fail, that banks had grown too quickly and borrowed too much, and that so-called 'light-touch' regulation hadn't prevented any of this."

– Former Governor of the Bank of England, Mervyn King, on the pre-crisis situation in global banking

"Icelandic banks pass the FME stress test," announced the Icelandic Financial Supervisory Authority (FSA) on 6 February 2008, seven months before the disaster. It had calculated the effects of simultaneous shocks on the capital ratio of the largest Icelandic banks. The banks were tested on their ability to retain a capital ratio above 8% even after 'certain setbacks'. The test covered a change in the value of shares, market bonds, nonperforming loans and the ISK.

The stress test showed a possible drop in Kaupthing's capital ratio from 11.8% to 11.2%, Glitnir's from 11.2 to 10.4% and Landsbanki's from 11.7 to 10.5%.

In short, a modest impact.

"It is a question of the assumptions," one of the authors of the FME report now says when I ask how such analyses could be made. "Our methodology was based on the European standards. From 1990 to 2007, the annual losses of the housing finance fund were always between 0.1% and 0.2% of the loan book. There was no basis for going way higher.

"Historic data didn't suggest a number anywhere close to the 5% we saw as the crisis hit."

Yet another important bit of wisdom. Don't trust the concept of stress tests. They are only as good as the assumptions applied. If one uses data from a period of stability, then the stress test will show the impact of shocks based on a period of stability.

Even Glitnir itself apparently didn't trust the stress test. In April 2008 representatives of Glitnir Norway called the Norwegian Central Bank, Norges Bank. Their ask was very practical: what are the application procedures one needs to follow to get 'S-loans'.

The 'S' though means 'on special terms', which refers to Norges Bank's role as lender of last resort. S-loans are emergency loans. They can only be given if the stability of the financial system otherwise is threatened. Now, after this call on practical procedures, some really got stressed.

"Why borrow at a high cost when you can wait, and then do it less expensively." This was the response of the Central Bank Governor according to the confidential minutes, made by and handed to me by an external party, from a meeting in April 2008. He was asked why the authorities did not increase the Central Bank reserves.

"The depositors will be saved if necessary. The same will not apply to the owners, and most likely not the creditors either," he stated.

Already then. But only in a closed meeting.

The SIC stated that the Icelandic financial market acted with a sense of impunity, a freedom from consequences. The FME did not use its authority. It did not respond in a formal way to breaches of the law. In some instances, even serious violations were not reported to the police.

An on-site inspection by FME at Landsbanki in 2005 showed that one of the bank's loan exposures was way above 25% of the bank's capital base, stated the SIC. Fifty per cent, in fact. The loan was made to a large owner in the bank. The finding was not brought up to Landsbanki until February 2007. Now, corrective action was demanded.

In September 2007, the large exposure at Landsbanki was still unchanged. The breach did not have consequences for either the bank or the owner.

Well, until everything collapsed, that is.

The FME had not laid down precise rules. When the FME tried to intervene, it met strong resistance from the banks. In sum, enforcement of regulation on large exposures was very weak.

"Weaknesses in the legal framework was not what stopped the FME," said the SIC. "But the FME had serious funding and staffing problems."

The banks grew 900% as a share of GDP from 2003 to 2007. The staff at the FME grew about one-twentieth of this. It did not grow at all from 2002 to 2006. Its budget was financed through fees charged from the banks. The budget had to be reviewed by a special oversight committee that included the three commercial banks, savings and loans institutions, insurance companies, pension funds and investment funds. Most members argued against any budget increase.

Internationally, the FSAs can send experts into the banks to inspect their practices and review the books. They can even conduct raids and seize documents. Dubious banks fear the inspections, while well-run banks use them to improve further. In Iceland, the Prime Minister appointed a committee to oversee these control operations. With representation from the banks. Hence, political decisions systematically restrained the FME.

"It was difficult to get even gradual increases in the budget and approval for on-site work," says a former member of FME's board. Apparently, the banks and the markets were largely expected to regulate themselves.

"The people in FME were all in their offices. They didn't engage. They didn't go into the banks."

'Who are we to question the operations of the banks?' was the feeling in FME and Seðlabanki. "The bankers were treated like gods," says a Seðlabanki interviewee.

Only 16% of the FME staff had prior experience in banking. Staff turnover was 50% higher than among other Nordic regulators. Three quarters of those who left landed jobs at a financial institution.

Better paid. More prestigious. With a stronger political backing.

IT'S A CONSPIRACY

"It was no surprise that the Icelandic banks would be the first to go. They were the ones most exposed."
– Rating analyst

Through the last part of 2007, the price of the CDSs on the three Icelandic banks started to escalate, especially on Kaupthing. It first reached 3% at the end of 2006 and then jumped to 4% at the end of 2007. Now it took $40,000 to insure $1 million worth of Kaupthing bonds. For a short period, the cost even bounced to $60,000.

"Early in the crisis we made a tragic mistake, which increased attention on the Icelandic banks," wrote a former Kaupthing executive.

In 2007, the ones believed to be on top of everything had launched an effort to buy a Dutch bank, NIBC, that had exactly the same weakness as Kaupthing and FIH, the Danish bank that Kaupthing bought in 2004.

A dependency on market funding.

NIBC had a CDS cost of 10%. Kaupthing had hoped that their interest would reduce NIBC's funding costs. Instead, Kaupthing's CDS costs climbed. Kaupthing clearly misread its position. It targeted the wrong acquisition candidates and didn't see its own weaknesses.

The two other Icelandic banks followed. Funding costs rose way beyond the costs for banks with similar ratings. The cost of a one-year insurance contract grew relative to the cost of a five-year contract. In short, a fire in year one was considered more likely than a fire further out.

"We had issued so many bonds in recent years, creating a significant supply of our bonds, and now demand for them was becoming scarce," wrote the Kaupthing executive. "Those that had cash, but didn't want our exposure, could buy the bonds at a discount and then buy protection in the CDS market."

"That lifted the spreads, which in turn made other bondholders concerned."

Kaupthing now had to pay more for its funding compared to other banks.

And it caught the attention of the media.

It soon got worse, with the CDS cost reaching 10% by the end of March 2008. No bank can operate at such levels. In effect, the business was no longer viable by early 2008, six to eight months before Lehman collapsed.

A PR effort was launched. The Kaupthing chairman claimed that four named hedge funds based in London had instigated a systematic attack on the Icelandic financial market and Icelandic banks. He said the funds had systematically contacted the UK media and analysts from UK banks to widen CDS spreads and bring down the share price of the banks.

"Truth be told, he could not be sure they had done anything, but it was intended as a deterrent," wrote the Kaupthing executive.

The Central Bank of Iceland attributed the recent rapid devaluation of the Icelandic currency to a speculative 'attack' by 'unscrupulous dealers'. While in reality it was partly a consequence of the three banks' own sale of ISK for FX, ISK they partly got as they tapped the same Central Bank.

The Prime Minister stated, "It's clear that there are people out there trying to make money at our expense, and we want to get them off our backs.

"There is no doubt that the Treasury and the Central Bank could provide assistance if a serious concern were to emerge in the banking system."

The reaction was similar to what others have chosen to say, as their weaknesses were exposed. They blame it on George Soros and the hedge funds.

The CDS costs dropped to 4%. Lower, though still unbearable for any bank. Still, there were sighs of relief. Many thought the markets previously had overreacted.

"We've already seen a degree of turning in the situation," said economics Professor Richard Portes, in *The New York Times* 17 May 2008, four months before the disaster, quoted as an expert on Iceland.

"People are waking up to the fact that these are well-run banks."

When CDS rates rose the next time, Kaupthing was ready with yet another innovation.

SPY VERSUS SPY

In Cold War spy novels, spies sometimes turn out to be working for the party they are spying on. But then, their counterpart may also turn out to be a double agent. In the most sophisticated novels, yet another level of deceit is revealed in the last chapter. It turns out that they are both conducting counterespionage against whoever hired them to conduct counterespionage.

A bit like finance.

On 2 February 2017, John Cryan, the CEO of Deutsche Bank, sent out a message to the bank's employees, updating them on the bank's activities over the previous year.

"Last but not least, we made a lot of progress resolving litigation matters," he noted.

"Last year and over the past few weeks in particular, we have resolved important legal matters including civil cases related to US residential mortgage-backed securities and precious metals, a long-running legal case with the Icelandic bank Kaupthing and parts of the Russia-related proceedings about our anti-money-laundering controls."

Quite a list. And it doesn't even mention Deutsche's dealings with a certain highly leveraged New York property magnate.

A list which brings us to the Kaupthing and Deutsche Bank debacle.

As the CDS prices rose, a new scheme emerged. Getting Kaupthing's cost of borrowing down was a matter of outmost importance. First Deutsche advised Kaupthing to buy back some debt. Then a scheme to lower CDS costs was designed. Both the SIC and the Kaupthing executives credit Deutsche as the mastermind, something Deutsche forcefully denies.

Two SPVs based in the British Virgin Islands were mobilized, Chesterfield and Partridge. One was owned by four old friends of Kaupthing. The other by one of Kaupthing's main owners – the same person, Mr. OO, who had tricked Icelandic authorities through the Hauck & Aufhäuser construct and who was the second-largest borrower of Kaupthing.

These SPVs had one task. They would borrow from Kaupthing and buy Credit Linked Notes (CLNs) from Deutsche.

Deutsche would receive euros in return. Money that originated from Kaupthing. Money Deutsche would have to repay if the SPV returned the bonds to Deutsche. Not if Kaupthing went down, though, said the contract. If that happened, Deutsche could keep the money. It thus had a reserve in case Kaupthing defaulted.

Deutsche could now use this position to create a product, something like CDSs, that would offer a payout if Kaupthing went down.

With Deutsche now selling these new CDS-like instruments, supply would increase, and the price of risk insurance would fall.

Kaupthing could not, as the Kaupthing CEO later wrote, issue insurance on itself. "The solution was to get clients we trusted well and with whom we had had a long relationship, built on trust and loyalty, to make these transactions on behalf of the bank," the CEO wrote. Sure. Someone like Mr. OO.

With more CDS issuance, the cost of borrowing could then decline as the bank was perceived as less risky.

Which it was not, naturally. Especially as the SPVs had very limited equity and were financed with loans and guarantees from Kaupthing.

As Kaupthing fell, the payments to Deutsche came due. Since Kaupthing had guaranteed the SPVs, it became liable. Interestingly, even as the world was falling apart, paying Deutsche was prioritized. Kaupthing paid €50 million to Deutsche on 7 October, two days before it collapsed. The special prosecutor later charged that a loan from Seðlabanki enabled this payment. A loan approved by the then Prime Minister and the Governor.

What's more, some claim that Deutsche itself bought the newly constructed CDSs. In that way, the new supply was matched by new demand. Maybe Deutsche saw how risk was increasing and seized an opportunity. Maybe the CDS-like position was used to hedge a broader portfolio. Maybe a buyer within the bank simply acted independently. Maybe it was a spy versus spy situation.

The fact is, the board charged with winding up Kaupthing after the collapse ended up suing Deutsche in Iceland and the UK. It claimed that the Kaupthing payment to Deutsche Bank was improper. Its purpose was to allow Kaupthing to influence the market in its own CDS spreads and thereby in its listed bonds. They also claimed that Deutsche knew or should have known. The estate demanded repayment of €509 million, plus costs and interest.

In 2016, Deutsche Bank and Kaupthing settled on a payment of €425 million from Deutsche. The German bank surrendered almost completely.

By the time the payment was made in the first quarter of 2017, the Kaupthing winding-up board had been dissolved. It had reached a so-called 'composition agreement' with the creditors, as we will see in more detail later. With this, all the payments from Deutsche flowed through to the creditors. When the composition agreement was made, the claim on Deutsche was booked at 'zero'. Now, suddenly it had a value of €425 million.

What's more, supposedly in part, the payment from Kaupthing to Deutsche in October 2008 was enabled by funds accessed by Kaupthing from Seðlabanki. Money that Seðlabanki partly lost in the end. In this way, taxpayer money went from Seðlabanki to Kaupthing, on to the SPVs, to Deutsche Bank and then through the settlement, to the creditors of Kaupthing, which were by then largely US hedge funds.

" ... this is 100 billion, the hospital and Sundabraut," the Prime Minister said in worry to the then Central Bank Governor Oddsson when they discussed the Icelandic krona loan from the Central Bank to Kaupthing, referring to the planned new hospital and the planned new traffic system.

The leader of the operation in Deutsche Bank moved to become the leader of its Asian trading operations. Later he was dismissed as the bank battled the lawsuit. But he then sued Deutsche. He declined a request for an interview for this book, even though I offered to meet him in Calcutta.

The UK Financial Supervisory Authority, FSA, considered bringing a lawsuit against Kaupthing and Deutsche Bank, but decided to let it go, as the CDS market was unlisted and partly unregulated and therefore a market manipulation charge would be difficult to prove.

"Cases touching on CDS trading are still among the cases we look at," says the special prosecutor.

Who said international finance is boring?

Complicated yes, but boring no.

THREE BANKS THAT ONLY PRETEND

"But, the bankers and their regulator should have understood the Central Bank's limited ability to aid them and incorporated those limitations in their business plans."

– "Iceland's failed banks: A Post-Mortem", prepared for the SIC
by Mark J. Flannery

All three banks claimed to have considered moving their headquarters out of Iceland. If so they would have placed themselves under the umbrellas of larger Central Banks that could provide support and liquidity. Kaupthing considered buying a Dutch bank, NIBC. It could then turn itself into a subsidiary. The new bank would get support from the ECB. Placing itself under FIH in Denmark was another option. Landsbanki considered merging with Straumur and moving the international part of both out of Iceland. Glitnir considered placing itself under BN Bank in Norway.

Some claim this would never had worked, as none would have welcomed the banks. But, what's clear is that no real effort to address their problems was made by the banks and no clear requirement to do so was set by the Icelandic authorities.

"There was talk of a dual listing in Norway," says a former executive of Glitnir Norway. "Moving to Norway was never a real project, though. A formal project was never established, a timeline was never defined."

According to the interviews for this book, the Norwegian FSA was never approached to clarify potential terms and conditions for moving the banks out of Iceland.

It was, in other words, all smoke and mirrors.

"The large amount of lending to the companies of the owners made it all complicated. The Norwegian regulator was already suspicious," says a Seðlabanki advisor.

"There would have been a lot of red flags if the Icelandic banks sold off the loans of their owners."

"It was a disaster waiting to happen. Iceland ran a huge deficit. We needed a constant inflow of capital. Suddenly, we might be without market access," says a former Seðlabanki economist.

"In hindsight, it is obvious to me that funding was a bottleneck," says a former leader of the credit department in one of the three banks. "It is hard to run a manufacturing process with no raw material. For us, funding was no competitive advantage. We ran a bank with no raw material advantage. Our competitive thinking did not work."

"The funding managers in Landsbanki and Glitnir screamed at us. They wanted us to provide money," recalls a Seðlabanki employee, Sturla Pálsson.

"The Seðlabanki Governor, Davið Oddsson, then called the Prime Minister who then called the bank CEOs. They said all was well. They feared that otherwise they would have to hand in the keys to the governor."

"Already in the spring of 2008 we saw that October 2008 would be hard. A large loan was due for repayment in October. The next big maturity was in 2009," says Tryggvi Pálsson, the former Head of the Financial Stability Department.

The first attempt to build backup lines of credit was at the IMF spring meeting at the end of March 2008; the second was in a parallel meeting with the UK Governor Mervyn King; and the third was in a meeting with Timothy Geithner in early April.

In May, a meeting was held among the governors of the largest economies, the G10, at the bank of the Central Banks, BIS.

"We didn't know what was discussed and still don't know," says the director of Seðlabanki's market department, Sturla Pálsson. "But from then on, the G10 representatives stopped taking our calls."

"Iceland wasn't on the agenda," says the Swedish Governor. "Everyone was aware of the vulnerability of Iceland, though."

"On 15 April 2008, Mr. Davið Oddsson sent a formal request for a currency swap agreement to the Bank of England," wrote the SIC.

"Mervyn King, Governor of the Bank of England, replied to Mr. Oddsson's letter on 23 April and rejected the request by the CBI (Seðlabanki)."

"However, he declared that foreign Central Banks could help Iceland find an effective way to reduce the size of its banking system. In his opinion, this was the only practical solution to the problem."

In closing, King said that he offered all the help he could provide to tackle the issue at hand, wrote the SIC. The CBI did not accept this offer. Instead, a reply was sent to the Bank of England, kindly asking it to revise its position regarding the said swap agreement. There was no reply to that letter, the SIC reported.

"We were already working with the IMF. A secret IMF mission came in May 2008. An IMF team came in June. Some Swedish experts came," says one person in Seðlabanki at the time.

"Our control could have been taken away if the Brits had been there. Our options might have become more limited."

In late April, the chairman of Kaupthing wrote a letter to the Icelandic Prime Minister, copying the governor, stressing the need to strengthen the currency reserves by up to €10 billion.

In April 2008, a representative of one of the largest international investment banks met with the Icelandic Central Bank.

"My presentation had three slides. The first said 'Your banks will fail', the second said 'This is why', and the third said 'There is nothing you can do to stop it.'"

"They didn't seem surprised," says the advisor.

By May 2008, the króna had depreciated by 26%. The Central Bank raised interest rates to a record 15.5% in April, but the ISK continued to slide against the euro. Inflation rose to an annual rate of 11.8%, the highest in 18 years.

Issuance of a €1 billion bond on behalf of the state was attempted in May and early June.

"We could have issued a €1 billion state loan," says the lead in JPMorgan, Michael Ridley. "But it wouldn't have helped. Its costs would also have been high and the reputational risk of trying and failing significant."

"We could have done €300 million at a high rate, but it would have been a desperate move," says the person in Seðlabanki overseeing state borrowing.

"We had still not ruled out issuing long-term financing in early June, but then Trichet at the ECB announced a rate increase. In early July, the ECB raised its rate by 0.25 to 3.25%."

The ECB had been watching the crisis emerge since August 2007. But it also saw June inflation numbers of 4%, well above its 2% target.

At the press conference on 3 July, after the interest rate increase, Trichet stated, "Inflation is now the number-one concern of our 320 million fellow citizens. They are counting on us to be the anchor of price stability in a period that is obviously very demanding. They can count on us."

Bold words to describe a faulty decision.

I attended Trichet's retirement event in the Frankfurt Opera House on 19 October 2011. Its highlight was when two of the grand old men of the EU, Helmut Schmidt, who was in his 90s, and Giscard d'Estaing, in his 80s, entered the scene, with the first in a wheelchair. They compared the euro crisis to the challenges of their time in post-war Europe. And they told the younger generations, all the EU heads of state, to get moving and solve their minuscule problems. Rarely have I been more impressed.

In Trichet's speech, he defended his move to raise interest rates in 2007. A separation principle had been applied. The higher interest rate was meant to stabilize prices. 'Nonstandard' measures were to solve other problems.

A year after Trichet made that move, the interest rate had sunk to 0.25%. Inflation was –0.7%. The world was in crisis, or, as said by Trichet in his recollection of his eight years in office, "After four years came the financial and economic crisis."

As if it were by destiny.

The workings of the market obviously did not include such a thing as a separation principle. And the risk of having just one performance indicator, price stability, for a Central Bank was demonstrated.

"The ECB rate hike blew all prospects of issuing bonds out of the water for Iceland," was the general opinion in Seðlabanki.

"While we were on a roadshow, all the cell phones of the team members stopped working," recalls the Director of Market Operations in Seðlabanki.

"Now Europe has pulled the plug, we commented. Is it coming now? We were almost certain."

"In August 2008, while on vacation in Tuscany, I raised €300 million from a German bank for the Republic of Iceland," he continues. "In 2010, we bought back the €300 million loan for 240 million."

"While I got beaten up for my Tuscany phone bill."

JUST FOUR DAYS AFTER LEHMAN

"Financial waters, already extremely chilly, then froze solid. Banks found it almost impossible to finance themselves because no one knew which banks were safe and which weren't."

– Then Governor of the Bank of England, Mervyn King, on the financial markets after the Lehman collapse

The Central Bank governors of the most developed countries meet once a quarter in Basel, in the bank of the Central Banks, BIS.

In addition, the governors may meet in regional gatherings. The five Nordic governors meet every quarter. These meetings rotate among countries. Once a year, they meet in a particularly nice location, chosen by the host. It is all friendly and collaborative.

Normally.

They met on 14 May 2008 in Rådhusgata, in the old part of Oslo. Here, a 16th century building has been integrated into the new headquarters of the Norwegian Central Bank and the Oil Fund, now the largest sovereign wealth fund in the world. The medieval setting provided a nice atmosphere.

But this time, the surroundings offered no comfort.

"It was an inflamed meeting. Iceland had asked for a Nordic swap. We needed certainty that the situation of the banks would be addressed with force," says a Nordic governor.

"It was a cumbersome evening," says another.

"We demanded a call with the Icelandic Prime Minister Geir Haarde," says Svein Gjedrem, then the Norwegian governor. "The Icelandic governor was upset. We got Prime Minister Haarde on his mobile. He gave the guarantees we demanded.

"We requested an immediate downsizing of the banking system, aiming for a reduction by half in the long term."

The next day, the Central Banks of Sweden, Denmark and Norway provided a funding line to Iceland. Seðlabanki could now pull FX if it placed a similar amount of ISK into the accounts of the other Central Banks, adding 10% as a buffer.

Each provided €500 million, raising the Icelandic currency reserves from €2 billion to €3.5 billion.

"In times of uncertainty and turmoil, it is the responsibility of Central Banks to cooperate to achieve their overall goals," stated the Swedish governor, correctly, in a press release as the May agreement was signed.

"The Swap Agreement aims to support Seðlabanki Islands in its task of safeguarding macroeconomic and financial stability."

He and the other Nordic governors were ready to support Iceland, but they were not impressed with Iceland's efforts at reform. Some were of the view that the Icelandic authorities did not take forceful enough action nor engage in real discussions on how to resolve the problems.

" ... unclear ownership, along with the banks' rapid balance sheet growth, had led to a dangerous situation, and that the Icelandic government did not seem to fully grasp nor understand how to deal with," read a letter the SIC received from the Swedish governor.

The Nordic lenders had asked for three conditions for the swap agreement: that Iceland should reduce the size of its banks, run a prudent fiscal policy and make changes to the housing fund.

The SIC says that the Nordic Central Banks felt the Icelandic authorities did not pursue these challenges with adequate vigour.

"You can argue whether there was enough time to do anything," one of the governors now says, "or whether it was too late already. But as far as we could see, no action had been taken to scale down the banks. We will never know if the crash could have been avoided if there had been real cooperation, but most probably the problems could have been reduced."

"Sometimes we were told that things weren't that bad. On other occasions, that the Central Bank had no influence."

The SIC saw a pattern of behaviour that triggered severe consequences.

"The aforementioned promises by the government in the summer of 2008 were not kept," said the SIC. "That did not improve the reputation of the Icelandic authorities with foreign Central Banks."

"At this time, the Icelandic authorities had become very isolated in the international community. Therefore, they had few to turn to when the Icelandic banks collapsed in October 2008," wrote the SIC.

The next meeting of the Nordic governors took place from 11 to 13 June in Egilsstaðir, on the east coast of Iceland. Again, a nice venue. The whole group went off to see the new power plant being constructed to deliver power to a giant aluminium smelter. Many were impressed.

"I see there is no lack of collateral," said one guest.

Some Icelanders were not sure if he was joking. One saw it as a sign of praise and hope.

"Now there was war. Nothing had been done with the banks," says an attendee.

"The criticism was hard. These folks had no control," says one of the governors.

"If you have no money, you have no choice," says a then governor. "It only gets worse."

"We sat together for what seemed hours, only us five governors," recalls Gjedrem. "The mood was bad. Then it got worse."

"The location was beautiful, the Icelanders friendly and hospitable as always. This made the impressions even more lasting.

"But maybe it was too late. There were no measures. There was no plan. The legal basis was insufficient. Paralysis ruled."

"'Landsbanki is well run, though. Less so the other banks.' I remember that as a statement from the then Icelandic governor," says Gjedrem.

"The next meeting of the Nordic governors took place after Lehman collapsed. Now all were clear."

"None of the conditions set in May had been met. Not again," says Stefan Ingves.

As late as 19 September, Seðlabanki had prepared a confidential memo with no named author. It summarized the status and the follow-up of the Nordic agreement. It referred to the metric used internationally to measure a bank's solidity, the Capital Adequacy Ratio or CAR.

"The three major Icelandic commercial banks delivered respectable results in the second quarter of 2008 and thus in the first half of the year taken together," stated the memo. "At the end of June, they all had satisfactory CAR ratios and they all met with a comfortable margin the routine stress tests conducted by the Supervisory Authority (FME) on their mid-year balance sheets."

The memo further stated: "The governors meet regularly with the CEOs of the commercial banks and the Central Bank monitors the activities of the banks very closely, as does the FME. At the present time, the liquidity position of the banks is under control and sufficient for them to be able to meet their obligations well into next year."

A notable assessment, written four days after Lehman, one week before what would be known as the Glitnir weekend and two weeks before the long weekend that led up to the week of the ultimate disaster.

The Nordic governors were not pleased. They were hearing the same tales they had been hearing for a long time. Even now, right after Lehman.

"By this time, most had gone to hell," says Governor Ingves forcefully as I ask him about the memorandum. "Entirely. No one believed a word of what was said and written."

A forcing device was needed.

"No IMF, no money," said Ingves.

"Yes, Central Banks do cooperate," says Gjedrem. "But this cooperation is not based on kindness. It is based on self-interest. There is no strict coordination. Small countries, especially, depend on trust. They need to work to be connected. Norway was the first to enter into a dialogue on a swap agreement with the US. Sweden, not Norway, was part of the coordinated reduction of interest rates by seven countries on 8 October 2008."

Nothing happens automatically.

A week after the crash, on 14 October, Denmark and Norway responded positively to Seðlabanki's request for money. Both provided €200 million. Sweden did not join.

Rejecting, as Sweden did, a request to execute on an established agreement between Central Banks is highly unusual, to say the least.

"Sveriges Riksbank is the entity in Sweden that decides if a loan is to be given," firmly states Governor Ingves. "That's what the law says. It's on our books. It's our risk."

"We had no evil intentions. But none of the conditions for the swap loan had been fulfilled."

Never again.

"A third party was needed."

The IMF.

ENVIABLE PROSPECTS

"The IMF, too, gave a positive assessment of Iceland in the summer of 2008."

This was a comment I heard from many, including current senior policymakers in Iceland, as I interviewed people for this book. They clearly wanted to make the point that others, too, failed to see what was coming.

"IMF said Iceland's prospects were enviable," many quoted, again and again, referring to the IMF reports.

It was time for a fact check.

In June 2007, an IMF report on Iceland concluded, "The *medium-term* prospects for the Icelandic economy remain enviable."

The 4 July 2008 report reads, " ... the *long-term* economic prospects for the Icelandic economy remain enviable."

Quite an indirect way of communicating the possibility of a multiyear deep economic depression, one might say. Still, the IMF was onto something. And it was right.

"The Icelandic economy is prosperous and flexible," stated the 2008 report. Per capita income is among the highest, and income inequality among the lowest in the world. Labour and product markets are open and flexible."

"The remarkable management of the country's natural resources has enabled Iceland to diversify the economy and help ensure sustainability," the report continued.

But then comes the harsher part: "Economic activity is expected to slow significantly from unsustainably high levels.

"Uncertainties surrounding the outlook are unusually large, with significant downside risks dominated by external considerations. Despite efforts to address market concerns, the banking sector still faces significant risks.

"Policy options to mitigate these risks should continue to be pursued with vigour."

And lastly: "The authorities should strengthen the crisis prevention and resolution framework further, building on the progress already made."

But then the IMF had a dilemma. When it first made a report on the financial sector in Iceland in 2001, there had been a discussion on whether the report should be made public. In the end, as one would expect in a democracy, it was made public. Hence IMF knew their mid-June report would be shared with all.

Certainly, the IMF, too, would not want to be the trigger of any crisis.

JAZZ, FREDDIE, FANNIE, LEHMAN AND WAMU

"In fact, neoliberalism's regime of restraint and discipline operated under a proviso. In the event of a major financial crisis that threatened 'systemic' interests, it turned out that we lived in an age of not limited but of big government, of massive executive action, of interventionism that had more in common with military operations or emergency medicine than with law-bound governance ... They would do whatever it took to keep the financial system afloat. And because the modern banking system is both global and based on dollars, that meant unprecedented transnational action by the American State."
– *Crashed*, Adam Tooze

"I was at a jazz festival in late July 2008. It was vacation time. That was when the US Undersecretary of the Treasury, David McCormick, called," says the then highest-ranking official in the Norwegian Ministry of Finance, Tore Eriksen.

"We have everything under control," McCormick said. "Your government has no reason to be worried."

"That was when we did get worried," says the official.

McCormick called again the day after. Now he asked to speak to the Minister of Finance. She was also on vacation.

"Everything is under control," McCormick again said. "There is no reason for the Norwegian Oil Fund to sell its positions in Freddie Mac and Fannie Mae," referring to the two US house financing institutions.

"He more than implied that the US would not let the two organizations fail," wrote the minister in her memoirs. "But we did not call the Oil Fund," says the official. "We never did."

In early September, the US government took control of Freddie Mac and Fannie Mae.

"The Americans did just what McCormick had promised," wrote the minister.

On 15 September, Lehman Brothers, among the largest investment banks in the US, collapsed.

"This time, we received no call from any undersecretary of the Treasury," says the official.

"Every Friday, we sent all funds of Lehman Brother's banking operations in the UK to the headquarters in the US, which sent it back before start of business Monday," says Glenn Kim, then a Lehman employee. "On that Monday, no money had been sent back."

On 10 September 2008, the Chief Financial Officer of Lehman Brothers, Ian Lowitt, had told shareholders and the public that the bank had $42 billion of available cash, or liquidity. The bank's position, Lowitt reassured, "remains very strong." But, despite the statement of the bank, and contrary to the belief of the regulators and rating agencies, the liquidity pool wasn't, in fact, all that liquid.

With this collapse, no one knew who might be next. Banks reduced their lending to other banks. Transactions were halted. They all cut financing lines to build buffers. Money was stuck. Glenn worked full time for an entire year just to clear the interface between Lehman and the Oil Fund.

A law firm was assigned the task of running the Lehman estate.

On 16 September, the European financial supervisory bodies met on a phone conference to coordinate their responses.

"There is no one in charge over there," said the Belgian regulator, Peter Praet, referring to the US. "A law firm is running Lehman."

Next in line was Washington Mutual, the sixth-largest bank in the US, with assets of more than $327 billion.

In a mid-September nine-day bank run, $16.7 billion, 9% of deposits, left the bank.

On 25 September, the United States Office of Thrift Supervision, OTS, seized Washington Mutual Bank from its parent, Washington Mutual, Inc.

The Federal insurance scheme, FDIC, then sold the bank to JPMorgan Chase, which acquired all the banking operations, including $307 billion in assets and $188 billion in deposits, for $1.9 billion plus debt assumptions. All Washington Mutual (WaMu) branches were rebranded into Chase branches by the end of 2009.

FDIC had solved its problem. The depositors and secured debt holders of the bank now had their rights guaranteed by JPMorgan.

Washington Mutual Bank was placed into receivership on 25 September. The next day, the holding company, Washington Mutual Inc., filed for Chapter 11 bankruptcy protection. Measured by total assets under management, Washington Mutual Bank's closure and receivership was the largest bank failure in the financial history of the Americas.

The US actions defined a new model for bank restructuring, the WaMu model. US law granted priority to the FDIC over other claimholders and legalized the move. Here the authorities had the right to intervene directly to secure depositors and prevent losses otherwise to be borne by taxpayers.

The other lenders took a beating. Some weeks later, the WaMu model became the model for Iceland. And, yes, after some searching, I managed, as will be seen, to find a creditor that had bought debt in both WaMu and in one of the Icelandic banks. With this, the brutality of the two can be compared.

"We had a patchwork of legal structures," says Timothy Geithner, then the President of the New York Federal Reserve and later Secretary of the US Treasury, when interviewed for this book.

"If you have complete legal authority, your desires are clear. When a banking crisis hits, you want to protect the core of the core of the system."

When large accidents occur, the emergency rooms in hospitals put in place a triage process. Patients are prioritized based on the severity of their condition and the probability of their survival. The emergency room staff then focus their efforts where they can do the greatest good.

"A triage-type process is also needed when handling a banking crisis," says Geithner.

"First, are the institutions regulated as banks? Yes or no?

"Second, where are the banks with regards to their solvency?

"Third, how important are they to the system?"

Then he continues: "The ones that will not make it must be put out of their misery at the least cost. You can force an auction. Sell off. Or nationalize. However, we did not have the authority to do that. We came from 70 years with no meaningful crisis.

"On Bear Stearns, we could help run an auction. Fannie Mae and Freddie Mac had to get priority. Here, we knew we had liabilities. But the bailout aversion grew and peaked just before Lehman.

"And Lehman was so weak we could not find a buyer."

The UK bank Barclays was the last to consider an acquisition. But the UK regulator and the UK Ministry of Finance provided no support.

"He said he didn't want to 'import our cancer,'" said the then US Secretary of the Treasury Hank Paulson, quoting the UK minister Alistair Darling.

"The British screwed us," Paulson continued.

Darling's first reaction had been to ask, "If this is such a good deal, how come no American bank is going to go near it?"

"Lehman was the game changer," says a Fed employee.

"Lehman fell on Monday 15 September. On Tuesday the outflow started."

"By Wednesday we had a full-scale bank run."

On 17 September 2008, Lloyds TSB took over the UK's largest lender, HBOS.

"I do not have the vocabulary to describe what happened. It was an unlimited crisis," recalls a US Fed official.

"The demand for dollars was enormous," says another.

"And in a contentious and problematic way, it had the effect of recentring the world financial economy on the United States as the only state capable of meeting the challenge it posed," wrote Adam Tooze in his massive book *Crashed*. "That capacity is an effect of structure – the United States is the only state that can generate dollars.

"Hidden below the radar and barely discussed in public, what threatened the stability of the North Atlantic economy in the fall of 2008 was a huge shortfall in dollar funding of Europe's oversized banks," continued Tooze. "And a shortfall, in their case, meant not tens of billions, or even hundreds of billions, but trillions of dollars."

Options were analysed on both sides of the Atlantic and the Pacific through the night. On Thursday 18 September, the swap lines to the ECB and the Swiss were extended to $137 billion. This was the amount of dollars the Central Banks could access by placing a comparable amount of their own currency in a US Fed account.

New lines of $100 billion in total were added to the Bank of Japan, the Bank of England and the Bank of Canada.

Six days later, Denmark, Sweden and Norway followed with another 30 billion – $267 billion in total.

In another two days the ECB and Swiss limits were increased from $137 to $290 billion.

Then came another painful weekend of crisis meetings. The total limit more than doubled, to $620 billion. And Australia was added as an eligible recipient.

Unlimited beat enormous.

By 13 October, there was no limit for the ECB, the Swiss and the UK any more. Japan had unlimited access when it woke up the next day. The inner perimeter of the fortress of money had been set.

" ... the Federal Reserve made dollars available to these four Central Banks in quantities not subject to prespecified limits," is the wording Central Bankers used when they gave someone unlimited access to their vault.

Soon after, New Zealand, Brazil, Mexico, South Korea and Singapore were added to the list of recipients. Now the outer perimeter had been set.

Seven OECD countries were left outside in the dark, among them Iceland and Turkey. A preamble to the 2018 Turkish crisis.

Brazil, Canada, South Korea and Singapore did not use the facilities provided. The ECB, Switzerland, the UK, Japan, Australia, Denmark, Sweden, Norway and Mexico pulled dollars. In total, $540 billion at the peak. Clearly, the mechanism was of use.

These Central Banks got dollars. The Fed got local currency in an account in the respective Central Banks, a claim on the authorities of each of the ten currency areas using the swap.

Many dollars were thereafter passed on to local banks. In return, each Central Bank received claims and collateral from *their* banks. And each Central Bank bore the risk associated with the dollar funding of their local banks.

"The foreign Central Banks, in turn, made dollar loans to financial institutions within their jurisdictions and took on the related collateral and counterparty risks," wrote the US Federal Reserve dryly.

In other words: the Federal Reserve supported the Central Banks and took the country's risk. Each national Central Bank could then choose to support its local banks, and if so take on the associated risks.

Ideally, all would have calmed down for Iceland if Seðlabanki also had obtained a swap line. If so, Iceland could, in principle, have joined the four non-takers.

More likely, though, the funding of the three banks would still have dried up as borrowers took their money. In this case, the Icelandic Central Bank would have had the option of joining the group of ten countries that made use of the facilities.

Sweden and Denmark pulled $25 and $15 billion, respectively.

By pulling dollars, Seðlabanki would then have had the choice of keeping the dollars in its own vaults or passing them on to the three banks.

In the latter case, the US would suddenly have had some ISK 100 billion as claims against the Central Bank in Reykjavik, which again would have had even more claims on the three banks.

If all had calmed down then, the challenge of the Icelandic banks could have been resolved in an orderly fashion. Possibly, that is. Alternatively, the banks could still have gone down.

A scary thought.

"The key point was to save the state, the sovereign. There were different views," says a former Seðlabanki Islands employee.

"I was happy we did not get exposed to the temptation of having money that could have been used to try to save banks that couldn't be saved."

The markets, however, reacted very negatively to the exclusion of Iceland from the system of swap agreements.

WRONG NUMBER, CALL THE IMF

"Lehman fell on 15 September. The next day I called Bill Dudley at the US Fed," says Audun Grønn in the Norwegian Central Bank.

"I requested a swap line. On Friday, they were ready to discuss. On Monday we had a call, together with the Swedes and the Danes."

"We got access to dollars. As we used them, we had to place a matching krona amount in a Fed account.

"No one mentioned Iceland."

The call from Norway, a country with massive surpluses and its oil fund, did nothing to calm the nerves of the US Federal Reserve. Referring in an internal meeting to Norway's request for $5 billion in liquidity support, Dudley said, "The fact that Norway is doing this suggests that the situation has broadened quite a bit further."

On 24 September, Australia was given access to $10 billion; Sweden, Norway and Denmark 5 billion each. Five days later, the quotas increased to 30, 30, 15 and 15.

"It is incorrect to say Iceland was the only country that was turned down by the Fed. Some major economies, like Turkey, also got no offer," says a Seðlabanki employee.

The Turkish lira depreciated about 40% to the dollar during the next six months, from August 2008.

Diplomatic cables leaked through WikiLeaks indicate that Indonesia and Turkey did request swap-lines but were turned down. In the Fed leaders' judgment, they were not important enough to American economic interests to warrant participation, wrote *The New York Times* on 23 February 2014.

A Cornell University economist, Eswar Prasad, has studied the US policy on the currency swaps and the transcripts of the Fed meetings.

"To the rest of the world, I don't think these transcripts are going to be very reassuring," quoted *The New York Times*. "What they show is that the US policymakers are very narrowly focused on US interests, and their actions are not so much determined by any moral obligation to save the world economy, but rather a clear self interest in preserving US economic interests."

Many in Iceland have asked why their country was excluded. Hence, off I went to New York to ask Timothy Geithner about the matter. I met him in a high-rise building just south of Central Park.

"Before the 2008 crash, everyone pointed to Iceland when big financial bubbles were discussed," said Geithner.

"But there were many others. We had no Iceland team."

"Iceland came to us and requested a swap line of approximately $1-2 billion," Nathan Sheets, an economist at the US Fed told the Federal Open Market Committee when it met 28 October 2008, "which would have been 5-10% of Iceland's GDP, so it was fairly large relative to the size of the country.

"But the liabilities of the banking system were in the order of $170 billion, and the underlying problem was really that there was a loss of confidence in its banks."

The US held the view that the Icelandic banking system was too big in relation to the country's GDP. Iceland did not pass the requirement that a swap line would 'actually make a difference'.

"We came to the conclusion that a $1-2 billion swap line was very little ammunition to use against a potential loss in confidence in this $170 billion financial system," said Sheets. "For that reason, we on the staff recommended against a swap line for Iceland."

"The US is the centre of the dollar world. We had to provide dollars to the system," said Geithner.

"European banks ended up being our largest borrowers in 2007 and 2008. But the three Icelandic banks never really turned up.

"The Icelandic banks were not active in the US. They were not our borrowers. We never feared they could create a contagion, negative repercussions for the larger system.

"So, the Icelandic banks did not rank among our many problems," said Geithner.

But the Federal Reserve still took the request from Iceland seriously. Staff interviews confirm that the Icelandic request was received, considered, analysis conducted and tested against the Fed criteria.

"Iceland did not rank well," says a senior staff member.

"What Iceland needed was credit lines, not a swap."

Some memories of the analysis conducted by the US Fed remain, even after ten years. "A diagram was drawn up that showed the interlinkages of the ownership of the Icelandic banks," says Terrence Checki, Head of the Emerging Markets and International Affairs Group at the Fed, who was responsible for the prep work. "It is one of the most convoluted systems I have ever seen.

"The US Fed is accountable to Congress. Its decisions must withstand scrutiny. Actions from the Fed toward the US market are understood. Actions in support of the main financial centres can be understood. But, from a US perspective, neither Sweden, Denmark nor Norway rank as economic centres," he continues.

"The triage model also applies to countries," said Geithner.

"The idea was to have a short list of countries. You judge based on fundamental strength. You consider what risks a problem in a specific country may create for the wider financial system and for the US. You judge if it may work at all."

On the top were the G10 countries and the main emerging markets, Brazil, Mexico, South Korea and Singapore.

"Then all is considered on a case-by-case basis. Denmark, Sweden and Norway were not seen as priority countries, but could easily be included," said Geithner.

"Some countries solve their problems themselves. In some instances, we can help with financing. Some need the IMF," said Geithner.

"I cannot remember any foreign policy debate when it came to Iceland.

"And, if a request is grounded in foreign policy objectives, then the IMF is our answer. Foreign policy does matter for our support through the IMF, not for swap lines.

"And on a general basis, assume someone called with a banking system nine times the size of GDP and asked for a swap line, there would be one likely answer," said Geithner.

"Sorry, wrong number. Call the IMF."

KEEP THE INFECTION AWAY

Sweden, Finland and Norway all experienced their own banking crises in the early 1990s.

In Sweden, a housing bubble burst in 1991-1992.

"We created our banking crisis ourselves. It did not come from abroad," says Ingves, the Swedish Central Bank Governor. He was the one who led the bank support unit at the time. Informally, it carried the name *bankakuten*, the bank emergency ward.

"In contrast, the 2008 crisis was international. Our priority was to keep it out of Sweden."

"The Swedish government had an emergency exercise at Harpsund in February 2008 on how to handle a financial crisis," says the then Swedish Minister of Finance, Anders Borg. "What actions would be needed? Who had which responsibilities?

"The crisis wasn't unexpected.

"Kaupthing Bank in Sweden had been a worry for a while. They offered higher interest rates than all others. They attracted deposits, but at a high cost. This was not going to end well, we thought.

"Ingves had 30 lawyers ready. When the Icelandic banks started to collapse on 6 October, all were ready," says Borg. "We even asked an employee from the ministry to be outside the branch office in the morning, to see if there was a bank run.

"But not one anxious depositor turned up."

"We were on the alert," confirms Ingves. "We required that any payment we made to Kaupthing Sweden be matched with funds from the parent. On top of this, we asked for collateral. Krona by krona. We wondered how long we would have to sit on Kaupthing.

"Then Ålandsbanken came and said they would take care of it all. They bought Kaupthing Sweden."

Many large Nordic banks had chosen Sweden for their headquarters, including Nordea, Handelsbanken, SEB and Swedbank. All had large FX positions and needed FX for their funding. Sweden has its own local currency, the Swedish krona. Now, the Swedish Central Bank itself had to borrow FX to build buffers.

In addition, the Swedish banks had grown widely in the Baltics. The Swedes, Finns and to some extent the Danes had aspired to make the Baltics their new home market. They competed by handing out loans. It was the opportunity of the decade.

To lose money.

A banking crisis developed in the Baltics, with the Swedish banks in lead roles. The Swedish Central Bank, Sveriges Riksbank, had to provide liquidity loans to many banks, and to Lithuania, Estonia and Latvia.

"Our balance sheet grew from SEK 200 billion to 800 billion. We handed out loans in euro and krona, some of this we borrowed," says Ingves. "The US swap line helped.

"We were not averse to supporting Iceland. Our main fight, however, was to not let the infection into Sweden."

On Sunday 12 October, Norway passed a bylaw giving its bank regulator the authority to seize and restructure assets.

The bylaw was tailored to the Kaupthing situation.

It only applied in cases where a bank with a headquarters in another country and with a branch in Norway did not meet its obligations in Norway while continuing to meet its obligations in its home country. Or, if the measures implemented in the home country did not resolve the situation in Norway.

The Norwegian FSA seized all of the assets of Kaupthing Norway, a branch of Kaupthing, and established a separate unit to wind up its affairs.

When its Icelandic parent bank collapsed, Glitnir in Norway lost a source of support. The Norwegian deposit insurance fund granted a liquidity loan of €590 million. The loan was valid for seven days. The fund turned down a request for prolonging the loan. Glitnir needed cash. Selling its subsidiary, Glitnir Bank ASA, which also included BN Bank and Kredittbanken, was Glitnir's only option. The divestiture had to happen there and then. Glitnir retained an advisory, Arctic Securities.

One buyer, a consortium of Norwegian savings banks, planned to bid half the book value. But then the buyer's advisor prepared benchmarks that showed that some buyers in the Lehman and Bear Stearns cases paid as little as 10%.

"Why not offer 10%?" asked an experienced member of the buyer's group. And 10% was bid.

"We feared there would be other bidders, but there were none," says a person close to the process. "Everyone was scared in October 2008."

The consortium bought BN Bank for NOK 300 million. Four months later, it booked a profit of NOK 1.3 billion on the transaction.

THROWING PENSION FUND MONEY INTO THE FIRE

The single largest pile of financial assets in Iceland lies in the Icelandic pension plans. In other countries, pension plans are routinely underfunded. Not so in Iceland. Here, the aim is for the plans that cover future pensions to be fully funded at all times. Eleven of the 100 largest pension funds in the Nordics are thus Icelandic.

The Icelandic pension system has three pillars: mandatory occupational pension funds being the most important; taxpayer-funded pensions; and tax advantaged voluntary plans for individuals.

Most of the funds are invested in Iceland, some abroad.

The funds invest in shares and bonds of banks and companies, including companies that in turn invest in banks.

On paper, the funds gained when Icelandic equity and asset values grew. The maximum percentage of stocks the funds were allowed to hold was increased in stages from 35% of net assets to 60%, most recently in 2006. This facilitated, one could also say required, vast holdings of bank equity.

A later report on the funds' investments based on findings by the SIC said, "A substantial share of the domestic investments made after mid-2007 was based on data that would not have withstood closer examination, if this had been possible."

"There were, admittedly, rumours during the period leading up to the banks' collapse that the banks had made loans for the purchase of their own shares."

The report continued, "Consideration must also be given to the mood that prevailed in Icelandic financial circles at this time, which were dominated by the influence of the investment banks and commercial banks, the views of leading politicians, the feebleness of regulatory institutions and the Central Bank's policy of maintaining a high ISK exchange rate as long as possible without ensuring that other economic forces were in step with this.

"In this connection, it could be mentioned that the mood was much more conducive to boosting the Icelandic banks' expansion abroad than to restraining it," the report stated.

The funds lost big time in Iceland. They could have lost even more. At the peak of the crisis, the pension funds sat on €3.5 billion in foreign assets.

In the last pre-crisis days, this stock of FX had the attention of many.

"The discussion of what role the funds should play was on the table," says a board member of one of the funds.

"Some banks and fund managers worked to make the pension funds take a role. Some fund managers gathered in Reykjavik."

Could the funds help to resolve it all? Was there an opportunity for the funds? Five funds looked at acquiring Kaupthing but passed on the idea.

IN NEED OF A GENERAL

"On all sides there was a failure of imagination to appreciate the scale of the fragilities and their potential consequences. No one could quite bring themselves to believe that in our modern financial system, the biggest banks in the world could fall over. But they did."
– Then Governor of the Bank of England, Mervyn King,
on the global financial crisis

"I worked in the fire brigade at Keflavik airport when I was a student," says Tryggvi Pálsson, who led the financial stability department in Seðlabanki through the years of crisis.

"Its chief was known as 'Patton', after the US General. In 1973, a lava flow threatened to close the port of Vestmannaeyar. From the US, he brought in the largest imaginable water pumps. He fought the lava. He just did it. And it worked."

The crisis group of Seðlabanki was formed on 14 November 2007. A joint group that included representatives of the ministries was established on 28 January 2008. Among its tasks was to define and describe a worst-case scenario.

All were functionaries. The group did not have a real mandate. It surely had no general Patton.

"An Emergency Act was needed. We started to work on it, but in bits and pieces. Some feared that any complete version could leak," says a key member of the joint group.

"We looked at various options," says another key member of the team. "We were making drafts.

"The ministers did not want to believe that the party was over. Some believed the minister in charge of the banks couldn't keep a secret, and that he was too eager to please some bankers."

Whatever the reason, he was the last to be informed.

The inability to act with competence and in confidentiality frustrated Seðlabanki. "There was a fundamental mistrust," says an advisor to the government. "The attitude toward keeping minutes of meetings was casual. All this explains why the coordination broke down."

"Working for one of the banks, I saw a strong need for coordination, but there was none," says a former employee of one of the three banks. "Coordination is needed, even when no problems can be seen. Here there were lots. But there was absolutely no coordinated response."

He continues, "Maybe the privatization process influenced the attitude of the authorities. The banks had been released. Now any problem was for them to solve. And the banks distrusted the political system and some politicians."

THE TOWER COMES DOWN

By now, most market participants knew that the Icelandic banks were gigantic by most measures: their absolute size, and their size relative to the size of the economy. Participants could also see the banks' weaknesses, the warning signs and the growing strength of the forces that could take them down.

It soon also became clear how much havoc their collapse would cause and how much rubble they would leave behind. Luckily, the rubble would later be encircled by a fence and the encircled area turned into a construction site.

But for most people, the abstract talk of billions of ISK, euros and dollars is hard to grasp. So let us experiment with a visual.

If you have been to Pisa and seen the Leaning Tower, you will understand. If you have not been there yet, you should go.

I was there 30 years ago, and the image still sticks. To me, it was a mystery that the tower was still standing.

So, head off to the lawn in front of *Fontana dei Putti*, order *un caffè corretto*, observe the tower and picture an imaginary banking tower next to it. Then, open this book and reread the following:

The Leaning Tower of Pisa is 55.7 meters tall.

Imagine that our banking tower has 1 meter of height for every 1 billion dollars managed by the Icelandic banks, as measured by their balance sheets.

Our tower would be more than three times the height of the Leaning Tower of Pisa, 182.1 meters.

The Landsbanki part alone would almost match the Pisa tower, at $50.1 billion or 50.1 meters. Glitnir would add another 48.7 meters, and Kaupthing topped it up with another 83.3 meters.

The banks grew to this height at an astonishing pace. Lending by the banks' parent companies grew by an average of nearly 50% per year from 2004 until the collapse.

You may think that each bank should have its own tower, as they were individual entities. But that was not really the case. Remember the spiderweb of linkages, the tightly interwoven net between the banks and their owners and their cross-lending.

And even if there had been separate towers, they would all have been located on the same small square, where the fall of one would also take down the others. A bit like falling dominoes. That is, unless the bricks had been deliberately placed to be independent of or even to stabilize each other.

Which the banks clearly were not. No real attempt had been made to differentiate the profile of the three banks. On the contrary, each picked up the tricks of the others, and they largely drew money from the same sources and issued loans to the same customers.

The size of a country's economy is often measured by the total value of all work done by its inhabitants and all profits earned by its companies in a full year, what we call Gross Domestic Product, GDP. In 2007, Iceland's GDP was $21.3 billion.

Now, imagine that every billion dollars of GDP is a square meter of space. The Pisa tower's base is about 188 square meters. Even the Pisa tower has a reasonable proportion between its height and its base. The banking tower not so.

The Pisa tower leans because its foundation is merely 3 meters deep, set in weak, unstable subsoil. The foundation was flawed from the beginning.

A bank's societal role is to gather money that depositors and others have available in the short and long term, and to disburse those funds for the use of homeowners and companies, usually over the long term.

To be able to invest in a building or a machine, a company needs long-term financing and predictability. Through a bank, this need can be met, using funds from deposits that the depositor may want to access tomorrow. This exposes the banks to mismatches of time and size. Buffers are needed.

These buffers form the foundation of the banks.

The buffers come in two forms.

First is the bank's own net value, its equity. In simple terms, the bank's assets should be greater than what it owes to others. That excess or equity is the result of capital contributed from its owners and any retained surplus from decades of banking.

Second is the bank's access to liquidity. It must be able to access additional 'money' if necessary.

The three Icelandic banks were said to have strong buffers. They reported making money and having access to more if needed.

However, as we have seen, a major part of their equity consisted of loans from themselves.

Still, what ultimately made the Icelandic banking tower fall was exactly the trigger listed in the overview of the five phases of a financial crisis. A lack of liquidity.

At the end of August 2008, the three banks reported an expected outflow of funds of €28 billion for the period from September to October 2008. An immense figure. But they also reported that there was almost €42 billion in liquid assets, i.e., 'money' they could access from various sources. A more immense figure. And oddly enough, exactly the amount Lehman Brothers had claimed in available liquidity. That turned out to be not so available.

Hence, the three banks claimed to be covered both in ISK and FX. In August 2008, the three banks all said they had sufficient liquid assets to cover loan payments over the next 12 months.

But these figures included money they expected to be able to borrow from Central Banks against collateral. The figures also included money promised from other banks, through so-called lines of credit. The banks claimed that these were secure, but they were in fact conditional. As later documented by the SIC. And the figures included funds that would have been immensely expensive to use.

A very different story from the one the banks were telling.

Not only was the 'new money' uncertain, the existing base was also unstable. Customers could pull their deposits. Existing funding could be shut down if the banks' credit rating dropped. As could happen with a weakening of the Icelandic economy, the ISK, the Icelandic stock exchange or the other banks. The banks had also already borrowed huge amounts from the ECB and Seðlabanki. The three banks had already eaten their emergency rations.

Glitnir was the first to go. Not such a big surprise.

On 4 July 2008, Seðlabanki's financial stability department submitted a memo to the board of governors. The memo carried the prophetic title: "Why do we worry about the liquidity of Glitnir?"

The reasons for worry were soon visible to all. Glitnir had a large loan expiring mid-October, for €550 million.

The gap could have been filled if Nordea had decided to buy Glitnir's stake in BN Bank in Norway. But on Tuesday 23 September, Nordea said no. Furthermore, some of Glitnir's other loans had expired already. Bayerische Landesbank had been allowing a weekly rollover of €300 million since early 2008. Over the summer, it stopped the loan to Glitnir and gave a similar sized loan to the Republic of Iceland instead.

Remember the Tuscany phone calls?

Bayerische was no longer willing to roll over the loan. It had moved to lower its risks. Now the loan was to the Republic, not to Glitnir. Of its €300 million loan it got 240 back. If kept with Glitnir the figure could have been 15.

"Glitnir had previously said they had credit lines, among others, from Deutsche Bank," says the director of Seðlabanki's market operations. "Now they came to us and asked for liquidity support."

He continues: "They had said earlier they had collateral, including a portfolio of loans to Norwegian oil service companies. Now they came and said those loans had already been committed. They said they had some others, though."

"But those we had already rejected."

And, later the SIC verified that two of the credit lines Glitnir had claimed were unconditional, in fact couldn't be relied upon. One from Citicorp and one from Deutsche Bank. Glitnir had given the Central Bank a false impression. In early 2008, the Central Bank had asked to see the terms, but Glitnir had refused. The Central Bank believed it had no legal basis to force disclosure.

To make things worse, the ECB called and said they would issue an irrevocable margin call. The ECB wanted larger buffers. With no right to appeal.

"This is when we understood that there was no hope," Jón Sigurgeirsson says.

Over the last weekend of September, the so-called Glitnir weekend, multiple options were considered. Sigurgeirsson and Sturla Pálsson, Seðlabanki's Director of Market Operations, worked on a memo through Saturday 27 September.

The memo was not about making suggestions. The memo was a description of the options.

Actually, the memo was, in effect, a listing of options: "Do you want to be crucified, hanged or shot?" as Sturla put it, according to the SIC.

"The memo also included the nuclear option," Sigurgeirsson recalls. "Of taking the banks down."

A solid, solvent bank can get liquidity support from a Central Bank. Such support is within the mandates of the Central Banks, even a main reason for their existence. But Glitnir was no longer considered solid enough for a Central Bank loan. Instead, Seðlabanki suggested a state equity injection of €600 million. In return, the state would take 75% ownership of the bank. The equity values of others would be almost wiped out.

The new equity would be a budgetary outlay for the state. Hence, with this, the destiny of Glitnir had become a matter for the government to decide, not for Seðlabanki.

The memo had warned of a possible run on both Landsbanki and Kaupthing if depositors panicked in the wake of a Glitnir collapse. It suggested seeking assistance from the Bank of England and the UK Financial Services Authority, FSA, reported the SIC. The board of governors decided not to ask for such assistance, said the SIC.

As word of Glitnir's struggle for survival and the impending equity injection and write-downs got out, it set off a chain reaction. The credit ratings of Glitnir and the Republic of Iceland were downgraded. Lenders with loans contingent on the rating asked to be repaid. Companies owning Glitnir shares, such as Baugur and Stodir, lost value. Their lenders, mostly Kaupthing and Landsbanki, saw losses.

Among all the questions related to the crisis, one is still among the most disputed: did the decision to 'nationalize' Glitnir trigger the crisis? Yes, some still say. And then blame the Central Bank, which made the proposal, for the demise of both Glitnir and even of entities such as its holding company Stodir.

Others say the hole was already too big to be filled. Glitnir commanded zero liquidity and zero trust. Surely when a bank unexpectedly asks for emergency support, its ratings will suffer. Glitnir now faced the harsh consequences of its prior misreporting of its liquidity position and of misleading the Central Bank and the rating agencies.

It is worth noting that a bank crisis can usually be averted if the state injects equity. Here, the planned equity injection just highlighted the weaknesses of the system: the state's questionable ability to support the banks as well as the banks' exposures and vulnerabilities due to the spiderweb of cross ownership and lending between the three banks, which was of a magnitude that few knew about, even in Seðlabanki.

Crowded around a copy machine. That was where the Seðlabanki governors learned about Glitnir's largest loan exposures. Shortly after the Glitnir weekend, one of the governors had got hold of a list of Glitnir's 20 largest loan exposures. But the list was printed in tiny type. They were trying to blow it up to make it legible. Soon the group, which by now included the chairman and another governor, could see that most of the largest borrowers were family members and friends of the bank's largest owner.

"The chairman was as furious as a wild animal," says an eyewitness.

Depositors continued to pull their money from the banks. Landsbanki owned a bank with internet-based deposit accounts, Icesave. It was launched in October 2006 in the UK and as late as May 2008 in the Netherlands. Kaupthing had launched something similar called Kaupthing Edge.

The UK online deposit accounts worked wonders in attracting money to Landsbanki, in total about €6 billion. But the online accounts also allowed customers to pull their money out at any time, even at night and on weekends.

The ISK also weakened, and the stock exchange fell. The ECB ruled out the possibility of new ECB loans.

On Friday 3 October, the three banks combined needed €5 billion in emergency funding. The total currency reserves of Seðlabanki were about €2.6 billion. In sum, the banks' international deposits added up to €15 billion. And other loans totalling €5 billion were due to expire in 2009.

As the bricks fell from the tumbling tower, an immense number of events played out. Meetings were held. Calls were made. Rescue efforts were attempted.

The triggers for Landsbanki and Kaupthing had many similarities with Glitnir's. With one important difference. For Kaupthing, the final blow came when its UK subsidiary, Kaupthing Singer & Friedlander, was short of liquidity. The UK regulator intervened and closed it down, triggering the default of the mother company.

Although these efforts and the stories behind them are all spectacular, in the end, the systemic weaknesses and the lack of support sealed the destiny of the banks.

Since the German banks were the largest creditors of the Icelandic banks by far, some had hoped that the Germans and the ECB would step in at the last minute, but both were conspicuously absent.

The Bank of England had also previously provided liquidity, or cash, against collateral. Now both the ECB and the Bank of England (BoE) tightened their terms. As did the UK FSA.

The Nordic swap agreement was still in place, but the amounts it provided were not sufficient.

In Pisa, corrective action was taken eventually. The bells were removed from the Leaning Tower to relieve it of some weight, and cables were cinched around its third level and anchored several hundred meters away. Apartments and houses in the path of the tower were vacated for safety. Then soil was removed from under the high side of the tower.

There was a plan.

In the case of Iceland, when the crisis hit, the banks and the country were almost completely alone. No real partnership was in place with either the EU or the ECB, the US, the UK or the Nordic countries. Some international partners felt they had been kept at a distance. Some even deceived. No cables had been fastened.

The banks had promised to scale back, but two out of three had continued to build the tower ever higher instead. All three banks prioritized lending to their owners ahead of the banks' health and risk levels. They put their own interests ahead of the interests of the country.

Some excused themselves by saying that if they had gone after the worst problems, like loans to their owners, the holding companies would have fallen and become a trigger for a larger collapse. But from a search of the record, it is hard to see any evidence that the banks or their owners made any material attempts to build resilience.

"Gambling for resurrection in Iceland: the rise and fall of the banks" is the title of an article on the banking crisis by Professors Fridrik Mar Baldursson and Richard Portes. When the problems first surfaced in the mini-crisis of 2006, they argued, the banks chose to double down instead of cutting back.

The tower in Pisa never fell, and the latest reinforcement efforts are expected to give it at least another 200 years of life. It even lost 4 centimeters of tilt in the two decades before 2018, leading some to fear that the Italian city, within a few centuries, may lose its number-one tourist attraction as the tower may no longer lean.

There may well have been building inspectors on site when the Pisa tower was erected. In that case, the builder is still the main culprit, but the inspectors also carry some responsibility.

Just like in Iceland.

A bank inspection manual highlights six or seven simple questions: how robust is the bank's funding? What is the quality of the loan book? What can be said regarding the quality of the bank's largest exposures? Are there any entanglements with the owners? How strong are the processes that govern the bank and its risk management? What can be said about the quality and accuracy of the reporting? Are the owners 'fit and proper'?

According to Icelandic law, the above matters were under the remit of the Icelandic FSA. It is still unclear what the FME knew, but the Central Bank did not know a week before the collapse that amounts equalling almost half the capital base of the entire banking system had been lent to the companies and the family of one banker.

At the peak, close to 90% of the capital of one of the banks had been provided to the companies of the main owner, his 'related parties'. The three banks had 23 loans that were each more than a tenth of their equity.

Lastly, not to be forgotten, the drama of the global financial crisis and the extent to which the markets dried up and funding lines were cut also exceeded the expectations of everyone in Iceland and beyond.

The tower was tall, the fundament tiny and its vulnerability vast. And the earthquake that hit exceeded all expectations.

Some weeks after the banks went down, in early November, I met the CEO of a large, robust Nordic consumer goods company known for its frozen ready-made pizzas, even more in demand as the crisis hit. While I was there, out of the blue, his bank, one of the Nordic top five, called him and said it was cutting the company's lines of credit.

It was clearly a time when the weakest tower with the least support could collapse. As it did.

The wreckage from the collapse reached far beyond the city square, leaving a mountain of rubble.

In Rome, the Colosseum was abandoned after the 1349 earthquake. Debris accumulated inside, and its south side became a place to pick up building materials. Rome was partly built from the rubble of a collapse.

As would be the Icelandic recovery.

HEROES IN A TIME OF CRISIS

"The Emergency Act is short and concise. It saved us. We made it in the last minute. It is something to learn from. But the key learning is to get this in place earlier."

– Lawyer, Reykjavik

The crisis group convened at 5pm on Friday 3 October in Seðlabanki. There had been a run on the banks. There was a sense that the weekend they had all feared had arrived.

"But it was all so disorganized," says one. "It was not as if there was some plan."

Not even then, at the start of a restructuring some had been expecting for at least a year and some for almost three. Still, some got ready for an early start on Saturday.

"We had long since planned for a family dinner at Grillið, a posh Reykjavik restaurant," recalls a member. "I went there. The dinner could not be cancelled.

"I looked around in the restaurant. It was packed. 'How can they spend this much money?' I thought. But I could not tell anyone.

"I have been told that I really looked weird."

Early Saturday, it was time to turn the bits and pieces that the crisis group had worked on into law. Likely the most important legislative effort in Iceland ever.

"Glitnir will go bankrupt on Monday," read the summary of the meeting at 8.45am Saturday morning on 4 October. The attendees were the government representatives and the governors.

The legislative team worked all through Saturday and through the night until 5am on Sunday. And restarted at 9am.

"Writing legislation on how to place banks under government administration is not straightforward. There must be provisions for everything," said one member of the team.

"We had forgotten to include provisions on who should govern the restructured banks. Luckily, we noticed," she continues.

"We worked until 5-6 on Sunday. Only then were we told the bill was needed."

The cabinet was gathered at its representation house next to the pond in downtown Reykjavik at the Ráðherrabústaðurinn. An old wooden building, moved in the year 1910 to Reykjavik all the way from the West Fjords.

As the group made its way there, the specialist team of economists stopped at an ATM. Soon, it may be closed, they thought.

"I stopped and called home," says another member of the team. "I asked my family to go and buy groceries. 'We have already been to the store,' they replied. 'Go again. Buy something. Everything.' We were all worried about the payment system."

Next, the head of the Reykjavik Police received a call.

"Have all your personnel ready for tomorrow," he was told.

"The achievement of the team that made the Emergency Act is spectacular. Not least in the light of the chaos at the time," says a leading lawyer. "It should have been passed earlier, ideally when the world was still calm. It should have been prepared.

"But as Icelanders, we are raised in a free manner. Our parents open the door and let us out in the open, most often with no steering and guidance.

"A bit like how we ran our banks."

"I was in Switzerland at a meeting, but flew back on Friday," says Guðmundur Kr. Tómasson, the person in Seðlabanki who oversaw the payment system and bank operations. He received a message telling him to prepare for the possibility that the banks wouldn't open on Monday.

A crisis specialist flew in. "All had red, swollen eyes after days with little sleep," he observed. "All were worn out, hungry and sweaty."

All had worked extreme hours. And despite all their efforts, now everything was about to fail.

A communications centre was established for up to 250 journalists. On Sunday and Monday, it was empty. By Tuesday, it was full.

"I got a call early Sunday morning from Seðlabanki telling us to get to Reykjavik immediately," says a London-based JPMorgan banker, Michael Ridley. The Central Bank had had the foresight to retain an advisor.

Ridley recalls "I asked, 'tomorrow?'

"'No, today.'

"All planes for the day had left. We chartered a private jet, a Learjet, from the old Royal Air Force base at Biggin Hill in Croydon."

But, somewhat symbolically, Reykjavik was too windy and stormy as the plane arrived from the old Spitfire base. The jet was redirected to Keflavik airport, the former US Air Force base an hour's drive southeast of the city.

"Then we waited. At 2am on Monday morning, we were called into the cabinet meeting. We explained how bad things were. That there was no liquidity.

"They asked, 'Can we save the three banks?'

"'No,' I replied.

"'Can we save two?' they asked.

"'No.'

"'Can we save one?'

"'No. There are only two things you can do. Save the depositors and ensure that the payment system works.'"

Some say it was only then that the cabinet understood what was about to happen.

" ... and then we met with these guys from JPMorgan, and it was actually crucial, because the decision was really made to introduce the Emergency Act," the then Minister of Finance said in his SIC statement.

He then continued, "They actually said there was nothing else to be done about it but to prepare ourselves to have to go into the banks and divide them up, using this Washington Mutual method, that this was a recognized method in such a situation, and they described it."

"So that, somehow, it was really a surreal moment; all of a sudden, it was as clear as day to us," recollected the then Minister of Business Affairs. "Just all of a sudden. It was like a moment of truth after this crazy rollercoaster weekend, which was perhaps more or less built on wishful thinking – certainly in retrospect."

Printouts with examples of how to restructure banks had been prepared.

"Priority one was to protect the depositors. Priority two, to ensure a functioning payment system. And then we had to find a model where litigation would be avoided," says Ridley.

"Alternative models were drawn up on the board and tested."

Even then.

"We had to find a simple model," he continues. "No one knew the value of the banks. Assets abroad were seized one by one by the authorities in those countries.

"One option was to put all the deposits in a new bank along with the assets needed to back them all. This model had its supporters. But you can't just strip assets away from creditors."

JPMorgan advocated a model where the deposits would be carved out, backed by a claim on the estate. Combined with a declaration from the government that it would support Icelandic deposits, everything could have stayed stable. The remaining part of the banks could then have been carefully disposed of and the proceeds distributed to creditors, in what's called a winding up process.

A more radical model was chosen, where each bank was placed under administration by the FME and then chopped in two.

One part of each was a new *domestic* bank, the 'new banks' as they were called in Iceland. The domestic lending of the banks exceeded their domestic deposits and borrowing. Hence, paradoxically, the new, carved-out, domestic banks were well capitalized.

Islandsbanki emerged as the domestic carve-out from Glitnir, Arion from Kaupthing, and NBI from Landsbanki, with the latter shortly again taking the Landsbanki name.

The old banks retained the *foreign* borrowing and deposits and the international loans. But, here the liabilities exceeded the assets. Hence, all three 'old banks' were placed under administration. In common parlance, they went bankrupt. With this, all three of the old banks were gone into bankruptcy. Institutions Icelanders had come to know over the years.

Deposits that had been made in Iceland went into the new domestic banks. These banks reopened the next day. All three new banks had more loans to Icelanders than deposits. Since loans to customers are assets and deposits are liabilities for a bank, all three new banks had a positive balance.

The international deposits and the funding and lending stayed in the 'old banks'. These all went down, and the remains were entered into a restructuring process. Deposits placed into branches abroad were given priority. They would be the first to be paid back, but only as the money was eventually recovered.

GOD BLESS ICELAND

"The risk is real, fellow Icelanders, that the Icelandic economy could, in the worst-case scenario, be sucked together with the banks into the violent surge of the financial crisis and consequently into national bankruptcy. No responsible government jeopardizes the future of its nation to such an extent, even if the nation's banking system itself is at stake ... God bless Iceland."

– Speech by Iceland's Prime Minister Geir Haarde on 6 October 2008

"There was a creepy silence. The streets were empty. People quietly passed by, walking close to the walls. Everyone spoke in a soft voice," says a professor who otherwise immerses himself in the history of the Viking Age. He arrived in Reykjavik one day in early October.

Monday 6 October at 4pm, the Prime Minister spoke to the nation on television. Serious, seated in front of a dark background.

His last words were, "God bless Iceland."

"Few understood what happened. They heard 'God Bless Iceland' and understood that this was serious. But the speech was very indirect. It made everyone even more scared," recollects a member of the crisis group.

"I took a taxi to the hotel some hours after midnight. The taxi driver was in deep shock," says one of the advisors. "He was filled with anger, sorrow and fear. I could not leave him.

"He was concerned about the future, the country, his family and his money."

But all faith had not been lost. The advisor was allowed to pay with his credit card.

"On Thursday 7 October, when Kaupthing fell, came the moment I remember the best," says one of the Prime Minister's advisors. "Geir Haarde sat with tears in his eyes. The last hope was gone.

"All the promises he had received up to the crisis and all hopes had by now been proven to have no basis."

"It was a double shock," says a former executive.

"The *Þetta reddast* approach, finally, had not worked. The situation had not miraculously resolved itself. The country was overtaken by a feeling of insecurity and despair. Everyone went to bed that night wondering what the morning would bring.

"It was like a war where we had no weapons."

Gudmundur Þór really wanted to blame the crisis, or the *kreppa* as he called it, on the Americans. They were the ones who invented the process of packaging dubious loans, what they called '*subprime*', into packages with a nice wrapping. He had heard that 60% of the packages issued in 2007 had investment-grade Icelandic bank bonds as their topping. Hence, the Icelandic banks only provided what the US investors asked for. Then, the Americans themselves let Lehman go down. And, while other allies got support, Iceland was left out in the cold. Iceland was a victim. But what would in the end anger him the most was what came next from the UK.

He was, however, not all that sure about the banks themselves. He had heard rumours that three of the ten largest borrowers in one of the banks were the owner, his father and his mother. He hadn't heard that the owner's spouse had joined the list. Þór felt treated like a fool.

Everyone had said everything was just fine.

And Þór and others had for long discussed who really ruled the country: the Prime Minister Haarde or the former Prime Minister, the then Central Bank Governor Oddsson. One soft spoken, one direct.

"How can you take a house-trained cat and make it into a lion?" Oddsson had commented as Haarde became minister. And Þór and his friends had all seen a picture of the two in the front seats of a car as they left a crisis meeting.

Oddsson held the wheel.

Ambiguity on who is responsible for economic and monetary policy, the head of the executive arm or the governor, is rarely a recipe for success, he thought.

WE ARE NOT TERRORISTS

Iceland is outside the Eurosystem and outside the EU. However, through the European Economic Area (EEA) agreement, Iceland, Norway and Liechtenstein were fully included in the EU/EEA inner-market from 1994.

Banks and other financial institutions headquartered in any EU/EEA country receive a European passport. They can freely open branches in any EU/EEA country and take deposits. They can also open daughter companies.

Kaupthing launched Kaupthing Edge. Landsbanki launched Icesave.

The marketing material for both stated that deposits were covered by the EU-mandated deposit insurance plans. Many customers made deposits that exactly matched the maximum amounts covered by such guarantees, noted the SIC.

Both offered interest rates above the market rate.

The money that came in through Icesave was funnelled into the British and Dutch branches of Landsbanki, meaning that Landsbanki could send the money straight back to Iceland.

The UK regulator, the UK Ministry of Finance and the Bank of England had long worried about the Icelandic banks. They had two main concerns: the liquidity of the Kaupthing-owned bank in the UK and the protection provided to UK depositors in Landsbanki.

Iceland was clear that it would seek to safeguard Icelandic deposits, and it had the necessary tool for this through its access to ISK. Less so with regards to the UK deposits, as here FX would be needed.

As the banks collapsed, they were cut in two, based on the authority of the Emergency Act. The domestic part was ringfenced, while the largest, international parts were pushed into bankruptcy.

Deposits made in branches in Iceland went into the new domestic banks. These banks reopened the day after the collapse. Deposits made in branches abroad went into the old banks, with a priority. They would be the first to be paid back, but only as money was recovered during the bankruptcy process.

The UK was desperate and furious.

It was desperate because the UK banking system itself was under threat. This was not the time to tell depositors that they could not have access to their funds.

It was furious due to what it saw as a lack of dialogue with Iceland and a mistreatment of UK customers.

Urgently, the UK sought to block transfers from the Icelandic bank branches and subsidiaries in the UK back to Iceland, but no suitable legislation existed.

On 8 October, at 10.10am, the largest Icelandic bank, Landsbanki, was put on the UK's list of terrorist organizations. With this, transfers of funds to Iceland could be blocked.

"I couldn't believe they did it," said a UK lawyer on the evening of the decision. "I guess speed was needed. They used whatever legislation was available."

The terror provision of 8 October also named Seðlabanki and the FME, the Icelandic Financial Supervisory Authority. Any funds in the UK owned, held or controlled by those two entities were blocked from moving to Landsbanki.

Landsbanki, as shown in the list, found itself in the company of Al Qaida, the Taliban, Iran, Iraq and North Korea, all to which transfer of funds from the UK was prohibited.

"After the collapse, all the phones in the Central Bank were ringing," says Jón Sigurgeirsson. "Now they all went silent. We then called some bankers with whom we had worked for years."

"Sorry, we can't talk with you any more," they answered.

"Some were blocked, some just gave an excuse."

"We were appalled. For some, any action is okay if it is in the national interest," says a later member of the InDefence grass-roots movement. "With this move, the UK lost the moral high ground.

"We started a campaign," he recalls. "'Icelanders are not terrorists.' Many sent pictures; 80,000 people signed up."

The use of the anti-terrorist law enraged, inspired and helped to organize many who later would lead the revolt against any settlement with the UK and the Netherlands.

OMX Iceland, the stock market index that had risen to almost 8,000 in 2008, fell to well below 500. On the last day the banks' shares traded, Friday 3 October, the three banks together had a stock market valuation of about €5 billion. On Monday 6 October, their value was zero.

Other losses were widespread. Domestic bank deposits were insured through the actions taken by the Icelandic government, but money market accounts received a haircut and property values soon fell by 40%. Few could buy, and few would want to sell.

The Icelandic króna had been backed up by the capital inflow to the banks. Now, everybody rushed for the exit. The value of the króna dropped.

Everything was falling. At 6.45am on 7 October, the Russian Ambassador to Iceland called the Central Bank Governor to discuss a possible loan from Russia.

A press release was sent out just over an hour later. Clear and specific.

"The Russian Ambassador to Iceland, Victor I. Tatarintsev, informed the Chairman of the Board of Governors of the Central Bank of Iceland this morning that Russia would grant the Central Bank a loan of the amount of €4 billion. The maturity is three to four years on terms in a range of 30-50 basis over LIBOR."

"Prime Minister Putin has confirmed this decision," it continued.

"Considering history, turning to Russia wasn't as strange as it might appear now," now says the author of the press release.

Throughout the 1950s, Iceland fought with the UK over the right to fish in the waters off Iceland. The UK banned the landing of Icelandic fish in British ports, the entry point to Iceland's largest export market. Iceland, however, was soon able to land its fish in the Soviet Union. The US, in response, also opened its ports, encouraging its European allies to follow. Possibly some hoped for a similar reaction in 2008.

Shortly after the announcement, a press release from the Central Bank set a stronger ISK as the target and signalled further measures: "Measures will be announced to support an appreciation of the króna and to restore exchange rate and price stability."

Within just two short days, the UK had put key Icelandic institutions on its list of terrorists and Putin had apparently stepped in.

"Remember, Iceland is the largest non-sinkable aircraft carrier in the North Atlantic," some said. A €4 billion loan would cost way less than the last US carrier, USS Gerald R. Ford, with a cost of $14 billion.

Seðlabanki said it would engage in foreign exchange transactions based on a reference rate of 131 króna per euro.

"The figure was decided ... based on nothing," the Chief Economist of the Central Bank was quoted by the SIC. "It was just arbitrarily picked and some numbers just thrown out, and then was the decision."

" ... the bank was honestly out of control, totally out of control, that was just it," said the Central Bank economist to the SIC.

There were few transactions, though. The markets were shut. The interventions to back the króna only reached €6 million.

At 11.23am, news agencies released the next announcement from Seðlabanki: "Further to the announcement from earlier today about negotiations between Russia and Iceland, it should be emphasized that the countries have decided to start in the next few days negotiations on financial issues."

Deutsche Bank had called the Icelandic Central Bank and said that the Russian Minister of Finance, Alexei Kudrin, had stated that no loan facility was in place.

Either there had been a misunderstanding, the Icelanders had been too forward leaning, or someone had changed their mind, based on their own judgment or the judgment of others. One day we may know whether the conspiracy theories are right, that a European minister called Russia and said, “Keep your hands off. Iceland is our real estate.”

The person who supposedly made the call has so far rejected my request for an interview.

The next morning saw yet another press release referring to the target of ISK 131 per euro: “It is clear that there is insufficient support for this exchange rate; therefore, the bank will not make any further such efforts for the time being.”

The Icelandic króna dropped to ISK 340 per euro before trading was suspended.

Unfortunately, many had done as Gudmundur Þór.

Seventy per cent of the loans in the corporate sector were denominated in foreign currency. Households had consumer credit and car loans in foreign currency. Thirteen per cent of home mortgages were in foreign currency.

In addition, 70% of household loans were indexed to inflation, with the principal of the loan to be increased as inflation kicked in. As it did as the krona dropped.

As loan values changed, about one third of Icelandic companies were in reasonable shape, one third were in distress and one third were in default.

In many cases, the debt was held in the holding companies of the owners. Most of these structures fell apart.

Unemployment, which had reached a record low in 2007, kicked in and rose to almost 10% within weeks.

In September 2008, Þór’s bank statement showed that every yen of loan repayment would cost him 77 Icelandic króna, up from 54 a year earlier. He had already been called for a meeting at his bank.

His November loan statement listed a yen rate of 123, up 60% from September. Þór’s trick of contracting to pay his Polish assistant, Kacper, in euro had also backfired. Kacper now earned the most of anyone, measured in ISK.

Þór’s bank statement showed he was broke. Now he really feared for the future.

Most of his friends were in similar straits. He had known them for a long time. And his father knew their fathers. And his grandfather knew their grandfathers.

He would pay his friends with what he still had, and he was sure that they would pay him. But he had no intention of paying the bank. It should not have talked him into linking his fate to the volatile yen.

Someone now even told him that the currency loans were, and always had been, illegal.

Some of his friends had gone to Reykjavik to protest. One had found one of the cars of one of the bank managers. The car got a new coat of paint. All red.

A PACK OF WOLVES

In England, the farthest point from Reykjavik is Kent County, known as the 'Garden of England', which is all the way down on the southeastern tip.

No fewer than 93 cities, boroughs and counties in the UK made deposits in Landsbanki and Glitnir. About 25 made deposits or bought bonds in the two UK subsidiaries of the Icelandic banks, Heritable of Landsbanki and Singer & Friedlander of Kaupthing. At least eight police departments had entrusted Landsbanki and Glitnir with deposits. These departments cover 35% of all British police officers. The total exceeded €800 million.

Kent County Council had the most money at stake. Among the police forces, only the Dorset police were ahead of the Kent Police Authority in terms of money at stake per officer. Kent was also number two in absolute exposure to the Icelandic banks. It was only surpassed by the London Metropolitan Police, with its army of 33,367 police officers.

No wonder the fate of the claims on the Icelandic banks had the attention of the public.

All EU/EEA countries were obliged to have a deposit insurance mechanism in place to provide compensation of at least €20,887 for each account. In some countries, higher limits were set, for example: £50,000 in the UK; €100,000 in the Netherlands; and NOK 2 million in Norway.

If a bank had a *subsidiary*, a daughter company, in another country, the rules and the deposit insurance schemes of the foreign country would apply. In this case, supervisory agencies less accommodating than Iceland's FME might interfere.

By operating in foreign markets through *branches*, banks could avoid these more onerous rule. Branch operations also had other benefits for the banks. No separate stock of equity or reserves would be needed. The money from the depositors could be sent straight back to Iceland, or wherever else it was needed. However, deposits in a branch are not guaranteed by the host country scheme, but the scheme of the country where the bank is headquartered. This detail became critical for the Icelandic banks, as we shall see.

Since Icesave was a branch, it was under the supervision of Iceland's FME. As required by the EU/EEA rules, Iceland had established its own Depositors' and Investors' Guarantee Fund, DIGF. The DIGF was to secure any foreign deposits Icesave had taken in.

"In hindsight, this was a major mistake by the management," wrote the then largest owner of Landsbanki in his memoirs. He was referring to the decision to organize Icesave as a branch linked to the DIGF rather than a part of its UK subsidiary, Heritable.

"I have to admit that right up to the weekend of the collapse, I was unaware of such technicalities," continued the Landsbanki owner, who co-owned the stake with his father, the chairman of the Landsbanki board.

Shocking.

In a meeting on 1 October between the FME and representatives of the prime minister and ministries, there was a discussion on the possibility of moving Icesave into a UK subsidiary.

"Isn't that taken care of already?" asked the Permanent Secretary of the Ministry of Finance.

Even more shocking.

The DIGF had only €130 million on hand. The law governing the DIGF stated that its balance should at minimum be 1% of the deposits of the preceding year. When Landsbanki went down, the tiny deposit insurance fund was emptied, eventually providing coverage of just 2%.

The Emergency Act, though, gave priority to the Icesave claims and other deposits. Whatever funds were recovered would go first to the collateralized debt holders, then to the deposit holders.

All other claims would be put aside, even the nonsecured debt due to Seðlabanki.

But the British and Dutch governments would not let their depositors wait. No further uncertainty could be allowed in the midst of the crisis.

The UK government stepped in and established a mechanism to allow immediate repayment to the UK depositors with no limit. The Financial Services Compensation Scheme (FSCS) eventually paid out about £4.5 billion to 228,516 customers, with each customer receiving £15,215.53 on average. In the Netherlands, a limit of €100,000 was set. The Dutch Central Bank, De Nederlandsche Bank, paid out about €1.6 billion.

The UK and Dutch governments then aimed to send part of the bill to the Icelandic people. They asked for repayment, with interest, of up to €20,887 for each account. They argued that the deposit guarantee fund was obliged to pay, and that the Icelandic state was obliged to come to its support. They argued, in parallel, that the actions taken by the Icelandic authorities were in breach of the EU/EEA principle of nondiscrimination.

Depositors at Icelandic branches had free access to their deposits. Depositors at UK and Dutch branches were locked in, and some might never see their money.

In the words of the statement issued by the UK as they froze the Landsbanki assets: "The exclusion on the grounds of nationality is discriminatory and unlawful under the rules governing the European Economic Area."

Iceland said the model had been created out of need, not desire. Iceland had fulfilled its obligations by establishing the DIGF. ISKs were available to re-establish the domestic banks, but there was simply no means to ensure payment to FX depositors. Iceland had done what it could, the Icelanders said, namely establishing the DIGF and passing the Emergency Act that gave priority to depositors. A mechanism that, as time eventually showed, would yield a result that surprised most.

The EU sided with the UK and the Netherlands.

Sweden was to chair the EU in 2009 and was reluctant to oppose two of the EU's then leading member countries.

Norway was caught in the crossfire. It wanted to come to Iceland's support. However, the EEA agreement is a cornerstone of its foreign policy and the most important agreement of all in ensuring its market access. No one with any influence was ready to side against the EU in the first truly heated EEA/EU dispute. Especially as at least some of the Norwegian government's own legal advisors also were of the view that Iceland had gone a step too far.

The ministers of finance of the non-EU countries in the EEA meet the ministers of the EU countries in the Economic and Financial Affairs Council meeting (ECOFIN) every six months. I was there myself in 1993 when Norway, ahead of its 'no' in the 1993 EU referendum, was a trial member. Normally these meetings are slow, polite and follow certain rituals.

Not this time.

Not when they met in early November 2008.

"We sensed it when we entered the meeting room. There was the scent of blood," says an attendee.

"It was like a pack of wolves. The Dutch. The Brits. The Germans," he says.

"Christine Lagarde, the French Minister of Finance and chair of ECOFIN, led the meeting. She had a hard time managing the pack. All the EU countries were there.

"The last time I saw anything like it was when Argentina defaulted in 2001. Argentina had been beaten up in an IMF meeting." On 26 December 2001, Argentina had defaulted on a total of $93 billion of sovereign debt. Now it was Iceland's turn.

"The ECOFIN meeting went on and on. The other Nordics left to catch a plane home. Norway stayed, in an act of solidarity."

"It did not seem as if the Icelandic Minister of Finance, Arni Mathiesen, had been prepared for what was coming."

"We had a pre-meeting that was completely surreal," wrote the former Norwegian Minister of Finance in her memoirs. "Arni had no reality orientation at all. He was not prepared."

"Iceland wasn't on the agenda for the ECOFIN meeting, but we thought a debate might be raised. We wanted to be prepared, to understand how we could help. But Arni talked about polls and internal politics. He said the support went up and down," says Tore Eriksen, the former Secretary General for the Norwegian Ministry of Finance.

"Either he just didn't want to share his thoughts, or he didn't know what was awaiting him. He talked about everything except what mattered the most. I have never seen anything similar in my 40-year career."

"It was a bit like the meeting in late September, after Lehman went down," Tore continues. "We met the Nordic-Baltic team for the IMF. Everyone else saw that the situation of the Icelandic banks could become a challenge. But the Icelandic representatives were clear in saying there were no problems."

50 BANKS, 20 COUNTRIES, ONE BIG CRASH

On 10 October 2008, a telephone conference was held among the EU/EEA FSAs of the 14 countries where the three large Icelandic banks and the fourth, Straumur Bank, operated. In total, 39 entities – 17 subsidiaries and 22 branches – were operating across the 14 countries. Add in Iceland and some non-European countries, and the number reached about 50 entities in about 20 countries.

Internationally, the Icelandic banks had played across the full register of banking formats. They had acquired many European banks. These were run as subsidiaries. All three banks also had subsidiaries in Luxembourg, allowing them to tap liquidity directly from the ECB.

Kaupthing had its own version of Icesave, through Kaupthing Edge. It was marketed in no fewer than ten European countries.

In Norway, Kaupthing Edge was run as a branch.

At 7.10am on 9 October, the Norwegian FSA was informed that Kaupthing had collapsed. Its internet bank and ATMs had to close, as Kaupthing Iceland couldn't provide any money. It had been placed under administration.

The Ministry of Finance was informed at 7.20am. Around 9am, the Minister of Finance announced that the NOK 2 million guarantee rule would apply. Only five of the 6,000 deposits in Kaupthing Edge exceeded this limit, though. Even the depositors had recognized the vulnerability of Kaupthing.

The branch was placed under administration on 12 October. Luckily, the payments to all depositors were covered. Kaupthing's assets had been frozen. This included a 20% stake in the country's largest insurance company, Storebrand.

A board of the estate was appointed. It would lead the winding up process. The board demanded an insurance policy to protect it against litigation. Which it got.

But which expired way too early.

THE FIGHT OVER HISTORY

"In statements by ministers and representatives of the governmental institutions before the SIC, each pointed a finger at the other concerning positive obligation, and no one assumed responsibility."

– SIC report summary

The Icelandic saga literature that originated in the 7th century and was written down in the 12th hails the importance of one's reputation; one's reputation is immortal, fame imperishable.

The old book of *Hávamál*, written on parchment in the 12th and 13th centuries, states, "Cattle die, kinsmen die, one day you die yourself; but the words of praise will not perish when a man wins fair fame."

Back when I was in high school, our teacher told our class that Iceland stands out with regard to the importance it places on history. Based on my own scattered observations, she was right.

A simple soul might have thought that by now, more than ten years after the crash, some sort of consensus would have been reached on its causes. On its root causes, the triggers, and on who was responsible.

But no.

Even when among Icelandic friends, a discussion of Iceland's recent history can bring up differences. Look in Wikipedia, for example. Here, the collapse of Stodir is explained solely by the Icelandic government's partial nationalization of Glitnir. Even today, some of the people involved, bankers and politicians, hire and pay historians to tell their stories and shape the narrative. With their own or with taxpayer money. Others just write books.

The short version is that the big mistake was in building three banking towers on top of each other, instead of ensuring that each was completely separate in funding, ownership and assets. With this, and with the enormous height of each, it added up to a tower that was just too high, too unbalanced. Especially given the cracks in the structure, the instability of the Icelandic economy, and the limited support capacity of the authorities and the Central Bank. An instability and limitation that were well known to all, including the banks. And, remarkably, neither the authorities nor the banks themselves had established real alliances with institutions elsewhere. To sum up: too high and interdependent; too many cracks; no diversification; too weak a base; and an absence of alliances. And, eventually, a downfall triggered by an external shock that was just too much.

The Icelandic government, the Central Bank and the FME were all found by the SIC to have neglected their duties. Some, the SIC believed, had even broken the law.

Looking back, some observers dwell on the build-up to the crisis. When the banks were privatized, the owners financed their acquisitions with loans from the other banks, establishing a pattern for the connected lending practices that followed. Others dwell on the failure to steer the overall economy, including the failed mix of budgetary tightness and high interest rates. Some even say that the lack of forceful regulation of the banks was not just an oversight, but was intentional, based on a philosophy of self-regulation and free markets.

The SIC report laid it out clearly: "The operations of the Icelandic banks were, in many ways, characterized by their maximizing the interests of the larger shareholders, who managed the banks, rather than running solid banks with the interests of all shareholders in mind, where due responsibility was demonstrated toward their creditors."

And: "The SIC is of the opinion that the financing of owners' equity in the Icelandic banking system had been based, to such a great extent, on borrowing from the system itself that its stability was threatened. The shares owned by the biggest shareholders of the banks were especially leveraged. This resulted in the banks and their biggest owners being very sensitive to losses and the lowering of share prices."

When the holding companies of the owners lost access to alternative financing in 2007 and 2008, " ... Glitnir, Kaupthing Bank and Landsbanki responded by taking over the financing so that loans in foreign banks could be repaid. The Icelandic banks thus lent substantial amounts while experiencing considerable liquidity problems at the same time."

And the banks continued to finance the ventures of their owners or owners of their holding companies. Early warning signs had not led to restraint: " ... In the second half of 2007, lending to foreign parties grew by €11.4 billion. Lending by the banks' parent companies to foreign parties increased by more than 120% in just six months."

And worse, Central Banks were a primary source of funds: "Collateralized loans increased substantially in all three banks as the liquidity crisis became more widespread. In the autumn of 2007, the banks' collateralized loans were some €2 billion, mostly from the CBI. When the banks collapsed, they had grown to roughly €9 billion and nearly half that sum was from the European Central Bank. Collateralized loans were chosen rather than financing through the issue of medium-term bonds with maturity of three to five years. They were mostly granted for a period of a few weeks, although individual loans were granted for a period up to six months. For the banks, this increased financing through short-term collateralized loans escalated their financial risk substantially."

To simplify, short-term Central Bank funding was used to finance long-term lending to the banks' owners and their Icelandic and international ventures. Especially after other banks refused to provide such loans.

The SIC said: "When the banking system had become far too big relative to the size of the Icelandic economy, the governmental authorities needed to respond. No later than 2006 it would have been necessary to take action if there was to be any chance of preventing the collapse of the banks without severely impacting upon the value of their assets. Neither that year nor the next did the authorities try, in a decisive way, to have the banks reduce the size of their balance sheets."

Some of the people I interviewed say it is possible to zoom in on the exact hour when Iceland's destiny was sealed. That was a day when the involved parties left a meeting believing they had solved the problem. They should have left the meeting thinking there was a huge problem looming.

"Sunday, 26 March 2006 marked Iceland's point of no return," says a bank employee.

Landsbanki had notified authorities that it could not meet a payment due the next day. An emergency meeting was held that day at the home of the governor of the Central Bank. With all three banks.

"We knew there was a problem," says a Central Bank employee. "Back in November 2005 we had gotten a call from a contact in a London bank. 'Have you seen the pricing of risk of the Icelandic banks?' she asked. 'The CDS price is going through the roof.'

"I pulled out my books and got familiar with CDSs."

In the middle of the 26 March meeting, Landsbanki announced that its financing problem had been resolved. Money was available.

The opportunity to take decisive action was missed.

Instead, it was after that meeting that Landsbanki launched its Icesave deposit-taking entity, dramatically increasing systemic risk. Normally, deposits solidify a bank's funding base. Not here. Icesave grew from nothing to a balance of £4.5 billion. But it was hot money, chasing high interest rates. Half the deposits disappeared in early 2008. Furthermore, it was after the March meeting that the banks increased their reliance on Central Bank financing and increased their lending to the holding companies.

Had the financial system been tamed at that time, the bust could have been averted.

Instead of reducing the size of their assets, the banks bought their own equity, increased their lending to their owners, and stepped in with more money as the owners came under pressure, with their business conglomerates, yachts and jets. And with much of that spending spree funded by short-term, Central Bank financing.

"This is completely wild," says Trygve Young, an experienced Nordic banker. "Central Bank financing is to be used to meet short-term emergencies. It is simply not a source of funding for growth.

"The banks carry the main responsibility, but the FME and the Central Banks should have known."

"Yes, if a bank had asked me for Central Bank funding beyond what I would consider normal, then I would have set requirements," confirms Svein Gjedrem, the former Norwegian Central Bank Governor and now chairman of the OECD's Economic and Development Review Committee.

"We would have moved in, presumably jointly with the FSA."

"I find it strange that anyone would even raise a question about the rights of the Central Bank as a lender of last resort," Gjedrem continues. "Obviously, it has rights. Even to the point, when most people wouldn't think there was even a need for a law saying it has such rights. A Central Bank that lends money as a lender of last resort has every right to impose requirements on those asking for money."

"The Central Bank runs the payment system. All its participants need to be robust. There is no clearer sign of crisis than a bank requesting excessive amounts of liquidity," says the Swedish governor, Ingves. "If anyone does, then alarm bells should ring in the Central Bank. And we will send someone in.

"Remember, the FSA has no money. The Central Bank has money. The person heading the Central Bank has to look after the money."

Some say there was little the authorities, the Central Bank and the private banks could have done in 2006 or 2007. This is simply not true.

As just one example, effective legislation banning FX loans could have dialled back a practice that later caused huge pain for many. Households that ended up in distress held an unusually large portion of the foreign currency car loans. The car loans were disproportionately burdensome and, as later court rulings showed, even illegal at the time. But, still the schemes were continued, even though the banks, the Central Bank and the policymakers all knew the risks.

For this there is no excuse.

Sixteen per cent of the total sum of new loans in January 2007 to September 2008 was granted to already distressed households. The banks had hedged themselves for years and the Central Bank had been warned by senior London bankers as early as 2005. The SIC is brutal in its description of the actions prior to the crisis: "Nothing suggests, either from the government's minutes or the accounts of those who reported to the SIC, that the ministers of the Icelandic government responsible for economic affairs (the prime minister), banking affairs (the minister of business affairs) or the state's finances (the minister of finance) submitted to the government a specific report on the problems of the banks or its possible impact on the state's economy and finance when the banks started to face constraints in their operations and until the banking system collapsed in October 2008."

The blame game of discussions about *who* among the ministers and officials is responsible, though, is a distraction. All present who saw what was about to happen should have voiced their concern and taken action to ensure a better outcome. Or resigned. A government minister can't blame other ministers. Government officials can't blame other officials.

Remember why the world admires the Icelandic football team? It's because its efforts as a team make great individual players even better. A player can't blame a poor team effort on the others. It's the same in economic policy formation and execution.

There should also have been a dialogue between Iceland and its neighbours. If your house is about to catch fire, you should notify the people who live next door. Even if they might tap water from the same reservoir or get in the way of the firefighters. Here, the Icelandic authorities blame the foreigners. The foreigners blame the then Icelandic authorities. Someone should have called out. There should have been a plan.

The SIC report then continued: "It is the assessment of the SIC that the government's actions concerning matters relating to the banks were unfocused when the situation became more dire in the beginning of 2008. The ministers focused too much on the image crisis facing the financial institutions rather than the obvious problem; that the Icelandic financial system was far too large in relation to the Icelandic economy. When the ministers intended to improve the image of the banking system by partaking in public discussions, mainly abroad, it was done without any assessment of the financial capability of the state to come to the banks' assistance and without information being available on the cost of a possible financial shock."

Even in the final days, things were no better. The SIC stated: "After it became clear that the government's measures in the Glitnir affair had been unsuccessful, a certain chaos seems to have ensued as regards to contingency planning on behalf of the state. The CBI and the government did not act in harmony and overall leadership was lacking. No decision was taken with regard to what course to take."

It is all neatly summarized in the article, "The Rise, the Fall and the Resurrection of Iceland":

> *First, the banks' new owners were very closely connected, and they lent each other large amounts of money right from the start.*
>
> *Second, this kind of equity funding seriously weakened, in a nontransparent way, the banks' ability to suffer losses, and hence notably increased their systemic risk.*

Third, from the beginning, the banks' ownership was murky, and supervisors and policymakers seemed complacent.

This was the backdrop against which the banks started to expand.

In the spring of 2008, two UK economists suggested forceful action. The immediate crisis had to be addressed through a range of actions, they argued.

Their fixes included borrowing from foreign central banks, swaps arranged by Seðlabanki, borrowing from the IMF, mobilizing the resources of the Housing Finance Fund and of the Pension Funds as collateral for external borrowing, and, last but not least, securitizing future energy revenues from Iceland's hydro and geothermal resources.

Hence, going all in.

Perhaps a more conspiratorial view of Iceland's strategy in that last year may one day arise. Namely, that the inactivity and apparent complete lack of coordination was actually a deliberate or at least an intuitive response, as it led to an outcome that wasn't the worst possible among many horrible outcomes. Including the scenarios that could have resulted if Iceland had followed the advice of the two economists.

↳ The Icelandic cartoonist Halldór Baldursson's view on the journey of the banks: To be born and to die as an egg; the saga of the private banks in Iceland as they originate from and return to the state (Rikið)

I LOOK

I look at the whitish sky,
I look at the clouds, blue-grey,
I look at the bloodshot sun.
So this is the world.
So this is the planets' home.
A raindrop!

I look at the lofty houses,
I look at a thousand windows,
I look at the far away spires.

So this is Earth.
So this is the home of mankind.

The clouds, blue-grey, are gathering;
the sun's gone away.

I look at the well-dressed gents,
I look at the smiling ladies,
I look at the tired horses.

Now the clouds, blue-grey, thicken.

I look and I look ...
I must have come to the wrong planet.
It's so strange here.

(Sigbjørn Obstfelder)

CHAPTER 3

THE HAVOC AND THE RUBBLE

DEAR VISA AND MASTERCARD: STAY OPEN OR FOREVER LEAVE

In a strong, functioning economy, a shortage of money is almost impossible to imagine. Even though money is just an artificial construct.

There is an implicit trust that money you deposited in the bank yesterday will still be there tomorrow. That when you pull your credit card out to pay in a restaurant, the transaction will be completed without a hitch. As we saw in Iceland, these bedrock beliefs can be overturned.

"On Monday 6 October, the breakfast buffet had everything. Fresh strawberry, pineapple, other fruits," says a Seðlabanki advisor from JPMorgan.

"On Tuesday, the strawberry was gone. On Wednesday, there was no pineapple.

"On Thursday, no fresh fruit. Only tinned. But that too was soon gone. But medical supplies were a larger worry."

The IMF sent its expert to Iceland. Straight from Iraq. The Indiana Jones of market operations.

The FX had to be taken from the Seðlabanki reserves. Any interbank trade required tapping of the reserves. Medicine, food and fuel were the priority. "As payments were due, the oil importers called one of the Central Bank governors to get foreign currency," says the now Head of Seðlabanki Reserve Management.

"No, our banks do not allow payments to your Icelandic bank account." That was the message a large fish exporter got from his European customers.

"The European banks do not trust the new banks. They fear you won't get their payments," was what he was told.

Seðlabanki had ISK 13 billion worth of notes in circulation. The vault was filled with another 15. And some old notes that otherwise would have been burned.

Almost ISK 11 billion in ISK 1,000 notes had been ordered in early 2008 from the UK-based money-printer, De La Rue. In October, the order was changed. Now it was for ISK 5,000 notes only. Worth ISK 55 billion.

But the notes would only arrive from the print shop in February 2009.

"Within a short time, there were almost no notes left. We could barely meet one more day of demand. We feared the reaction," says Guðmundur Kr.Tómasson, the Seðlabanki payment system manager, who kept his eye on the dwindling pile of notes.

"We prepared a scheme where notes could be handed back to the Central Bank. People would get certificates in return."

Queues would have looked ugly. All feared widespread panic. Preparations were made to open the first floor of the Seðlabanki building in Reykjavik to avoid any queues. The citizens could then exchange their bank notes for certificates of deposit. Next, the notes would have been taken to the basement. And thereafter carted out the back door and trucked to the banks for recirculation.

"We also called the police," says Tómasson. "They were asked to make a statement saying it was dangerous to have too many notes lying around. The government also stated that all deposits were secure. It was just statements, but the outflow stopped. In the last moment."

Now, at least there were notes.

Your credit cards carry the name of your bank, called the 'issuer' in payment-system terminology. You use them to make payments to the 'merchant'. The payment is validated, executed and the money transferred by an agency, the 'acquirer'. Valitor and Borgun ran this function in Iceland. Last come the owners of the systems, like Visa or Mastercard, the so-called 'schemes'. They live off a fee charged for each transaction. They operate in all countries and have rules and procedures to handle even the strangest situations. But at some point, even they may give up.

Now, assume the banks, the issuers, go bust. Then the whole system may shut down.

"We in Seðlabanki could not give a guarantee, and the new banks were not up and running," says Tómasson.

"Visa said yes, the system can stay open. Mastercard said no."

"'If so, you will never again be permitted to operate in Iceland,' was our response. Now, both said yes. Maybe because they couldn't have stopped it anyway."

"The system had been built from scratch in Iceland. All arrangements were domestic. The transactions were cleared and settled in Iceland. The coding systems were under the control of the acquirers. We knew the schemes could not have closed the cards, even if they had wanted to," says Tómasson.

He continues: "Today everything is globalized. Everything is under the control of the schemes. Now we can't cut off the schemes and run things from home. But, hopefully, a similar meltdown won't occur again.

"Unless, of course, there is a cyberattack."

In 2008, the next step was to make sure the new banks met their obligations. All domestic payments had to run smoothly, every millisecond.

International transactions were a battle. An ISK 400,000 limit on card transactions was introduced to cap the flows. And the schemes took the ISK out of the 'vector', the list of convertible currencies. Also, there were situations where merchants abroad did not accept the cards of the Icelandic banks. Furthermore, as the three banks went down, they lost their access to the payment system. Lastly, some banks would simply not pay the 'new banks' or its customers if the 'old banks' owed them money.

The Central Bank stepped in. It set up a war room. Each bank sent employees to Seðlabanki and payments were routed through its accounts, its SWIFT. Some days later, the banks themselves were able to route payments through the Central Bank system.

"There were a lot of payments. All through 2009 and 2010. Millions of transactions," says Tómasson.

"The UK freeze order caused hell. It made a big difference. Especially as others followed. Deutsche Bank refused to clear transactions."

"Banks shut down their lines. German banks feared problems. The UK freeze also blocked the Central Bank for some time, as they had even listed the Central Bank alongside terror organizations. Both UK payments and payments to and from banks associated with or with subsidiaries in the UK were blocked. The mighty Bank of America ceased allowing payments, fearing the UK."

Seðlabanki mobilized JPMorgan, which routed the payments through its system.

"I got a call from someone working for the UK Government," says a former JPMorgan employee.

"'You are a British citizen?' asked the government representative.

"'Do you know that you are working on tasks related to an entity that is on the list of terrorist organizations?'

"But then, who knows, maybe he was just curious," says the JPMorgan banker.

"Despite all problems, we were pleasantly surprised," says one of the Seðlabanki employees who made it all work. "We thought all exporters to Iceland would ask for upfront payments. But they didn't.

"It might have been out of sympathy, it may have been due to their long-term relationships, or they may just have run it all on autopilot."

"Maybe they didn't have time to read the newspapers.

"Or, if they did, maybe they didn't connect it to their world."

Some even offered better deals. Payment terms were extended. "We renegotiated 20 contracts," says a business executive. "We got better terms on 17. Such support is never forgotten."

"The need for backup systems had been discussed among the Nordic countries when we met in 2006, 2007 and 2008," says the Seðlabanki manager. "We thought we might need to do something. But in the end, we only started to solve the problems on 3, 4 and 5 October. It was in real time. Everything."

"But I didn't hear any stories of people stranded in China with no money."

WHEN THE IMF COMES MARCHING IN

"My first post-crisis memory is of an advisor marching into the room late in October 2008," recalls Bjarni Benediktsson, a former member of parliament and later Prime Minister. "'Nothing has happened in the last two weeks,' the advisor said. 'Get your act together, or nothing will happen in the next two.'"

The collapse shocked everyone. Many were preoccupied with all that had happened and with arguments about who was to blame. There were payment system emergencies daily and new entities on the brink of collapse. Seðlabanki handed out FX as emergencies surfaced, but there was no plan nor process.

The Seðlabanki staff worked around the clock, as did other officials. The effort started in March and April 2008 in the run-up to the crisis, then through the collapse and finally through the efforts to keep what was left up and running. All while protesters on the outside were hammering on pots and pans.

Day and night.

Eventually, Iceland had no choice but to take shelter in a programme run by the International Monetary Fund, which steps in to support countries, often developing countries, when their economic systems collapse.

"Some really hated the idea of an IMF programme. Ending up on an IMF programme was seen as a disgrace," says an Icelandic economist.

But there was no alternative. The market trust was gone. The coffers were empty. There was no alternative plan, despite all the warnings. All potential contributors made their support dependent on Iceland agreeing to an IMF programme.

"The timing was perfect. What the IMF now had to deal with were bread-and-butter issues. Had the IMF been here earlier, they could have tried to save the banks," says Jón Sigurgeirsson. "Who knows what schemes they would have tried to lure us into. Look at Ireland. At least Iceland had more degrees of freedom."

"Imagine the situation if the IMF programme head had been tasked with making a plan in mid-September. Could he have gone to the IMF board and said he had a great plan? To take down the banks and incur tens of billions of euro losses for the German, Japanese and US banks?"

"We have seen 136 crises," said the IMF as its team landed in Iceland post-collapse.

"What is different is only the height and angle of the lines showing where the economy is heading," was the IMF statement that made the most lasting impression on Benediktsson.

"The entry of the IMF marked an important change. Now there was structure. On everything, from A to Z," says a former economist in the Central Bank.

"But, as I once told the IMF," she continues, "if you want to add more success stories to your résumé, you had better focus on countries with fundamental strengths. Like Iceland."

"A country with state debt or debt to other countries normally has it for a reason," says Anne Krueger, a former IMF deputy director. "The debt is due to a prior deficit that had its own specific cause."

The deficit could be due to a weak economic base, weak institutions, insufficient political legitimacy or a desire to weaken what some call big government. Or, the authorities might simply not have had the ability or will to tax their people or to ensure efficiency. They might have squandered money. Robbing the state may be considered legitimate in said country. Maybe the economy is dependent on the stimuli from the deficit.

Similarly, external debt may be due to a weak economic base, high costs, excessive domestic spending or just mismanagement. And again, the economy might have become dependent on the deficit.

"Paying down debt may be the least of the challenges," Krueger says. "Fixing the deficits, replacing the artificial stimuli with sustainable activities and resolving the root causes may be the biggest."

Hence, when reviewing deficits and the plans for addressing them, remember to consider the root causes of the deficits, their prior impact, and whether the new plans address these challenges.

"Iceland, however, didn't historically have a deficit in the state budget, and the depreciation had largely brought the imports and exports back into balance," Krueger summarizes.

On 24 October, the IMF announced the programme for Iceland. It was supported by a $2.1 billion IMF loan and a Nordic loan package. An Icelandic Professor in Economics, Fridrik Mar Baldursson, made important contributions as an advisor to the government and helped establish a balanced programme.

A key element were the Letters of Intent, the LOI. An interesting construct.

First, the IMF makes a complete draft. Then the authorities in the programme country comment, approve or fight, negotiate and finally settle on the text. Then the IMF steps aside and the result appears in the form of a letter from the country's authorities to the IMF. A letter where the authorities list all their commitments. Their letter.

The first LOI was formulated as a letter to the Managing Director of the IMF at the time, Dominique Strauss-Kahn. It was signed on 15 November 2008 by the Icelandic Minister of Finance, Árni M. Mathiesen, and the Central Bank Governor, Davið Oddsson.

Well, actually, another LOI had already been signed. It had been agreed upon between the Icelandic authorities and the IMF staff. But, when it was circulated in the IMF, the UK and the Netherlands rejected it. "Sorry, it's not strong enough," they said. While thinking about Icesave. The next day, the minister and the Central Bank governor got a revised version to sign.

This set a pattern we would experience again and again through 2009. The IMF hurdle was set ever higher. At first it was a source of irritation. In the end, as we will see, it turned into a blessing. One of many paradoxes.

"The programme was special," says Murilo Portugal, a Brazilian who was then one of three IMF Deputy Managing Directors, with responsibility for the Iceland programme.

"Along with Hungary, it was the first programme after Lehman. It was huge, relative to the size of the economy. Three to four times the normal. It was frontloaded, with large disbursements up front."

"The requirements were lighter relative to the standard set in prior programmes," says Portugal. "Poul Thompson, the IMF programme lead, convinced the IMF that the budget tightening ought to be gradual. Instant tightening would have meant a deeper recession. And the pre-crisis surplus allowed for a delay."

"We were sceptical, but he convinced us," says Portugal, who himself became a very influential and strong supporter of Iceland.

The Asian programmes each called for eight to ten reforms. Never waste a crisis as an opportunity to get things done. That had been the view of the IMF. Unrelated reforms were launched.

"But we got distracted. Before Iceland, we had learned our Asian lesson," says Portugal.

"We agreed on capital controls. Such rules would block the right to exchange ISK to foreign currency. Without them, there would be no interest rate high enough or fiscal policy tight enough."

To hinder nervous holders of ISK from rushing to exchange them for more stable euros or dollars.

"In emerging markets, we have seen many countries with controls. They are not such a big issue," Portugal says.

Imposing capital controls in a developed economy, however, is a much bigger deal. The accepted orthodoxy is that free markets benefit from the free movement of capital. This is what allows funds to flow to the places of greatest opportunity and it has been a cornerstone of IMF policy. So allowing Iceland to break that policy during its period of crisis was indeed controversial.

Measures to restrict FX exchange were first put in place in October 2008. The remains of the banks were short of FX and it couldn't be bought at reasonable terms in the market. Instead Seðlabanki simply handed out whatever FX that was needed. Now controls became a part of the programme. Gradually, they were tightened ever more. Later, as will be seen, they became an even more important policy tool. A tool that even made the leading US hedge funds kneel.

Along the way, the experience in Iceland, once and for all, changed the IMF's view on capital controls. Iceland changed global policies.

Later, the IMF even searched for measures with a similar impact to capital controls for use in countries without their own currency. Such as Greece and Cyprus. The emerging market countries' representatives applauded as the IMF turned.

"The IMF had advocated capital control liberalization," says Annamaria Kokeny, the IMF specialist on capital controls.

When I ask who decided to introduce the controls, which became one of the most important policy tools of all, she responds, "It's really difficult to say."

"By the time we came, the Central Bank had already asked what remained of the banks to ration their use of foreign currency. In addition, international payments were hindered by all sorts of problems."

She continues, "We tried to understand the situation. Things couldn't be kept as they were. More clarity was needed."

"The top management of the Central Bank was receptive. No one knew where it would all end if there were no controls. Having them was just safer."

"There were not that many people who knew how to manage them. The informal measures had to be managed. We in the IMF provided technical assistance."

"It was the first time ever that the IMF advised on introducing capital controls," says Kokeny. "I spent a nice Thanksgiving evening in 2008 on the phone with Iceland."

"The capital controls law was passed in November 2008. It was a milestone."

"It was as if we were conducting heart surgery," says the Seðlabanki Head of Reserve Management. "All had been cut open and the ribs sawn away."

"Now we stood there with the heart in our hands. Pumping. Leaking FX."

"We had to put the patient into a coma. By introducing capital controls."

All trade-related transactions and current transactions were allowed. Interest payments and dividend payments were also allowed. The base capital, the principal, could not be exchanged. Financial transfers out of Iceland were disallowed. Forbidden.

At first there was no apparatus for this in Seðlabanki. A unit was established. The detailed regulations were drawn up.

"The reactions to the controls were very mixed in the IMF. Some research had been done internally that had advocated the use of controls," Kokeny says.

"It was, however, quite a shock when the IMF recognized their usefulness."

And even more of a shock as the IMF became a hardliner.

"I suppose there was some satisfaction among the emerging market country representatives, even silent applause."

"When they commented on the programme in the IMF board, they always made sure to add a statement," she recalls. "'We find it very useful and appropriate that capital controls have been included as part of the programme,' was the standard phrase."

The interest rate at which banks could borrow from Seðlabanki had been 15.5%. On 15 October, before the IMF entered, the rate was reduced to 12%.

"A stable króna was our main objective," says Portugal. "Here we had nothing to give. A further depreciation would increase the debt issues and risk hyperinflation. To avoid this, high interest rates were required. Even with capital controls."

"Controls work for a while. Soon everybody knows how to circumvent them."

"I called the Seðlabanki governor," recalls Portugal. "There will be no programme if the rates are not increased."

The IMF programme was announced on 27 October. On 28 October, the governors hiked the rate for banks wishing to borrow from Seðlabanki to 18%, up 6 percentage points.

On Icesave, the IMF was torn. "We were careful that Iceland should not take on new debt," says Portugal. "We did not want to push Iceland. But we could not lend if there were no negotiations in good faith."

"The British were understanding. The Dutch resisted the most. They could not block it, though. The US wanted the programme."

AT THE OSCARS NIGHT OF DEBT

In an odd coincidence, the international community of insolvency lawyers had its annual charity dinner on 7 October 2008 in London. The prizes for the leading lights in the world of insolvency were to be awarded.

An Oscars night of debt. And all had heard the news from Iceland.

"The room was very busy," says said an attendee. There was a buzz in the room. "This will be our golden age."

Royal Bank of Scotland, RBS, and Barclays were struggling. Monday 6 October had been the worst trading day in London since 1987. Then came the news from Iceland.

"A large US insurance company called," recalls Barry Russell, who later became the leading lawyer for the claimants. "I was asked to run a conflict check. I could not have any competing assignments."

When you insure your car, your insurer generally requires you to prepay the premiums. To keep premiums down, while earning a profit, the insurance companies invest the prepayment in the capital markets. Some companies prioritize solidity. In this case, by buying Icelandic bank bonds. To diversify risks, one of Russell's prospective clients had invested in all three banks. To spread it out further, it had even invested in Iceland's fourth-largest bank, Straumur. No wonder an insolvency lawyer was needed.

The following week the claimants gathered in Reykjavik. The Heathrow Icelandair lounge, previously filled with lenders and *útrásarvíkingar*, the Viking conquerors, was now filled with creditors.

The German banks were there. As was the Belgian bank Fortis, itself a later victim of the crisis. And their insolvency lawyers. All fresh from the dinner on 7 October.

When the creditors and their lawyers landed in Reykjavik, a bus was there to meet them. It stopped first at the headquarters of the four banks. A traveling band of creditors. With billions at stake. "The Icelanders had not established any process," says an attendee. "There was no structure."

Next, the entourage went to Seðlabanki.

"I was waiting on the fifth floor outside the elevator," says Jón Sigurgeirsson. "Our stance was to meet everyone who requested a meeting.

"First the door of one elevator opened. It was packed. Then the next. Also packed. Then the first returned. And the second. All full of creditors and lawyers."

While extra chairs were being brought into the meeting room, the creditors started quarrelling. Some banks claimed priority ahead of the bondholders.

For the chairs at the table. And the money.

"Some were knowledgeable, especially the bondholders' representatives. Some knew nothing," says Jón. "One creditor was eager. 'Just give us the cash flow from the fisheries and from the power plants,' the creditor said."

A German bank tried to intimidate a lead bondholder. "You will be second in line," said the bank's representative.

"That one got nasty," says an attendee about the next meeting at the Ministry of Finance. "The ministry had no idea. 'I want my money back,' one creditor said."

The last stop was the FME. "They had no clue," says a creditor representative.

The creditors met for dinner at Hotel Holt. Here they organized themselves. All present agreed there needed to be a creditors' committee.

The following day, they went back to the three banks to meet the debt sellers.

And, yes, in Iceland the largest insurance company, Sjóvá, also went down. Its owner, Milestone, and its subsidiaries had tapped its funds. The financial Vikings couldn't resist the temptation of such a cookie jar, stuffed with the policy holders' prepayments. Sjóvá had also committed itself to investing $100 million in a tower in the Chinese gambling capital of Macau.

Luckily, however, the number of car accidents in Iceland dropped by a third from 2006 to 2008. The bankers were reckless; the drivers less so.

IN THE SMALL TOWN OF ÁLFTANES

The small municipality of Álftanes lies on a peninsula just south across a bay from the Reykjavik city centre. It has a population of about 2,500. Next door lives the Icelandic President, in his residence at Bessastaðir.

This was the neighbourhood in which Frjalsi Investment Bank won a house in a forced auction in November 2008, right after the crash. The former owner demolished the house on the Icelandic National Day, 17 June 2009. He had just received a final eviction order.

"I saw what was going on and called the police and the house owner," said a building inspector. The house was almost completely destroyed. Only the garage was left standing.

The demolition became a symbol, attracting international publicity. Even today, some abroad refer to it when discussing the crisis.

The owner said he felt he had nothing to lose. To him, it made no difference if he went bankrupt owing 60 million króna or 120 million. The loans had been in foreign currency and had increased from ISK 36 million ISK to 78 million. He had tried to negotiate with the banks, but they had not listened. He said.

The sentiment in Iceland, however, turned as the homeowner was sentenced to 18 months in prison for robbery, failure to pay taxes, fraud and breach of accounting laws. There was simply no way the collapse in October could have been the main reason for the auction only a month later. But it was a selling story.

The municipality of Álftanes had earlier decided that an FX loan was the way to finance its new swimming pool. Its sole revenue, however, came from income taxes and real estate taxes. All in ISK.

The pool was stylish from the outset, with a wave pool and water slide tower that can be seen from a distance. Now the FX loan doubled. The pool supposedly became the most expensive ever built in Iceland. Post-crisis, the income of the municipality plummeted. In 2013, Álftanes merged with another municipality due to a lack of better options.

In 2007, the debt and monetary assets of all Icelandic municipalities approximately matched. By 2013, the debt had doubled, and the monetary assets shrunk.

The debt crisis that was engulfing Iceland's businesses and households was about to become much deeper.

ECB IS OFF THE HOOK. SEÐLABANKI TAKES A HIT

In the meeting room in Seðlabanki, where I conducted interviews for this book, all the expensive Danish design chairs are of different shapes and colours – red, yellow and green.

"They came from the banks. They were collateral," said my interviewee.

In 2008, as markets dried up, Seðlabanki became the banks' main domestic source of new liquidity. By submitting collateral, the banks could get fresh liquidity, or cash.

In January 2008, the rules had been changed to allow for a broader range of collateral.

Now, bonds issued in US dollars, pounds or euros were allowed. Bonds issued in ISK and backed by housing portfolios, so-called covered bonds, were allowed. Also, bonds packaged by the banks themselves.

Yet more doors were opened in August 2008. Debt backed by assets was accepted. Also for the covered bonds. No rules were set as to what assets could be securitized.

Like chairs.

The banks had also used bonds of other Icelandic banks as collateral. Remember the 'love letters'.

But, Seðlabanki knew it was on a slippery slope. Hence, even when it eased the terms, it also announced a provision saying that such collateral should be accepted at only 90% of its market value as of 1 September 2008, 80% as of 1 October and so on, until 1 January 2009, when the 50% limit was to be reached.

Which never happened. By then, all three banks had collapsed.

The ECB acted more quickly.

The ECB had provided liquidity to only five entities that defaulted in 2008: Lehman Brothers, the Dutch bank Indover NL and the three large Icelandic banks. The total ECB exposure was €10.3 billion. A buffer of €5.7 billion was created at the end of 2008 to cover possible losses.

The ECB, however, recovered its money through disposal of the collateral. Hence, the Eurosystem did not in the end carry any losses on collateralized lending to the five entities that defaulted in 2008.

An email I received from the Bank of Finland, 1 August 2018 read, " ... the governing council reviewed annually the appropriateness of the outstanding provision and decided to dissolve it at the end of 2013 when the Eurosystem had been able to dispose of the collateral. Hence, the European System of Central Banks, ESCB, did not have any losses on collateralized lending to any of the defaulted counterparties."

The ECB had cleaned up its portfolio, terminating love letter structures, and thus avoided losses.

For Seðlabanki, the choices were more stark. It could either put a great deal of taxpayer money at risk or initiate actions that would put even more pressure on the already fragile banks.

The SIC quoted the Director of the Central Bank's Market Operations department as saying that asking for collateral of better quality would simply have been too "difficult." And besides, it had relied on the banks and FME.

The SIC said the Central Bank should have taken more forceful action to limit the love letters and that it should have insisted on better quality assets as collateral.

At the end of 2007, the balance of collateralized loans at the Central Bank stood at ISK 302 billion, the highest level up to that point. Then it rose further, peaking in October 2008. By the time the banks collapsed, Seðlabanki had lent them ISK 520 billion, up from 50 billion in early 2007. Clearly, the Icelandic banks were having trouble obtaining liquid funds well before the fall of Lehman.

Fifty-eight per cent of the underlying collateral consisted of bonds issued by Glitnir, Kaupthing and Landsbanki.

Seðlabanki fought to become a prioritized claimant. First, the FME nodded, but then said no. The FME upheld the principle of equal treatment of nonprioritized creditors. Seðlabanki became a creditor like all others.

From the banks that were still alive, the Central Bank demanded more collateral. This limited later losses. And, as we will see later, it took Seðlabanki into even more exotic structures. Including one alongside Dresdner Bank.

At the end of 2008, the Treasury took over the Central Bank's claims against the financial institutions.

The Central Bank had also gone bust. It needed a recapitalization of ISK 170 billion, 11% of GDP.

The bank boards are responsible for the operations of the bank. The FME is responsible for the supervision. But, as the banks' largest provider of liquidity, the Central Bank could have set requirements and asked for rights. It could have asked to see the books. It could have set conditions for the banks' scale and activities as a prerequisite for funding. Which it did not.

And as events unfolded, this was where the largest losses to the Republic of Iceland occurred. Either because the risks were unknown or taken on in a desperate attempt to save the banks, or both.

There was worse news. What the banks needed in late 2007 and through 2008 was FX. Hence, when they borrowed with 'love letters' from Seðlabanki, they got ISK that they then turned into FX. This weakened the ISK. The banks then made money as they were hedged. While Seðlabanki was trying to shore up the krona by raising the interest rate.

THE FIRST TO GO TO JAIL

The permanent secretary in the Ministry of Finance is usually one of the most influential government officials. In Iceland, he also was a prominent member of the special consultative group on financial stability and preparedness. And a lawyer by training.

And a sizeable shareholder in Landsbanki.

He did not see that as a reason to step out of the discussions.

On 13 August, the permanent secretary met with the CEO of Landsbanki. All the problems of Landsbanki were described and discussed. On 2 September, he met the UK Minister of Finance to discuss Icesave.

On 17 and 18 September, the permanent secretary sold all his shares in Landsbanki, freeing up ISK 192 million. In his view, all the information he had when selling was also in the public domain.

In October 2008, FME started an investigation of the sale. In February 2012, he was sentenced to two years in prison by the supreme court. He received the first insider trading related jail sentence ever handed out in Iceland.

"We were amazed," says a former employee at another Nordic financial authority. "The sale and the sentence were remarkable. But even more so, the fact that the regulations allowed him to sit on the shares and still be in lead on the discussions in the first place."

CLIMBING THE STAIRS OF THE PALACE OF JUSTICE

I was summoned to Paris. I was to be there on a dark cloudy day, 10 May 2019.

Ten years, seven months and three days after the crash of Landsbanki.

I was to meet next to the remains of another tragedy. The fire of Notre Dame. In the Chambre Des Criées in the Palais de Justice on Île de la Cité, the small island in the river Seine. In a courtroom normally used by the French Supreme Court.

I had been called as an expert witness. To be questioned for more than three hours.

Forty-seven plaintiffs had raised a civil case, many after years of suffering. Some felt they had lost a decade of their lives. Fifteen had by now retired. The group also included shopkeepers, a doctor, two nurses, a truck driver and a kindergarten assistant. They had all placed their trust in the same bank.

Landsbanki.

↳ **The lawyers of the Landsbanki customers and their advisor climbs the stairs of justice at the Palais de Justice.**
Source: Author

Landsbanki Luxembourg and nine individuals met as defendants. The most prominent being the prior chairman of Landsbanki. The other eight I list by their initials; RA, VF, TJ, OL, PM, MN, TN and GT. Most were non-Icelanders. All were respectfully present as the court proceedings started on 9 May, in the courtroom of a building that dates back to 1240.

Except the chairman. He might have had other matters to attend to. Together with his son, the chairman had been the largest shareholder of Landsbanki. The father and son owned just over 40% of the bank but controlled over 50%. The latter 10% was in several offshore companies, controlled by the bank itself.

The court case followed from what I personally believe is the worst of all traits of the three banks, as least when considered based on what's morally right or wrong.

In the old-fashioned world, banks gathered deposits from savers and then lent the money to individuals and companies in need of funds. As an example, middle-aged workers saved through deposits for their pension, and the bank then lent their money to young families building their first houses. The interest rate payments from the borrowers were paid to the lenders, with a small margin for the bank. The bank owner was rewarded as she has injected equity to safeguard the deposits and as a buffer in case many depositors suddenly need their money.

Not so, though, in the Luxembourg banking operation of Landsbanki.

From here, the bank's salespeople had knocked on doors and offered an innovative financial product: Equity Release.

If your house was worth €1 million and was debt free, then you could take a loan of €600,000, spend €200,000 and invest €400,000. With the €400,000 placed in high-return investments that could pay the capital cost on the €600,000 and earn back the €200,000. With this, you as a homeowner could increase your spending at no cost. This was their sales pitch.

The bank could then give the homeowner a high-security loan. That could be placed as collateral in a Central Bank, as mortgages were eligible collateral.

Even better, the bank's equity need could be met if a part of the homeowner's equity investment fund, the €400,000, was used to buy shares in Landsbanki.

Hence, no deposits are needed here. Equity is created, not required. Fees and margins can be charged. No wonder some claimed that the three banks reinvented banking.

As they surely did. Landsbanki had its own appraiser, the plaintiffs claimed. The plaintiffs had reviewed ten properties. In this sample, the houses on average had been overvalued by 70% when the borrowing quotas were set. That meant some customers could borrow more than their property was worth.

The loan documents showed that some loans were issued in Swiss francs. This lowered the interest rates, but also exposed the borrowers to currency risks. As Landsbanki had done with its Icelandic customers.

But, here Landsbanki took things one big step further. It placed some borrowers' money mostly in Kaupthing and Landsbanki securities. It had placed 82% of the money of one customer in such securities, showed the exhibits presented to the court. With the largest purchase made on 6 September 2008. One month before the tragedy of October 2008.

The second-largest purchase, €228,050 of Landsbanki bonds, was booked on 10 October 2008. These bonds were de facto almost worthless, worth just €3,050 when the securities were booked on the customer's account.

One may surely wonder whether it was the interest of the customer that made Landsbanki Luxembourg make such a transaction, or whether it was a part of the last attempts to save the bank and the owners' source of funds.

Many customers had been uneasy. Some asked to receive a copy of the Landsbanki annual report with the auditor's report of PWC. As if that provided a fair representation.

The Landsbanki estate itself sued PWC. With an ISK 100 billion claim. The estate's board considered that the bank's auditors had caused damage through their actions, omissions and wrong advice.

A German customer, one of the 47, had for a long time been worried. He asked to see a version of the contract in German. He was told it wasn't available.

Similarly, French customers had received contracts in English, as the French version was not available. The English customers received contracts in French, as the English version was not available. Supposedly.

OL, one of the eight, could, though, share his words of comfort in a mail dated 17 January 2008. "As TN said to you November last year ... we can say the investment part of our Equity Release will earn yield in height of the cost of the loan and repayment (after term)."

He then added, "The market values based on indices produce adequate yields to pay these costs, so don't worry about putting extra money on that."

The reality, though, was the opposite. The analyst, Jean-Michel Matt, was called as a witness to the court. He had assessed the mechanics of the structure on behalf of the plaintiffs. He had reviewed 60 scenarios. Only one delivered a satisfactory outcome for the customers.

Which didn't materialize as both Landsbanki and Kaupthing defaulted.

The impact can be seen from the account statement of the German customer. The value of the 'risk-free' portfolio of bank bonds fell from €664,487 to €22,437.

While his portfolio value evaporated, the euro value of the money he had borrowed in Swiss francs increased. Some time later, the estate asked to be repaid. Foreclosures and personal ruin were to be expected.

The Icelandic language, the language of a country of honesty and trust, got a new word as the practices of the banks were unearthed: Kaupthinking. It can be used as a noun, a verb or an adjective. Or even to characterize a state of mind or even a political or an economic system. It is used to characterize smart, but dubious, borderline criminal behaviours.

The equity release scheme of Landsbanki was worse.

Apparently yet another word is needed. In the Luxembourgian dialect.

It should cover a situation in which a Luxembourg-based bank puts the assets of its customers at risk through an insane allocation of their investment funds. Fund managers rarely invest more than 10% of a portfolio in one company. In many countries, a higher ratio is actually illegal. Furthermore, asset managers normally lower the risk of customer portfolios as the customers near retirement. Not here.

This new word should also cover situations in which loans to customers also carry extra risk. Many borrowers were, as in Iceland, exposed to currency risks.

The word should also describe cases where the bank systematically hunts for customers with only limited knowledge of financial markets. Exactly the group that laws normally seek to defend.

And situations in which the risks are hidden. On purpose.

And, where the authorities' main response is to hunt the victims and not the offenders.

"Luxembourg is the worst place in Europe to take a bank to court," said a person who has followed the cases closely. "In Spain and France, there were rulings favouring the customers of equity release schemes. But Luxembourg makes its living from the banks."

The structure of equity release, the portfolio allocation and the customer communication reveal a horrendous culture, with little understanding of risks, and either an absence of guidelines or an absence of mechanisms to ensure compliance. All such shortcomings are ultimately the responsibility of the board.

But, what the chairman knew is unknown. He decided not to answer questions when he finally turned up in the Palais de Justice on 22 May.

However, on 7 June 2019, the French state prosecutor stood before the French court. Here he made a landmark call for a verdict.

The time set for the court's ruling is 4 December 2019 at 1.30pm.

EXPLAINING WHAT CAN'T BE EXPLAINED

The last chapter was simple compared to this one.

Therefore, you may skip it and move on to the next. Unless you really want to understand something that almost defies human understanding. Modern banking.

And, frankly, there are some people who really do not want you to know how it all works and how they operate.

"I can't claim I understood how it all worked," said a former leader at one of the trading houses. He asked to be anonymous. So, let's call him Zevs. "I didn't understand it all. Those who did understand didn't share all the information. It was a lucrative niche. There was a lot of money to be made for the few who understood it all."

If you opt to skip to the next chapter, all you need to know is that, over time, transactions took place that resulted in non-Icelandic residents sitting on large holdings of ISK. A lot of it parked in banks outside Iceland. After the collapse, most of these account holders wanted to turn their ISK holdings into FX.

This created what was called an 'overhang', a vast potential outflow of ISK. Possibly named after a feature sometimes seen in Icelandic mountains, a snow formation created by the wind on the lee side of the mountain top. Ready to slide down the mountainside in an avalanche. And destroy everything in its way.

Much like the pile of ISK waiting to be exchanged.

Which would result in downward pressure on the value of the ISK. Hence, the imposition of capital controls. Now the money was locked in. This ISK could not be exchanged.

This chapter explains how it all started. So, if you like sudoku or chess or aspire to become a derivatives trader, give it a go. Explore the creation of what came to be known as 'glacier bonds'. Another celebrated financial instrument that turned into a weapon of mass destruction.

In the summer of 2005, interest rates in Europe in general were modest. In Iceland, however, rates were high. And the ISK had gained value relative to the euro over many years. Each ISK could buy ever more euros.

Hence, you could turn your euro into ISK and receive the highest interest rates around. Then turn it around after a few years and receive an even larger pile of euros. Hopefully. An opportunity too good to be missed in 2002, 2003, 2004, 2005, a bit less with the mini-crisis in 2006, and again in 2007. But not in 2008.

Even more spectacularly, though, the high Icelandic interest rates could also be turned into a tool to reduce the funding costs of the European banks to even lower levels. Just by playing around with money that never entered Iceland.

Financial alchemy, some may say.

Here's where the financial engineers enter the scene. Toronto Dominion was the largest, with its securities arm TD Securities, which had a 60% market share. Deutsche Bank was the second-largest. Surprise, surprise.

They teamed up with solid banks, so-called triple-A banks, that could issue bonds. International state-owned banks accounted for 34% of the volume, commercial banks 31% and multi-state development banks 27%. Hence, the game I am about to describe was largely enabled by government entities. The largest participants were the German state bank KFW, Rabobank of the Netherlands and the European Development Bank. In fourth place came the Republic of Austria. Others included the World Bank and Kommunalbanken of Norway, and even Toyota Motor Credit Corporation.

Let us call our imaginary bank AAA.

Belgian dentists and others with money to spare got an offer. They could buy bonds issued by AAA.

The bonds were denominated in ISK. They could, as an example, have a three-year duration and a 10% annual interest rate.

Let's now say the dentist buys this 'glacier bond', denominated in ISK, all paid for with euros.

AAA now has euros from the dentist. Euros it could lend to its own customers. These could be regional development projects, call them RDPs. The RDPs would then pay these euros back after, say, three years with 2% annual interest added. Hence, the money stayed where it was. This money never entered Iceland.

However, AAA still owes the dentist ISK through the glacier bonds. ISK, that it must repay in three years, with high interest on top. AAA must therefore earn interest and manage the currency risk on the dentist's ISK-denominated glacier bond. Because, in three years, AAA will receive the euros from RDP loans but will need ISK for the dentist.

The initiator of it all, let's call him TD, finds a solution for AAA. TD helps AAA buy a right to convert the euros from the RDPs to ISK three years in the future. At a predefined price that yields AAA 10% interest, which covers the amount owed to the dentist, plus a bit more. Let us say 12%.

TD establishes what is called a currency forward. This instrument predefines the transaction that is set to happen three years in the future. Now AAA is happy.

TD must now find a customer that can honour the forward contract in three years' time. It seeks to find someone willing to guarantee payment of today's price plus the 12% annual interest in ISK in three years.

TD knows the Icelandic interest rate is at 14%. TD finds an Icelandic bank, let us call it III, that is willing to be on the other side of the ISK forwards. It commits to delivering the ISK, with interest added, three years in the future. And to get euros in return. III could thereafter pass a part of the right to access euros on to its customers. Some it could keep itself. Now it knows it will have euros. As a hedge for the FX risk of its equity.

Hedges they all had, remember.

"The schemes wouldn't have worked without the participation of the Icelandic banks," says a person involved. "In order for it all to work, someone would need to take the forward position. We scanned the world and tested high interest rate countries. We couldn't trade in Serbia as no banks in Belgrade were ready. We tried Malaysia, but that didn't work."

"However," he continues, "in Reykjavik there was a massive appetite."

"Sure," says a then Kaupthing employee.

"We were told to grow.

"'Yes, we can do it,' would be our answer, 'if someone comes and proposes a deal many times larger than what we were doing.'"

Now III is happy, as are TD, AAA, the dentist and the RDPs.

And if you ever wondered how the Icelandic banks managed to be industry leaders on interest margins and fee income, you now have part of the answer. In this case, partly thanks to the high Icelandic interest rates that were meant to cool down the overheating created by the banks themselves.

"In 2005, the upper limit for FX trades was €1.5 million," says a former Kaupthing banker. "Two years later, a €10 million trade was considered small."

"I worked with two trading desks when I started working in London around 2000," says an employee of one of the three largest US investment banks. "One desk was called 'Scandis'. It traded the Scandinavian kronas. The other desk was for 'emerging markets.'"

"We traders didn't at first even know which desk was supposed to trade the ISK. Then in 2005, the ISK trade took off. The volumes exploded. I never saw anything like it. For us it was great, especially as a lot was with hedge funds, like Millennium and the macro funds. We had trading lines with them. While the competing Nordic banks didn't."

The chain of transactions on the AAA bonds was then supposed to reverse when the bond expired. The first part worked. The dentist got back a nice big stack of ISK. However, when the banks defaulted, followed by the threat of a massive flight of capital out of the country, capital controls were imposed and the dentist could not exchange the ISK into FX in the local market.

The last glacier bond that's been identified hit the market on 10 September 2008, issued by Rabobank and facilitated by Toronto Dominion. ISK 13 billion at an interest rate of 10.25% for a one-year bond, while the comparable yield on Icelandic government bonds was between 13% and 14%. Only a month later, the buyers would find themselves locked in.

Dentists who bought toward the end fell into a hole. They had expected to get a convertible currency in return when buying an AAA bond issued by a large Dutch bank, Rabobank, the largest glacier fund issuer of all.

That was not the case. Repayment was made in a currency subject to capital controls. The retail investors' possible assumption that the issuer had worked out all the risks associated with issuing a bond denominated in ISK was unfounded.

To add to the misery, some other funds were also brought to Iceland and placed directly in deposit accounts. Some were imported to buy government bonds and government guaranteed bonds.

A billion dollars had been invested in bonds issued by the Housing Finance Fund, HFF. The Quantum Fund, headed by George Soros, was supposedly among the big buyers. HFF paid 6-7% interest, with a full adjustment for inflation. Even better, the buyer could hand the bond over to an Icelandic bank and borrow 90% of its value, through so-called repo agreements. Using this strategy, only one tenth of the money had to be kept on hand to earn the full margin. A money machine. For a while.

Along the way, the demand for the ISK created upward pressure on the ISK, adding to the stabilization challenges.

Most of the glacier bond activity, quite paradoxically, was enabled by international state-owned banks and state development banks. In hindsight, one may wonder why no one tried to intervene.

The Central Bank of Iceland's initial assessment in 2005 was that the impact would be small. "The small size of the Icelandic securities market limits the available hedging opportunities, which will gradually erode the gains from ongoing transactions of this kind," it wrote.

An assessment of the development in the Seðlabanki's monetary bulletin concluded that, "There are a number of indications that króna bond issues could have a very positive impact on Icelandic financial markets and strengthen their infrastructure in the long term."

Hence, the Icelandic authorities supported this 'carry trade'. The trade made Iceland a bigger market, increased the liquidity and the size of trades and built Iceland as a financial centre. Besides, an inflow of capital was needed, given the country's gigantic trade deficit.

"Usually, when I come to a new country, I am not welcome," one carry trader was quoted as saying. "Here I was. My employer was happy."

"I remember once I returned from Reykjavik," he now recalls. "'Wow, they hiked the rate again,' I could report. My boss was happy."

"In Iceland, few people were interested in how the trade worked and its impact," Zevs says. "We could continue making money. The margins were huge. As they often are for financial instruments aimed at the retail market."

The Icelandic ISK was now traded alongside the Turkish lira, South African rand, Brazilian real, Indonesian rupiah and the Mexican peso. Currencies of countries between 15 and 70 times as large, as measured by 2007 USD GDP.

"In size, the Icelandic trade out of our hub in London was comparable to the size of the trades in these currencies," says a trader. "Of the total trade in these G20 countries, the Icelandic trade commanded a 10-20% market share".

The trade, however, also increased the money flows, the size of the financial holdings, the stabilization challenges and the vulnerability of Iceland's financial system. Imagine a giant warehouse full of financial positions denominated in ISK. With immense flows in and out. Stacked from the floor to the roof with 'positions' held by traders in the world's financial capitals. What's more, a large part of the money never entered Iceland. And a large part was derivatives, positions built on top of the primary positions. Thus, the true size of the trade and the warehouse of money were partly invisible in the official statistics. They operated largely outside the view of Iceland's economists and regulators.

"The carry trade positions were huge," says a former Icelandic derivatives trader. "But such derivatives largely don't show themselves. If someone invests in a country, usually it will show up. With the derivatives, all the risk is there, but none of the capital."

At some point, the Central Bank made an attempt to curb the market. "We called the World Bank and asked them not to contribute to the trade," says an employee in Seðlabanki.

But by now it was too late.

"In hindsight, one may wonder why it all was let loose in the first place," says the employee.

When I later came to Iceland, I was amazed by the level of knowledge many people had about even the most advanced financial instruments. In the strangest places, I met people ready to discuss the most sophisticated tools. I had never experienced anything like that in my ten years working in economics and 15 years in business, working in dozens of countries.

TD Securities in London now fills two floors in a high-rise building at 60 Threadneedle Street, close to the Bank of England. It sits behind a vast glass facade and a huge foyer. Internally, many feared it would take a hit as Iceland collapsed. Not because TD bought any instruments for itself, but because some of the counterparties in its many transactions might implode. But, in the end, TD did well. It had bought massive amounts of CDSs on Kaupthing. Not because it had Kaupthing debt. But because those CDSs had become the instrument to buy for anyone afraid of or eager to make money on an Icelandic collapse. Yes, once again, the scale, apparent success and innovation of Kaupthing came back to haunt it.

Today the TD Securities web page lists the currencies it trades. In emerging markets, it lists 13 countries, still including Brazil, Turkey, Indonesia, Mexico and South Africa.

Plus Iceland.

LOSING A QUARTER OF THE PENSION SAVINGS

A quarter of the assets of the Icelandic pension funds disappeared into the black hole of the financial crisis.

Almost half of the losses were on Icelandic shares, one fifth on bank bonds and one fifth on corporate bonds.

One reason for the losses was the increase in the risk profile of the funds in the years leading up to the crisis.

"Most or all of these amendments expanded the funds' investment authorizations," read the 2012 report on the funds' losses. "Most of these amendments were not made with sufficient care, and it is questionable how well conceived some of them were."

Normally, when a stock market drops in value, one can always hope that values will fully recover one day. Not so in Iceland. About 75% of the market value of Icelandic listed companies at the end of March 2007 were in entities that later went bankrupt. Another 15% were in companies that were taken out of the open market just after the crash, typically by majority owners buying at a deep discount.

A lot was lost, never to be recovered. The funds were increasingly inadequate to cover future pensions. New money had to be collected from employers and employees who were already stretched.

CALLS FROM ALL CORNERS OF THE WORLD

The Icelandic bank creditors were disorganized at first, but they soon formed a creditors' committee. "I was put there as the bondholders' representative," Barry Russell says. "The organizer even put my mobile phone number on the web page as the number to call."

"My phone was about to explode. People called from everywhere – Japan, China, Thailand, everywhere."

"The banks knew the buyers of the privately placed debt. Who held the other debt was totally opaque. People just called."

On 4 and 6 November 2008, the post-collapse price of the bonds was set through CDS auctions. They defined the compensation to the CDS holders.

The price of the Landsbanki bonds was set at 1.25% of face value, Glitnir's at 3% and Kaupthing's at 6.625%. The payments to the CDS holders reached $7.6 billion, exceeding Lehman's $5.2 billion and WaMu's $1.3 billion.

"The prices were even lower on some days prior to the auction," says a buyer at one of the large hedge funds.

In other words, if someone bought bonds at $100, after Armageddon, those same bonds would have traded at as little as $1-7 a piece. Many of those original bondholders just wanted to get whatever money they could, take their losses, and get out of the market. That's where hedge funds come in. After studying the corpse left behind by the banks, they bought the distressed bonds at a steep discount, betting they could extract enough value from the estates of the issuers to make a profit.

"Goldman Sachs was among the first to enter," said an interviewee. And yes, Deutsche Bank was active too. In Kaupthing, it was by far the largest player in the CDS auction, followed by JPMorgan, UBS and BNP. They traded on their own behalf or on behalf of others.

"Deutsche came in through its distressed debt unit," says another buyer. "Even before the auction."

"We didn't have a lot of data," says a buyer. "We only had the year-end 2007 accounts and the mid-2008 preliminary accounts. We subtracted what we knew had been lost or taken to cover deposits in Iceland and abroad."

"We saw a clear picture. Normally deposits represent a large part of the financing of a bank. This was the case for WaMu. Not so for Kaupthing and Glitnir. Instead, they had large market loans."

This had been their weakness. Now it made their bonds especially attractive.

Only a small share would be taken by the depositors, even after paying full coverage. This meant there was a lot left for the bondholders. Some hedge funds spotted this as early as November 2008.

Most others wouldn't fully believe in it until 2013.

"I calculated a 30-35% recovery," the buyer says proudly. "With the very low price in the auction, a lot could go wrong and we would still make money.

"I got some things right and some things wrong. In sum, it evened out.

"The global economy and asset prices recovered faster and stronger, beyond any prudent assumptions."

But the buyer continues: "The estates didn't manage to capture as high a ratio of the value as I had expected. The policy measures also ended up being costlier. And it all just lasted longer. We spent a lot on lawyers and advisors."

"The hedge funds really started to come in after the auction," says Russell. "The first creditors I represented left in 2009, 2010 and 2011," he says.

"Think of it as sailing," said a hedge fund manager, when I met him in Boston, where the sailing is great. "On sunny days with gentle winds, lots of people want to sail. It gets crowded and the cost of renting a boat goes up. On cloudy, windy days, fewer people want to sail. The price goes down."

"Some people may get a great ride at a low price, while the vessels of others may break and sink.

"In the capital markets many invest when the sailing is expected to be smooth. Returns go down."

"Fewer, like ourselves, are there when it gets rough," he continued. "And I mean rough. In some spectacular cases, as in Iceland, we get fantastic returns. Those are the cases that get attention. But it's not free money.

"Sometimes the investment just goes sour. Even in Iceland, the authorities could have been more draconian. Taxes could have been imposed and the claims could have been recalculated to ISK.

"Then people would say, 'How come you didn't know? Are you crazy?'

"The outcome is never obvious."

And, yes, in Iceland, the result could only be seen after a long battle.

48,580 POSSIBLE LOSERS

From early 2009 to 2012, the creditors of the three failed banks reported their unsettled claims to the winding-up boards. There were 27,620 such claims in Kaupthing, 11,880 in Landsbanki and 9,080 in Glitnir. In total, about 48,580. This did not include the small depositor claims in the UK and the Netherlands.

About 28,000 claims by individuals and companies were placed in the non-prioritized category, called paragraph 113 claims.

Kaupthing alone had about 15,000 creditors in 100 countries in this non-prioritized category. One of the law firms engaged, White & Case, had more than 280 lawyers in eight offices working on Kaupthing claims.

In late spring 2012, the winding-up board met to review the claims and their priority. The paragraph 113 claims added up to about ISK 9.6 trillion, or almost €60 billion at the official exchange rate of mid-May 2012.

The Landsbanki list of paragraph 113 claims had a median size of about €25,000. Kaupthing was at about €85,000. Glitnir was more than 100,000.

Among the almost 50,000 claims on the bank spreadsheets were some Norwegian claims. Of the nonprioritized Norwegian claims on the list, The Oil Fund, designated with its organization number 937 884 117, was the largest, with 11 different subclaims. Adding up to ISK 7.34 billion. The Oil Fund had gone short in 2006, but, according to the 2012 lists, the pension fund of all Norwegians had also become a creditor.

And, as we know, the Revenue Equalization Reserve Fund of Kiribati also had its place on the spreadsheet.

TURNING A FUND INTO SHIT

The Revenue Equalization Reserve Fund's losses from the global financial crisis amounted to 25% of Kiribati's GDP.

The 2011 IMF report for Kiribati cites the investments in the Icelandic banks as a primary cause.

Since the Icelandic incident, the management of the fund was transferred to two US fund managers.

"On Kiribati, no vegetables can grow. The soil is not suitable," said its UK consul as I met him in Wales. "The islanders' diet consists of fish, coconuts and breadfruit.

"The story of how the phosphate resources were exploited by the colonialists is a very nasty one," he said, commenting on the book he is writing on the history of Kiribati.

The Kiribati UK consulate is not, contrary to most embassies, to be found in the posh Mayfair, Knightsbridge or Belgravia neighbourhoods in London. To hear the history, one needs to travel to Llanddewi Rhydderch, a village in the rolling green hills of Monmouthshire in south Wales, about three hours by train from London.

Here the consul has a small plantation of exotic trees, including one planted by the President of Kiribati.

"For a country as small and poor as Kiribati, formal London-based overseas representation is just too expensive, and despite our colonial history, the UK is no longer of much relevance to us," the honorary consul said.

BARRICADES AT SEÐLABANKI

In early 2009, the police were called to stop protesters from entering the Central Bank. I had seen in a newspaper the picture of the police blocking the Seðlabanki reception. They were fully equipped with shields and helmets. My predecessor had a bodyguard for some time, even in peaceful Iceland.

Now it was my turn.

↳ The Central Bank, and especially the profiled Central Bank governor Davíð Oddsson, became a main target for the protests. Some protested against the political direction he had chosen for Iceland, others its consequences and the decisions of the crisis days. Demonstrators broke into the bank, and the police had to barricade the doors.
Source: Júlíus Sigurjónsson

When I woke up on 27 February 2009, I woke up to my first day as governor of the Central Bank.

I had not previously met anyone from the bank. I knew that no one would have any idea about me when I turned up. I was in a country I did not know and where I had never really worked before for any significant length of time. Naturally, the bank is run in Icelandic, a language I do not speak or read. Only about a dozen people knew what was coming.

And, I had just moved to a new country, a country in the depths of its worst crisis.

And off I went. To meet up at the reception area at the bank on Friday 27 February 27 at 8am.

The protesters were gone.

They had achieved one of their goals.

The director of the Central Bank governor's office, Jón Sigurgeirsson, was there to greet me.

He was not happy. He had tried to keep everything in order in the time after the collapse, and now this. Within a short time, though, he became my most trusted advisor, taking on some of the most demanding tasks in the months to come.

My first decision was to spend time only on the challenges ahead, not on past events. What happened before day one was none of my business. No employee in the bank should waste precious time or attention on that history. It was time to focus on the tasks ahead.

Many in the bank had been traumatized by recent events. Many were exhausted by stress and long hours. "Since October, the days had been absurd," says one Central Bank executive.

"Six hours of sleep, and then work, only work."

Many wondered what had happened and who was to blame. But at that moment, when there was so much to do, the past was just a distraction. We couldn't change what had happened. Committees and historians should be the ones to review and make sense of the history. Dozens of books would be written.

Many people wanted my thoughts on what had led to the crisis. Some journalists even tried to put words in my mouth, eager to get one more voice to comment on the spectacle and to place me in some box. But it was easy for me to deny those stories, as I never said anything on the history of the crisis. Being an outsider became an advantage. I had no history to defend.

Given the hardships people were enduring, as well as the broader troubles and the long way forward, the time saved by not dwelling on the past could be much better spent.

Since my days at the Central Bank in Iceland, I have frequently been asked to make speeches on what I learned about managing in a time of extreme crisis.

This is my day-one learning: let the past stay in the past. Be clear on your priorities, on what is your business and what is not. And define the story you want to tell.

Iceland has the highest labour force participation of any country in the world. Work morale is strong, entrepreneurship widespread. Up until the crisis, state finances had been sound. Many businesses would do well in the new environment. Some sectors had benefited from the boom. But some had suffered. Now, their time had come.

I tried to formulate my message.

The first part was obvious. The second part a stretch. "Iceland has become a symbol of the global financial crisis. Let us make it the symbol of the recovery."

That same day, Reuters, the news agency, quoted me saying, "Even though Iceland is now a symbol of the financial crisis, my hope is that through our joint efforts, it will also be a symbol of a country able to regain momentum and establish new growth."

Reuters, unfortunately, put this at the end of the article, while their chosen title read, "Iceland picks little-known Norwegian to run c.bank."

Other reactions were a bit more positive. "It is great to have a governor who at least understands half of what I am trying to tell him and who isn't in denial," thought the Swedish Central Bank Governor, Stefan Ingves.

My oldest brother was a bit harsher in his words of congratulations; "Why not take on a real challenge? Like leading the Zimbabwe Central Bank." In November 2008, the Zimbabwe inflation rate peaked at 79.6 billion per cent month-on-month, or 89.7 sextillion per cent year-on-year.

By coincidence, all the Nordic prime ministers were meeting that day at the Blue Lagoon, about an hour from Reykjavik. Here the excess geothermally heated water from a power plant is directed out between the lava, forming an arctic lagoon.

The Norwegian Prime Minister at the time, Jens Stoltenberg, attended the meeting. He called and asked me to come to the Blue Lagoon, which would give us a chance to discuss the actions needed and how the Nordics could lend support. And allow him to catch his plane home.

I turned down his request. My obligation was to head the bank. We were short on time. This was not the time to head out anywhere.

Stoltenberg called me again and asked if he could meet me in the bank instead. I was reluctant. I asked him to get the advice of his Icelandic host.

Stoltenberg made his jet wait and came to the bank.

The impression the meeting made was not good. One key employee arrived for work as usual at the Central Bank. "I was met by Norwegian police, the bodyguards of the prime minister," she says. "I was asked about my errand in the bank."

"I was extremely sceptical," she recalls. "What was happening?"

I made the mistake of discussing issues with Stoltenberg in Norwegian. In Seðlabanki. A proud and independent Icelandic institution.

"This was the darkest moment ever," Jón Sigurgeirsson still recalls. He was there. And he had seen quite a bit and would see even more.

But, Jón did get his revenge. At my farewell party.

Later I moved into my flat in the main street of Reykjavik, Laugavegur. I asked for a lease to sign. But I was told no contract was needed. The flat's owner said he knew me and probably his father had known my father. I said I doubted that, as I was Norwegian.

He responded that then our ancestors had known each other.

"In Iceland, we all know each other," he said. "There is trust. We need not spend time on formalities."

Maybe this Icelandic attitude explains a bit about how the country's banking practices evolved as they did. And also how the economic system could continue to function in some way through the years of crisis and default.

Some people, even some presumably insightful people, said they hoped I had made sure to get paid in euros. Really, being a Central Bank governor and not getting paid in the currency of your own bank!

Surely I was to be paid in ISK, the ISK that toward February 2009 had depreciated 50%, cutting the international cost and value of the ISK in half.

That is how a depreciation works. And why many economists believe depreciation is such an effective tool. It cuts the costs for all employers, even Central Banks. It improves the cost-competitiveness of the economy. Companies that export can grow and companies competing with imports prosper. Imports fall, as import prices increase and buying power declines.

Other, also presumably insightful persons, asked if I would move to Iceland. As if there could be any other option.

As a governor of a country in crisis, the regular workdays are used for running the basic Central Bank operations. Weekends are spent on bank restructuring.

Gudmundur Þór had mixed feelings.

He really disliked seeing the foreigners swarming the Central Bank. However, he thought there might be some value in having the bank rise above the domestic feuds. He believed that all three banks had belonged to power clusters, or even clans. It had been hard to see where the world of finance ended and the world of politics began.

Politics had derailed any chance that appropriate action could be taken, he thought. And some of those actions, when attempted, had been misread, with various factions claiming that they were part of the power battles of the modern *goð*. All the discussions Þór had with his friends in the heat of his *heitur pottur* on the past actions of the Central Bank had ended in speculation about the motives of the bankers and the governor.

Events five, ten or even almost 30 years back in time were brought into most discussions, in typical Icelandic fashion. The main owner of Glitnir had successfully worked to oust the governor from his prior position as Prime Minister. Kaupthing had helped the same Glitnir owner take control of the bank. While Prime Minister, the Governor had publicly withdrawn his deposits in Kaupthing, protesting the share option scheme put in place for its key employees. And because, as Þór believed, the Governor's old party had its ties to Landsbanki.

Þór saw a poll in a newspaper. It asked: "Was it right to get a Norwegian in Seðlabanki?"

And 78.2% responded yes.

Þór nodded.

But the Norwegian's talk about recovery was weird, he thought.

Totally off.

THE ONE-PAGE PLAN

From the outset, the Icelandic crisis had some similarities with the crises that hit Norway in 1992 and Sweden and Finland in 1993.

All three countries suffered from a financial crisis, macro crisis, increased unemployment, a state budget crisis, state debt problems and a debt crisis among households and businesses.

Though most people have forgotten, Sweden and Finland were the only western European countries to experience a crisis between 1990 and 2007 that triggered a decline in GDP of more than 10%.

It was clear that Iceland would be hit by all the same elements that had beset its Nordic neighbours. But way harder. And all concurrently.

Before I left for Iceland, I set out to develop a one-page plan I could memorize and that could steer my actions. I wanted it to show all the main policy fronts, how they were all connected, what we wanted to achieve along the way and what the recovery programme could lead to.

Issues related to monetary policy had to be in the forefront for the Central Bank. However, all the policy fronts Iceland faced were connected. I needed to see the full picture and to identify how the Central Bank could contribute to all.

A McKinsey colleague and Icelander, Klemens Hjartar, volunteered to help. He cancelled all other commitments and flew in from his hometown, Copenhagen. We got to work in a locked office, with the shades pulled down.

No one knew that the scribbling on the whiteboard was the new governor's version of the economic plan for Iceland.

We mapped all the actions the Nordic countries had taken in the earlier crises. We studied the outline for the IMF programme from November 2008.

We reviewed all recent economic indicators and we made our one-pager. And then we drew it out neatly.

We started with the main fronts: macroeconomic adjustment, monetary policy, fiscal policy and management of state debt. We then added the turn-around of the banking sector and the resolution of the corporate and household debt crisis.

The macro and monetary policies had to reduce the inflationary pressure that followed from the weaker króna. With no further inflow of capital, we needed a plan that would increase exports and shrink imports.

Absolute confusion reigned with regard to the Icelandic state finances. Some took it as a given that the state had already defaulted or would default. Few distinguished between the state, the country and the banks. Some believed it all would collapse.

We did not share that view. On the contrary, we were optimists. Maybe the only ones in those early days.

We made reaching some clarity on the state debt status an early priority. Containment and predictability in the cost to the state of the banking recapitalization was therefore needed. The recapitalization had to be completed as soon as possible.

We believed speed to be of the essence, to ease the pain of unemployment and modest GDP growth. We thought half a year would suffice to set the direction. Gradually, our one-pager was refined as we added new elements and took out others. The overview we produced shaped the approach, the structuring of the work, and the statements I made from day one.

On 1 April 2009, we got it printed in one of the Icelandic newspapers, *Morgunbladid*, together with an article on the way forward.

To my surprise, it did not spark any controversy or even attention. There was no appetite for discussions on aspirations, structures and plans. The day-to-day debate centred on power structures, a search for the One Big Problem or conspiracy that had caused the crisis or the One Big Solution of the day.

"Get used to it. Don't get distracted," was the advice of Klemens.

"Can you help me translate the specifics of what is written here?" I asked the head of communications in Seðlabanki one day, when an article in an Icelandic newspaper caught my attention.

"The article is written by person NN," he said. "It is a response to an article last week by person YY."

"Interesting," I said, "but what does the article say?"

"The father of NN went to university with the father of YY," he responded. "And they had a dispute."

"Interesting," I said again. "But what does the article say?"

"The grandfather of NN also had a dispute with the grandfather of YY," he continued.

"Hmm, interesting," I responded once more. "But I only care about what's written in the article."

"Why are you asking about that?" he responded.

"That's not what is important," he continued. "No one cares about that. Everyone only wonders why he decided to go on the attack now. Remember, we live on an island with a 1,000-year uninterrupted history."

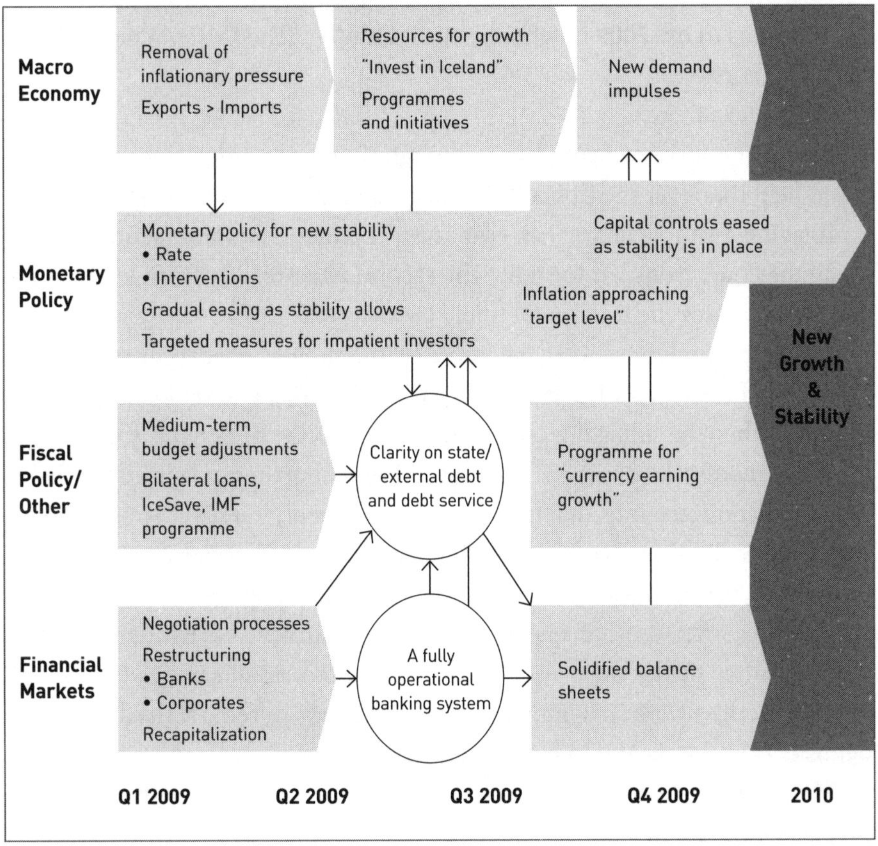

↳ **The response.**

STILL NOT AT THE BOTTOM

Plans are great. Reality is something different entirely.

In the Central Bank, I met the bank staff first. Then came the IMF team. They were all there waiting for me.

I sensed it already in the first meeting. All looked at each other. It was as if they wondered who was to pass on the sad message.

That we had still not reached the bottom.

But I also sensed an eagerness. Some were almost like kids who had waited too long for Santa Claus. They were impatient. The change of government and the fight between the government and the governor had brought many of their efforts to a halt. Months had been wasted.

Now they wanted to get the formalities completed and move on. Immediately.

The notes in my 2009 notebook state it bluntly: "The IMF not pleased with the lack of progress."

Now, I was there.

Not in the form of Santa Claus, though. Rather as a decision maker who could help them get the difficult, but necessary, processes moving.

Imagine a simple chart with two lines. The first is horizontal and runs all along the chart from left to right. The second falls steadily from left to right, and soon crosses the horizontal line.

The horizontal line shows the liquidity, the money, needed to run a bank. The falling line shows what is available, from deposits, market loans and other funding. When the falling line crosses the horizontal, the bank has run out of cash.

When there's a lot of market funding and large short-term deposits combined with market uncertainty, that falling line drops steeply. Or dives straight down. As it did for the three banks in September and early October 2008.

Banks work in networks with other banks. If one goes down, the others suffer. Now, after the collapse of Kaupthing, Glitnir and Landsbanki, half a dozen other banks were also under water. Even small savings banks with strong practices were struggling; some being banks in remote fjords and with deposits from locals and loans to their neighbours.

My 2009 notebook brings back the desperation of those early days: "The savings banks are in a severe situation."

And continued, "May need to act quickly. The crisis is coming faster and deeper than foreseen."

One bank played a key role, *Sparisjóðabanki Íslands*. Also called Icebank.

It served as the hub for Iceland's savings banks. Many of Iceland's small savings banks held shares, bonds and deposits in Icebank. It provided access to international sources of credit and was the entry point to foreign and domestic settlement systems. But Icebank had also bought a significant stake in Exista, the largest shareholder in Kaupthing. To top it off, Icebank had also bought bank bonds and placed them as collateral in the Central Bank. It held a vast portfolio of bonds issued by Kaupthing, Glitnir and Landsbanki.

"Icebank was a collateral machine," two sources say.

"It bought bank bonds, used them to borrow from the Central Bank and then passed the money back to the three banks that had issued the bonds," says one. "It was the most prominent intermediary of the love letter transactions."

Icebank, with its ISK 10 billion in equity, had ISK 200 billion of loans from the Central Bank, backed by bank bonds.

The largest increase occurred in April 2007. Of the 200 billion, 57.5% was lost in the end. Relative to the size of the bank, this would turn out to be Seðlabanki's greatest loss.

The Icelanders, used to bad news by now, could only expect more.

Priority one for us in the Central Bank was to try by whatever means possible to bring the struggling banks back to life. The boards of the banks had the primary responsibility, but we helped as well. We called on the current and potential new owners and the biggest creditors and asked them to make concessions. Many of the German banks ranked among the top lenders. Once again, they trooped back to Reykjavik.

Creditors sometimes do offer delayed repayment and lower interest rates to save a customer, on the theory that they're worth more alive than dead. These are decisions that can be made by the folks in the credit departments.

But reclassifying the claims by converting some of the debt into equity would be more effective. By giving creditors a sliver of ownership, the debtor could duck the need to come up with cash to repay the debt. That kind of a concession, however, usually exceeds the authority of the credit department. They would need to involve other departments in the bank. Potentially even the board. This exposes their losses. Therefore, unfortunately, few such concessions are usually given.

A big mistake.

All could see the trajectory of the two lines. The boards, FME and we in the Central Bank received daily reports and forecasts. For each bank, we could actually calculate when the lines would cross. The doomsday of each. Most days the doomsdays got one day closer.

My notes from 2009 capture the banks' anguish. One bank's cry for help was simple and direct, "We have a need for cash," and "The time difference is impossible to meet." The latter referring to the impact of depositors asking for their money now, while the borrowers were repaying their loans gradually, on a schedule.

The notes from the meeting with the next bank are more technical, but the message equally dire: "The funding facilities of the bank are below the required level."

Soon, a third bank knocked on the door, one that was struggling with its equity. Here the notes read, "The subsidiaries are below the 8% requirement."

Many meetings were held, but progress was slow. No one was ready to inject enough new equity. Some debt relief was proposed, but no 'fresh' equity was available. Most creditors were not ready for a conversion. Possibly because a debt conversion went beyond the authority of the credit departments. Possibly the creditors had no mandate to hold bank equity. Possibly many were trying to figure out who would pay. All, however, seemed to agree that the FME, the Central Bank and the governor were the ones to blame.

As the final moment for the banks neared, the tension grew. As a governor, one must be available for any discussion that can make a difference. One must offer support and signal readiness to provide liquidity if a solution is found. And one must hope. But, at the same time, the governor must keep up the pressure and be absolutely clear about what's required and what is at stake.

At this stage, boards attempt to find a recapitalization solution, but most fail. When that happens, the board may avoid taking the final step of closing the bank. The regulator can force a decision, but the legal risks are way lower if the board itself hands in its banking licence.

It becomes a tug of war.

Sometimes a board announces something that looks like a solution and calls a celebratory press conference. Sadly, it may all just be based on promises instead of hard cash. Or they may just be trying to put pressure on the FME, the government and the Central Bank to keep the doors open. Sometimes they request a capital injection from the state or assume one will be forthcoming, typically through some complex mechanism or instrument that may blur the reality that they are asking to be bailed out. Some exhibit unprecedented levels

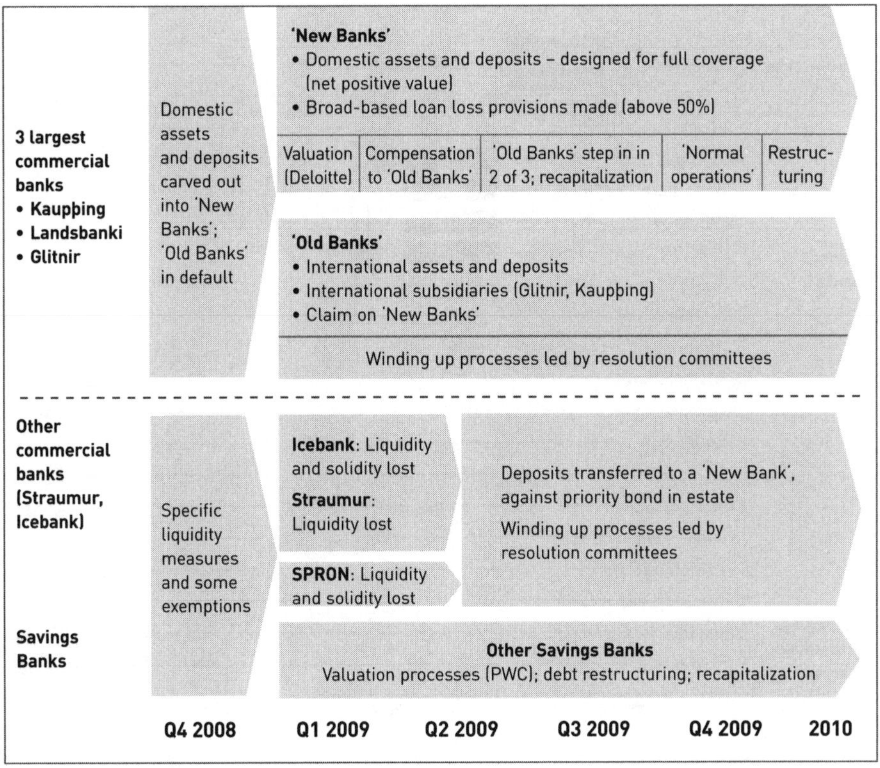

↳ **The default and restoration process for the banking sector.**

of creativity in the last moments, requiring complex analysis and review of legal and accounting-related issues.

In Iceland, we had intelligence that some were playing the system, with banks allowing customers to re-categorize market loans as deposits, which would move them to the head of the line for repayment in the event of a default. Or in general, just chasing high-interest funding from the market and labelling it as deposits.

The discussions go back and forth, most often late into the night and over the course of long weekends.

Which is how my first weeks in the bank were spent.

In hope and despair.

In the absence of equity, we in the Central Bank cannot provide liquidity. But this is a hard answer to give. It's the only possible answer, but in the short-term, it will deepen the crisis and lengthen the line of the unemployed. And once again, many will seek to blame the Central Bank.

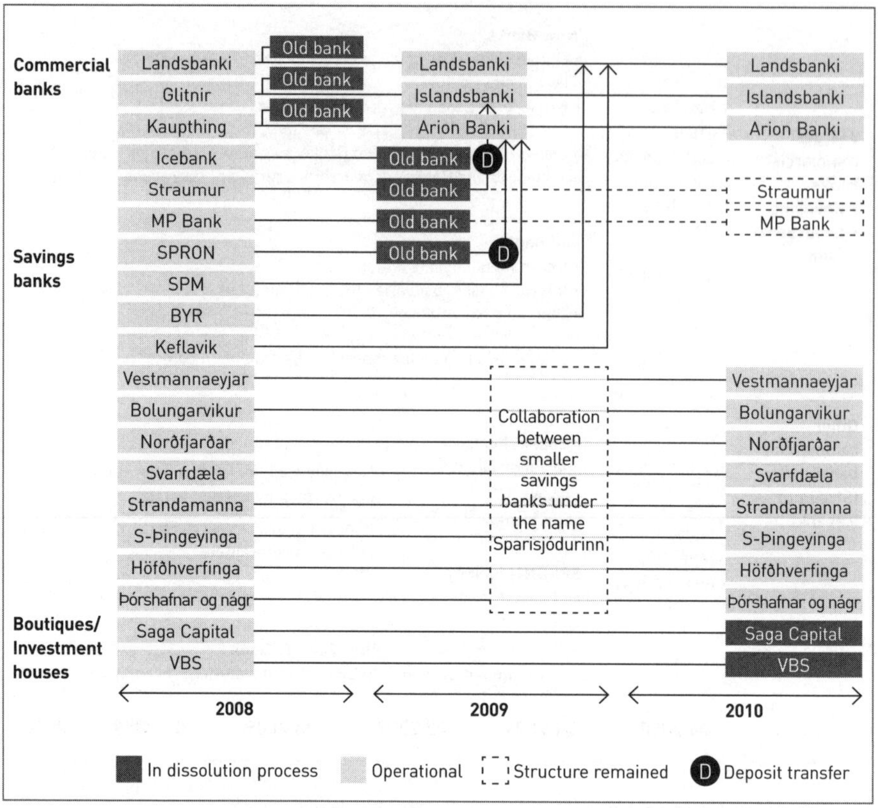

↳ **Overview of banking sector restructuring.**

In Seðlabanki, everyone knew someone who would be harmed. They had been at university together, lived in the same neighbourhood or had kids at the same schools.

The situation was difficult for all of us, but even more difficult for some. I could see the pain as I looked around the table. Seeing their anguish, I believed I understood why Seðlabanki had failed to make some of the difficult but necessary decisions in the past.

Now, the man from the mountains came in handy.

In the Central Bank, backup plans were prepared for cases where no solution could be found. Priority one was, again, to keep the payment system running and to protect depositors.

One alternative was to move deposits to another bank. If we did that, the receiving bank had to be solid on all fronts, able to take on expanded operations.

It is a bit of a paradox that the new banks, created from the domestic parts of Kaupthing, Landsbanki and Glitnir, became the safe havens. Their offspring had all been well capitalized. Hence, most moves throughout the crisis increased the domestic market share of the offspring of the banks that had fallen first.

There are no notes and coins, and surely no gold in a bank vault somewhere backing your bank deposits. Every transaction is just a series of numbers in a data file. In Iceland it was even simpler. All the account files were held centrally, by the common caretaker agency of the banks. The banks had copies, and made regular reconciliations throughout the day, with smaller payments 'netted' out by each individual bank.

Each bank had its unique identification code. By changing these codes, the deposits could be moved.

This partly explains how all the restructuring could happen. In real life. And it carries an important lesson. The regulator must be able to control the system. Something that may become increasingly complex in our age of globalization and cloud computing.

In Iceland, a bank restructuring could be done over a weekend. No trucks with notes, coins or gold had to pass through the streets of Reykjavik. An identification code was changed and billions were moved.

The ZZZ15XXX in the data file was changed to ZZZ08XXX.

When a bank receives ISK 1 billion in obligations to its new depositors, it needs to be compensated. The receiving bank needs to get a promise of payment from the bankruptcy estate of the fallen bank. As a prioritized claim. Furthermore, it must be prepared to hand over cash if depositors wish to take their money.

Hence, plans are needed, and a competent staff.

The board of Straumur, Iceland's fourth-largest bank, handed in its banking licence on 9 March 2009. The FME then placed it under administration.

Icebank and the Reykjavik Savings Bank, Sparisjóður Reykjavíkur, also called SPRON, followed on Saturday 21 March. SPRON, partly controlled by Kaupthing, had lost on large loans to Baugur, Kaupthing and Exista – with Kaupthing being SPRON's owner and Exista being the owner of Kaupthing. The last of these was provided just two weeks before the collapse of Kaupthing.

No fewer than four different models were used in Iceland to address the banking collapse, as illustrated in the two charts in this chapter.

The SPRON restructuring was particularly abrupt. Here, all deposits were transferred to the Kaupthing carve-out, Arion, over the weekend. The employees were asked to meet at the Grand Hotel in Reykjavik on Sunday 22 March. Here, they were told that the bank had ceased to exist. Not by the CEO, though. He refused to convey the message and had already left. On Monday, customers and employees found the bank closed.

Two other banks, Byr and Keflavik, were also discussed regularly and their crisis plans prepared. The latter being the one that had planned for a New York branch. The two banks fought for survival throughout 2009 but followed the others into restructuring in 2010.

Þór read the news of all the bank closings and transfers in the newspaper. He saw that he would now have to go to Arion, the new Kaupthing, to receive his SPRON deposits. He was a bit sceptical. He had moved his money out of Kaupthing because he disliked its practices. And now, as his own bank was closed, partly due to Kaupthing's misbehaviour, he had been transferred back to the Kaupthing offspring.

But by this time, he had seen a lot. And yes, he found what he was looking for when he turned up at the bank to check if his money was there.

WALL STREET, THE CITY AND FRANKFURT COMPLAIN TO THE IMF

Many at the Central Bank worked endless hours.

If no viable model for recapitalization is found and a restructuring is necessary, it has to happen when markets are closed.

The team needs to know by Friday afternoon at the latest if a restructuring is to be carried out over that weekend. By late evening the preceding Thursday or early on the same Friday, the bank's board and FME must reach an agreement on the course of action. By late evening the preceding Wednesday or early on Thursday, all stakeholders must be told that they have one last do-or-die chance to try to avoid being wiped out. Deadlines must be defined and enforced to trigger the necessary decisions.

The IMF has specialists on almost everything. With years of experience from the most remote places. In March 2009, many of them were sent to Reykjavik.

The IMF advocated the need for proactive restructuring to ensure that all banks that were open for business were viable. It was also concerned about Iceland's future ability to service all the debt it owed to foreigners. On these matters, the IMF only cared about the interests of Iceland, the integrity of the Icelandic financial system, and the Republic's ability to make timely payments on its remaining debt.

And to repay its IMF loan.

The IMF became a hardliner. It advocated taking out distressed banks quickly, and placing the debt, largely foreign, into a restructuring process that would wipe out the banks' nonviable parts and thus trigger vast write-offs. This would support many IMF objectives.

One surprising question emerged: What can count as equity?

Is it only the money inserted by the owners plus the retained earnings? Does it only include hard cash, or is it rather an accounting figure? The difference between assets and defined liabilities? If a debt write-off reduces the bank's liability, it would strengthen the equity, most agreed. Even the IMF.

But what if interest rates were cut on a fixed-term part of the bank's borrowing?

Which is exactly what the creditors offered in one of the processes. I was in doubt. I found the book stating the rules. They were ambiguous. I called some old friends, all professors in finance and accounting. "This adds to the equity," they said. But the IMF said no. As did the FME. With this, the bank couldn't be saved.

One day the entire IMF team was assembled in the war room on the fifth floor of the Central Bank. They filled one side of our long table. Over their shoulders, through the windows, I could see the still bustling harbour of Reykjavik. We had just received a letter from all the main creditors in one of the struggling banks. Many prominent names were among the signatures, including leading banks in Germany, BeNeLux, the UK and the US. They complained about the government's and the Central Bank's refusal to inject additional capital into a defaulted bank. They wanted the government to contribute. They threatened to lodge a complaint with their governments and with the IMF board.

It was a situation I disliked. At that point, I didn't yet know the IMF's mode of operation.

The lead IMF representative in the room put the letter aside calmly. "This we can disregard."

Then he archived his copy of the letter.

In the waste bin.

In April 2009, 27 banks sued the Republic of Iceland and the FME for pushing to restructure SPRON while they were still working to increase its equity.

In 2009, I was told that they were also considering a lawsuit against the Central Bank and a personal lawsuit against its governor.

Me.

The district court dismissed the case.

"The district judge was incredibly hostile," says the lawyer for the international banks. "At least nine or ten reasons were found to dismiss the case.

"There was no interest in opening a line of attack on the authorities."

A small Norwegian savings bank, Sparebanken Øst, had made a large profit through a 20% stake it held in BN Bank, which was sold to an eager Glitnir. But Øst considered the margins it could make by using the proceeds to make loans to Nordic companies too thin. Instead it put the money in a portfolio of what turned out to be the worst possible investments. It sent the money to Reykjavik, where it was used to make loans to SPRON, to the Baltics and to a Danish bank that was later to implode. Roskilde Bank. Øst lost all the profit from the sale to Glitnir.

Now it joined the group of 27.

And later, as one of ten, it also appealed the case to the Icelandic Supreme Court. And lost.

THE AILING KRÓNA

On day one, I learned that the banking system had still not bottomed out. Next, I learned that the króna was a patient with an ever-weaker heartbeat. Despite being in a coma.

Every day at noon, the three new banks reported their net daily FX trades, the market was cleared and the exchange rate set. Though there were some buyers of ISK, there were always more sellers. The ISK was about to sink.

This had been countered through the fall as Seðlabanki had provided FX and bought ISK, depleting its modest FX reserves. These purchases stopped in March 2009.

Now, the patient's pulse weakened further. Through March, the stack of ISK needed to buy one euro increased from 142 to 160, a depreciation of more than 10%. On top of the 30% depreciation of the preceding year.

Further intervention was needed. We wanted to freeze the exchange rate to hinder further inflation and to contain the cost of the FX loans. Ideally, we might have wanted to strengthen the ISK somewhat, but such a goal was clearly beyond our reach. But, even though it would have been hard to prove analytically, we were of the view that a ISK 160 to €1 rate could be defended.

As a rule, we met in the Seðlabanki trading room just before 12 noon every day. By then, some information on upcoming trades was available. We could decide to intervene or stay out. Our reserves were modest. But the market was shallow. Even a move of just €1 million could make a big difference.

It was a heavy responsibility. Either to decide to let the ISK weaken, raise the interest rate, or to tap our tiny currency reserves to try to defend the last barricade. Using the last ammunition. A decision I had to make then and there. With hardly any information available on what may follow next.

At one point, we feared a new attack. We moved in to defend the ISK. I called the Ministry of Finance, which convened the leaders of the largest political parties.

I made a statement on the challenges. The leader of the largest party, Benediktsson, provided constructive comments and suggestions.

Another raised his voice and made a lengthy speech denouncing the government, the Central Bank and the global financial system. It was

Sigmundur Davíð Gunnlaugsson, who in 2013 was to become Prime Minister of Iceland.

He spoke almost as if he was out campaigning, even though there were only a handful of people in the room and me, the only one with no affiliation to any Icelandic political party. And with no right to vote. Again, the desire for conflict surprised me.

I could see the contrast to what I had experienced years earlier. On Thursday 19 November 1992, the Swedes gave up their defence of the Swedish krona and let it float. It lost about 10% of its value.

The Norwegian Minister of Finance at the time, Sigbjørn Johnsen, and I had planned for a weekend in London. A meeting with the UK Chancellor of the Exchequer on Friday, a speech to the Norwegian business community on Saturday, then a Premier League match and a musical. Almost a typical Norwegian tourist package.

But as the Swedes gave in, the traders attacked the Norwegian kroner. They assumed Norway would be the next to go. Early Friday morning, as we landed in London, Sigbjørn called the then Norwegian Central Bank Governor Hermod Skånland, who had decided to intervene by buying kroner.

While we were in the taxi from Heathrow to the Exchequer, the intervention reached NOK 50 billion, about $8 billion at that time.

"We just had the most expensive taxi ride in London ever," I commented.

The minister flew home. I had to make the speech to the business community in his stead. In my fumbling English. Thirty-two years old. Maybe half of the people present had sold kroner the preceding day. I talked about the strong fundamentals of the Norwegian economy.

Many smiled. Sarcastic smiles.

On Monday, the interventions reached another NOK 10 billion.

Then the Norwegian kroner was, as ever since, allowed to float.

But it resurfaced. The traders lost their sarcastic smiles. The fundamentals were not that bad. But the episode had shown us that a fixed rate regime is a phenomenon of the past for open, market-based economies with no limitations on the movements of capital.

But, among both political supporters and opponents, there was just one objective. To provide support.

STEMMING THE JÖKULHLAUP

Initially, no medicine seemed to help the ailing króna; neither interventions, high interest rates nor capital controls.

When all is stable, the Icelandic glaciers grow and shrink through the seasons. But the ice cap stays. Unless a volcano erupts from below. Then the ice melts underneath. A large and abrupt release of water may follow, a *jökulhlaup*.

That is when things get really dangerous.

In the period before the crisis, the ISK holdings of foreigners grew ever larger, due in part to the glacier bonds.

In the heat of the crisis, most investors wanted to exit. Many ran for the door. The ISK lost half its value. A financial *jökulhlaup*.

But only some positions could contractually be released immediately. Others were locked in for the short-term, and some could only be released long term.

A further outbound flow was expected as the holding periods expired. The ISK could slide to ever-lower levels, increasing inflation and further exposing those with FX and indexed loans.

The government decided to close the exit. Capital controls, rules to block the right to exchange ISK for foreign currency, were imposed. A dam was built.

Usually seen as a proponent of the free movement of capital, in this case the IMF supported the measure. Iceland became the only OECD country that locked in the money of its citizens and investors.

A system of a dual 'official' (onshore) and 'unofficial' (offshore) exchange rates emerged. ISK could be exchanged at the official rates, the onshore rates, for trade, dividend and interest rate payments. Exchange in support of financial repositioning was forbidden.

Some financial investors, however, really wanted to get out. While the official exchange rate required 160 króna for each euro, some were willing to pay up to 240-250 and, on occasion, even more than ISK 300 for each euro to leave.

Price differences north of 30% for the same product, in this case the euro, create tensions. Circumventing regulations appeared like a profitable business to some: would exporters selling Icelandic goods abroad take their foreign currency back to Iceland or would they exchange it abroad at the offshore rate? Would they use their FX earnings to buy locked-in glacier bonds at a discount and tap the water from the dam?

In the Central Bank, we had to make a tough choice; either take the hit and let the onshore and offshore rates converge at a weaker level, or impose ever stricter regulations, surveillance and penalties. The first option would add to the immediate pain. The second would keep controls in place year after year.

We chose the latter option.

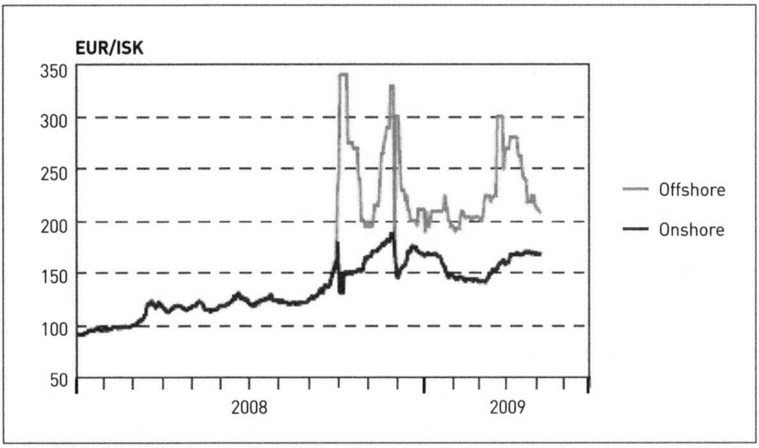

Amount of Icelandic króna needed to buy €1 in the two markets, the 'official' (onshore) and the 'unofficial' (offshore) from January 2008 to May 2009.
Source: Seðlabanki

SICK OR ONLY PLAYING GOLF

"Eventually, currency exchanges were prohibited unless they were explicitly permitted," says the current leader of the capital control unit in Seðlabanki. "That was how the capital movements were regulated. We established a monitoring department, an investigation department and an exemption department.

"Yes, we got many applications."

"You needed a good reason to get an exemption. If you moved abroad, you could exchange money to buy a house, up to ISK 100 million."

Hence, if you moved to Spain or needed a house at a golf resort to recover, you might get a permit. But not for recreation.

Many were the complexities, as illustrated by the regulator's examples.

"If someone wanted to put money in an account in a foreign betting company by exchanging ISK for FX, that was considered to be buying a betting service and they could make the exchange. But then, some people put in a lot of money. Maybe together with a foreign friend. Who also had the right to pull the money from the account. All that is legal. But not if the friend was just a channel for converting ISK to FX at the more favourable official rate."

"Dividends on Icelandic investments could also be exchanged for FX. But not if they were huge and represented an export of value. Paying down old foreign loans was allowed. But not if the payment structure was changed dramatically and the borrower got another FX loan from some other bank."

These were just some of the issues the Central Bank faced.

"On some occasions, we felt like we had every finger in a hole in the dam," says the regulator.

"We got information from customs on exports and imports. We had access to information on all cross-border transactions. But it was hard to see what was going on outside the country."

Gudmundur Þór's father had told his son stories about the currency controls in the 1950s. Then, the scarce currency holdings of Iceland were supposed to be used to build the country, not to travel abroad for pleasure or for consumption. His father had been happy when he could get hold of a pair of imported shoes. They were brought home with enthusiasm. Even if they were mismatched, with one too big and the other too small, or both of the same wrong size.

Never had he thought that controls would reappear, although at least now they did not apply to goods or services.

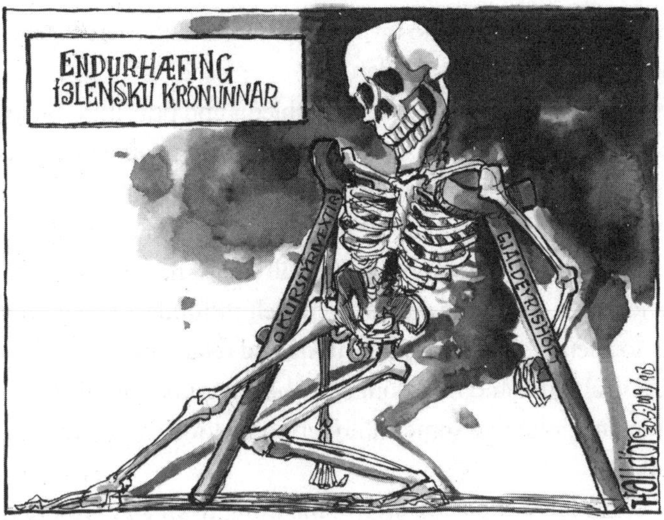

↳ Icelandic artist Halldór Baldursson's interpretation from March 2009 of the rehabilitation, the *endurhæfing*, of the Icelandic króna.

Questions were now asked when Þór needed euros to pay Kacper. Foreign tourists had started to reappear. Any FX they brought in had to be turned in. Reports had to be churned out.

But, even worse, Þór needed to invest to expand. Some international investors were ready to help. However, there was no way they would put their money behind the wall. Þór heard the talk about the recovery of the krona, *endurhæfing*. He heard that increased rates, *okur stýrivextir*, were needed. As were capital controls, *gjaldeyrishöft*.

He was not sure this was what he wanted.

A LEAKING SHIP

Yes, we were half desperate.

I have never been stuck in quicksand. But for us, wherever we stepped, the ground provided no foothold.

In early 2009, we saw a net outflow of money. Some currency-earning companies did not bring their earnings back to Iceland, but instead exchanged them in the 'offshore' markets.

Something had to be done. I decided to invite the 30 largest exporters to meet at the Central Bank, one by one. Two each day.

One objective was to get a better sense of their problems and priorities, and of how we could support them. Another was to ask them to bring home their FX. And finally, just in case someone was not fully following the letter of the law on currency controls, we believed that shining a bit of a spotlight would not hurt.

But the move also stirred up controversy. Some still claim that we brought a dark cloud of suspicion over entire industries. Some felt intimidated. Not only were they struggling to keep their businesses running and retain jobs. Now they were called to the Central Bank and questioned by the governor and his team. I still, most likely, owe an apology to some, although some today forget that we were fighting for survival.

We did find that some large exporters were benefitting from an exemption from the law. They were not forced to take their export earnings straight home. They could exchange them in the offshore market, where they could get even more ISK for each dollar. By doing so, they could pay their employees with ISK that had depreciated by up to 70%, not just by 40%. Employees who had seen prices increase, salaries frozen, interest rates rise and debts escalate.

I was upset. The November provisions had created an opening. They were meant to enable, among others, the large aluminium companies to operate without hindrances. Were businesses wrong to use it for their benefit, even though it was legal? Or do business leaders have an obligation to consider the bigger picture? Especially in a time of crisis?

We quickly moved to terminate the exemption.

SORRY, WE CAN'T SHIP THE OXYGEN

Imagine a country where half of all companies are in distress – in popular terms, bankrupt. On average, this would mean that half your suppliers are in distress, as are half your customers. And the chances are 50/50 that you are bankrupt, too.

Will your suppliers demand prepayment before they ship you goods? Should you ask your own customers to prepay? Can your suppliers deliver or will they run short of supplies? And will employees come to work not knowing whether you can pay them?

"I got an emergency call," tells the former CEO of Iceland's University Hospital.

"Our order for oxygen for our medical operations was blocked in Copenhagen," was the message. The supplier refused to make any shipments unless they got a signature from the hospital CEO and the health director."

"The oil importer was bankrupt," says another executive. "We had to prepay. When we exported, some customers were unwilling to make payments into our Icelandic bank accounts.

"We paid early but got paid late."

Some Icelandic companies suffered huge cash flow problems.

"Our decision on this was among the most important decisions we ever made," says a banker in one of the new banks. "We decided to let the system live. No one could bear a stoppage. We provided credit to let the machine run.

"It was a conscious decision. It was our decision. Everything had to move in parallel. If one bank had decided to tap the system, everything would have come to a stop."

"In Iceland, people still had faith," says a minister at the time. "In general, only some of the imports had to be prepaid."

"Many asked us to move fast," says the banker. "The theory was that bankrupt companies should be taken out quickly. There was quite some pressure to push companies off a cliff. Or to sell them to well-connected investors.

"Some had turned up with all the available cash they had.

"For me," he says, "the most important lesson from the crisis is that you need to wait. You need to let the dust settle. And think."

The amount of dust from the wreckage of the tower was vast. Some companies had extremely high debt, some not as much. Some could survive if their customers stayed afloat. Some were dependent on their suppliers.

Demand had shrunk dramatically in many sectors; in some retail categories by as much as 70%. Most likely, future demand would be higher, but stores had to survive in the present.

"Who should decide how many shoe stores Reykjavik should have? And which ones to preserve?"

One of the new banks had made an overview of its largest loan customers, with one page for each. The stack was 4 centimeters thick.

"We analysed but could not get the specifics. We decided to score in red, yellow and green categories. With this, we could buy some time. We only got decent figures in late 2009.

"By then we could see some movement under the layer of dust."

MOVING OUT FROM THE COGNAC ROOM

Old cartoons often depict bank governors with a hat, a cigar and a glass of cognac in hand. Even more so Central Bank governors.

In the cosy old days way back when, all three may have been part of the daily life of a Central Bank governor. That's also what some might have expected today.

And yes, we did have what I called a cognac room in Seðlabanki. I assume that the cognac had been rarely tasted, though.

Even without regular infusions of cognac, however, some processes had been less than ideal. Considering the small size of the agencies dealing with economic matters in Iceland, the level of coordination and cooperation to me appeared appallingly weak.

On this, the SIC had harsh comments. "It may be assumed that the representatives and administrators of those governmental institutions which had the role of monitoring operations in the financial markets and the effects of those operations on state economics were, in various cases, unaware of who was meant to carry out and take responsibility for certain aspects of these affairs in the government's daily activities."

Iceland is one among a few countries in the world with no military: no army, no air force, no navy. It has only a very effective coastguard and is otherwise protected as part of NATO. Hence, the concept of coordinated troop movements is unknown in Iceland and few, if any, have such training.

As became evident when a crisis loomed.

Even in early 2009, there were still some who said the Central Bank governor, appointed by the prime minister, should not cooperate with civil servants appointed by ministers, or even the ministers. What nonsense. Roles and responsibilities need to be clearly defined and divided, but that should not hinder cooperation. Especially in a time of crisis.

Some executives say that organizations can handle only one, or at maximum, two or three change programmes in parallel.

If you want a counter argument, look to Iceland post-crisis.

Here, more than a dozen programmes had to be executed as soon as possible, ideally within a period of six months. The magnitude of many of the programmes exceeded what normally could be delivered in years.

My Iceland experience and experience working on change programmes for 30 years also left me with other important learnings. First, it is an illusion to believe that it's easier to implement change if one allows for more time and dialogue.

Yes, one should allow for appropriate discussions and preparations, but clarity and direction is what an organization seeks. Change programmes of companies owned by private equity owners paradoxically most often advance quite smoothly. All know what to expect and act accordingly.

Second, an organization most often gets better as it trains its muscles. There is no such thing as a set capacity of any organization.

Third, communication is key. Gjedrem gave me one clear advice, "Reach out. Meet business leaders, unions, media, market participants and Icelanders. Present your plan!"

The team I met in the bank were individually very competent, but small. We needed clarity, allocation of responsibilities and mobilization.

When making presentations on 'crisis leadership', I always refer to how we worked in Seðlabanki, especially in those early months.

All initiatives had one and only one owner, with all the owners being on the management team. Ideally, each executive owned just one or two initiatives at a time and had to form their own teams for each.

We met daily to review progress and discuss issues related to one or at a maximum two of the initiatives. The management team attended, plus one or two members of the team whose initiative we were to discuss. I wanted to get to know as many of the employees as possible and leverage their capabilities and competencies.

And yes, we moved our meeting from the cognac room to the Seðlabanki boardroom, and we had a defined agenda and attendance. Structured meetings replaced informal afternoon gatherings.

As we got the system in place, it worked smoothly. Lilja Alfreðsdóttir, a highly competent young economist in the governor's office, managed it all. She defined the priorities and ensured that everyone was prepared. She had a strong sense of what was needed. We quickly gained speed. Somewhat surprisingly, we also quickly ran out of issues to discuss.

It soon became a question of execution and of accelerating the pace and enhancing the level of cooperation with other agencies.

RUNNING ON A KNIFE EDGE

The value of the currency kept sliding downward, despite the capital controls and high interest rates. The economy was suffering from debt escalation, recession and high interest rates. Inflation was running at 20%.

The next task was to set the interest rate.

Central Banks set interest rates, technically by determining the rate at which they will lend money to commercial banks. With adequate collateral, the banks can access liquidity. Fresh money.

This rate, the policy rate, sets the cost of borrowing throughout the economy, with upward and downward spreads, depending on the amount of risk involved and the mode of financing. It is the most important price in any economy. To differing extents, from a modest breeze to a stormy gust, it influences the economic choices made by all people and organizations.

The rate defines how much you will have to sacrifice next year to pay for the spending you do today. This influences demand and savings. It determines how much money a builder, for example, would need to earn next year to support an investment, in, say, a new condominium today. Again, this steers demand and the level of economic activity.

Add it all up, and you get to the 'transmission mechanism'. This includes all the channels through which the interest rate set by the Central Bank influences the real economy.

For someone sitting on domestic and foreign currency, the rate also determines what they can earn by keeping their local currency in the country. This influences their eagerness to buy or sell the currency, and thus its value. Which again feeds into the economy's competitiveness and the level of imports and exports that take place. All quite complicated; here grossly simplified.

In parallel, the Central Bank manages the liquidity in the system. It can hold money back, sell securities or increase the requirements for the banks' reserves if it wants the banks to lend less. Or it can loosen up to ensure that there is more money in the system. The level of liquidity determines how the market interest rates float relative to the policy rate. Add in the banks' mark-up, and you get the interest rate on your home mortgage.

By early 2009, the Icelandic króna had weakened 50% in a year and it stayed soft. Inflation approached 20% per year. Many prices were indexed. As one price rose, others rose with it.

There was a risk that inflation might stay high. This would further erode the value of the króna. Some restraint was needed. Without this, Iceland could again enter an inflationary spiral. Repeating a troublesome history.

On 1 January 1985, it took 3.59 Icelandic króna to buy a Danish krone. By 2009, 20 króna were needed. The Icelandic prices had risen six-fold in the meantime. In Denmark they 'only' doubled.

High interest rates are, normally, a mechanism for encouraging investors to stay in a currency. High rates also reduce demand in an economy and dampen inflation.

↳ There were many demanding days in the Central Bank. Difficult decisions had to be made. Many of the governor's days were only filled with new problems, and nights with little sleep.
Source: Kristinn Ingvarsson

At the end of 2008, the Icelandic Central Bank lending rate was set at 22%.

But the economy had already come to a standstill. Everyone could see what was happening. Investment projects came to a halt.

We had to balance on a knife-edge, or rather, to run a sprint on a knife-edge.

The Monetary Policy Committee, MPC, had unrestricted authority to set rates. The decision was ours. We could ask advice from many but could blame no one. While everyone could blame us, if they so desired.

The MPC first met on 18 March 2009, on the top floor of the bank. The committee had two outside members, Professors in Economics Anne Sibert and Gylfi Zoega. The bank also listed its chief economist, Thórarinn G. Pétursson, the deputy governor, Arnór Sighvatsson and me as members.

Anne probed in depth to get the full picture. Gylfi brought us the latest advances in economics. No meeting was held without updates from him on recent and relevant academic papers. We listened with interest and admiration. In a rare combination, he was also on constant lookout for practical actions we could take to accelerate the recovery. He followed all the debates in Iceland, considered the arguments, and brought valid, contrarian views into our discussions. Thórarinn guaranteed that under the new governor, the chief economist would be listened to. He gave no space to politics. Arnór scrutinized all economic data and took the lead in synthesizing it.

We took a bit of a gamble, at least that was what the IMF thought at times.

Sometimes I thought of the lessons from my first job after I graduated as an economist in 1985.

I started as an analyst on prices and wages, in the Ministry of Finance of Norway. I was responsible for estimating wage and price inflation and entering the data and assumptions, and for interpreting the results from the macroeconomic planning models. The results governed, among other things, the price adjustments of most tax and excise limits, as well as the state's allocations. The generals from the Ministry of Defence asked for meetings with small me, Private Øygard, to discuss the inflation adjustments of the allocations for bullets, gunpowder, tanks and vessels.

It was an unfair match. They controlled lethal weapon systems, but I controlled MODAG, the macroeconomic model. And what's more, it was my first job to consider the price and wage adjustment of the King's appanage.

The day I joined, the ministry got its first two computers. Its first IBM PCs ever. One was assigned to me.

Imagine that you are the only one with computing power at your workplace. When you turn up at meetings with complex calculations, people will tend to think you are smart and productive. A bit of luck never hurts.

I was able to build models. The models could predict price increases over the next month. To the last decimal. One simple lesson was to focus on the 'as is' inflation rate, not the 12-month rate.

In the MPC, we assumed that the one-time price jump from the depreciating currency had instantly made it into the inflation numbers, as import prices rose. Hence, the 20% year-on-year inflation; the multiple of a 50% drop in the value of the currency and a 50% import share of consumer goods, with some leakage along the way because of the economic shock. The inflation had ceased, we argued, even with the 12-month rate running at about 20%.

The Icelandic system also showed its strength.

The labour unions, the employers and the government came together to negotiate. The target was a three-year wage and price freeze, combined with a state budget tightening of 12% of GDP over four years. In short, one of the harshest adjustments ever in post-war western Europe.

The trade union leader stated that this was unacceptable. He could not possibly agree.

"No way my members will accept this," he said.

Steingrímur Sigfússon, the then Minister of Finance, and I got worried; what did he want?

The union leader was firm in his voice, as only a union leader can be.

He put his ultimatum forward: all budget adjustments would have to be made within two years.

"Better to suffer intense pain for a short period than to have four years of slow torture."

I looked at Sigfússon while I nodded.

We had just in a glimpse seen the best possible illustration of why all the Nordic countries succeeded in their recovery efforts. A 10% drop in GDP and a 10% budget adjustment are harsh and painful. But splitting costs in a fair and equitable way is normally more effective than years of haggling and only pretending to act.

Simply put, it was like going to a restaurant with a big group and racking up a big bill. If you split the bill equally, everyone can pay their fair share and move on. Or there may be a few who have to wash dishes. But, paying up is better than quarrelling or, even worse, getting into a fistfight and adding damages to the bill.

In Iceland, a three-year wage and price freeze agreement was concluded, and an accelerated fiscal adjustment plan was made. Quite a feat with inflation running close to 20%.

On 19 March 2009, the MPC decided to lower the policy rate to 21%, in early April to 19.5%, in May to 17%, in June to 16%, and even further, to 11.5%, by the end of 2009.

Most Central Bank monetary policy committees meet six to eight times a year and, at most of those meetings, they decide to keep the rate unchanged. Sometimes they may make a small adjustment, raising or lowering it by 0.25%. This was not the time for such customary increments.

And, as predicted, inflation halted and the currency stabilized. Toward the end of 2009, the annualized rate of salary growth bottomed out at 2%.

By now, even the calm Gudmundur Þór had lost patience. Prices had soared. He had been proud of the króna. Now it would not buy him anything. The bank tried to get him to change his loans into ISK, as it struggled with maintaining deposits in króna and loans to its customers in euros, dollars, Swiss francs, Nordic kroners and yen. But no way would he change into ISK at its bottom and with interest rates hitting the 20s.

He was in no hurry. He could wait and see. Hekla's eruption in 1947 had lasted a year and a month.

The MPC rules also had to be decided. The MPC was a new construct. We had our own expert. Anne Sibert's field of research is Central Bank processes: how to proceed with decision making, how to structure the agenda and how to govern the voting. Should the content of the internal discussions be made public or just the overall votes? What about the votes of each member? Should the public get to know the hawks and the doves, the members voting in favour of a high versus a low rate?

We decided to make the MPC statement public as the interest rate decision was announced. The minutes were to be made public two weeks later. The overall voting figures were to be shown. How the individual members voted would be published in the bank's annual report the year after. We considered it a compromise between the principle of accountability and transparency, and the desire to moderate the heat of the moment.

With this, everybody would get a chance to identify the hawks and the doves, but not that same day. And by the way, in the end, the hawks and doves both flew high and low.

Interestingly, the procedures we defined in the midst of the crisis still apply. With this, Iceland has a system that is more transparent and accountable than most.

For each rate setting, the MPC met a day in advance to review the relevant economic information and forecasts. We considered all aspects. The next morning we made our decision and thereafter the announcement. Four sessions over two days was all we could allow ourselves, given everything else that had to be done.

MCDONALD'S CLOSES, LEAVES ICELAND AND BECOMES PART OF THE SOLUTION

On 31 October 2009, McDonald's closed its three Icelandic outlets. Iceland joined Albania, Armenia and Moldova as the only countries in Europe with no McDonald's.

Davíð Oddsson, then the Prime Minister and later Central Bank Governor, had opened the first outlet in 1993 and eaten its first burger.

McDonald's operated in a franchise model. The restaurants were bound by the chain's requirements. All supplies, from packaging to meat and cheese, had to be imported from Germany.

With high capital inflows to Iceland, the value of the króna was boosted and Icelanders could buy euros, as well as European meat and cheese cheaply.

↳ Icelandic cartoonist Halldór Baldursson's caricature of the downfall of the symbols of the past.

As the króna lost half its value, the McDonald's model ceased to be viable. Icelandic ingredients were way cheaper. Furthermore, the purchasing power of the locals had plunged. Expensive hamburgers were out of the question.

The franchise owner was clear: "It just makes no sense. For a kilo of onions, imported from Germany, I'm paying the same as for a bottle of good whisky."

Probably not Scotch, though. As that also is imported.

The Big Mac, long a symbol of globalization, itself became a victim of the global financial crisis.

A new chain, Metro, was established. Icelandic meat, salad, potatoes and cucumber filled the plates.

Our friend Þór was surprised. Out of the blue, he got a contract to supply vegetables from his greenhouse.

He had no doubt that the veggies he grew, tapping into Iceland's geothermal heat, tasted way better than anything shipped in from Germany.

In most other ways as well, the economy behaved as macroeconomic theory predicted, before, during and after the crisis, making Iceland a textbook case.

"In 2007, our average ISK salary cost was 18-19 per hour when calculated in euros," says a fish company manager. "In 2009, it was down to 11."

"We hired 100 employees. We had exported whole round fish. Now, we started to process it all. Everybody wanted to work 8, 10 or even 12 hours per day. On workdays, Saturdays and Sundays. We thought there was a boom."

Car sales in Iceland had doubled from 2002 to 2008, with the large Toyota Land Cruiser a bestseller.

"Don't exaggerate," says one of my Icelandic friends. "It wasn't the 200 series with the V8-engine. It was the 150 series."

The apparent cost of financing was low. Foreign currency loans could be bought from street vendors. They were backed by the Icelandic banks.

The increased sales created jobs, salary increases, tax revenue and positive expectations. The inbound flow of capital made it all possible.

In 2008, the current account showed a world record deficit. Equally remarkable, except for positive blips every six or seven years, the country had been running a deficit since the mid-1960s.

Iceland's savings had not matched its investments, leading to a vast gross net debt toward other countries. All Icelanders, all Icelandic companies, its banks and the Icelandic state combined were in sum indebted. The so-called International Investment Position, IIP, was negative, amounting to a full year GDP.

What most people had bought pre-crisis were cars, electronics and appliances. This is what economists call discretionary spending. The category is called durable consumer goods.

Then it all turned. The króna fell and the outlook blackened.

In 2009, car sales fell as much as 89% at their worst year-on-year comparison. The small Suzuki Swift became the top-selling car.

Three cars were parked next to me when I fuelled my car when I last was in Iceland. A Toyota Land Cruiser. A Suzuki Swift. And, yet another Land Cruiser. As an economist I didn't need a closer look to guess in which era each of the three had been bought. Happily, the closer look verified that one of the Land Cruisers was brand new.

Other indicators showed a similar pattern. Supposedly Icelanders cut back on foreign vacations by 70%, while camping in Iceland grew 40%. Luckily, many found that camping with friends was just as fun. Most import categories fell. Sewing machines were an exception. The old saying that necessity teaches the naked woman to spin came true, with a modern twist.

Many zoomed in on the bad news. Reduced activity, higher cost of capital and a worsening outlook halted the construction industry. Unemployment soared to almost 10%. Tax revenue fell. Government spending increased. A budget surplus turned into a deficit.

But there were also some positive signs, even in those early days.

Iceland has a large fishery sector and is a large exporter of metals purified with the help of low-cost renewable energy. These sectors were cost-competitive, even more so after the depreciation. Both ran full speed even in the middle of the global financial crisis, now with the new aluminium plant adding a vast capacity.

It takes scale to manufacture most durable consumer goods. Iceland does not have scale. It does not manufacture durable consumer goods. Almost all are imported.

Well, after the crisis they were not. Sales plummeted.

Half of the contraction in consumption manifested itself in lower imports. Being a small open economy was part of what caused the crisis. Now it became half of the solution. As a share of GDP, imports minus exports declined by more than 10 percentage points from the average of 1980-2009, to Q4 2009-Q3 2010.

For Iceland, having an independent floating currency accentuated many of the elements that had led to the crisis. Now, the currency's value got cut in half and that also made it part of the solution. Import prices rose, and people cut back on their purchases. Icelandic costs and salaries fell when counted in international currency, and people started substituting locally made goods for imports. Exports, which now cost less for foreign buyers, grew.

Proponents of a fixed exchange rate or of linking the Icelandic króna to a broader currency area pointed to the pain caused by the pre-crisis run-up in value and the sacrifices caused by the sharp drop. The proponents of a floating rate pointed to the self-adjusting mechanisms.

And, sorry, I was wrong when I wrote that no McDonald's burger was to be found in Iceland post-2009.

On 30 October 2009, the day before the last outlet closed, Hjörtur Smárason bought one. He kept the burger and fries stored in their original bag. Three years later, all was donated to the National Museum of Iceland. Now, it sits on display at the Bus Hostel Reykjavik. From there it is livestreamed by web cam, probably the only burger in the world with live coverage.

And, even during the crisis, Icelanders found a way through the dark.

Statistics Iceland gives one indication. It tracks the number of births in Iceland from 1853 to 2016. In August 2009, nine months after the dark of November 2008, the number was the highest monthly total ever.

A new generation of stubborn Icelandic fighters were born.

A EURO ISLAND DOWN SOUTH

One of the most distinct memories of my childhood is watching day after day on TV as red hot lava emerged from a hillside and flowed in a slow river toward the town below.

Glowing sprays of molten rock soared into the darkness in a fountain of fire. Ashes and steam followed.

As the river of lava flowed slowly toward the small town, house after house was engulfed by lava, burning as we watched. Those that were spared were covered by layers of ash. Almost half the town was destroyed.

The tragedy could have been worse. The lava flow had threatened to pour into the fishing harbour, which would have been destroyed. The small town could have lost its livelihood.

As we know, one person, acting with the authority of a general, the leader of the Keflavik airport fire brigade, was there, leading the efforts. He made sure that seawater in immense quantities was sprayed onto the lava flow, to steer mother nature.

We watched these efforts and wondered if they would really work. We collected money for new houses and emergency shelters. As Norwegians, we never felt closer to Iceland, the archipelago of Vestmannaeyar and the island of Heimaey, than during the Eldfjell eruption in 1973.

As I landed on Iceland to become governor, there was one thing I absolutely knew I would do: visit Vestmannaeyar.

With the eruption and the lava flow, the island grew, in the same way that a small island a bit further south, Surtsey, had risen from the North Atlantic in 1963 and as Iceland itself had, long ago. In 1973, the harbour survived and was even improved, strengthening the island's role as one of Iceland's main fishing ports.

One that, de facto, largely lies within the eurozone.

Almost the entire wild catch of the fleet of Vestmannaeyar is taken ashore on Heimaey and then sold to western Europe. During the crisis, it was also processed on Heimaey, less so before and after.

The fishing crews are paid through profit sharing, or *lott.* In euro. As were many onshore employees. Here, even the banks were in reasonable shape, with regard to the business on the island.

The fishing companies did well. When looked at in euro, their earnings were on a steady upward trajectory. Catch levels varied, but this was largely offset by price changes.

In ISK, their results looked like what the seismographic images possibly looked like in 1973. The ISK only added volatility and risk.

When competing based on innovation, entrepreneurship, hard work and suitable regulations, these companies were competitive. After being sent through the macro-policy rollercoaster, even they were challenged.

Ecuador, with its 16 million inhabitants, gave up its own currency, the *sucre*, in 2000. It had lost 67% of its value during the financial crisis of 1998-99. Ecuador eventually adopted the US dollar.

"If you manufacture a car, you can't decide who will buy it second hand," explained an economist. "If you issue a dollar or a euro, you can't stop others from using it."

"The pre-crisis years had been very difficult," said a banker as we chatted in Guayaquil, the economic capital of Ecuador. "Inflation was high, the banks were struggling."

"I worked in Banco Popular," he said. "Every evening we met at the centre where the payments between the banks were cleared. We could see which banks would struggle the next day."

"The transition from sucre to dollar was horrendously hard," he said. "Deposits were converted to dollars at a deep discount and frozen, as the banks didn't have dollars. Loans also shifted to dollars, again at a discount. Albeit smaller. This was the mechanism used to help the banks build a buffer."

Montenegro, with its 600,000 inhabitants, decided to use the euro. Without being part of the eurozone. Many other countries have the dollar or the euro as a shadow currency.

Typically, four arguments are presented for why a country should have its own currency or belong to a currency area where it is a contributing member. Like the Eurosystem.

First, you can print and mint your own notes and coins. In some countries, the authorities even run the printer overtime, typically in countries with limited political legitimacy. The extra notes appear to be the simplest way of providing buying power to a dictator, the military or a weak government. But with extra notes available, demand for goods and services exceeds supply. Prices are bid up. Inflation follows. What first seems an easy solution turns into a plague. As in pre-dollar Ecuador.

And as seen as early as the 12th century in Norway under King Harald III Hardråde, 'the hard ruler'. He ruled from 1046 to 1066. He was inspired by Byzantium, today's Istanbul. He sought to promote trade.

To make this happen, he issued coins. The unit was the *mark*, each equal to 214 grams of silver. Each mark was equal to 240 *penninger*, each of which should thus have contained 0.9 grams of silver. But due to all his wars, Harald ran short of silver. He started to substitute copper for silver, among others, in the coins paid to his soldiers, his *hirdmenn*. A classic case of inflation followed.

One hirdman, an Icelander, Halldór Snorrason, threw Harald's coins away in disgust. The Icelander disliked the Norwegian monetary inflation. Harald's response was tough. He imposed the death penalty on anyone who rejected the king's currency. Medieval monetary policies included harsh measures. Halldór, however, confronted the king in his bedroom with drawn sword. He demanded the queen's gold bracelet as payment. Halldór got his wages and managed to escape King Harald's revenge, while forever winning the respect of the Icelanders.

Today, however, Iceland, like the other Nordic countries, knows how to tax its people and has the political legitimacy to do so.

Here, still, as in other countries, the state has another less obvious form of funding. The currency it prints is actually an interest-free loan from the people to the state. This benefit to a government even has a specific name, *seignorage*. In past centuries, this used to be a major source of funding for the state, and it still is in some countries. Hence, when you sit on a US dollar or a euro note, you are providing an interest-free loan to the eurozone countries or to the US. As Ecuador does.

Second, countries that have their own currencies also have Central Banks to control that currency. The Central Bank can itself make all the money it needs. Thereby it can fulfil its role as the 'lender of last resort'.

Well, that's the old theory. It is partly obsolete in the modern world of cross-border banking. Seðlabanki could provide ISK, but the three banks needed euros. They took the ISK and exchanged it for FX, putting the ISK under pressure and forcing Seðlabanki to raise interest rates. Even large countries such as Sweden were put under pressure as the huge Nordic banks headquartered in Sweden screamed for dollars and euros. In 2009 and 2012, the Swedish Central Bank, Sveriges Riksbank, had to borrow FX in order to have enough to feed its banks. Since then the largest, Nordea, has moved its headquarters to a eurozone capital, Helsinki. It has done what the Icelandic banks never managed to do. And most likely, the Riksbank wasn't completely saddened. Today, the Riksbank has about $30 billion in FX lending. It has become, partly, a 'lender of last resort' of foreign currency, financed through state borrowing. And, as we saw, even the giant ECB had to get support from the US to access dollars. The US Fed ended up being the only unconstrained 'lender of last resort'. Hence, even for a country with its own currency, there is a limit.

But, the countries with no independent currency do face a tougher challenge. In Ecuador, the banks themselves must now ensure their liquidity. They must maintain larger buffers. That has a price. Lending becomes more expensive.

In principle one could, though, rely on foreign banks, benefitting from their Central Banks.

Third, an independent currency allows for an independent monetary policy. The Central Bank can fix interest rates and determine the banks' access to funding. It can decide their required reserve levels to create the desired level of liquidity, the 'amount of money', in the economy. In theory, this puts one more tool into the hands of economic policymakers.

Finally, an independent currency can adjust. It can strengthen if there is a surplus toward other countries and weaken if there is a deficit. This is the argument most economists consider the strongest.

The Icelandic case shows that this can work, but also that there is no guarantee. Post-crisis, the ISK weakened and enabled adjustments. Pre-crisis, the capital movements created too much noise, undercutting the economic fundamentals as the main driver. Similarly, pre-crisis, the independent monetary policy strengthened the ISK and kept inflation down. But it also enabled the monstrous capital inflows.

In short, an independent currency carries benefits. But with capital movements becoming increasingly important, it also brings with it the risk of overshooting or undershooting and a greater need for discipline.

For Iceland, as it struggled to stabilize the economy, shifting to a fixed point of reference, a stable currency, could have been an option. Iceland and its businesses would then have been able to compete in a stable environment and on equal terms with adjacent countries. In those conditions, Iceland would have been well positioned to win, given its work ethic, productivity and resource base.

Back in 2009, however, the flexibility of the exchange rate and monetary policy was of value. Also, the banks were transformed back into ISK banks. So, I saw no big need to push for a major currency reform.

And I had faith that the Icelanders, after the rollercoaster years of the past, and with the new, professionalized MPC, would run a wiser monetary policy in the years to come. As has been done.

But the Vestmannaeyar currency remains an option for the larger island.

In economics, anyway, there is never a silver bullet. Whatever the model, what's needed is professionalism and discipline.

"In Ecuador, the government continued spending money it didn't have, even after shifting to the dollar," said the Ecuador banker. "It pre-sold oil, emptied pension funds and took on debt. It continued all its mistakes from the past."

He summarized the situation: "The *sucre* had collapsed due to lack of discipline. Giving up the sucre didn't itself establish discipline. Hence, the foreign banks were reluctant to enter.

"Things are beginning to improve only now.

"But one thing is for sure. No one wants to leave the dollar."

A DANGEROUS SPIRAL

In October 2012, a US hedge fund seized the proud sailing vessel *Fragata Libertad* from the Argentinian navy. The three-masted 102-meter-long school ship had pulled into the Ghanaian port of Tema.

Argentina also has its own *Air Force One*. A Boeing 737. Naturally called *Tango 01*. In 2010, its flight to Germany was cancelled. For fear it would be seized by creditors.

Both events had their roots in Argentina's default a decade earlier. One hedge fund refused to settle.

Although spectacular, such cases are rare. One reason for this is the inability of creditors to seize the largest source of revenue of any state.

Its taxpayers.

Still, the soundness of the state finances sets the tone when investors assess the country, its businesses, banks and households. A state in distress can, in principle, always tax its people and its companies to solve its problems. Or it can borrow from its Central Bank, which can always print more money, creating inflation and reducing the real value of all nominal debt.

A state with financial strength, on the other hand, can support its companies, bail out its banks and help resolve the real challenges in the economy. It also serves as a symbol of discipline and the ability to get things done.

In the Icelandic collapse and the later crises in Ireland, Greece, Italy, Portugal and Spain, a fear emerged, just as it had in Sweden and Finland in 1992. A fear of a meltdown of the state finances.

With productivity growth, economic growth and population growth, the tax base of a country will grow. Future taxpayers can pay more taxes. Government investments in education, research and infrastructure may lead to future growth. It is therefore reasonable for a state to have some debt and run a slight deficit.

The debt instruments the state uses, especially government bonds, play an important role in capital markets. They are the mechanism the Central Banks use to manage liquidity, and their rate sets what by convention is called the risk-free rate.

When I was deputy minister of finance of Norway, we turned the budget deficit into a surplus. The then head of the state debt office knocked on my door.

"We must issue debt instruments," he said.

"Why should we?" I answered. "We will never run a deficit again."

"We need state debt instruments so that banks and companies can manage their portfolios," he answered. "And for the Central Bank to buy and sell to inject and withdraw liquidity from the markets."

"And to set the risk-free rate," he continued. "How else can we calculate the WACC?"

WACC is an acronym meaning the weighted average cost of capital, a metric used by many financial analysts when comparing project returns and project costs. The calculation starts with the interest rate on risk-free debt, which is typically equal to the interest rate on government debt. Then additions are made to reflect the specific company or project risk.

Anyway, almost all states have debt. The EU has set a 60% limit for the ratio of gross governmental debt to GDP. Most also run a deficit, year after year. Here, the EU has a limit of 3% of GDP.

But once a recession hits, things change. First, tax revenues shrink and expenses grow. A 10% weaker GDP may mean a 5% point weakening of the state finances. A deficit of 3% grows to 8%. And, in year two of the recession, the 60% debt rises to more than 76%.

If GDP drops by 10%, a bank crisis is usually the main or at least a contributing reason. Or a banking crisis may follow. The state may have to bail out the banks.. Here, the costs can vary. In the case of Ireland, the 2009 cost of the bailout reached 40% of GDP.

Suddenly, state debt may climb north of 100%. This escalation drives up interest rates, the deficit and adds yet more debt.

With higher state debt, higher interest rates and competition for funds, the market interest rates will increase further.

Down go investments, consumption and GDP. Up go the deficit and the debt level.

Looking back, the government debt-to-GDP level of ECB member countries on average grew 26% from 2008 to 2013, of which 6% was due to bank rescue operations.

Iceland's starting point was better than most, with a budget surplus and modest debt. The size of the shock, however, exceeded anything experienced by any ECB member countries. The costs to the state were also unpredictable and nontransparent. The big threat was the liabilities related to the banks, given their immense size. And worse, many of the public were not able to distinguish between the situation of the banks, businesses and the state.

Sorting out the facts and the formalities had to be a top priority.

Even though we had our numbers straight and the facts were clear, analysts, international news reporters and rating agencies viewed us with suspicion.

TWO TECTONIC PLATES SLIP APART

It is March 2009.

The red numbers on the alarm clock show the time is some hours past midnight.

The room is rumbling. There is smoke and steam. I sense the smell of sulphur and the heat. The two tectonic plates of Eurasia and North America just slipped apart. I sense that I am falling into the deep. Together with Iceland.

I have taken all possible precautions, but there is nothing to hold on to.

No foothold. No tree branches to cling to.

Then I wake up from my bad dream.

To an equally harsh reality.

It is time to wake up to a new day as Central Bank governor.

Economists have long since swung round to the view that Central Bank governors should be fully independent. Monetary authorities should make their decisions without political interference. This ideal has steered Icelandic legislation in regard to its Central Bank.

If conditions call for raising the interest rate, it should be raised, even during an election year. Fiscal stimuli should be countered with monetary tightening if the economy is at risk of overheating.

Independence equals full accountability. As a governor, no one can tell you what decisions to make, and no one can relieve you from your responsibilities or take the blame for a poor decision.

Under normal circumstances, this has its benefits and challenges. It is worse when everything is falling apart, when there is nowhere to hide and all reserves are gone.

I have never before or after had as many sleepless nights as in Iceland, lying awake, thinking about whether all that could have been done had been done. And wondering what bad news the next day might bring.

Environment, Health and Safety, or EHS, is a top priority for any top executive. The governor is also the chief executive of the bank, in addition to everything else.

Hence, on a rare quiet day, I called on the head of operations of the bank. I wanted to review and inspect the safety procedures for the handling of notes and coins in the bank. I also wanted to inspect the vault.

When I was deputy minister of finance, we were invited to inspect the vault of the Bank of Norway.

First, we watched where the worn out notes were incinerated. The central heating system of the bank consumed millions of kroner per hour. The most expensive fuel imaginable.

The next stop was the vault. Parliament had just decided to grant NOK 1 billion to elder care, 'The Billion For the Elders'.

This equalled one wooden warehouse pallet stacked full of 1,000 kroner notes.

"Here is what a billion kroner looks like," said the then governor.

Then we turned around. The pallet warehouse was five stories tall. All filled with billions. It even had shelves with backup notes that had a different design, in case of an enemy invasion. If the invader brought with him fake copies of the existing notes, the new notes could be introduced overnight.

The last stop was the gold ingots vault. Whoever managed to lift one straight up would be allowed to take it home, promised the governor. But they were just too heavy, as he well knew. If we had only known in advance. Then we would have been regulars at the gym, working on our finger strength.

The Seðlabanki operations manager asked why I wanted to see the vault. I responded, "What if someone tries to break into the bank?"

"Why would they?" he asked.

"To take the money," I replied.

"What money?" he answered. "It is empty. I thought you knew that by now.

"Now you know why a Norwegian could be trusted in the role of governor," he said with a smile.

"The vault has no FX reserves or gold. And if someone took our ISK, we would know within a day which of the regular suspects in Iceland was suddenly cash rich."

I guess he was joking. Anyway, I never got to inspect the vault.

We considered filling up the vault with some 10,000 króna notes. My predecessor had started the process of getting those printed. But I cancelled his order. It was time to bring an end to the inflation cycle.

↳ **1,000 króna bank note.**

Now, more 1,000 króna notes were needed. I got the chance to sign what some said was the first OECD-country banknote ever signed by a noncitizen. And, maybe also the only note anywhere. Possibly soon to become a collector's item.

The Central Bank museum took the first 200. I bought the next 200 for friends and family. A small injection of foreign currency into the system. The others were put into circulation.

Some can now be bought on eBay. They already trade at a premium. Which might soon rise.

When I agreed to take the job, no one had thought about the need for an exemption from the 1262 legislation that banned foreigners from senior civil service positions. No language on this was included in the first version of the new legislation.

But the McKinsey risk team had signed up an Icelandic lawyer, who had raised an alarm back in February. I had to call Iceland and raise the matter. Some legal wisemen were called upon by the government, and the provision was added. The wisemen said the amendment would suffice, as my role was interim.

Some, however, claimed that the appointment of a non-Icelandic Central Bank governor was constitutionally invalid, among others the respected law Professor Sigurdur Líndal.

But, to my knowledge, no one has ever commented on what such a breach might have implied for me, the monetary policy decisions I contributed to, or the validity of the decrees and the 14 million Icelandic bank notes that later carried my signature.

As an independent governor, I could oversee all parts of the Central Bank's activity. But there is a limit to everything. After some time, I moved out of my apartment into the bank's guest apartment, normally used for visiting dignitaries, even Luciano Pavarotti, but now made available to the interim governor. But, here, finally, my authority was constrained. The bank had made sure to lock the liquor cabinet the day I moved in. Even though I had no time to empty it.

Naturally, there was a limit as to what could be entrusted to the man from the mountains.

A NIGHTMARE CALLED CDS, GOVERNMENT DEBT AND FISCAL AUSTERITY

Textbook economics states in simple terms that a company will only invest if the expected returns of an investment exceed the interest payments and other costs of the capital needed to make it happen.

The expected returns are determined by the costs of the inputs and the price the final product can command. The latter is again influenced in large part by demand. In Iceland, domestic demand after the crisis was weak. Few products could be sold at a good price. This capped the profitability of investments. Projects focused on exports could move forward, while those for the home market were halted. Demand for construction was modest. In sum, investment demand stayed low.

The textbook method to calculate the cost of capital, again in simple terms, starts with the risk-free interest rate.

For some reason, this is defined as equal to the interest rate on US government bonds. In short, even the most right-wing financial analyst believes that the most certain thing in the universe is the US (or German) government's continued ability to tax its people.

Added to this is the country risk of the country in question, in our case Iceland. An investor will expect to be compensated for this risk, according to the textbooks. Finally, there is the risk associated with the project, based on its fundamentals, financing, owners and so on. This adds up to the long-term cost of capital.

Policymakers can ensure supportive regulations and improve economic fundamentals. They can also, to some extent, influence the country risk. Here, as seen, the strength of the government finances is key.

Country risk is often measured by the cost of the CDS. That cost equals the cost of buying an insurance policy against a default of the state. The higher the cost, the greater the perceived risk. Yet again, the opaque and nonregulated CDS becomes a metric of great importance.

The CDS price is quoted regularly, listed by data providers such as Bloomberg, and can be plugged into the calculations made by any project analyst.

After the collapse, the cost of the Icelandic Republic's CDS went to 1,000 basis points. In everyday language, the annual cost for an insurance policy against a default of the Republic of Iceland was 10% of the face value of its bonds.

Adding it all up, with a risk-free interest rate of say 2 percentage points, the CDS of 10 and a project risk of, say, 5 percentage points plus a little profit on top, the annual return required to make a project worthwhile ends up at around 20-25%. Combine that very high required return with lagging demand. The result was no investments, no growth and continued recession.

This had to change.

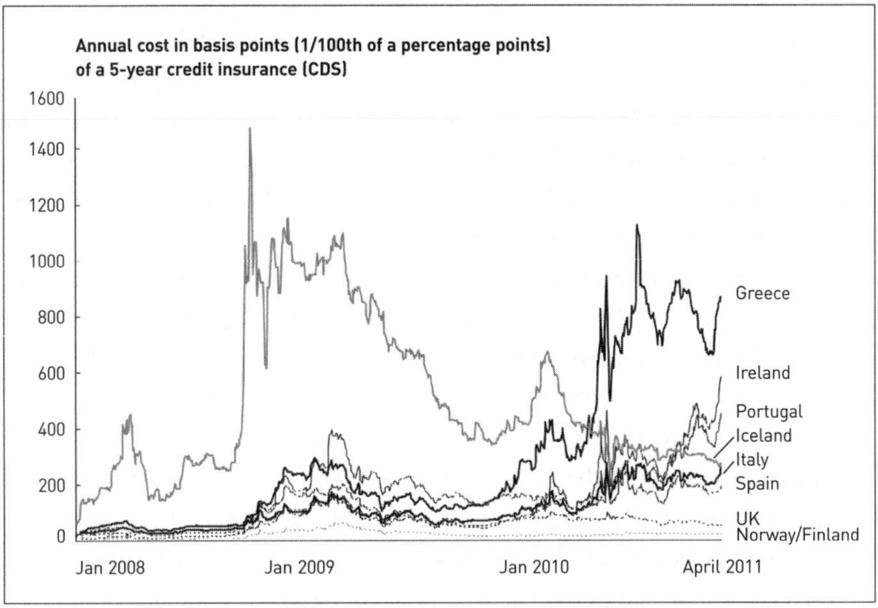

↳ **Country cost of credit insurance.**
Source: Bloomberg

We first asked how the CDS figures were calculated: how did the market work, what were the concerns of the market participants and what could we do to ease their concerns?

We called a key data provider and found it was all made up. Trades in debt insurance on Icelandic government bonds post-crisis were rare, happening maybe once or twice a month. The numbers were therefore filled in with data on trades in credit insurance instruments in countries in the same risk category, at that time typically central Asian offspring of the old Soviet Union.

However, even with these extra data sources, there were not many trades. Thus, the data providers' next trick was to use a ruler to interpolate and extrapolate.

The result was a number that was treated with the utmost seriousness, regularly commented on by analysts, commentators and professors, but which really was completely made up, a guesstimate. It was tempting to start shouting 'fake news'.

But even though the CDS figures were phony, they did reflect a serious concern. Many believed that the Republic of Iceland, that is, the state itself, would collapse.

We repeated our arguments against such a view again and again. Pre-crisis, the state finances of Iceland were sound. The government debt-to-GDP ratio had been about 27%, way below the European average. The 2007 state budget delivered a surplus of 5%, rare in Europe. And the pension system was targeted to be fully funded and independent of the state, financed largely through employer and employee contributions. These funds added up to about 120% of GDP, even after adjusting for what was lost during the crisis.

Still, many people had concerns. In Nordic welfare state economies, the state plays a crucial role. Indirect and direct tax rates are high, often with escalating rates tied to the increased unit prices of cars, wine, salaries and whatever. Furthermore, the state foots the bill when unemployment kicks in.

The state's readiness to be a buffer acts as a huge automatic stabilizer. Tax income shrinks and expenses of the state increase as a crisis hits, leaving more for the citizens. In many cases, the impact of the automatic stabilization mechanisms has by far exceeded the impact of all the deliberate decisions. This is the good news.

Then comes the bad news. The state needs to be strong enough to carry this burden. When Sweden had its crisis in the 1990s, state finances absorbed 70 cents of each dollar of lost GDP, according to estimates. Countries with similar economic systems need rock-solid state finances to carry that kind of burden. As Sweden very impressively has managed to build up over recent decades.

Icelandic finances were solid, but not rock-solid. The country ended up with a deficit of 13% of GDP in 2008, and about 10% in both 2009 and 2010. And this occurred even after a fiscal tightening that was among the most extreme in Europe.

Textbook economics argues that government spending should increase and taxes decrease when an economic crisis hits, to help stimulate the economy. This makes sense but is hard to do in the absence of very sound state finances. Stimulus is of little help if there is a lack of trust, which will inevitably lead to sky-high interest rates and a halt in investment.

To solve this problem, all the Nordic countries found similar solutions when they had their crises: Denmark in 1982, Norway in 1992, Sweden and Finland in 1993 and Iceland in 2009.

Specific and credible budget measures were put in place to restore market confidence. These had to include measures with immediate effect, but even more important were the decisions that changed the balance long term.

With the right measures, countries can eliminate a government deficit of 10-12% of GDP in just three or four years; in the Nordics, independent of the parties in power, typically half of the deficit reduction came from spending cuts, a quarter from increased direct taxes and another quarter through increased indirect taxes.

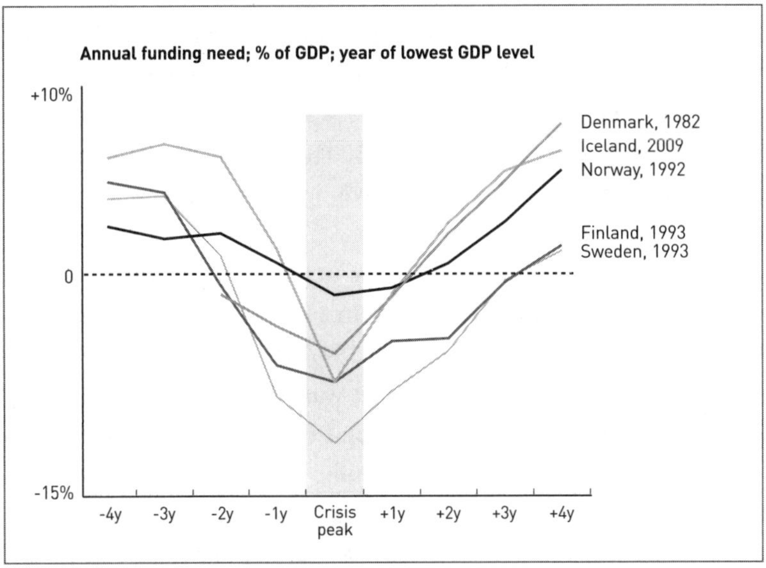

↳ **Public sector financial balance before and after the year of the deepest crisis.**
Source: IMF Iceland; review 16 April 2010

Credible budget reforms, for example of pension systems, which can have a big long-term impact and moderate short-term impact, were favoured.

Through this, loss of demand can and must be reversed; budget cuts that re-establish confidence can, despite their tightening effect, thereby strengthen demand as citizens consume more and companies invest more.

In Iceland, the government also looked at private pension funds that were overfunded and found ways to free up excess funds that otherwise would have been locked in. Next, the hit that individual borrowers took from the increase in the size of their indexed loans as the ISK sank in value was eased. The payment periods of loans were extended.

Furthermore, the government encouraged the investment capacity that remained to be utilized. Investors were invited to invest in infrastructure, contributing to an increase in employment. Some tasks, such as certain infrastructure projects, were transferred to private actors.

Very importantly, we curtailed the cost of the bank recovery. The responsibilities of the state were clearly spelled out, which had the effect of limiting them to a degree. And, in the end, the state injections of capital for the bank restructuring even turned into a profit.

Göran Persson, the Prime Minister in Sweden during that country's turnaround, has been clear on what countries should do: "Use the 'worst case' as the base case."

As was done in Iceland. The CDS market responded to the measures the government took and the price fell rapidly, by 600 basis points in some months. Luckily, we had not shot the whole metric down, which now allowed us to use it as a measure of our progress.

Þór's family knew all about how difficult the world could be. They had seen eruptions and hardship. When Hekla erupted in 1104, 1158, 1206, 1222, 1300, 1341, 1389, 1510, 1597, 1636, 1693, 1766, 1845, 1947, 1970, 1980, 1981, 1991 and 2000, their communities had mobilized. Shelter was provided to those harmed, and they got assistance in recovering all the land that could be recovered and support in rebuilding all that needed to be rebuilt.

In Þór's view, a tough, short recovery always beat a long period of pain. He could eat mackerel many days in a row, if needed. A natural disaster could really hurt.

Still, the financial crisis, or *kreppa* was, he thought, worse in many ways.

When nature hit, no one was to blame.

And everyone worked together.

THE TRUCK DRIVER AND THE FLIGHT ATTENDANT

Iceland's minister of finance in the post-crisis years from 2009 to 2013 had been a truck driver in his youth. The prime minister, a flight attendant. Now, after decades of political experience, Steingrímur Sigfússon and Jóhanna Sigurðardóttir were tasked with taking the country through the roughest of terrains. Two left-wingers cleaning up after the forces of finance went wild. Seeking to limit the pain, while respecting the importance of fairness and equality. All while running an austerity programme among the harshest western Europe had seen in decades.

The collapse caused vast damage: claims for government unemployment benefits grew by a factor of seven. State revenue fell. The foreign reserves of the Central Bank were largely lost. And the state had to help bring the three failed banks back to life.

In Iceland, the crisis triggered a spending increase of 5% of GDP as compared to the pre-adjustment spending level. Tax revenue fell by a similar amount. The state debt increased, as did interest payments. From 5% to 16% of state revenues.

If you ever need an argument in favour of robust state finances and low state debt, look to Iceland. When the crash hit in October 2008, it had virtually zero debt.

Therefore, the immediate weakening of the state finances could, for some time, be allowed to translate into a deficit without imperilling the state's underlying soundness. But eventually, stronger medicine was needed.

"Only in mid-June 2009 did we start the effort to balance the budget," says Steingrímur.

"We searched for measures to retain purchasing power. Locked pension funds were released."

"We set four targets," says the then Minister of Finance.

"Top priority: make public finances sustainable and thereby lower the debt and interest burden.

"Second, reduce the public sector gross debt to less than 60% of GDP long term.

"Third, protect the social safety net.

"Fourth, increase equality in the distribution of income."

"This comment makes me very proud," says Steingrímur, referring to a UN Human Rights Council report. "It states that international organizations and countries could learn from the path chosen in Iceland. In the end, it is the social side that matters the most.

"The IMF accepted our position. 'We understand your desire to maintain a social safety net,' the IMF said. 'You need to deliver, but you can decide how.'"

However, even the hospitals got a taste of the bitter medicine.

"'It must be a joke,' was my response when I first saw the budget figures," says the then CEO of the largest hospital in Iceland. "We spent 60-70% of our money on salaries and the rest on medicines and equipment. Most of the latter was imported. Now their costs counted in ISK had been doubled. But we had no extra money. We decided to stay quiet and not add to the panic. Every month we scratched the bottom to see what we could afford."

The total tightening of the budget added up to 11-12% of GDP; 43% was achieved through tax increases and other revenue measures, 57% through expenditure cuts. Expenditure in real value was down 13% from 2008 to 2012.

"By 2013, we were back on the road," says the truck driver.

LET'S SCRAP THE PLAN – IT DOESN'T WORK

"We expect you to join the coordination committee for the bank restructuring," Tryggvi Pálsson said as he entered my office on one of my first days. He headed the financial stability department of the bank.

The first IMF Letter of Intent, LOI, promised that such a committee would be established. It had multiple roles. One was to ensure the momentum of the recapitalization process. Another was to have an arena where the bank creditors and stakeholders could voice their many concerns.

But the committee clearly did not function. Some people used it mainly to tell everyone else what to do. Some discussions only scratched the surface, as if we were only pretending to be doing something.

Among many priorities, we discussed whether to chase the money that the main bank owners and managers might have taken out of the banks before the crash.

All the large Icelandic banks were infected by connected party lending. Many loans had been made based on sound banking judgment and appropriate procedures, but not all.

If a bank, a state or a bankruptcy estate is to recover such funds, it needs to go all in. Vast resources are needed, full dedication and professional support from specialists with experience in chasing funds. The money will often have made its way to tax havens and countries with no transparency on ownership. Many located in the Caribbean, many former British colonies. These jurisdictions regard some claims as legitimate, and some as not. They provide information to some parties but say no to most. Heirs are typically seen as legitimate claimants. Tax authorities and ex-spouses often aren't. Hence, to have any hope of recovery, you need people with specific skills who will be recognized as having legal standing with legitimate claims. In my view, the estates of the failed banks were in the best position to track down the elusive funds.

I advocated a full-blown effort. In a Norwegian case, the Ministry of Finance sponsored a chase that lasted a decade. The specialists were paid a share of whatever they recovered. In the end, the recovery was sizeable. But we only got there when the ministry was classified as an heir. Tax claims were not prioritized by the tax havens. Claims of heirs were.

When I met resistance, I asked for my opposing view to be recorded in the minutes. That did not make me popular. And I still consider that the estates should have done more to chase funds that may have been hidden away.

Progress lagged on some other matters as well. The committee was on the verge of collapse. Some simply refused to meet face-to-face.

From day one, we in Seðlabanki had decided to actively support the committee, to conduct analysis and prepare proposals. I was soon asked to chair the whole effort. I changed the group's name from the 'Coordination Committee' to the 'Execution Committee'. My intent was to signal a desire to get things done. Some saw an alternative interpretation.

When the three systemic banks collapsed, they were each split in two. The domestic parts with domestic deposits and lending were carved out as the new banks. They had a positive value. Their loan books were larger than their customers' deposits.

One snag remained. The positive equity value of the new banks belonged to the owners and creditors of the old banks. They had a right to be compensated.

The plan of October 2008, as summarized in the IMF LOI, stated that each of the new banks should commit to repaying the fair value of the new bank to the creditors. Technically, by issuing a bond transferring the value to the creditors. In reality, by giving the estates and thereby the creditors IOUs.

However, such bonds would, by design, wipe out the equity of the new banks. The plan, therefore, stated that the Icelandic state should inject ISK 385 billion in fresh money into the new banks.

On paper, it all looked possible. But I always thought another approach should have been chosen back in October. The plan had three significant weaknesses. In sum, it was simply not workable.

First, the capital injection would be a huge drain on public finances.

Next, it would make the state the main owner of all three systemic banks. Some degree of state ownership in a banking sector may be workable and even a plus. But not full ownership. Especially not as we were entering a process of debt restructuring for households and companies. In my view, such a process requires a bank owner with its own money at stake that can work to find the right solutions in cooperation with the debtors and the bankruptcy estates.

On paper, a political system may be able to run such a process, but not in the real world. Especially not in Iceland, with its history of entanglements between the world of politics and the world of business. And where a lot of the loans and other transactions that had contributed to the banks' downfall were highly dubious, even criminal.

Finally, it was impossible to put a value on the new banks and therefore on the bonds that were to be issued to compensate the old banks. A value that all the parties could agree on and where litigation could be avoided.

Deloitte was brought in to conduct a valuation. Then Oliver Wyman was brought in to review the Deloitte report.

The result was a disappointment to some, but they should have seen it coming.

The two advisories presented an enormously wide valuation range. What's more, the FME went further and stated: "Conceivable scenarios that may imply an even lower valuation lie outside the scope of the Deloitte analysis."

Some need for negotiation on the final value was to be expected. But here, almost everything had to be negotiated. A serious attempt was made. Weeks of negotiations passed, following the months spent on the valuation work.

After an eight-month process, someone had to say that enough was enough. We had to define a new approach. It was time to scrap the nonworkable model.

I suggested a debt-to-equity conversion, where the claimants would get the banks' shares instead of a bond.

The initial plan was to issue a bond, but only after an agreement could be reached on the value. Now, instead, with a debt-to-equity conversion, the estates could be given the banks' stock shares, which by definition equalled their value.

This required no agreement on valuation. The principles were agreed upon over a weekend. All three problems were solved in one go. The ISK 385 billion capital injection was reduced, easing our task of re-establishing confidence in the state finances. Responsible owners appeared, enabling the restructuring processes to move forward. The nonresolvable valuation puzzle was avoided. As was the risk of lengthy litigation.

No one with respect for basic business principles or for the rights and obligations of private owners should have had any basis for criticism. The positive residual value of the new banks belonged to the bank creditors. And that was what they received. Nothing less. Nothing more. By definition.

The first creditor agreements were signed. At a stroke, a great many risks disappeared.

The IMF was amazed. And pleased.

We were truly proud when we saw what we had achieved. We would have been even more enthusiastic if we had foreseen all the possibilities the model offered.

Gudmundur Þór was torn. His distrust of the banks was as strong as ever. But he had to admit that some of the folks who had left the banks and started to work in other industries now really made a difference. Previously, it had been hard to get hold of people who could help out with his hotel. Now, whatever skills he needed were available.

G4 MEETS IN SWITZERLAND

The Central Banks have their own Central Bank, the BIS, or Bank of International Settlements. It supports transactions between Central Banks. It shapes regulations. It is also a forum where the Central Bank governors meet.

The BIS headquarters is in Basel, in Switzerland. It is housed in a tower 69 metres high, encircled by the flags of the countries of its 60 Central Bank members. One being Icelandic. Within the building, all governors have their own permanent office.

Even I, for a short time.

When I turned up for my first BIS meeting, I was pleased to see my name on the door of my new Swiss office. All had been prepared, as you would expect from the Swiss.

For me, the plenary meetings were of limited interest, though. While crises steamrolled the world outside, most discussions in the tower focused on regulatory changes meant to hinder the next crisis. And the rules were largely built on the misperception that crises mainly are driven by insufficient bank solidity. Even though we see again and again that what really matters is liquidity.

Luckily, I had more pressing tasks to attend to in the tower.

The bank collapse wiped out the reserves of Seðlabanki. They had to be replenished. We needed foreign currency to backup the ISK and eventually reopen markets.

An Icelandic cartoonist made the joke: "There is only one solution to the problem of too much debt.

"More debt."

But this was no joke. New funds were needed, at least as a buffer. Steingrímur and I embarked on a tour of the world to raise funds. The first stop was Tórshavn.

The Faroe Islands are located almost exactly halfway between Scotland and Iceland. The beautiful green islands rose from the sea as we came closer.

In Tórshavn, it was clear to Steingrímur and me that we were among friends. The government of this country, of then 48,000 inhabitants, wanted to do its utmost to help.

The Faroes had their own crisis in the early 1990s. Its private sector debt had been too high. Along came a slowdown in the global economy and a reduced catch in the fisheries. A bank crisis followed, leading to a large-scale state bailout. After that came a surge in emigration and a crisis in the state finances. Then, Iceland helped. It gave way to allow for larger Faroe fishing quotas.

A Faroe loan agreement with Iceland was signed on 23 March 2009. All was to be paid to us at once. With no strings attached and no mention of the IMF, the Nordics or Icesave. And with a premium above the Faroe borrowing cost of only 0.15%. For no less than DKK 300 million. More than $1,200 from each Faroe Islander.

We discussed with a smile who would get to carry Steingrímur's suitcase back to Iceland.

Some Reykjavik stores offered special discounts for the Faroese. Some, supposedly, refused to sell to Brits.

On 1 July 2009, a further four loan agreements were signed between Iceland and Denmark (27% of the loan), Norway (27%), Finland (18%), and Sweden (28%). The total amount was €1,775 million.

Sweden had at first opposed the loan, but then reversed its decision and insisted on providing the biggest amount. As a symbol of its self-perceived Nordic leadership role.

The Nordics, however, insisted on making the IMF the gatekeeper, linking the loan payments to the IMF reviews. Hence, without IMF approval, no money. And the other way around. The Nordics became the main provider of funds for the IMF programme.

"Formally, there was no link between the IMF programme and the claim of the Dutch and the UK related to Icesave. There was no paragraph in the programme stating any requirement on Icesave," says a person working at the IMF at the time.

"But the IMF programme required financial assurances. The programme had to be fully financed."

It was all circular. The Nordic loans were dependent on the IMF. The IMF programme was dependent on the Nordic loans. Both could, rightly or wrongly, blame the other party.

In the IMF at that time, the Brits and the Dutch had more voting power than all of Africa combined.

The UK and the Netherlands dug in, demanding reimbursement for the funds they had paid out to depositors in their countries. And they got support from the rest of the EU. Sweden chaired the EU for half of 2009 and promoted the EU view. The Swedes also held the Nordic chair in the IMF and would thus normally have been a proponent of the Icelandic programme. Not now.

"A situation where the Nordic chair did not support the programme in a Nordic country would have been unheard of," says an interviewee with years of IMF experience.

The reviews were delayed. New requirements were added. The programme could have been taken to the board for a vote. Maybe the EU would have been voted down. But such a move was seen as too divisive.

At the IMF annual meeting in Istanbul on 6 and 7 October 2009, Steingrímur, the Icelandic Minister of Finance, tried to unlock it all.

"The Dutch minister, Wouter Bos, was a decent man," says Steingrimur. "With him we could discuss."

The UK minister, Alistair Darling, however, had no time for the Icelanders. Back then, the UK still had a say in the EU.

"There was no breakthrough even though the IMF started to feel awkward. Iceland was delivering. Still, the programme was stuck," says Steingrimur.

Soon though, Dominique Strauss-Kahn, DSK, acted with force. He was frustrated with the EU. Some non-EU and emerging markets directors equally so. Iceland had made progress. Now DSK threatened to establish a new programme, backed by the US. A breakthrough IMF meeting was scheduled.

DSK, the then head of the IMF, wrote on 13 November 2009, "The Icesave dispute did indirectly affect the timing of the programme's first review, since it held up needed financing from Nordic countries (for whom resolution of this dispute was a precondition)."

Among the ones to step forward and to proactively offer support to Iceland were the Poles. Poland offered 630 million Polish zlotys, the equivalent of $200 million. While the Nordics as a group set an agreement with the UK and the Netherlands as a condition for their loan, the Poles made no such demand. On the contrary.

"We do not require any such agreement," they said.

"Don't give in to the Brits," some Poles said in the hallway.

In the spring of 2009, the Chinese ambassador in Reykjavik initiated a discussion on support from China. At the next BIS meeting, after listening for some hours to a discussion that was going nowhere, I decided to knock on the door of the office of the governor of the People's Bank of China.

Why not?

His office was next to mine.

We were colleagues.

"A blatant breach of protocol," said one of my advisors afterward. "We were shocked. And laughed."

This time the man from the mountains had really gotten lost.

But the Chinese governor was very friendly. He knew every detail of the Icelandic crisis.

We started a discussion that later led to a currency swap agreement between Seðlabanki and China. Its value was ISK 66 billion, 3.5 billion Chinese yuan or $512.5 million.

Not bad.

For China, this was a step on its journey to establish a convertible 'national bank reserve' currency and to establish a predictable economic environment for trade. We in Iceland were the first in western Europe with whom they got a swap structure in place.

The Chinese governor was pleased when I said that it was only natural that the Chinese currency would soon find itself among the leading currencies of the world.

It took three years for the UK, as the next in line, to follow with a swap agreement. Iceland later also became the first country in Europe to sign a free trade agreement with China.

After the discussion, we went off for lunch. We were joined by the Russian governor and the president of the New York Federal Reserve.

A member of a Nordic delegation came by, asking me about the focus of a meeting of such prominent personages.

I replied that it was a "G4 meeting."

China, Russia, the US and Iceland.

All of us G4 governors laughed. A rare opportunity for some humour among Central Bank governors.

The Russian loan announced on 7 October 2008 never materialized. A delegation went to Russia on 14 October. It met the Deputy Minister of Finance, Dmitry Pankin.

"We tried to show the strong fundamentals of the Icelandic economy," says one of those present.

"The sentiment was positive. Not like in the neighbouring room where TV screens showed the price of oil dropping like a stone.

"Later we discussed a Russian loan under the IMF programme. But in October 2009, it was all called off. By then, no more money was needed."

A country with 38,000 inhabitants contributed, as did one with 1.350 billion. Some friends were supportive, some not. Many made the IMF the gatekeeper.

The ups and downs of working with the IMF require a chapter of its own. And how the money was eventually used may come as a surprise.

MUAMMAR GADDAFI, THE NUCLEAR PLANT AND THE PACIFIC ISLAND

"You control the debt, you control everything ... This is the very essence of the banking industry ... To make us all, whether we be nations or individuals, slaves of debt."

– The most frequent statement quoted by the Head of Reserves Management at Seðlabanki, from the film *The International*

First split a bank into two, into a domestic and a foreign part. Then split the latter in two again, into prioritized deposits and other creditor claims.

If your money ends up in the domestic part, you will get it all back. Tomorrow, if you so wish. If it is in the foreign prioritized part, you may get it back one day, but surely not tomorrow. If you end up in the last pile, then maybe you will get some money back. One day. Maybe 30% of it. After six to ten years.

So, where you end up matters. But the rules of the game were not known in advance. When the Emergency Act was passed, the money already sat in its respective bank accounts. In some cases, money that the depositor had locked in as term deposits.

Some were adamant that their claims had ended up in the wrong pile. Some questioned the whole law and its legitimacy. After all, it was passed in one day, and the ruling also dictated the treatment of old deposits that had been locked in long ago. Some people claimed it was applied retroactively. Many cases went to court.

Aresbank is a Spanish bank, owned by the Libyan Central Bank. The bank of the then dictator Muammar Gaddafi. As late as September 2008, Aresbank made wholesale deposits in all three Icelandic banks. One might wonder what made them do that – ISK 20 billion in total, or about €150 million. In Aresbank's view, the money was placed as interbank deposits in the Icelandic branches of the three banks.

The first opening balance sheet from FME of 9 October 2008 categorized the money as deposits in the new banks. With this, Aresbank would have the right to get its money back immediately.

That was no longer the case with the new banks' balance sheets from 14 October. Now the Glitnir and Kaupthing estates classified the funds as general claims in the old banks, putting them last in the last queue.

Landsbanki disagreed and continued to classify the funds as deposits, but the FME objected. The FME claimed that the money was to be treated as general loans, not deposits. In the old banks.

The case went to court. Aresbank took the case all the way to the European Free Trade Association (EFTA) Court of Justice and won on 22 November 2012. Now the money was moved into the deposits pile of the old banks. Aresbank got its money back, after some time. With penalty interest payments added.

Gaddaffi himself never got to enjoy the victory. By the time Aresbank got the money back, he was long gone, deposed and executed by an angry mob of countrymen.

About 100 UK counties and municipalities, 16 Dutch municipalities and a Dutch nuclear power-plant company had also made large wholesale deposits into Landsbanki. They wanted, just as Iceland did, to uphold the prioritization of their deposits. While nonprioritized creditors, some from the UK and the Netherlands, attacked the legitimacy of the whole Emergency Act and the prioritization of depositors.

At this juncture, the municipalities, counties and the nuclear plant moved in to support Iceland.

"There was huge tension," says a lawyer representing the municipalities.

He was to meet the creditors in Amsterdam. His Dutch colleagues had warned him. They expected a heated meeting in the high-rise building overlooking Beatrixpark where they met. They expected tough questions from the managers of the municipalities.

But there were no questions.

"The former managers are all gone," said the Dutch in the bar after the quiet meeting. They had been voted out of their positions.

The case went to the Supreme Court of Iceland. The judges had all been profiled. "Who is likely for, who will be against," says a lawyer.

"I profiled them all, but it was inconclusive."

"There was only one person whom I with certainty could say would support the Emergency Act. He had been a clear ally of the ruling party.

"But he was the only one against it. He said the law was in breach of provisions protecting against retroactive changes.

"The majority did not share his view, though. The depositors and the nuclear plant got priority."

Kiribati was less fortunate. Its claims were not prioritized.

WHEN SOCIALISTS TURN CAPITALIST AND CAPITALISTS TURN SOCIALIST

When a crisis looms, even some of the most principled private-sector bankers call on the state. There is one thing they really want to socialize.

Private-sector debt.

Meanwhile, some socialists turn into private-sector enthusiasts.

Depositors are usually protected, but for others, a banking crisis is often ruthless. Even for the innocent.

An investment-grade rating serves as an entry ticket to the global financial system. It gives the investment-grade institution the chance to sell its bonds to funds and investors that have no appetite for risk. Some buy based on knowledge, some buy based on the rating and some buy it as part of a package.

What's more, a bank with an investment grade is part of a global web. Transactions pass from bank to bank as banking partners execute and settle transactions. Every millisecond, international transactions are happening. Say you live in the US and have a friend in Kathmandu, to whom you owe money after your last trip to Nepal. You ask your bank to make a transfer. Neither you nor even your bank may know all the banks your payment will be routed through on its trip to the other side of the world.

One Japanese trading house was particularly unlucky. On 22 September 2008 the Bank of Tokyo-Mitsubishi and Kaupthing made a currency contract requiring the Japanese bank to deposit $50 million to the Kaupthing account at JPMorgan in New York. Kaupthing was supposed to deposit the same amount in yen to an account at the same New York bank.

Tokyo-Mitsubishi lived up to its part of the agreement and deposited $50 million into Kaupthing's New York account 39 minutes before its collapse. Kaupthing, however, never deposited any yen. Suddenly Tokyo-Mitsubishi was a creditor in a defaulted bank. Without even knowing.

Some months later, the New York account was emptied, leaving only $2.5 million. In 2010, the Japanese took Kaupthing to court and received $1.9 million.

The Japanese bank felt, not without merit, unfairly treated. It wanted Icelandic authorities to intervene or provide some form of compensation.

The minister in charge, Árni Páll Árnason, made himself available to meet the executives from the bank. "I referred to the processes put in place by the authorities to ensure a fair treatment of all claims, the integrity of the courts where the case was worked and the principles agreed to with the IMF," says Árni.

"But then a large group of Icelandic civil servants that had been lined up entered the room and pushed me out."

All measures were to be used to ease the pressure on Iceland's finances. The state should take on no additional debt or obligations. No one should be tempted to make any promises with state money, even to the unfortunate Japanese with whom everyone had sympathy.

And, yes, the ringfencing did help. Iceland did become the only country on an IMF programme that retained its investment grade rating from Moody's and Standard & Poor's, even in the depth of the crisis.

LIKE A PISTOL TO THE FOREHEAD

"Hello, what I was about to tell you, you see, we can in and of itself today scrape together €500 million, but of course by then we have come all the way to the bone – and then we can help Kaupthing four-five days, but then we can't also help Landsbanki, you see."

– Then Central Bank Governor, Davíð Oddsson, in the transcript of a call notifying the then Prime Minister, Geir Haarde, about the transfer of €500 million to Kaupthing

Being a lender of last resort is part of the job description of a Central Bank. Naturally it implies that a Central Bank must stand ready to lend money to banks, especially when no one else wants to lend as much as a dime.

This position is unpleasant. It is challenging, even when the banks operate and fund themselves in the currency of the Central Bank. It gets a lot worse if the banks, as in Iceland, largely fund themselves in FX.

Some rules apply. The banks must be 'sound' and they must provide collateral. The Central Bank also asks for a buffer. The bank's borrowing must be smaller than the value of the collateral, with a margin. A so-called 'haircut' is imposed.

But a bank that at first needs limited liquidity support may suddenly need more. And then even more. And more. In that case, the Central Bank and the banks will all be inclined to keep trying for just a little bit longer. Especially if the banks are of systemic importance.

Alternatively, the value of the assets provided as collateral may shrink. Especially if it consists of bonds from other defaulting banks.

Hence, the risk of a default of a privately owned bank may turn into a risk and cost borne by the Central Bank. This was what happened in Iceland. And in Luxembourg.

The Icelandic banks' access to international funding started to dry up through 2007. They then turned to the Central Bank for liquidity.

First, they offered their government-guaranteed bonds as collateral, then packages of loans to companies and households, and thereafter a general bank guarantee. But the funding shortage continued. Ever more exotic collateral was offered.

Despite all efforts, the banks went under. Now it was time for Seðlabanki to claim the collateral and recover its money.

Haukur C. Benediktsson was tasked with leading the recovery effort. At first it was run directly by the Central Bank, then through an asset management company of the Central Bank, Sölvhóll. Later an asset holding company, ESI, was established.

Running such a 'bad bank' is a task rarely managed by Central Banks. On top of all the other tasks, the man from the mountains suddenly found himself in charge of the largest bad bank in the OECD area, measured as a share of GDP.

A Finnish investment bank, eQ, had been provided as collateral for €50 million.

A tender was run and eQ was sold for €37 million.

In the last days before Kaupthing went down on 9 October 2008, in a last-ditch attempt to save itself, it offered all its shares in the Danish bank FIH as collateral and got €500 million in return.

In a conversation on 6 October 2008, first revealed in the fall of 2017, the then prime minister and the Central Bank governor of Iceland agreed to provide the funds.

" ... with this we are all the way to the bone ... " said the governor. "I do not expect we will get this money back ... we are just talking about the strictest collateral," said the transcript of the conversation, a conversation with many interpretations.

"The FIH case is the one that will haunt me to my last day," says one person who worked on the recovery of assets for Seðlabanki.

"Kaupthing had talked about FIH as the jewel in its crown. That was what the Central Bank thought it got. It was wrong. Real collateral should have been demanded back in 2008," says Már Guðmundsson, the Central Bank governor from August 2009 to 2019.

At the end of 2010, FIH had a loan portfolio of DKK 60 billion to Danish companies, about €8 billion. Part of it was to real estate development companies, following a push from Kaupthing to make FIH grow faster. FIH's lending was mainly financed by market loans and bonds. It's worth noting that when Kaupthing made its largest acquisition, it bought a bank that was even weaker on the one dimension where Kaupthing was weakest. Namely its reliance on market funding rather than on a strong depositor base. FIH did have a sizeable equity base but was completely dependent on market trust. Without trust, FIH would implode.

Ownership by the bankruptcy estate of Kaupthing was no winning model for FIH. Having its shares pledged as collateral to the Central Bank of Iceland did not help either.

For some time, the crisis, paradoxically, helped FIH survive. The Danish State provided a general guarantee to all Danish financial institutions, which included FIH. No other bank requested more guarantees, about €8 billion in all.

The state guarantee, although important, was temporary. The Danish regulator threatened to revoke FIH's banking licence. A change in ownership was a possible solution, but any buyer of FIH would face the risk of having to repay some of the bank's market loans right away, as some loans had a change-of-control provision. The largest provider of funding to FIH, ATP, was the most likely buyer.

Not the best basis for achieving a good price in a sale.

"The Icelanders had a gun put to their forehead by the Danish financial supervisory authority and financial stability, which wanted to have the bank in safe hands," wrote the Danish newspaper *Jyllands-Posten* about the case.

Jyllands-Posten continued, "The Icelanders could not make more money available to the bank themselves." Therefore, they had to sell.

"A bad negotiation situation, which the two Danish investors on the other side of the table took full advantage of."

The buyers took control of the bank in a deal announced 19 September 2010 for €255 million, with the possibility of additional payments to Iceland of €415 million. But the latter was to be deducted against the bank's losses, which were incurred, so Iceland never saw any extra payments.

The Danes first tried to get the bank back to normal operations through an improved rating from Moody's. But while Moody's had judged the three Icelandic banks to be flawless in 2007, having burned its fingers it now sent a rating of FIH as 'junk' in return. Even though the bank now had solid owners.

The Danes then put FIH into what many customers experienced as a brutal winding-down process. FIH held several priority loans. It could push for repayment, leaving the lower priority claimants and the borrowers to take a hit.

Despite the challenges, in the end, the new FIH owners earned three times what they paid.

They had tools Seðlabanki did not have. They received a state funding guarantee that covered the lengthy winding-down proceedings. They could also run the process in a way that would have been hard for Seðlabanki to match.

In the end, Seðlabanki took a loss of about €250 million. The Danes gained about 500 million.

"The FIH case is the one where we most clearly saw the brutality of the world of finance," Benediktsson comments.

And remember, most likely a part of the money provided to Kaupthing against the collateral possibly ended up with Deutsche Bank as payment for the dubious CDS transactions, which were later disputed and settled through payments to the creditors.

In the lead-up to the crisis, Straumur, Iceland's fourth-largest bank, had already pledged a loan package as collateral to Dresdner Bank. When Seðlabanki required more collateral in the fall of 2008, Straumur offered the Central Bank a second priority pledge.

In May 2009, Dresdner Bank, with priority in our joint loan package, called for a repayment of its part of the loan. It wanted its money back: €80 million.

To pay Dresdner would require an immediate fire sale. We would need to split up and sell the loan package. Dresdner would then get its money. Seðlabanki would not. And nothing would be left for other creditors.

Our only other option was to find €80 million for Dresdner and buy the whole loan package ourselves.

A hard choice. Our reserves were tiny. And more debt, bought for hard cash, was the last thing we needed.

"Governor Bails Out German Bank, Buys More Debt and Loses," was the headline I saw in my mind, splashed across the front page of some Icelandic newspaper. Or worse.

Who was I to authorize the expenditure of €80 million? I briefly recalled the stories of long ago justice in Thingvellir, when some of the accused were thrown into the icy river with rocks tied to their waists. Those who didn't sink were judged innocent.

We met the Straumur team in London. We reviewed the assumed recovery on the loan package. We saw that the assumed recovery rates on the individual loans were generally very low, for many just 30% to 50%. But many of the debtors were well-known Nordic companies, and many of those were owned by Nordic private equity houses. I knew many of the CEOs.

I picked up the phone and started to call around, asking, "Will you repay Iceland if we buy your loan?"

Jaan Ivar Semlitsch, then CEO of the Nordic gardening group Plantasjen, was somewhat surprised by the late-night call from Iceland. He had no idea that his loan was for sale. And that the seller of the loan had assumed it was worth just half its face value.

"Yes, we will pay," he said. "Everything. We are a bit stretched before the gardening season as we fill up the stores. But as spring comes and the gardeners start buying, all will be fine."

The others answered along the same lines. We added it all up, ran the math and bought the package.

No one can say the life of a Central Bank governor is without its challenges.

We got our 80 million back. With interest. And even more was regained. We ensured that lower-priority creditors also received some money. And, as one would expect, Seðlabanki was also in that queue.

"Wow, that was when I thought the governor might be a useful guy," says the head of the market operations department in Seðlabanki.

Even more amazing was the deal we later did in the Grand Duchy of Luxembourg.

WE CAN'T PLAY GOD

In the Central Bank, we knew that no material improvements would happen unless the debt challenges in the corporate sector were resolved.

As early as 2005, the Icelandic banks were making 85% of the loans to Icelandic fishing companies in foreign currency. By May 2008, the share was 95%. With income largely in foreign currency, this was a natural evolution.

From 2005 onward, other sectors followed, even industries that didn't earn income in foreign currency, as a response to the high ISK interest rate. For construction, the FX share rose from 30% to 50%, and for all firms, from below 60% to north of 70%. Including firms with no matching FX income.

Furthermore, the total loan-to-value ratios were typically high. In many cases, new owners had acquired other businesses, owning the companies through debt-rich holding companies.

Then the ISK lost its value, and the value of the foreign currencies rose. As did the loans when measured in ISK.

Ninety per cent of the holding companies went into distress, as did 66% of the corporates.

Three out of four non-life insurance companies restructured their ownership, as did both Icelandic airlines, both Icelandic mobile phone operators, the largest food retailer, the largest building-equipment provider, both shipping companies serving the shipping-dependent island, car rental companies, fuel distributors and power, water and heat utilities. To name just a few. Even pizza chains. Despite all the orders from the people working around the clock through the days of crisis.

All banks had large portfolios of distressed debtors, many with loans in multiple Icelandic banks, and some with loans in international ones.

A carve-out of the bad loans into 'bad banks', a typical model internationally, was not viable. There would simply be too little left over in the 'good banks'. In addition, most of the leaders of the future Icelandic industries would have found themselves in the bad bank.

The post-crash IMF-backed plan said that all three large banks were to be refinanced by the state. If so, the state banks would own almost the entire banking industry, which in turn would control the restructuring processes of most companies. That would mean that the state, its advisors and restructuring units would control the Icelandic economy.

A process was started to draft the regulations for an Asset Management Company, the AMC. This unit would be tasked with managing the restructuring of Iceland's most important companies. A special law was passed. A truly horrific situation – most companies in distress with the state controlling their destiny.

Even worse, many owners had been tainted by the past. Some were toxic. Many were innocent victims. Many had no capital. Some had some. Among the ones with capital were some that had tapped their banks. And some that for a while had hidden money abroad.

But luckily the banks were recapitalized in mid-2009 by another mechanism, without the state as the dominant owner. Suddenly there was no need for a big AMC.

The wrongdoings of the past could be left to the normal legal processes. Now the work on the debt issues could start.

The need for restructuring had been there for all to see back in October 2008. By mid-2009, the new banks had established structures to manage their portfolios and to begin assessing the value of what they held.

"First the dust had to settle," says a banker who worked on the debt restructuring. "Then we had to watch for the signs of life in the dust."

"Some people wanted us to decide on the right number of shops in every category in Reykjavik and decide on winners and losers. But we could not play God."

"Some said legislative change was needed, but here the IMF was good. They had a true expert. 'You have all the legal frameworks you need,' said IMF's expert. 'You are just not pushing forward.'"

"I went out every morning and worked until late evening. Half an hour at each company," says the banker.

Still there was criticism.

"By September 2010, nothing had been done," says a person deeply involved in the process. "Many companies had received loans from more than one bank. In many instances, no bank wanted to be the first to provide debt relief. They all wanted to sit it out.

"Even as late as March 2011, the banks were not moving. All were waiting for others to move. It was estimated that 1,800 companies needed debt relief."

"If no action is taken, I will view it as treason," a minister told the banks at that time.

On 7 April 2011, on the 50th anniversary of the Central Bank, the Minister of Commerce called for a faster process. The day after, the banks called and agreed on a process.

The IMF corporate-debt restructuring specialist got on a plane from Ireland and spent weekends in Iceland.

The specialist helped create a set of guidelines. For example, debt levels should normally not exceed 80% of book value. Valuations should be realistic. The banks would be allowed to claim a part of the upside to repay themselves for the forgiven debt if the value of the company later increased. But not all.

The valuations in the fall of 2008 assumed vast write-offs, 53.9%. The banks had made the first value assessments themselves. Arion had calculated a loss of 67.7%. The new rules allowed the banks to write up their loan values as the economy bounced back. Rounds of write-ups followed. The banks suddenly made huge profits. The strategy of patience proved to be the best one.

The banks benefited and along the way many companies in need got debt relief. But many suffered.

"A friend had a profitable franchise business selling fabric. Now he was in distress, and the franchise was terminated. He never got it back," says one.

"The bank forced a conversion of the loans from FX to ISK. For some, that happened when the ISK was at its weakest. They never saw the gain from the bounce-back of the ISK," says another.

Gudmundur Þór had many dilemmas to face. His company had borrowed in FX to build his hotel. He had expected foreign tourists.

Now they were gone, and the debt had doubled. His company was broke.

Would he be able to buy supplies or pay the electric bill? Should he keep the hotel open or shut it down? And whom should he pay with the little he had? Especially as his suppliers were bankrupt as well.

Furthermore, could he take guests and, if so, would they pay? Which contracts and approvals would be needed? Would anyone ask for guarantees?

In this case, the easy solution was the best. He paid everyone except the bank.

Half a year later, the manager of his bank came along to talk to him. But by then, the bank had gained new, faraway owners. The local team had decided to let Þór stay on and run his business, and one day they would agree on a repayment plan on whatever part of the loan they thought his hotel could carry.

Probably, this could not have worked in any other country.

DOWN, DOWN, DOWN, AND A THING CALLED AVENS

Many of the tools we ended up using in Iceland you won't find in the standard Central Bank toolkit.

Financial markets are brutally effective in reassessing values after a collapse. They set a new price on equity and bonds and determine the winners and losers. This takes a split second, a day, a week, a month or some other length of time, depending on the instrument, marketplace and response time.

The 'market' gives no weight to the question of fairness in the distribution of losses and gains. It is what it is.

Sometimes the market gets the new price right. Quite often it overshoots and reduces values way too much.

Typically, few investors want to enter a market or take a position in an entity in distress. Some fear the risk of entering too early. Many don't have enough knowledge or a willingness or ability to get that knowledge. For others, fear and panic dominate. Investors think *out, out, out* while they should be thinking *in, in, in.*

Others are restricted by their mandates. Many serious funds have mandates that only allow them to hold investment-grade instruments, preventing them from staying, contributing and benefitting from the eventual recovery. Other investors fail to evaluate the fundamentals that enable a recovery.

Instead, in many cases, hedge funds end up being the main buyers – these are called 'vulture funds' by some. Like vultures, they clean up and take what is left. Contrary to vultures, they bring money into the country and hinder a complete collapse of prices and values.

In contrast, public sector restructuring processes may be slow, tedious and political. It may take months or years to agree on valuations and agree on how to split the losses. Or it may take almost a decade, as in Greece.

We had no time to waste. We looked to the financial markets for inspiration. Sturla Pálsson and Freyr Hermansson, both in the market division of Seðlabanki, explored the options.

The IMF's initial contribution was to find arguments to shoot down our plans and reasons to do nothing. Gradually the IMF's sentiment changed, though, and the IMF machine helped us get the specifics right.

Our first move was to buy back government debt in the secondary market.

Despite our own conviction and the messages we repeated in our speeches, many participants in the financial markets still saw a risk that the Republic of

Iceland would default. This had never happened in Iceland's existence as an independent country, and we saw no reason for it to happen now.

Still, given their disbelief, some market participants were willing to sell us our old debt at a discount. Of their own free will. We bought it back.

Sturla and his team managed to free up some liquidity, and our global tours to raise new money yielded results.

Down went Iceland's net debt-to-GDP ratio.

A successful first step. Some were inspired. One advisor who had been with one of the three failed banks suggested that I should give a speech hinting that Iceland might not make it. That would have made the debt even cheaper, allowing us to buy it at an even larger discount.

I firmly said, "No way.

"We are running a Central Bank. Our priority is to ensure a steady recovery."

And I was left wondering what, if anything, the proposal indicated about the practices of the failed banks.

Next, Seðlabanki approached the market for 'offshore' króna.

The holders of offshore króna could not change their króna into foreign currency but did receive regular interest payments that could be converted at the official exchange rate. Moreover, the interest rate they received was high by international standards.

Some, however, really wanted to get out. We labelled them the 'impatient investors.' While the official exchange rate required 160 króna for each euro, some were willing to pay up to ISK 240-250 per euro to get out.

This difference caused us big problems.

Our plan was to remove the capital controls as stability was achieved at the level of the official rate. Few were willing to believe this could ever happen. Some just laughed at us. They observed the unofficial market rate and feared a weaker ISK and more inflation.

This was a self-fulfilling prophecy. No investor would enter at ISK 160 to the euro if the rate could go to 240. Many wanted to get out as soon as possible, fearing the 240. This limited capital inflows and increased the outflow, both weakening the króna.

Something had to be done.

We checked all available data, made interviews and tested the models. We came to believe that only a few investors really wanted to get out. But, in a thin market even a handful can drive the rate up and add tension. We set out to dry up the market.

The IMF was reluctant. "A Central Bank should rarely intervene in the currency market," they argued when we met. "And never in the grey market."

But that did not stop us.

Sturla and Freyr constructed a device whereby we could run auctions in the offshore market, offering investors Icelandic government bonds denominated in euros. With a price reflecting the offshore value of their ISK. We compromised with the IMF by not using any foreign currency that was part of their programme. Instead we convinced some Icelandic pension funds to exchange some of their FX reserves. And every now and then, some banks with positions to clear quietly called the Central Bank and offered FX.

Armed with new money, Seðlabanki could go to the market. The impatient investors bid down the amount of new debt in FX they needed to convert their ISK debt to euros.

In total, 22 auctions were held. Down went Iceland's debt-to-GDP ratio. Down went the unofficial exchange rate. The removal of the last control mechanisms eventually happened at a rate of ISK 120 to the euro, though only after a lengthy journey.

Sometimes patience pays off.

In between it all, the time was ripe for a big transaction.

We headed off to Boulevard Royal in the Grand Duchy of Luxembourg.

In 1998, the euro was established. Before that, Luxembourg used Belgian francs as its currency. Luxembourg was served by the Belgian Central Bank. When the ECB was created, however, all countries needed a Central Bank of their own to be part of the Eurosystem. The Central Bank of Luxembourg, *Banque Centrale du Luxembourg* (BCL), was founded.

The BCL aspired to make Luxembourg a banking hub. It aimed to be the most service-minded Central Bank of all.

As one would expect, Glitnir, Kaupthing and Landsbanki grasped the opportunity. All established themselves in Luxembourg. All were investment grade, and all could seek funding from the Eurosystem through the BCL.

In April 2008, the Icelandic banks represented 1.7% of the total banking system in Luxembourg. But they had more than 10% of the repo lending of the BCL, which gave them cash in exchange for collateral.

In fact, for some time the ECB became their largest source of new liquidity, exceeding the Icelandic Central Bank by three to one.

This happened even before the Eurosystem started its quantitative easing programme, to be discussed later. Under this programme, the ECB members started buying bonds and debentures left, right and centre. It is scary to think about how such a system, based on massive cash outflows even in normal times, would have fared during a crisis when banks and companies were truly desperate for liquidity.

At the peak in June 2008, the ECB loans to the three banks amounted to €4 billion. These loans were, remember, partly obtained through the 'love letters'.

When discovered, this practice was deemed to violate the spirit, if not the letter, of the ECB regulations. After an intervention from the President of the ECB in April 2008, the banks were required to limit such collateral to 40% of the total.

Naturally, one can get to 40% in two ways: by reducing the amount of love letters or by increasing the total amount of borrowing. As you would expect, the three banks chose the latter option.

This practice continued for some time. In mid-2008, the ECB intervened once more. The BCL took action, with the full backing of the Governing Council of the ECB.

"These exceptional measures are taken in view of your specific situation, which revealed the cross use of certain debt instruments among Icelandic banks," the BCL wrote in a letter to Landsbanki dated 30 June.

"In the event of difficulties encountered by any of the involved banks, there would be significant likelihood that the other banks would also be impacted, thereby rendering the risks which the Eurosystem faces substantially higher than usual," the BCL continued.

At the end of July 2008, the Icelandic bank bonds and love letters were tossed out of the European Central Bank.

Landsbanki again turned to its favourite partner, BCL. It needed euros. It now got them in exchange for a package called 'Avens'. The package contained one third bank deposits and two thirds bonds. These were bonds issued by the Icelandic government or with an Icelandic treasury guarantee. A large part were bonds issued by the housing financing fund, HFF. All of these bits and pieces were wrapped together nicely in a special vehicle. An ISK package.

In fact, this zero-employee construct called Avens now was the largest single owner of króna-denominated assets outside Iceland. Its ISK holdings equalled one-fourth of all króna-denominated assets owned by nonresidents.

Despite its general helpfulness, the BCL could not take ISK. Landsbanki therefore wrapped another mechanism, a swap, around the Avens package. This converted all the ISK collateral to euro. Landsbanki, remember, was still investment grade.

Then Landsbanki went down. Therefore, it could not honour the swap. Overnight, the BCL became the largest non-Icelandic holder of papers denominated in ISK.

An unpleasant situation.

With the capital controls, the ISK could not be exchanged to FX. The BCL could not place it in its books at any defined value. Neither could the ECB. And the controls could not be removed while vast positions, like Avens, were in play.

It was time to combine the three tested mechanisms: the buyback, the auction of government bonds and the mobilization of FX reserves.

The BCL got an offer to change its ISK into euro-based Icelandic government bonds. Naturally with more ISK required for every euro. The BCL could still avoid losses, as it had insisted on a 'haircut' when accepting the collateral. Hence, again, the bank creditors took a beating.

A group of 25 Icelandic pension funds got an attractive offer to buy the ingredients of Avens in return for some of their FX. At once, a lot of our problems were solved. Down went Iceland's debt-to-GDP ratio, starting with a reduction of 3.5% of GDP on day one. Away went one ISK risk.

Just as we found during our efforts to bring the banks back to life, market mechanisms proved to be the only viable tool.

"Everything we did later, we first learned on Avens," says a key state negotiator in one of the later negotiation processes.

The BCL negotiators had one more question as the Seðlabanki team was about to leave. "Now we have solved Avens," they said.

Then they asked: "What about its two twins, Haf and Holt?"

These were the Glitnir constructs. Avens lookalikes. The banks all played similar games, remember.

Glitnir had placed a part of its lending portfolio into Haf and Holt, which then, as two packages, were placed as collateral with the BCL. To access liquidity. But, Haf and Holt were registered in Ireland as Irish trusts. Hence, they had gone onto the books of the old banks as they were believed to include non-Icelandic assets. Seðlabanki thought they weren't its problem.

Two years later, however, it became clear that this question from BCL was indeed a first warning sign.

Of what would become Seðlabanki's largest problem.

A BIG HAPPY FAMILY

"Really, we run a pawn shop," says a Central Bank official. "Banks give us collateral, and we give them liquidity. Cash."

If that was true, then the European Central Bank, the ECB, was the world's largest pawn shop.

And, interestingly, it is run as a cooperative. All Eurosystem countries take part. Normally the countries act jointly. The rules of the cooperative are agreed to jointly. Among other things, the cooperative has agreed on rules as to what kind of collateral should be allowed.

In addition, each country runs its own pawn shop, which can take on some loans on its own. In some instances, an individual bank in a country may be in dire need. Its Central Bank can then decide to provide Emergency Liquidity Assistance, ELA. In these cases, that country's Central Bank takes on the risk and covers any losses.

The gains and losses that result from the standard operations are, however, shared jointly.

Imagine, then, the following:

The three Icelandic banks establish daughter banks in a Eurosystem country. The banks provide collateral that ends up having modest value, perhaps because it is a bond issued by one of the two other banks. The banks default. The local ECB pawn shop takes a hit.

That hit is then shared by all members of the big Eurosystem family. Each Central Bank gets a bill. In some countries, the legislation states that all such losses must be flagged in the national parliament or in the bank's supervisory board.

Hence, while I was governor, a colleague sat down with me in the bar after a meeting.

"I had a bad day yesterday," he said.

"I had to go to parliament. I had to ask for reserves for sizeable losses. It was all due to the Icelandic banks. The parliamentarians in my country did not really understand why they should pay up."

I had to buy him a glass of whisky and a cigar.

Luckily for him, in the end, none of his reserves turned into losses.

The Cypriot Governor, Athanasios Orphanides, was equally concerned. "How could you let this happen?" he asked the Icelanders.

THE EVEN LARGER CHALLENGE

From the first week of the collapse, one thing was clear: high unemployment and a household debt crisis would soon rank high on the list of collateral damage from the Icelandic financial crisis. And worse, we knew that a crushing level of household debt is among the most complex issues to resolve in a financial crisis. This we had learned from the earlier Nordic crisis.

The household debt problem was confirmed when I was first briefed after entering Seðlabanki at the end of February 2009. "[I]s a pressure on the government to cut the loans of households and companies," read my notes from the meeting.

And then the notes almost repeat themselves, as if my pen wanted to ensure I got the message: "[I]s a great pressure toward the government to resolve this issue."

Any responsible Central Bank must work to ease the pain of such a debt crisis. In addition, it needs to understand how the depth of the crisis and the choice of policy will affect state finances, the banks, and the consumers' spending decisions and thus demand.

Gudmundur Þór preferred to spend his free time with his horses, between the rivers and hills, and now and then in the vast and desolate interior.

He did not spend a lot of time on numbers, but he did have some numbers straight. Since the peak of the ISK rollercoaster ride, just before the ISK started its free fall, the price he paid for a bag of groceries at his local store had risen by almost 40%. His salary, meanwhile, had only risen half as much.

And his household wealth was wiped out. He could see from the ads in the newspaper that houses like his sold for 35% less than they did at the peak. His monthly bank statement showed that his mortgage loan, which was indexed to inflation, had grown by 40%. He had been careful to only borrow half the value of his house, and here he had stayed away from currency loans. Still, the value of his mortgage now exceeded the property value.

His Toyota Land Cruiser, with its Japanese yen loan, was another sad story. The car's value had fallen by half, while the loan had grown by 60%. He now owed twice the value of the car.

He had been hit hard. He is strong and persistent. He was working harder than ever, but his money couldn't buy as much as before, and gone was the wealth he and his ancestors had earned through generations of hard work. Because of events in which he had no part.

Still, he knew many who were worse off.

↳ The Icelandic Prime Minister, Jóhanna, and the Minister of Finance, Steingrímur, have set up a shield marked 'household debt'. They are attacked with spears marked 'tax increases', 'reduced purchasing power', 'indexing of loans' and 'reduced house prices', as drawn by the artist Halldór Baldurssons.

Some he felt needed and deserved help, some less so. Some, he thought, had squandered money. Some had lived high on the hog while accumulating debt. Some had aggressively borrowed to benefit from rising asset values.

Worst off, and the ones Þór believed should be supported the most, were the unfortunate ones who had lost their jobs, who had been forced to move, but could not sell their old houses. And the ones who had been able to sell, but at a steep discount, and now had nothing left to their name but their debt.

Financial crisis and debt crisis often go hand in hand. A heated debate on political measures to ease the crises emerged in Iceland, just as it did in the Nordics. Citizens were pushing hard for relief. When the shocks are as immense as they were in Iceland, it's critical that governments develop thoughtful policies that can help ease the pain and give hope.

"The pressure was on for a collective debt write-down," says a former minister.

The Nordic experiences from the early 1990s show that in this field, perception often deviates from reality. The facts and nuances rarely shape the debate.

Who do you think has the most debt, absolute and relative: low-income people or high-income people? What is more likely to push someone into poverty: unemployment and loss of income or debt? How many people are in financial distress, unable to meet monthly debt payments and cover minimum living expenses? How can they be identified and helped? How should policy measures be implemented? And who should bear the costs?

Poland, Hungary and Romania were other countries in Europe where FX borrowing represented a high share of the household debt. However, in Iceland, the percentage increase in FX debt as a share of total debt due to the crisis was double the level in those other countries. Simply because the ISK fell more than any other European currency.

Furthermore, most ISK loans were indexed to inflation, which was driven by FX. Hence, the more the ISK weakened, the bigger the ISK loans also grew. And even before the crisis, the debt-to-income level for households in Iceland was twice the euro-average.

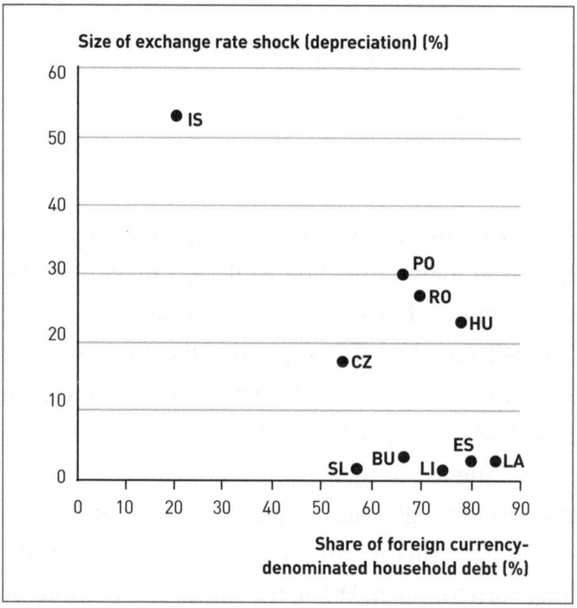

↳ **Share of foreign-denominated debt and size of exchange rate shock.**[1]
Source: "Households' position in the financial crisis in Iceland", Working Paper No. 59, Central Bank of Iceland, Þorvarður Tjörvi Ólafsson and Karen Áslaug Vignisdóttir

1 Share of household debt denominated in foreign currency in 2008 and the maximum size of annual nominal exchange rate depreciation from peak in January 2007-September 2008 to October 2008-August 2010 according to BIS effective nominal exchange rate indices. IS: Iceland, PO: Poland, RO: Romania, HU: Hungary, CZ: Czech Republic, SL: Slovakia, BU: Bulgaria, LI: Lithuania, ES: Estonia, LA: Latvia.

A team in the Central Bank, consisting of Þorvarður Tjörvi Ólafsson and Karen Vignisdóttir, set forth to build a unique database.

There is nothing like it, anywhere.

Many of the fundamental mechanisms it uncovered also apply to other advanced economies with high levels of consumer lending. Partly irrespective of time. Even today and probably when the next crisis hits. Or, if market interest rates for some reason skyrocket. The work, therefore, should, unfortunately, be of interest to many.

In Iceland, an incredible amount of data is available, both at the individual level and nationally. Tjörvi and Karen coded, anonymized, and, with special permission from the data protection authority, uploaded it all.

Hence, each and every Icelander had their own line in the model. With more data registered than most themselves have readily available.

The model had per person data on sources of income, taxes, loans, overdrafts, family size and composition, location, age, living conditions and housing. Even land registry data on the value of each property was added.

The model could link each individual and family, disguised, to consumer guidelines on minimum living expenses. A nationwide household-level database emerged. The only element that was missing was nonhousing wealth data, mainly a differentiator for high-income groups.

Next, they added profiles: payment profiles for each loan, income profiles and living-expense profiles for each household, and housing-wealth profiles for each homeowner.

The shocks that hit in the real world, that had rocked Iceland, could now also be simulated in the model. The currency depreciation and inflation, the rise in living expenditure, the fall in employment and the rise in unemployment, the changes in salaries, taxes and benefits. And, of course, the asset-price shocks.

The model could provide a clear view of how Iceland's citizens were faring. It answered questions that were critical to formulating policy: how many were in financial distress, with a disposable income insufficient to cover debt service and minimum living expenses? How many people were both in distress and had negative housing equity, and thus unable to mitigate distress by selling off assets or obtaining better payment terms? What were their characteristics?

It could also predict the effects of potential policy measures: how would the rates of financial distress and negative housing equity be affected? Which measures would be most effective?

Gudmundur Þór was right. He was a bit of an average guy. Many were better off than him, some worse.

At the end of 2008, about 90% of all mortgage holders held ISK-denominated mortgages only, 3% had foreign-denominated mortgages only, and 8% had a mix.

Roughly 19% of households with motor vehicle debt had ISK-denominated car loans only, while 47% had foreign-denominated loans only, and roughly a third had a mix.

Before the collapse, in early 2007, about one in ten households was in distress. Half of these were households in the lowest income bracket, the lowest fifth, where one quarter of the households were in distress. As with debt and income, a lot was out of order, even before the collapse.

And the collapse hit hard. At the peak, in the autumn of 2009, almost three out of ten households were in distress. Half of those in the lowest income group were in distress; one in ten in the highest income group.

Hence, the level of income mattered. Age also mattered, with the youngest hit hardest. Time of purchase mattered, with recent home buyers suffering the most. Location made a difference, too, somewhat surprisingly, with rural areas hit hardest.

Pre-crisis, 5% of Icelandic households had negative housing equity. That percentage rose to almost 40% by early 2010. Ireland, in comparison, reached a level of 30% in 2010; the US, 25% in 2011; and the UK, 10% in 2009.

Two out of 100 households were hit by both distress and negative housing equity pre-crisis. That number rose to 14% at the peak in mid-2009.

Simply put, low income was the biggest factor in determining whether someone fell into distress. On the other hand, having high levels of debt was the main prerequisite for negative housing equity.

Gradually the government formulated and enacted the first policy measures. These measures reduced the share of households in distress by the end of 2010 by 5 percentage points, from about 25% to 20%.

More measures followed. The chart overleaf shows the full list of measures from 2008 to 2010.

The measures included a moratorium on foreclosures, a temporary suspension of debt service for FX- and CPI-indexed loans, and rescheduling through payment smoothing and deferred payments of such loans.

About half the households with eligible loans took advantage of payment smoothing, which could reduce current debt service payments by 15-20% for CPI-indexed loans and by 30-40% for FX-indexed ones.

October 2008
- Moratorium on foreclosures
- Temporary payment freezing of foreign-denominated loans

November 2008
- Payment smoothing of ISK mortgages introduced by law
- Third-pillar pension payouts, later expanded
- Increases in mortgage interest subsidies

March 2009
- Payment smoothing of foreign-denominated mortgages introduced by law

May 2009
- Act on Temporary Mitigation of Residential Mortgage Payments

October 2009
- Law on measures for individuals, households, and corporations due to the banking and currency collapse providing a framework for decentralized debt restructuring
- Agreement on offering payment smoothing for foreign-denominated motor vehicle loans

November 2009
- Payment smoothing applied to all indexed ISK mortgages unless households opt out

June 2010
- The Supreme Court rules that indexation of motor vehicle leasing payments in ISK to changes in currency exchange rates is illegal

August 2010
- Office of the Debtor's Ombudsman created to oversee and provide advisory and mediation services related to debt mitigation procedures
- Measures introduced for households with two properties for personal use

September 2010
- Supreme Court rules that interest should be calculated on illegal foreign-denominated motor vehicle loans in accordance with general interest rates on ISK bank loans, published on the Central Bank of Iceland website

December 2010
- Law on recalculation of illegal foreign-denominated loans to Icelandic households
- Adjustment of mortgage debt to 110% of the underlying collateral value
- Expansion of the voluntary debt mitigation framework
- Enhanced and more progressive tax rebate on interest
- Special interest rebates for the years 2011 and 2012

↳ **Main debt relief policy and legal interventions.**
Source: "Households' position in the financial crisis in Iceland", Working Paper No. 59, Central Bank of Iceland, Þorvarður Tjörvi Ólafsson and Karen Áslaug Vignisdóttir

The most severely hit households were given the option of restructuring their loans out of court by negotiating with their lenders directly or with the help of the newly created office of the Debtor's Ombudsman acting on their behalf.

The negotiations were on a case-by-case basis, but used templates developed through a dialogue between the government and the financial institutions.

The templates provided for substantial write-downs, designed to align secured debt with the asset values, and debt service with the ability to repay.

The case-by-case negotiations took time. As of January 2012, 35% of the case-by-case applications had been processed.

Later, mortgage debt was capped at 110% of the collateral value. Large sums were written off. As no means testing was applied, high-income earners often benefitted the most.

Many foreign currency loan structures were ruled to have been illegal and were thus recalculated back to ISK, with the ISK values and interest rates set as they would have been at the time the loan was originated. In addition, a large share of mortgage holders received a sizable interest rate subsidy over a two-year period, financed through temporary bank taxes.

In late 2014, the government launched a new programme aimed at reducing household debt level by 20%. Half the reduction was achieved through a bank-tax financed cut in mortgages, and half by the tax-exempt use of the debtors' own voluntary pension saving fund.

The measures differed with regard to their cost and effectiveness.

The research indicates that popular demand and an urge to do something does not always yield the most effective result.

Most effective was the recalculation of parts of the FX loans to ISK. This was also a high-cost measure. Here, as we will see, the loans were judged to be illegal in the first place. The banks and their creditors thus had to pick up the tab.

Payment smoothing was judged to be effective and low cost.

Capping the mortgage debt at 110% with no consideration of income level was, based on research, expensive and ineffective, based on its impact on reducing the number of households in distress. Naturally so, as the largest proportion of the debt tends to be held by the highest income groups. Hence, it was the highest earners who benefited most from this measure. In a sampling of countries, the highest 20% of income earners held 42% of the total consumer debt, while the lowest 20% of earners held 6%.

Aligning the households' incentives to participate was complicated. The combination of indexing, inflation and falling home prices meant that the longer households waited, the bigger the write-down they got. The unconditional moratorium on foreclosures and the suspension of debt service also reduced the immediate need to resolve debt problems, and frequent revisions of the debt-restructuring framework created an expectation of additional measures.

It was only when a comprehensive framework with a clear expiration date was put in place that the debt write-downs finally took off.

As of January 2012, 15-20% of the principal of all mortgages had either been or was in the process of being written down.

To sum up, Iceland averted a spike in foreclosures by imposing a temporary moratorium and by working to find solutions to the household debt problem. Then the debt and the debt service costs were reduced.

Many Icelanders would say that along with the impact on people in distress, other outcomes also mattered. The write-down improved the financials of consumers and possibly strengthened demand. Many saw the adjustments as fair toward people seen as innocent victims. Some saw the finalization of the relief measures as the closing of a troublesome era. And that again allowed people, some will even say Iceland as well, to move ahead with hope for the future.

The 2014 programme also had another result. "This is it," was the message. Now no one could wait for more.

From the very start, the new banks' balance sheets anticipated the need for write-downs.

Remember the rubble left behind from the tower?

They had enough reserves to shoulder the costs of write-downs, and they frequently took the initiative. All of this, however, had an impact on the ultimate recovery for the bank creditors.

Bank taxes were also imposed, effectively further reducing the recovery rates of the creditors. This was considered by many to be fair.

"The banks should pay," was a refrain often heard in Iceland.

"The creditors should pay," was another saying.

The creditors that lent the money to the banks pre-crisis now bore part of the blame for what later happened, with the new creditors becoming the ones to pick up the tab.

For Gudmundur Þór, a mortgage indexed to inflation meant his debt continued to grow as inflation rose. He would now need to repay until his 60th birthday, not his 50th. And his Japanese car had suddenly gotten an ISK-loan, with a value of half of what the bank first proposed, but with a higher interest rate. He never really knew if the loan had been illegal in the first place, despite all the rumours. Although he was a law-abiding citizen, he was not sure he would have cared anyway.

"It's the provider of a loan that ought to check that what he offers is legal," he thought.

How the loans could have been given in the first place is another Icelandic banking mystery.

OFF TO THE WHALING STATION

My parents have never been particularly interested in shopping or cafés. So when they came to visit me in Iceland, I wanted to share a more spectacular experience. That we got. We also got some vivid illustrations of why the Icelandic economy had the potential to recover faster than anyone expected.

Hvalfjörður, meaning whale fjord, lies north of Reykjavik. Here, first the British and then the Americans operated fuel depots and naval bases during the Second World War. They built a camp and expanded the port, which later was turned into a processing station for a commercial whaling company, Hvalur hf., showing how resourceful many Icelandic companies are in using what they have. And their ability to adjust when market opportunities close or open.

When we were at the station, a 25-meter-long fin whale was brought ashore. With a weight of about 50-60 tons. First on deck was an inspector to review the workings of the harpoon. His task was to ensure that the kill was instantaneous. Next came a Japanese trader. His task was to cut out the most valuable pieces from the whale's tail. White and fatty. They were placed in a cooler and transported in a fast car straight to Keflavik airport. The next day, they would be served at the best Tokyo and Osaka restaurants.

Yet another illustration of the Icelanders' resourcefulness. Opportunities are pursued wherever they can be found. Icelandic fishing vessels are active in remote locations along the West African coast that few people will ever venture to. They bought the fishing rights and are there to harvest the wild catch. They work in the Arctic waters outside Iceland in one season, in tropical waters the next, and don't see this as particularly strange.

Next to enter the deck at the whaling station was the crew that carved up the rest of the whale while pumping away some tons of blood.

"I am used to blood," said the crew leader, standing in a fountain. "I used to be a bank manager running the derivatives trading desk."

This illustrated a more general experience. As jobs were lost, most Icelanders immediately did all they could to find new ones. Even if this required a change in industry, skills, profession, location, rank or apparent status. As they searched, friends, families and municipalities went to great lengths to help. This was what everyone expected. And, frankly, it was necessary. Icelandic state benefits are phased out faster than in the rest of the Nordics.

And, yes, bankers are useful. Thousands lost their jobs when we had our Norwegian banking crisis. The state holding company overseeing the support programmes pushed for cost reductions. A euphemism for firing bankers. About 5,000 lost their jobs. The Ministry of Finance attempted to help and asked the state employment agency to establish a support programme. The agency refused. Instead, we in the ministry established our own programme, financed with 500 million kronas, about $80 million.

But, only two applied.

Some time later, the whalers evolved yet again. With the growth in tourism, whale watching turned into a more lucrative industry. Some hunters turned into guides.

TACKLED AND SUED BY NEIGHBOURS AND FRIENDS

Gudmundur Þór's family had always fought. First, it fought for its land. Then it fought nature and the elements. His tale of Icesave is another tale about the importance of not giving in.

Þór could not see any reason why his taxes should be used to repay the UK and the Netherlands. Landsbanki was a private bank, taking deposits from voluntary deposit-holders. It was their decision to chase a higher interest rate. Now, the two countries were demanding reimbursement from the Icelandic state. The UK and Netherlands wanted compensation for the payments they made to cover the minimum deposit guarantees of up to €20,887 per account holder. The totals worked out to €2.7 billion for the UK and €1.3 billion for the Netherlands. In sum, equal to about 35% of Iceland's 2009 GDP.

The EU/EEA agreements had required Iceland to establish a deposit guarantee fund. As it had done. But no such scheme in any country contains sufficient funds to cover a full meltdown. That would simply have been too expensive. When the banks defaulted, Iceland did all that could be done by giving priority to all deposit holders. With no FX, a full payment or guarantee was simply not possible, Þór always believed.

And Þór would never forget what the Brits did. They had not come to the rescue of Iceland. Instead, they increased the capital requirement for Heritable, the Landsbanki daughter company. They cut access to funding. They placed

Iceland on a blacklist, equating it with Al Qaida. They then worked with the Dutch to persuade other countries to put pressure on Iceland. They even tried to use the IMF as their money collector, their torpedo.

Like many other Icelanders, Þór had read a lot on Icesave, even legal texts and EU directives. He and many others could make their points as expertly as any trained lawyer. With a persistence exceeding any lawyer. He knew and partly acknowledged the British and Dutch positions, namely that Iceland had discriminated against depositors in those countries and had not cooperated in the critical hours. Likewise, that, in the early days of October 2008, the UK and the Netherlands had their own problems, as their banking systems were in turmoil.

"ECOFIN, the council of EU ministers of finance, had its first meeting after Lehman's collapse on 7 October," recalls Anders Borg, then the Swedish Minister of Finance.

"I spent all night of the 6th on the phone after hearing about the Icelandic Emergency measures. As did many others."

Borg continues, "Normally ECOFIN meets for breakfast to discuss pending issues, prior to the start of the formal meeting. On the 7th, breakfast lasted until lunch.

"Many EU countries wanted a joint response to the post-Lehman crisis. Not the UK, though.

"Any country may have a crisis. That we all understand. But we found it strange that we received no pre-warning. We were only told around 9pm on 6 October. Here, the Icelandic government lost a lot of goodwill."

"It was traumatic," says an Icelandic minister at the time.

"The extreme bullying of the UK and the Netherlands was hard to swallow.

"And, yes, for a while we allowed ourselves to be bullied."

The numbers Þór had seen were scary. Yes, the Emergency Act Iceland passed gave priority to depositors and would reduce the amount Iceland might have to pay if it was to compensate the UK and the Dutch. But the depositor prioritization was soon challenged in court. Also, Þór was certainly not ready to trust anything he heard from Landsbanki or from any bankers on what part the bank assets could help repay.

He was afraid of what the crisis would do to Iceland. The UK and the Netherlands wanted to force Iceland to repay them in FX for the costs of the deposit guarantees they had covered. With interest. With an ever-weaker ISK, the ISK cost would keep rising. What the two were asking would drain the blood from the veins of Iceland, he believed.

Gudmundur Þór fought this fight for his future grandchildren.

In 2009, the then Icelandic government worked to settle the dispute with the UK and the Netherlands. An arrangement was negotiated whereby the Icelandic Deposit and Investors Guarantee Fund, DIGF, would reimburse the UK and the Netherlands for the two countries' payments to the depositors. In return, the UK and the Netherlands would lend a similar amount to DIGF, with a guarantee and interest payments from the Icelandic state.

The first agreement had been negotiated in secrecy. It was passed to the parliament for discussion and approval.

"We got suspicious when we sensed that the negotiations and the results were kept secret," says a key person in InDefence at the time, a movement formed in opposition to the agreement.

"But someone leaked and gave us a version of the agreement. We then started the fight."

According to Icelandic provisions, Seðlabanki must review and provide comment for all debt obligations to be taken on by the Icelandic State. In the final rounds in July 2009, the parliamentary budget committee asked for our position.

The Seðlabanki head counsel saw numerous flaws in the agreement.

"The agreement was in the format of the Paris Club," she says.

The Paris Club is a mechanism for resolving issues for countries with payment difficulties. Normally, these countries have taken on too much debt, and they approach the Club to seek a solution.

"It is simply not how debt agreements between countries on an equal footing are to be structured," says the head counsel.

The contract was a civil law contract with a focus on the interest of the lenders. It stipulated that British courts would resolve any disputes. It gave Iceland no clear right to renegotiate in case its situation worsened. It also included multiple other provisions that would weaken Iceland's position.

Seðlabanki presented its memo to parliament on 7 July 2009. Some people were surprised that I allowed a memo questioning a negotiated agreement to be submitted. I heard some grumbling: to which party did the author belong? Who was related to whom? Had I lost control of the bank?

But for me, it was quite simple. Holding back the views of the head counsel from the parliament on such an important matter was just not an option.

The Central Bank was also asked to assess the agreement's economic impact. Our base case assumed that asset recovery would cover 75% of the claims. With numerous other assumptions, the base case showed payments equalling 3.1% of Iceland's GDP in each year starting in 2016. A pessimistic case showed payments of 6.2%.

↳ There are different views on who put Iceland, here represented by Steingrímur, under pressure to sign the agreement on Icesave. Here the torpedo carries the iconic symbols of four powers.

Spurred on by InDefence, parliament added a payment cap to the bill. It capped payments at 3-4%, with possible remaining debt in 2024 to be cancelled.

This bill passed through parliament and was signed by the president on 2 September 2009.

The UK and the Netherlands, however, rejected the alterations, and thereby a settlement.

A new round of negotiations started. This time, Iceland had a debt negotiation specialist on its side.

Lee C. Buchheit was on the train between Washington and New York when the Icelandic Minister of Finance called him. "Please be in Reykjavik on Sunday," was the message.

Lee had worked on debt restructuring in about 25 countries.

"Some take a year, some take a decade," he explains.

"I arrived in Reykjavik thinking it was a normal arrangement. Steingrímur brought me into a room with the three leaders of the opposition parties."

"Here he is."

Bringing in Lee in one piece was what the three had asked for. They wanted a lead negotiator, a pro, who could take on the Brits and the Dutch.

Lee's first meeting with the two countries was in Iceland's London Embassy, in South Kensington. Here, one wall was decorated with cartoons from the 1974 Cod War. That was when Iceland had last confronted the UK, fighting for its 200 kilometre economic zone. The Brits were placed facing the cartoons.

"I was surprised by the extreme level of hostility," says Lee.

"I was surprised by the animosity and distrust.

"Normally country-to-country negotiations are a gentlemanly affair. Not here; the emotions had heated up on both sides.

"And rarely have I seen a situation where both parties have political constituencies at home watching their every step.

"The UK and the Netherlands said they had tried to get a dialogue going with Iceland prior to the 2008 collapse. Sometimes their calls were answered and they were told the banks were all fine. Sometimes the calls were just not answered," says Lee. "The Dutch claimed they had a piece of paper from the fall of 2008 when an agreement had been promised."

An amended agreement was negotiated.

But it was a hard sell.

"I flew to Akureyri in the north of Iceland. I was to present the agreement to the locals," says Lee.

"A woman stood up. She had moved from Ireland. To avoid paying taxes to pay for the collapse of the Irish banks. Now, even worse, she said, her taxes would pay the Brits."

The agreement passed parliament with a narrow majority and was sent to the president to be signed. Opposition was strong. A petition to the President to reject the law was signed by almost 30% of all Icelanders with voting rights. On 5 January 2010, the President announced his rejection of the bill. It was passed on to a referendum.

Only then did Iceland lose its investment grade rating from Fitch.

"No one called us to say we should punish Iceland," says a then rating analyst at Fitch.

"We respected Iceland's decision not to take on the losses of the banks and to ringfence the sovereign.

"But we did not see this decision as being in line with the spirit of an investment grade credit rating."

Gudmundur Þór was not alone in his views. Ninety-eight per cent of Icelanders voted no, while 2% voted yes in the referendum.

The agreement was renegotiated.

The interest rate was lowered, and the repayment period made longer.

Again, the proposal was put in front of parliament. Again, it passed with a narrow majority. Again, the President refused to sign. Again, a referendum was called.

On 9 April 2011, 60% of Icelanders voted against and 40% in favour.

ICELAND, THE UK AND THE NETHERLANDS FACE THE COURT

After the second referendum, no further attempts to reach an agreement were pursued. The case moved to the EFTA court.

On 28 January 2013, the EFTA court ruled that the state was obliged to ensure that its banks establish a deposit insurance mechanism, as Iceland had done. It recognized, however, that such a mechanism might not suffice in the case of a systemic crisis. That would simply be too expensive for the customers and banks to pre-finance. Furthermore, the judgment made it clear that a state has no obligation to step in and cover costs in cases where the mechanism is not able to fully compensate depositors.

On the contrary, such support might even have constituted a breach of the prohibition against state subsidies. Yes, consumer and deposit protection had been requested when the directives were written. But in the end, open markets and competition on equal terms had mattered more.

Hence, the Icelandic state was freed from any obligation to pay.

Next, the ruling said that DIGF did not discriminate based on nationality, because the deposits made in Iceland had been transferred to the new bank prior to the decision to have DIGF compensate non-Icelandic deposits.

The judgment also said that Iceland did not breach the overall principle of nondiscrimination. This principle states that equal cases should be treated equally. However, compensating for the minimum amount would not re-establish equal treatment, as the overall handling of the deposits had been very different from the outset.

Finally, the ruling pointed out that a state within the EEA/EU needs to have wide latitude to make its own choices in the face of a systemic crisis.

The judgment made no reference to the fact that the UK and the Dutch depositors were about to be compensated anyway. All deposits were given priority through Iceland's Emergency Act.

By 30 June 2013, the total value of the assets in the Landsbanki receivership, including what had already been repaid, covered more than the total amount of the priority claims.

Remember, deposits had been only about 30% of the total liabilities of Kaupthing, Glitnir and Landsbanki.

What the UK and the Dutch had demanded was a reimbursement, with interest, of their payment to the depositors of up to €20,887 per account, which is the figure called for in the EU directives. In May 2008, Landsbanki had also, voluntarily, signed up for the UK and Dutch schemes 'topping' up the insurance to £50,000 and €100,000 respectively. These amounts had also been paid out to depositors by the UK and the Dutch. The UK Treasury had even, for the UK accounts, reimbursed depositors who exceeded those limits.

Gradually, now everything was reimbursed. Even more, Icelandic bankruptcy law requires a penalty interest rate of 6% in the case of nonpayment. Hence the depositors even earned some interest.

In the beautiful world of finance, the claim of the Dutch Central Bank, De Nederlandsche Bank (DNB), was sold on 27 August 2014. With this, DNB's payment of €1.636 billion to depositors of Icesave under the deposit guarantee scheme was recovered in full. DNB was no longer a creditor of Landsbanki. The deal was made with, yes, Deutsche Bank.

Early in 2014, many British local authorities with claims on Landsbanki also decided to sell.

The whole British and Dutch campaign against Iceland had, in some sense, been both superfluous and of insufficient legal basis. The tension and ambiguity it created had slowed the recovery process by several years and turned former friends into foes.

The Special Investigative Commission, SIC, summarized its views on the Icelandic government's readiness to handle matters raised by Icesave as follows: "During the time leading up to the collapse of the banks, there were divergent views within the Icelandic administration on the obligations of the EEA member states in the event a guarantee scheme, established in accordance with the deposit guarantee directive of the EU, could not meet its payment obligations.

Despite this, the Icelandic authorities did not conduct an enquiry into the available legal sources for the interpretation of such obligations. The examination by the Investigation Commission does not indicate that contemporary sources on this issue provide definitive answers to the matter."

"It only started to dawn on me that this could be a difficulty when I spoke to the Prime Minister on 2 October," wrote the then largest owner of Landsbanki, referring to the impact of the decision to place Icesave directly under Landsbanki Iceland.

Amazing.

Other countries took note of what happened in Iceland. Some had looked with amazement at the overtures toward Russia, the UK decision to use the anti-terror legislation, and the fight over Icesave. Some time after my tenure as governor, I was asked to give a presentation to the top team of the Nordic Ministry of Defence. Some were puzzled by the actions taken by friendly nations in a time of financial crisis. Some wondered if anything could be read from this on what might happen if even more serious situations were to arise.

"In hindsight, the Icesave dispute was painful, but of help," says a person engaged in the later creditor negotiations. "That was when we learned that debts are flexible."

SOME SIMILARITIES, MANY DIFFERENCES

Just as in Iceland, everything looked great in Ireland in the early 2000s. Foreign companies in technology, pharma and finance had moved their headquarters to Ireland, appreciating its top-notch infrastructure, use of the English language and generous tax laws. There was an inflow of labour and incomes were rising. A construction and real estate boom followed.

The Irish banks saw a flow of apparently profitable long-term lending opportunities, which they chose to finance through short-term foreign borrowing. A classic timing mismatch.

International bond borrowing grew from €16 billion in 2003 to €100 billion in 2007. Well above half of Ireland's GDP. A lot, but still a tiny fraction compared to Iceland.

The markets and regulators took comfort in the strong equity ratios of the Irish banks. Their dependency on a single – and short-term – source of funding was less of a concern.

The total stock of mortgage loans in Ireland went from €16 billion in early 2003 to a peak of €106 billion by the third quarter of 2008. This led to a hike in property prices.

"We had a workshop in 2007, prepared by IMD, the business school," says a then Glitnir executive. "They had prepared a case on Anglo Irish Bank, one of the largest Irish banks. They suggested it as a role model for us."

The first signs of a recession appeared in mid-2008. Soon after, government deficits increased, businesses closed and unemployment rose.

The banks' problems started even earlier, in 2007, as markets started to dry up. The problems became acute post-Lehman.

First, no new loans meant no new property deals. This exposed the fragile cashflows of developers. And threw property values into doubt.

Second, with less money available in the market, banks started to feel a liquidity pinch as depositors withdrew money.

Finally, as their loan books, which held their biggest group of assets, started to decline with the falling property market, the six Irish domestic banks soon found that their liabilities exceeded their assets.

On 29 September 2008, the Irish Minister of Finance issued a broad state guarantee for the Irish domestic banks. In addition, the government promised to recapitalize the banks. It guaranteed all retail and corporate deposits, interbank deposits, senior unsecured debt, asset-covered securities and dated subordinated debt. Basically, everything except the equity-type instruments.

The government injected capital into the banks and took over ownership. It carved out distressed bank loans into a state-owned 'bad bank'. The government received bonds in return. In sum, it took on all losses not covered by equity, while also claiming the assets.

The cost to the government was vast, booked as a deficit. Add the impact of the associated recession, and you have a government deficit of 40% of GDP. Government debt surged.

The Irish citizens carried the burden. The unemployment rate rose from 6.5% in July 2008 to a peak of 15.1% in early 2012.

"Yes, after Lehman we did put pressure on the EU to guarantee the southern periphery. And Ireland was important," says Timothy Geithner, former President of the Federal Reserve Bank of New York and Secretary of the US Treasury. "The integrity of the EU was important."

The ECB put pressure on the Irish government to enter an IMF programme. It threatened to withdraw its emergency support for the struggling Irish banks.

In the end, however, there was good news. The economy recovered. The housing and real estate markets recovered. The bad bank regained value and was able to repay the government.

In 2016, the bad bank, the National Asset Management Agency, NAMA, started to offer financing to builders. Somewhat ironically, its aim was now to mitigate a chronic undersupply of housing.

Worth observing, the Irish banks fell after a boom and bust because of their reliance on market funding. As in Iceland. Even a smaller size relative to GDP and full access to the ECB system of liquidity did not offer sufficient shelter.

Along the way, both the chairman and CEO of Allied Irish Bank resigned. They had borrowed money from the bank to buy equity, with loans that were later hidden from the accounts.

THE REYKJAVIK SYNDROME

"He who is in debt is not free."

– The title of a book by Göran Persson, Swedish Prime Minister 1996-2006

"Some people really hated the idea of an IMF programme," said an Icelandic economist. "Some hated the idea of any international institution that might try to impose rules on Iceland. Some saw being in an IMF programme as a disgrace and feared what was to come."

Many saw the IMF as the tool of global powers, brought in to make Iceland succumb.

But the IMF was to become one of the most important mechanisms providing leverage for Iceland.

"Maybe it wasn't bad to be the first," says an economist. "Along with Hungary, being the first IMF programmes after the global financial crisis and the first European countries for a long while. The IMF had an interest in contributing to a successful outcome. And, despite all beliefs to the contrary, Iceland had strengths it could build on."

On 23 August 1973, a convict on parole attempted to rob Kreditbanken, a Swedish Bank in Stockholm. Unlike the big bank robbers, who empty the bank from the top or by excessive lending to themselves, he went in through the front door, armed with a gun.

His attempt failed. He then took four employees hostage and negotiated the prison release of a friend who would assist him. Together, they held the hostages captive for six days.

After their release, the hostages defended their captors and refused to testify against them in court. The term 'Stockholm syndrome' was coined as the expression for a condition in which hostages develop a psychological alliance with their captors.

In the case of Iceland, in a kind of reverse Stockholm syndrome, the captors ended up feeling sympathy for the captives.

The IMF machine started humming in early October 2008.

The IMF had experts on all possible topics. If we, on a Monday, defined a need for expertise, the expert would fly in from Washington on Tuesday. With, typically, experience from lots of the world's trouble spots. Often supported by young analysts. The best and brightest, especially from all corners of the world. All free of charge.

But, with strong views.

At the end of October 2008, the IMF had pushed Seðlabanki to raise its interest rate to 18%. On 19 March 2009, the MPC took the first step in lowering it. It was a cautious 1 percentage point decrease.

The IMF nodded.

On 8 April, the MPC took another step, lowering the rate by another 1.5 percentage points. The IMF registered what happened with a worried look.

In simple terms, a Central Bank sets two interest rates: a higher rate at which it lends money to banks, and the lower rate at which they can make deposits. This sets a corridor. If the market is liquid with excess cash, the market rate drifts down toward the deposit rate. If the market is short on liquidity, the borrowing rate steers. As is normally the case. Most market players and journalists therefore use the Central Bank borrowing rate as the reference. As was done above.

That was also the case in Iceland in early 2009. The market was short of liquidity and the market rate was in the upper part of the corridor.

Then two changes occurred concurrently. One, liquidity increased, and the market rate drifted downwards in the corridor.

Two, the MPC decided on 7 May to lower both the deposit rate and the borrowing rate by 2.5 percentage points. Now the IMF was grumpy. Some would even say they were screaming. Already then.

In my view, the reduction was well reasoned. Month-to-month inflation had stabilized. The economy needed all the easing possible. Our business was to stimulate growth, not to punish anyone.

The IMF vehemently denies that its intent was to punish Iceland. "The IMF does not try to punish Iceland or any other countries entering a programme," says Murilo Portugal.

↳ Halldór Baldursson depicts the head of the IMF office in Iceland, Franek Rozwadowski, with the Minister of Finance, Steingrímur, the Prime Minister, Johanna, and the Governor, right to left in the backseat as seen from the front. The text reads: "Relax there in the backseat. We don't want to take the policy rate to the bottom and interfere with a whimsical experiment in which many innocent passers-by are run over."

"You don't reduce the temptation of other countries to run an unsustainable policy, a moral hazard, by punishing a country already in crisis."

As I was in Washington for the IMF spring meeting, a top IMF executive called me into his office. And yes, this time the IMF literally screamed. He did not like us lowering interest rates. He did not like the actions we had planned to dry up the offshore ISK market.

Ahead of the MPC decision in June, the IMF representative in Iceland gave an interview to an Icelandic newspaper telling the MPC not to lower the rate further.

But this was not for him to decide. After reviewing the numbers, it was my view that the borrowing rate should be reduced. It would not matter a lot, as the market was long liquidity and the bank's weren't borrowers. But it would signal a continued easing.

Now, I did call a fellow governor. It was time to ask if I had gone crazy. Or, rather, to get his advice. He listened to me summarizing the facts and my reasoning and confirmed my sanity.

The day after, on 4 June, the MPC voted to lower the borrowing rate while keeping the deposit rate, which now mattered the most, unchanged.

"Iceland Lowers Key Interest Rate to 12%, Defying IMF," read the Bloomberg headline.

The IMF asked for an emergency meeting. They sent their representative to Seðlabanki to communicate their dislike. But theirs was a difficult case to make. They had a hard time mustering a factual argument for why the borrowing rate could not be lowered, as another rate now determined the market interest rate.

"Don't ever try to tell the MPC what to do," I added.

From then on, there were no further public statements.

↳ IMF found the lowering to 12% to be aggressive, but some wanted more. The swing is marked '12% policy rate' and the text reads, loosely translated, "This bully will not let us go down." The prime minister, the head of Iceland's employer organization and of the Icelandic trade union hangs on to the swing while a spokesman of the largest party, the Independence Party, has fallen to the ground. The prior governor swings in the background.

The tug of war did not go unnoticed. When the team went out some weeks earlier for a beer, half the people present would have liked to send me backup into the mountains. Or worse. Luckily, the other half moved to my defence.

On this Friday, everyone was welcoming.

Icelanders, too, do not like to be told by outsiders what to do.

Often, we sensed that the requirements for the upcoming IMF reviews were being set ever higher. Again and again we believed that we had fulfilled the requirements that had been set out for the disbursement of funds. But then the IMF would add some new condition or tighten the requirements. There was no firm evidence, but I suspected the bar was being raised to buy time for the IMF because the Icesave dispute made it hard for their team to get internal IMF approval or the necessary financial assurances.

And, possibly, given the controversy it would cause, the IMF did not want to blame the delays on the UK, the Dutch or on the Nordics. So, it just made it harder for Iceland to meet its requirements.

However, just like in the gym, if you keep adding more weights to a barbell, eventually the person trying to lift it collapses. Or gets stronger.

The latter was what happened in Iceland. The IMF set ever-tougher requirements. That Iceland fulfilled. To clear the higher IMF hurdles. Soon Iceland soared well above even the highest IMF requirements.

Despite the conflicts, the IMF support was hugely important. The IMF mission head, Mark Flanagan, the head of the IMF office in Iceland, Franek Rozwadowski, and their team members were competent, dedicated and supportive. They found numbers to support discussions where others were just speculating. A two-page memo was most often seen as enough by the Icelanders, while the IMF built a full model.

On some occasions, though, I did feel that IMF got stuck in its models. Maybe as I myself had ten years of experience from the public sector and 13 from business, I felt more could be done to leverage the 'best of both'. As illustrated by the tools we used, market mechanisms are often the most effective tools.

The IMF's presence gave greater confidence to many external parties. Its analysis added credibility. Its expertise was vast. And frustrated bankers and creditors had a hard time criticizing us, as Iceland could show that her actions were in line with the IMF programme and its policies.

There is, however, a bit of a paradox with an IMF programme. When the IMF brings funds in a crisis, it becomes a creditor itself. Its money may help. But the actual elements of the programme help more.

Many, but not all, measures that strengthen a country's ability to pay its debt are good for the country. The IMF often pushes for more austerity and restraint. This may result in less focus on investments and growth, and thus cause harm.

But quite often there is an alignment of interests, especially when dealing with private- and public-sector creditors that want the state to foot the bill.

Iceland made use of this support and refined its use to perfection. In the battle with creditors, the IMF increasingly turned into Iceland's strongest ally – paradoxically, especially as the IMF's loan had been paid back by then.

"In meeting private creditors, we are polite and encouraging. But we don't bail them out," says Murilo Portugal from the IMF.

A MISUSED PRECIOUS GIFT

"It is no big surprise that the German regional banks were deep into Iceland," says a senior banker.

"The German banks were loaded with deposits from German savers. They benefited from the implicit government guarantees. Now, all that money had to be placed somewhere."

As an example, 15 of the 27 banks that sued us were German.

Three events occurred as the eurozone was established.

First, the market expected a more 'German' monetary policy with more focus on restraint and on capping inflation. Inflation fell. Interest rates went down. In their search for yield, European investors had to look to other high interest-rate countries. Like Iceland. Yield seekers went in, led by the German banks.

Second, those countries in the eurozone that had previously had a high interest rate, most notably Greece, Italy, Portugal and Spain, got a valuable gift from the low interest rate countries: now their own rates fell. With this, yet further high interest rate opportunities for investors disappeared.

The markets believed that the German rates would be the new reference, and all were invited to join the new world of low rates. The risk of depreciation had disappeared and the potential for state default was assumed to be zero. Now all euro states could borrow freely, at a low rate. As they did.

As in Iceland, the lower cost of borrowing triggered a boom in consumption, real estate investments and state projects.

Third, add to the mix yet another celebratory event that opened up a path in the wrong direction. The Berlin Wall fell. All of Germany was cheering. While everyone was celebrating, the politicians should have provided a sobering reminder.

"Great, but this comes at a cost," they should have said.

"Everyone in the East must understand that their currency will have less value. Everyone in the West must accept that they will now pay higher taxes. Money will be needed to build the East."

"Great, and there is no cost," was unfortunately how their decisions could be read. "The currency unit of the East and the West shall have the same value, and there will be no tax increases."

Sometimes economists really should be allowed to be party poopers.

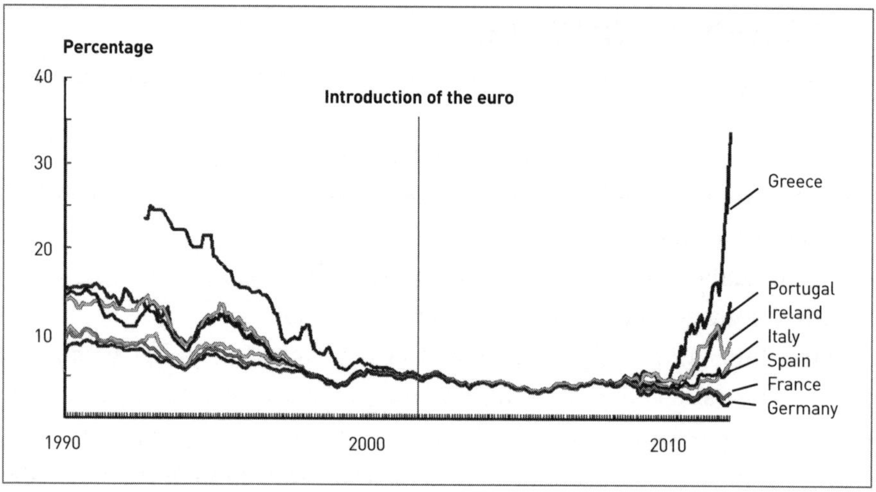

↳ **Yields on 10-year government bonds.**
Source: Bloomberg; Eurostat; McKinsey

The lack of a mechanism to differentiate between East and West led to unemployment. The unfunded costs of integrating East Germany led to a budget deficit. The EU had set limits on the size of the deficit a country could carry. But now the German politicians tried to sneak around the rules and ask for exemptions. And when the Germans started sneaking, just as the old prejudices would have predicted, France, Greece, Italy, Portugal and Spain became ever more brazen as they also flouted the rules.

All of them ran government deficits, partly above the agreed-upon limits, even in boom years.

Those countries failed to become more robust. Debt levels grew. Here, contrary to what happened in Iceland, in the form of government debt. The gift became a curse.

"Debt ratings had never been a great topic at parties," says a then ratings analyst.

"Then we downgraded France.

"Before I got to the pub, everyone knew.

"It was tough. I have rated 50 countries. In some it gets hostile. Not so in Iceland."

In Portugal, the debt level of the state-owned enterprises, as well as that of the state itself, had escalated. In Italy, both companies and the state had raised their debt levels. In Greece the state was the main borrower, ahead of other sectors and ahead of all other EU countries.

In both Italy and Greece, some of the state lending was passed on to the private sector, partly in the form of loans, partly by substituting tax collection with state borrowing and partly by government overspending on nonsustainable social schemes. Unfortunately, the exposure and the risk stayed with the state.

Especially Greece, then Portugal and Spain and partly also Italy, overspent through borrowing from foreign countries. Greece had deficits in its transactions with other countries, in the current account, at almost Icelandic levels. Greece financed the deficits with government loans from international creditors.

For the politicians in countries looking for an outsider to blame for their own sloppiness, the Germans and the reckless bankers came in handy.

SMUGGLED IN BEHIND TINTED WINDOWS AND UP THE FREIGHT ELEVATOR

In August 2009, Már Guðmundsson was appointed permanent Central Bank Governor of Iceland. He successfully took on the task of manoeuvring Seðlabanki through the lengthy process of the recovery.

"Now I got my revenge," says Jón. He arranged my farewell party at the Central Bank.

He brought in a great singer. And he instructed her to only sing the most patriotic Icelandic songs. One being *Draumalandið*, or 'the country of dreams'.

The next day I woke up without a job.

And, during my short tenure in Iceland, Ian Davis had left his position as McKinsey's Managing Director. I was now an 'outsider'.

If I was going to rejoin, it would require a 'direct elect' to senior partner, no easy feat, requiring a great many steps. Including 20-plus interviews. With my former Icelandic colleagues and leaders, who would offer assessments of the impact I had had in Iceland.

I asked Steingrímur to testify, which he happily did. Although not without asking first, "How can this be necessary? You worked there for 15 years. They should know you by now."

Next on my list was Mark Flanagan, the IMF mission chief.

"Iceland has advanced on all agreed-to priorities," he said.

"What Iceland agreed to has been delivered. On areas of disagreement, both sides were clear and solutions were worked out.

"Often programme countries say 'yes, yes and yes', and do nothing. This was never the case in Iceland."

In mid-September 2009, I rejoined McKinsey.

A month later I received a call from the office of the Norwegian Prime Minister, requesting a meeting. I was picked up in a car with tinted windows and taken to the basement of the high-rise building where the Prime Minister's office was located. There I was smuggled up the freight elevator to avoid being seen by any of the journalists outside, all trying to ferret out the composition of the new government. I was asked by Prime Minister Jens Stoltenberg to become Minister of Finance of Norway.

But this time I answered no. The challenge would not have matched the challenge in Iceland.

I promised to never mention his request. But then Jens revealed it all in his memoirs.

On 5 August 2009, we had called for a press conference. Just before I stepped down from the role as interim governor. We were to present the future strategy on capital controls.

A journalist who was present was disappointed. He asked, "Why did you call for a press conference?" He found the plans vague, with no firm dates. Supposedly, this was all boring and as expected. "A meeting about nothing," one of the newspapers wrote.

In a moment of inspiration, I remembered and paraphrased a quote of Mervyn King. "A successful monetary policy should be boring ... successful Central Bankers should be seen neither as heroes nor villains, but simply as competent referees, allowing the game to flow and staying out of the limelight."

Then I added, "Frankly, it is great if a press conference in Seðlabanki is once again boring. That has not been the case for some years."

The statement was shown on the national news that evening.

When he saw it, Gudmundur Þór supposedly nodded.

CHAPTER 4

THE RECONSTRUCTION

I WILL PRETEND I AM YOUR FRIEND

"In the spring of 2007, no one cared about politicians. The banks and private sector carried the hopes and dreams. In November 2008, all looked with hope and expectation to the politicians. The anxiety was enormous. We were hugged on the street. In January 2009, everybody hated us."
– Icelandic MP in interview

The number of protesters at the weekly Saturday protests in front of Althing peaked in October 2010. Unemployment was high. There were no signs of growth. Companies and households remained mired in a debt crisis.

The SIC said the former Prime Minister of Iceland, the Minister of Finance, the Minister of Business Affairs, the three pre-crisis Central Bank governors and the Director General of FME had been negligent.

But then, on 28 September 2010, the parliament decided to dismiss the charges against the ministers. It did, however, vote 33 to 30 to bring several charges against the Prime Minister. He was later found guilty on one. For not convening the government. Apparently, a trifle. But in reality, the lack of proper procedures, plans and systems were major contributing causes of Iceland's fall.

Gudmundur Þór commented on the outcome with sarcasm: "The bankers had their love letters. I lend to you and you lend to me. Here came the political version: I vote to release you and you vote to release me."

All got off the hook except one, and they charged him on what many, wrongly, believed was a minute charge. Even the Minister of Banking was released.

Maybe because he was found so untrustworthy that he, as banking minister, wasn't even invited when the destiny of the banks was discussed.

Þór had been surprised, as had most other Icelanders, when he got to read the SIC report. He had heard rumours of the wrongdoings of the banks. But never, ever had he believed it to be as systemic as it was. And with such a clumsy response from the authorities in the years preceding the October crash.

He was off to Reykjavik the next Saturday and joined in the largest of all the protests.

"An old friend visited me at my home," says a minister at the time. "My friend was among the best actors in Iceland. He had won many prizes.

"'Today I will pretend I am your friend,' the actor said.

"'They could not send an amateur to play such a demanding role,' the actor continued. 'It's such a hard role to play.'

"On many other occasions, I felt as if I were jumping between the patches of ice on the pond in the centre of Reykjavik in early spring," continues the then minister. "The patches were melting. The water was still cold.

"In every break of the parliament, we met to discuss which new things we could come up with to speed things up."

The crisis, and especially the Icesave conflict, once and for all changed the political mood in Iceland.

In the April 2009 election, the party of the Prime Minister Geir Haarde and Davið Oddsson lost in a big way, with the Social Democrats and especially the Left-Green being the winners.

In the April 2013 election the two latter lost, among other reasons, as they were seen as supporters of an Icesave settlement and now carried part of the blame for the hardship. The winner was an Icesave hardliner and a 'the creditors should pay the households' debt proponent': the new Prime Minister Sigmundur Davið and his Progress Party.

The actions of the Brits and the Dutch had created a result not foreseen.

SO NERVOUS THAT I COULDN'T HEAR

A handful of court cases were critical to Iceland's recovery.

The banks had sold loans in many forms. Some were in ISK with fixed or market-dependent interest rates. Some were in ISK indexed to inflation and with fixed or floating interest rates. Some, especially those made to companies, were in FX with FX rates. Yet others had been paid out in ISK but were indexed to and had an interest rate based on the interest and exchange rates of some foreign currency.

Many households with ISK-based indexed loans saw their loan values escalate as inflation kicked in. However, such loans had existed for decades and had been tested thoroughly. Even now in 2019, they have by far the highest market share in Iceland. They have once again become attractive as inflation has fallen.

The pain in 2009-2010 from the indexed loans was severe. It was, however, eased somewhat by the fact that the indexing usually did not increase the monthly loan payments. Instead, the repayment period was extended.

The FX loans hit borrowers harder. Those loans were looked at closely. There were disputes as to whether the ISK-denominated FX loans had even been legal in the first place under Icelandic consumer protection laws. The case went to court.

In July 2010, the Supreme Court first judged the construct to be illegal. With four votes against three. In September 2010, the court, in a second ruling, decided that the Central Bank interest rate for non-inflation indexed domestic loans should apply to these loans. In a case from June 2011, this principle was applied for the first time to some corporate debt as well.

The banks had to recalculate all the FX loans. Their values were reset, as if they had been in ISK all along. The equity value of the banks fell, as did the recovery of the bank creditors. The debt burden eased for many households. But less so than some had hoped and expected after the first ruling.

"The banks would need money from the state again." That was Moody's and Standard & Poor's belief after the first ruling. They downgraded Iceland.

After the second ruling, this risk ceased. The regulators had already written down the loans when they transferred them to the new banks. These buffers were big enough to cover the combined impact of the court rulings.

Remember the rubble left behind from the tower?

Here, yet another failure of the old banks and the regulators became evident. The structures for a vast part of the loan portfolio, loans sold on the streets in Reykjavik, had been illegal. Neither the auditors, regulators or bank managers had seen this one coming. Few customers, if any, saw any point in questioning the structure while it yielded benefits. Once the ISK imploded, that was no longer the case.

The next Supreme Court ruling was even more important. In October 2011, it ruled on the validity of the Emergency Act. The prioritization of the deposits ahead of other claims had been challenged. A loss would have split the recovery among all creditors on an equal basis, and less would have remained for the depositors.

If this had happened, the Landsbanki estate would not have had the funds to fully cover the Icesave claims. But, with a supportive ruling, it would become almost certain that all depositor claims toward Landsbanki would eventually be covered.

"I was so nervous that I couldn't hear the ruling even when I listened," says a legal expert.

"We were all in the emergency room," says a then minister.

"This time we were prepared for anything.

"We were in a constant crisis-preparedness mode."

"What people have forgotten is that Iceland took a huge risk through the Emergency Act," says a then key person in InDefence. "The law gave all deposits priority. We did not stop at ensuring payment only of the €20,000 demanded by the EU/EEA directives. If the Emergency Act had been ruled invalid, we would have been exposed to a huge loss."

"And for this we got beaten up by the Brits and the Dutch."

IN THE ECONOMIST'S MODEL

After the collapse, the brakes slammed on throughout the Icelandic economy.

Icelanders reduced their consumption. Austerity programmes and weak local government finances reduced public consumption and investments. The numbers for 2009 and 2010 showed a 10% drop in GDP.

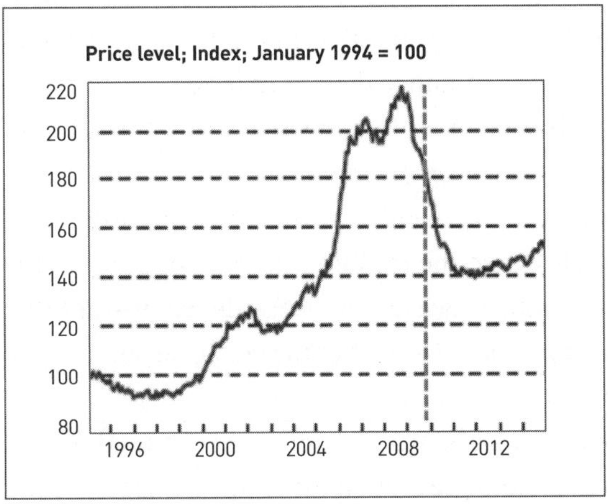

↳ **Real house prices**. Monthly data, January 1994-February 2014.
Source: Registers Iceland, Statistics Iceland, Central Bank of Iceland

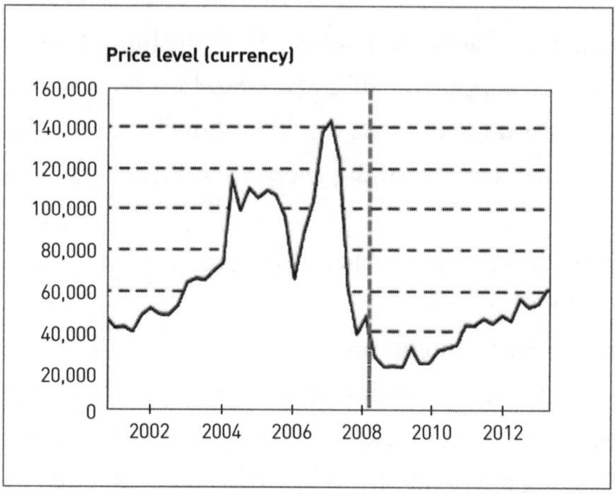

↳ **Housing market turnover**. Q2 2001-Q4 2013.
Source: Registers Iceland, Statistics Iceland, Central Bank of Iceland

As the charts show, house prices dropped by 30-40%, and the number of house sales dropped by 80%. Few wanted to sell at the bottom. Few could buy.

But just as economic models predict, the depreciation of the currency increased the cost-competitiveness of Icelandic companies and workers. Higher import costs reduced purchases of imported durable consumer and investment goods, which played right along with consumer instincts to cut back and retrench. Half the demand drop was offset by fewer imports. Factories abroad that manufactured cars and other exports to Iceland took half the hit. Put simply, half the job losses from the Icelandic crisis occurred abroad rather than in Iceland.

"I have no doubt that it was the collapse of the currency that turned it all around," says a business executive.

At the time, the pre-crisis capital inflow and growth in banking were considered a plus for the economy. However, the resulting strength of the ISK, the cost increases, and the fight for labour squeezed the Icelandic companies that were exposed to international competition. Now, after the crash, resources were available again and costs came down.

The constrained industries bounced back. The domestic production and service sectors grew. The export sectors grew at about twice the speed of the export markets. Tourism grew, too, accounting for half the extra growth. The other half was due to aluminium and other products. The new power and aluminium plants were now running at full speed.

This paved the way for the second phase of the recovery, which ran roughly from 2011 to 2014.

The continued shrinkage of the financial sector was still a heavy drag on the economy. But gradually the reduction of public consumption and investments ceased, followed by modest growth. For the first time since 1960, Iceland's savings exceeded investments. The country now ran a surplus in its trade and payments.

For Gudmundur Þór, the challenge was clear. Prices were up about 40%, only half of which was matched by salary increases. His debt was huge. Luckily, though, his bank did not hound him.

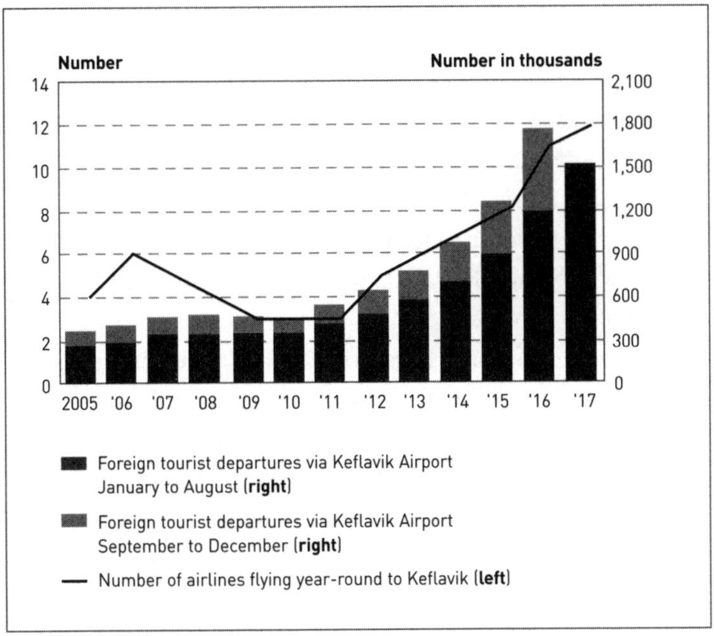

Number of airlines flying year-round to Keflavik, and foreign nationals' departures.
Source: Icelandic Tourist Board, ISAVIA

He won some contracts to supply vegetables from his greenhouse, and Icelanders who decided to skip their usual vacations to Spain were starting to fill his hotel. Some foreigners had begun to turn up, too. And they even came in winter.

Nature had offered him both challenges and blessings. Now, it came to his support. On the horizon he could see *Eyjafjallajökull*, which began to erupt in March 2010. A month later it was spreading its ash across northern Europe.

Some see the drama of the eruption and the curiosity it inspired as the trigger for the start of Iceland's tourism boom.

Which came in handy, as the government had neither the will nor the capacity to take on any additional measures for attracting tourists or shaping growth policies.

In the spring of 2009, I had taken the liberty of inviting some companies to Iceland. We wanted to bring in long-term investors to accelerate growth. But at that time, there was little interest among companies and even less among Icelandic policymakers.

Huge investments in metals and power generation had added to the 2005-2008 super-cycle, but now the brakes were on. International markets were weak. The memory of how the *Kárahnjúkar* power plant had split the nation was still fresh. Besides, the Icelandic power companies were loaded with debt and incapable of making further investments.

Even the draft IMF Letter of Intent of June 2009 failed to include a chapter on growth. Something that for me always was a mystery.

Domestic interest rates were three to four times higher than comparable international rates. The international capital markets were closed to Icelandic companies, except for a few exporters.

At one point I was asked to visit a local power utility that was struggling. Pre-crisis, it had easily found long-term financing, up to 30 years, from a Belgian bank at a 0.5% interest rate. Now, there were no lenders to be found at any price.

Many investors had been burned earlier. Many did not feel comfortable with the risks. Many struggled to figure out how to approach a system with dual exchange rates, capital controls and incomplete restructuring of most industries.

Most investors were simply not ready to spend the time needed to understand it all.

THE JAMES BOND MOMENT

"If you don't investigate, you ask for a chaos of criminality. It isn't just the cases brought forward that matter."

– The special prosecutor

"If you enter a room and find a dead body with a knife in its back, then it's safe to assume a crime has been committed," says Eva Joly.

"Most probably, there is something to investigate."

In 1990, she had joined the High Court of Paris as an investigative judge. Soon after, she started an anti-corruption campaign. She took on ministers, the bank Crédit Lyonnais and the French oil giant Elf Aquitaine, now part of Total. She received death threats but continued her investigations, securing dozens of convictions.

"At first, many in Iceland were surprised when I said some individuals had committed economic crimes," she says. "Early in 2009, I hadn't familiarized myself with the details. But fraudulent accounting, suspicious share purchases and money transfers could be spotted."

"The government really wanted to understand what had happened," Eva continues. "It was ready to start investigating. Remember, a furious people had placed the new government in office."

The SIC was tasked with reviewing the actions and possible negligence of policymakers. Now, after some fumbling, the Icelandic authorities also made a dedicated effort, with additional funding, to investigate and prosecute 'bankers'.

In February 2009, the Icelandic government appointed Ólafur Hauksson to be special prosecutor. At the time, his unit had a staff of only five. In March 2009, Eva Joly was also brought in.

Soon after, Eva and I met at the Central Bank.

"The Central Bank will provide all possible support to all investigations," I said.

"Great," she said. "But let's also go after the big criminals."

"Sure," I answered. "Who?"

"The IMF," she responded.

I was a bit puzzled. Later I realized what she meant: the spotlight should also be put on the IMF's role as the driving force for the Icesave money collection and for the privatization of Icelandic natural resources. Power plants were purchased by owners who provided only one thing: debt.

And she believed that an even bigger bank also should be investigated. A large German one.

While preparing this book, I met with Ólafur, who is now district prosecutor. He and his team of investigators occupy offices on the second floor of a building on the north side of Reykjavik. Their interrogation rooms are on the first floor. Even in 2018, his conference table was still covered with binders and documents related to an ongoing case stemming from the financial crisis.

I counted about 30 binders.

"Think about it as a matrix," says one of the investigators. "On one axis, you split between the small fish and the big fish. On the other, you split between the crimes with a moderate impact on society and the ones with a major impact. Most people would say you should focus on the upper right corner, but remember, even Al Capone was convicted for tax fraud."

He continues: "It is hard, and should be hard, to secure a conviction. There are many filters. A clear legal basis is needed. A clear breach is needed. It needs to be deliberate. One needs proof. And the court needs to be convinced beyond a doubt."

"The executives typically get all the attention," says the prosecutor.

Formally, the board may have more responsibility, but they seldom make the specific decisions. Even less so the owners. Unless they are steering the executives, that is.

By coincidence, exactly as in the court case, he was preparing with the help of the 30 or so blue-grey files on his table.

By 2012, the special prosecutor had 110 employees, with 140 cases under investigation.

"For this, Iceland deserves credit," Eva Joly comments.

"A major investigation normally takes between 1,500 and 9,000 man hours. In Iceland, the resourcing gradually increased, including many new team members with strong competencies," says one of Eva Joly's international experts as he talks me through the course of events.

"Early on, a structure and methodology were put in place, enabling later investigations to cover the full matrix. That was important. One cannot measure impact just by the number of sentences.

"Experience tells us that with limited resources and a lot of pressure for quick convictions, the investigations will focus on the small crimes of the small fish.

"The SIC did a good piece of work. They helped to clarify what had happened, almost like a truth commission. You need to place the SIC report and the results of the investigation next to each other to see the full picture."

"Our experience shows that a team like ours can have impact," says the special prosecutor.

"Initially there were rumours," he says.

Some evidence came from the Resolution Committees of the banks. By now the board of the FME was also stepping up the pressure. The estates had been told that they could be held liable if they didn't report wrongdoings.

Even I, when I was governor, received documents from whistle-blowers. In thick brown envelopes. Anonymous. That I passed on to the right authorities.

One of the international advisors to the special prosecutor, Jean-Michel Matt, had worked on bankruptcies, litigations and investigations since 1984. Among others, on the French Elf Aquitaine corruption case. "This case was huge," he says. "Hundreds of millions of euros were going here and there."

"What we saw in Iceland were patterns we recognized," Matt says. "After one week, I said, 'this is what you will find.' And, yes, 90% was exactly that. Maybe it was a bit more sophisticated in Iceland. Maybe a larger share of the transactions bordered toward criminality as compared to what I had expected."

"Often things aren't black and white," says Jean-Michel. "First, a decision of a bank manager may be borderline. But then, at some point, the situation may worsen. A cover-up is launched. And, then all is taken one step further."

The politicians did not make it easy for the investigators. Resourcing was ramped up late and reduced early. From 110 persons at the end of 2012 to 70 in September 2013 and 50 in September 2014.

"The inmates were also allowed to go on probation earlier," says the special prosecutor. "I found that timing strange."

Criminal cases that were related to a breach of the capital controls were largely dismissed. In the autumn of 2008, Seðlabanki had made a draft of the bylaws. The draft had been sent to the Ministry of Commerce. It had provided its comments by email. But formally, the bylaws had not been signed and hence they were not valid!

"The *Þetta reddast* practices still hadn't been replaced," says one. "The Icelandic expectation is that all will resolve itself."

"The steps needed in economic investigations are often similar," says Eva Joly. "Follow the trail of money. Search the premises. Review the bank statements."

"All investigations had to start in Iceland," she says. "No authority outside the country will volunteer unless you have built a case from home."

"We did get strong international support," says the special prosecutor. "In Luxembourg the authorities put in a lot of effort. They allowed us to be on the premises when the searches were conducted. Only in the Madoff case had this been allowed previously."

"Maybe that was one," says the special prosecutor when I ask him for a James Bond moment.

"Otherwise the days are filled with heaps of documents, emails and tape recordings."

ENTERING AT FULL VALUE, STAYING AWAY AT QUARTER VALUE

Who are the investors who decide to enter a market when assets are fully priced?

Apparently, it's the big crowd. That's what drives the prices upwards.

Who are the investors who decide to enter a market when assets are priced at a quarter of prior values and when guaranteed returns are set at 18%?

Apparently, almost no one.

At least in Iceland.

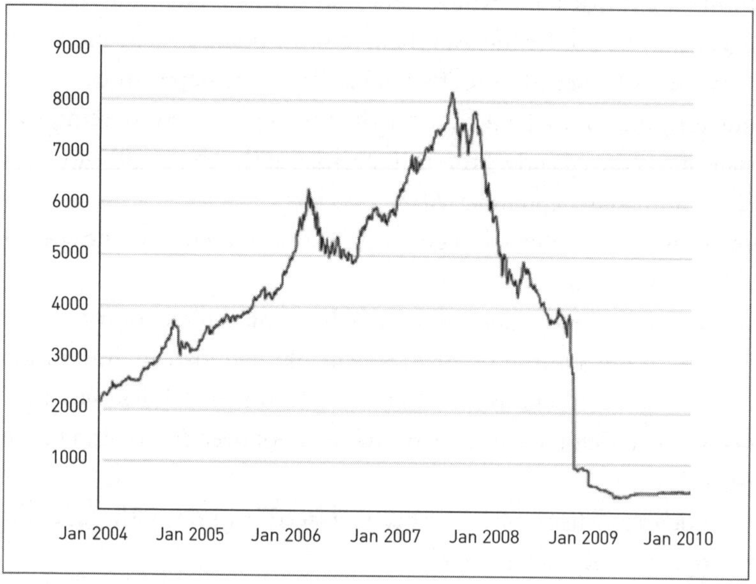

↳ **Iceland All-share Index**. 2004-2010.

Pre-crisis, the capital inflow was vast, mainly through the three banks. A range of smaller banks, utilities, municipalities and industrials also received capital market funding.

The equity market index entered the new millennium at an index value of 1,512 and peaked on 18 July 2007 at 8,174.

And then it fell. Within a year, it had plunged by more than half to 3,778. The market sensed that something was amiss, well ahead of policymakers, rating agencies and financial market supervisors.

Then came the crash, and the index hit bottom on 1 April 2009 at 379, a mere 4% of its pre-crisis peak.

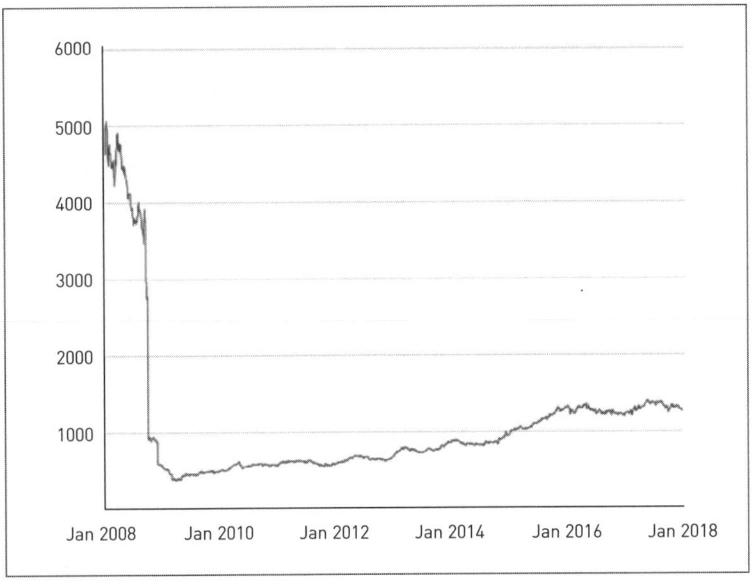

↳ **Iceland All-share Index**. 2008-2018.

By early 2009, most investors had left the country. Despite multiple efforts and some isolated successes, our efforts to entice new capital to Iceland were largely in vain.

Even more so as the Icelandic restructuring processes were slow and often opaque.

Old owners tried to hold on to whatever they could retain and let time work in their favour. The banks that controlled the loans were slow, for a range of good and not-so-good reasons.

In addition, many funds were restricted in their ability to invest. Their market value had shrunk as international equity markets nosedived. Their buffers were gone. They did not dare to sit on positions and even less to take new ones. They ended as net sellers at a time when the markets were searching for the bottom. Clearly not an optimal way of creating long-term value for you as a future pensioner.

A handful of international investors turned up in Reykjavik, though, including some old, almost aristocratic, US East Coast families. They were convinced that the printing of money in the US would undermine the value of the dollar. They believed in the lessons from King Harald III Hardråde, who mixed copper into his coins. They searched for a safe haven outside the US.

And expected to find it in Iceland.

The capital markets and debt markets worked effectively to restructure the banks. For corporate Iceland, little help was provided.

Still, from its low point in April 2009, the value of all listed Icelandic companies climbed steadily, more than tripling in the period up to January 2018. In euro, the value rose more than four-fold when using the official rate.

The impatient investors who exited the Icelandic market through the auction of government bonds gave up a six-fold return.

Across a sample of countries that had weathered a financial crisis, a pattern emerged in which the equity markets hit bottom two years, at the latest, after the pre-crisis peak. The median time was seven quarters, exactly the time it took for Iceland to move from peak to trough. The average drop among the crisis countries was 50%.

The average increase two years after hitting bottom was 80%. Investors can surely themselves benefit from investing into a country in a recovery process. Most of the countries were back above pre-crisis level after five years, as counted from the pre-crisis peak. Only one of the ten countries in the sample was still below the pre-crisis peak after eight years, namely Thailand.

Iceland will join Thailand.

In Iceland, the ownership rights of the old owners were terminated through defaults or restructuring of entities that made up at least three quarters of the March 2007 market value of all publicly traded Icelandic companies. Interestingly, many of the operating companies were doing reasonably well. But the holding companies that owned them were staggering under enormous debt.

"Yes, we looked at buying one of the Icelandic banks, Islandsbanki," says a then employee of a large Nordic bank.

"Some of our customer representatives said there was a market need. The Icelandic companies were not served as well as they could have been. Their interest rates were high and market access weak.

"We liked the Icelandic people and the companies we met. We asked someone from the IMF what he saw as the most important enabler of recovery.

"'That you buy the bank' was the response."

"We liked the professionalism of the organization," says the possible buyer. "But it was unclear where an acquisition would take us.

"Was there a natural next step? What would our exposure be? Is the economy sufficiently diversified?"

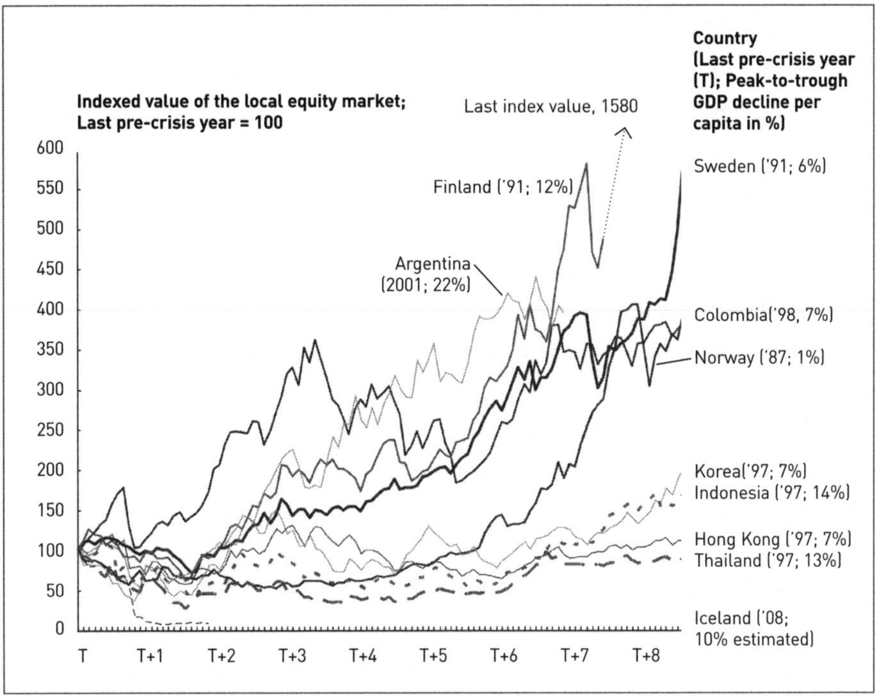

↳ **Post-crisis development of equity markets.**
All reached bottom of cycle latest in T+2; average/median is 7Q.
Majority above pre-crisis level in T+5.
Only one of nine below pre-crisis level in T+8.
Average of last index values is 310, with T = 100.
Average is 570 with bottom value = 100.
(If Finland capped at 400).

Source: Datastream; Last pre-crisis year from Reinhart, C.M. and K.S. Rogoff (2009), except for Iceland; Sparebank 1 Markets.

"We were a bit torn, but still positive. But then a load of new Nordic regulatory requirements with regards to banks' equity ratios were imposed and our attention drifted," he says.

A bit surprisingly, judging from the interviews for this book, the estates never gave anyone a really good deal to buy one of the banks with FX.

"The winding-up boards were not equipped to conduct a sale. And the creditors thought they would be able to sell the new banks at full value at some point," says an advisor.

Another billion-dollar mistake, as will be shown.

ONE JAILED BANKER IN THE US, 25 IN ICELAND

In a remote location 100 kilometres north of Reykjavik lies a building that resembles an old farmhouse. It faces the harsh North Atlantic on one side and barren fields with snow-covered lava on the other. The house is part of the Kvíabryggja Prison. Its inmates are housed in white barracks. Each cell measures about 6 square metres.

"Up here, you find bankers, tax avoiders and sex offenders," says a banker with first-hand experience.

"Many are sentenced for drug-related crimes," says a former inmate and ex-banker.

"Kvíabryggja is not such a bad place, though.

"My time at Kvíabryggja wasn't what hurt me the most. The day I was taken into custody and the time from when I was charged until the day I went to jail were way worse. And the time after my time in jail.

"I was educated to be a banker. But now I can never take such a position again."

"A total of 212 cases were looked at," says the special prosecutor when we met. "After filtering, 35 were investigated. Twenty-five were taken to court.

"Seventy-three individuals were investigated; 38 have served jail time, 11 were found not guilty, 11 cases are under appeal, 11 are in the district court and one was pulled back."

The *Financial Times* counted bankers only. Their research showed 47 convictions globally after the financial crisis, of which 25 were in Iceland. The UK had none. Spain had 11, Ireland 7, while Cyprus, Germany and Italy had 1 each. So did the country that originated the global crisis, the US and its subprime mortgage market.

That lone US banker was sentenced for artificially inflating the price of subprime mortgages. Even as the banker got his verdict, the judge said his conduct "was a small piece of an overall evil climate within the bank and within many other banks."

Hence, the largest man-made economic catastrophe in the US since the Great Depression yielded one verdict, on one second-level banker in a second-tier institution. In contrast, 839 people were convicted after the US savings-and-loan scandals in the 1980s.

Barclays Bank also received Qatari money, with provisions paid to its Prime Minister. This case was taken to UK courts in 2019.

"The Supreme Court was in general more punitive in its rulings than the district courts. It was ready to take a holistic view," says the then special prosecutor.

The largest group of prison inmates had a prior career in Kaupthing. The percentage sentenced was highest among the CEOs, likely because that was where the prosecutor focused the most attention. Five bank presidents or CEOs were convicted. The top executives of all three Icelandic banks at the time of the crash were charged, with two convicted and one case pending.

The level-one managers and the operators in the trading and debt departments were also prominent on the list of convicts. Less so the bank owners.

Most were charged with manipulating share prices through loan-financed share purchases. Kaupthing, Glitnir and Landsbanki all had such cases.

Some cases were related to the approval of loans from the banks to companies that bought assets, allowing friends and family to cash in their shares. A Kaupthing executive borrowed ISK 570 million from Kaupthing to a company, so that the company could buy the director's Kaupthing shares.

Some cases were related to insider trading, most notably the sale of shares just before the collapse of the banks.

Some civil lawsuits were also filed, especially in cases where the banks lent money to the owners and their companies.

On 7 June 2019, the French state prosecutor stood in front of the French court in the Equity Release case. He requested in total 16 years of imprisonment for six members of the Landsbanki staff, including five years for the chairman and largest co-owner. Depending on the outcome, he may be the only large bank owner to go to jail. Globally.

"Wow, that was quite something," I commented, when I heard of the prosecutor's request.

"What do you mean? responded Eva Joly. "The bankers have destroyed the lives of hundreds. A youngster last week got five years' imprisonment after attempting to rob a coffee bar."

"The 2007 reports gave a false assessment of the banks' own funds," says a former FME employee, speaking of the required annual filings made by each bank. The banks' shares had fallen in the latter part of the year. Margin calls had been made. The banks sold shares to structures that were not real buyers.

"The financial statements should have revealed this."

However, two international accounting giants, PWC and KPMG, signed off on the accounts without further comments.

Two auditors worked with the special prosecutor on the accounting and auditing. In an article, they wrote, "The collapse was primarily of domestic origin and the banks' extensive purchase of their own shares was a large part of the reason."

"We found the relevant legislation too weak when we considered the basis for possible cases against auditors and rating agencies," says the special prosecutor.

Hence, the Icelandic experience also contains a more complex lesson. Excessive risk taking, as well as negligence and decisions that ultimately led to vast societal risks and costs, deserve criticism. But it takes a lot for a criminal code to provide a basis for a verdict. Hence, the possibility of criminal investigations can only be one among many mechanisms to ensure that financial institutions, managers, owners and the authorities act with prudence.

"It was often difficult to prove what had happened," says the French investigator Jean-Michel Matt. "From what I saw, the three banks had the same laxness and level of informality as in France 20 years earlier.

"A lot was very informal. It was often difficult to identify who had made which decisions."

"Why did an owner get a loan?" asks the investigator. "Because management decided, based on its best judgment, or because the owner gave a direct or indirect order?"

"Nobody whom I met in the banks had bad intentions," said a bank executive who knows Kvíabryggja well, when I met him in a quiet corner of a hotel coffee shop in Reykjavik. I had to promise not to reveal his identity or to write anything that may identify him. All quotes had to be double-checked.

"We just had limited experience and were too optimistic about a turnaround and that credit would always be available," he said.

"We did not foresee the crash any more than bank executives in the US or the UK did.

"We wanted to grow, the rating agencies said we were doing well, everyone wanted to lend us money and we wanted to go international. Everyone said we were doing the right thing."

Rhetorically he asked, "Were we inexperienced? Yes.

"Were mistakes made? Yes.

"Was there negligence? Yes.

"Was there a criminal intent? No."

"It is in some way understandable that the investigation centres on the banks and the executives, but of course it was a systemic crash," said the ex-banker.

"And remember, society will learn nothing if it's all turned into a question of individuals. Right now, everyone is showing a great level of hindsight."

"But back then, no one wanted us to stop."

IT WAS A CIRCUS

If you have had a pension plan for a while or live in a country that bailed out one of its banks, it may be that you were among those who lost money on the Icelandic banks. But most losers will never know.

On most questions related to the crisis and its impact, data do exist. The ultimate allocation of the losses, however, mostly remains a mystery. The easy answer is that 'the shareholders' and 'the creditors' lost, some of whom had bought bank bonds, and some who had provided loans to the banks.

The difficult part is to find the individuals who held the losses in the end.

Stakes in companies and banks in the form of share ownership are usually publicly known. Stock markets are closely regulated. Ownership information is made public by the companies or can be found in public registries. The winners and losers can be identified as the values of the companies shift.

When new equity is needed, the key stakeholders can usually be identified. They also often contribute by signing up for new shares, either voluntarily or under pressure.

If they do not, the company can issue new shares, diluting the stakes of the existing shareholders, who are left with the choice of injecting funds or becoming marginalized. A choice that is often brutal, sometimes unfair, but often very effective in supporting the survival of the company.

When a company or a country enters distress, the debt holdings matter the most, though. The creditors are the ones that matter when countries, companies and jobs really are at risk. The creditors' holdings appear in many shapes and forms, as company-to-company debt, debt certificates or bonds. For such instruments, information on ownership is harder to find. Few public registries exist.

The difference in the availability of information on equity and debt is one of many peculiarities of the financial markets.

Also, in the Icelandic bank restructuring, it was the debt holders who mattered most as the equity got wiped out already in the first weekend of October 2008.

Lots of the debt holders spoke German. Bayerische Landesbank was prominent. In late October 2009, it became the first German bank to ask for government support. To the surprise of many, in total the German banks received more dollars in bailout support than in any other ECB-member country, about €250 billion.

The French-Belgian bank Dexia, which was bailed out a bit later, listed losses on Lehman, the Icelandic banks and Washington Mutual among the causes of its plight.

An elegant lady introduced herself to me at Seðlabanki.

"I am the director of the Icelandic debt restructuring division," she said.

I was a bit puzzled that such a permanent position would exist in a German bank.

She clearly knew better.

"A US asset management fund had the largest pre-crisis exposure," said an interviewee. "More than $2 billion." Its name is still not public, though.

The May 2012 creditor lists show that one Icelandic pension fund had almost 7% of its assets in the bonds of the defaulted banks. Another almost 10%.

Even after many had sold out, the list from May 2012 included more than 190 pension, life insurance and health insurance funds. More than €1 billion altogether.

At one point, I reviewed a top 100 creditor list. Names from Germany, the UK, the US and Japan were prominent. Nordic names were notably absent, counting a mere two or three.

All had had access to the same data from the banks and the rating agencies.

But the Nordic banks and investors had seen how the three banks operated in the Nordic market, buying assets at prices way higher than offered by others.

They also saw the kind of growth rates, both in the Icelandic economy and for the banks, that are often associated with later busts. The Nordics decided to impose restrictions on their Icelandic exposure. Some say out of envy, others say out of experience.

Some people said the incumbent Nordic banks did not understand the new Viking model of banking. But, as always, there is reason for caution when there is talk about a new economy or a new paradigm. Most often, it ends in disaster.

As happened globally around the year 2000 when the internet started to take off, and the asset value of technology companies skyrocketed. Some claimed the world would never again see recessions and productivity crises.

Then it crashed.

And as happened in the 2006-2007 boom, when demand from China and other markets was expected to drive growth for decades.

Before it crashed.

Like in Iceland. And as in 2019, when many expect that we forever will have zero nominal interest rates.

The positions sold after the Icelandic default were picked up by other investors. Many of these had their home address in the US hedge fund capital of Boston. All very professional.

Funds carry the hedge fund label if they can also invest in assets other than common stock, regular bonds or real estate. Basically, the label covers funds that can make any sort of investment, governed only by their internal rules and investment strategies.

Like buying bonds in defaulted companies.

Some invest on behalf of pension funds. Yes, this might also include yours. Even if you are Icelandic. The guidelines of some Icelandic pension funds do allow for hedge fund investments.

The most active fund in late 2008, Baupost, mostly has endowments and charities as investors. Almost $1 billion comes from Yale University. Yale's lead investment executive sits on Baupost's advisory board.

At least 20 of the 50 largest US hedge funds were engaged in Iceland for some time, including Och-Ziff, BlackRock, Soros, Baupost, Davidson Kempner, York Capital, Canyon, Eton Park, Anchorage Capital, Centerbridge, Grantham Mayo Van Otterloo, Taconic, Marathon Asset Management, Third Point, Highfields, Paulson & Co., Angelo Gordon, Farallon Capital, King Street and Fortress Investment.

For a while, Baupost was the hedge fund with the greatest dollar amount of claims in Iceland, 3.7 billion. But that was hard to see. Baupost established a range of shell companies with Icelandic names: Thingvellir Fund, Thingvellir SARL, Gulfoss Partners, Geysir Advisors, Silfra and Grindavik Fund.

"We only came in after the crash," said the Baupost investment manager when we met in Boston. "I went on the Golden Circle tour to Thingvellir, Gullfoss and Geysir, and went diving at Silfra in the cracks between the tectonic plates of the two continents."

The water in Silfra is the clearest in the world. It has been filtered for 100 years as it passes through lava rock.

"It was not as if we were trying to hide or to go undercover," said the investment manager.

"I just preferred those names."

The leading debt investors were represented in the bodies providing input and guidance to the bankruptcy estates. Many investors, however, also wanted to trade the debt. They wanted the option to buy or sell, or maybe both, on a daily, weekly or monthly basis.

Therefore, they were not interested in any information or roles that would make them insiders and thus prevent them from trading debt. And many preferred secrecy to public prominence. They would not take governance roles.

Few would step forward and defend their positions. They could not and would not become spokespeople on behalf of the creditors.

Instead, the creditors engaged an army of lawyers, advisors and banking professionals. But the professional advisors had a hard time. The bonds were traded. Every month, a new group of owners arrived and changed the direction.

It was a circus, a circus with the most amazing ensemble of super-smart professionals.

In the years that followed, again and again, in the strangest places, I have come across fund analysts that know every detail about Icelandic bank debt. They have all served their time.

They observed the rulings on the prioritization of deposits and money market funds, on the illegal foreign currency loans, the 110% cap on mortgages, the household and corporate debt restructuring and the later de facto hand-over of Islandsbanki and Kaupthing to the state.

In sum, the creditors with the big losses left early and in silence. New creditors entered at bargain prices, with moderate ability and willingness to engage. There was never any real spokesperson to represent the interests of the widows, the elderly or the Pacific islands who had taken the big losses.

The feared hedge funds were not well positioned for the next battles.

THE ONES HAILED

Corporate restructuring is not a smooth process and fairness is often no determinant, here illustrated with the help of one of the then President Ólafur Ragnar Grímsson's success cases.

Bakkavör's origin was as an owner of companies producing ready-made foods.

But Bakkavör also turned itself into the largest owner of a holding company that owned a large part of Kaupthing. Bakkavör owned 45% of Exista, which in turn owned 22% in Kaupthing.

And who can be found in a leaked 205-page list of Kaupthing borrowers?

Yes, the two brothers owning Bakkavör, with €1.86 billion in loans. And Exista, with €791 million. The latter accompanied by a note: "The bulk of the loans are unsecured and with no covenants."

Basically, the loans to the owner had been given without collateral and restrictions.

The actions of the two brothers in Exista earned one of the brothers an eight-month prison sentence, imposed by the Icelandic Supreme Court.

He had received ISK 50 billion in shares in Exista, while only paying ISK 1 billion.

Exista later collapsed, as did Bakkavör. Kaupthing carried huge losses.

And who later got the opportunity to buy what was left of Bakkavör?

Yes, the two brothers.

Who set up a new company. With money coming from somewhere. They received the rights to 25% ownership. The company promised to pay about €600 million to the claimants. The latter included an Icelandic bank, the Kaupthing offspring Arion, and half a dozen Icelandic pension funds.

The new company also struggled, due to its vast debt burden. It had limited value, except for its ownership of the daughter companies, which also had debt. And the daughter companies had created what some may call poison pills. Someone had given their banks the right to request debt repayment if certain persons were no longer in charge of the companies.

The two brothers.

The brothers then teamed up with one of the first hedge funds to enter as a creditor in the Icelandic banks, which was also among the first to leave. With supposedly almost $1 billion in profits. Baupost Group, the one that Yale University has entrusted with almost $1 billion.

Arion and a range of Icelandic pension funds were bought out in January 2016 for £163 million. A new company, Bakk AL Holdings Ltd, now held 89% of Bakkavör.

And who were the two controlling shareholders in Bakk AL?

Yes, the two brothers.

Finally, Bakkavör was listed again in 2017. This time in London. Now with the brothers' position tripled in value.

With the two largest shareholders, the two brothers, now owning 25.1% each.

In many other cases, banks and other partners that committed new capital or wrote off debt required prior management and owners to be given positions in the restructured companies. In some cases, they required prior owners and managers to be released from the personal guarantees they had given, while providing them with ownership stakes and options.

As I heard all the stories while in Iceland, I often got upset. "If only media had known," I often thought. Many globally leading, respected branded goods companies had franchises in Iceland. Some of the franchisees had taken on vast debt, not all for such good reasons. Now some of the branded goods companies threatened to cancel the franchise contract unless the banks wrote off the claims. The man in the street had to struggle to repay the debt. Some others less so.

Which explains how old bank owners managed to turn millions in debt into millions, if not billions, in fortunes. While others suffered.

And the bank requesting the largest release of all was, naturally, Deutsche Bank. With the beneficiary being the largest pre-crisis owner of Landsbanki, who is now, thanks to Deutsche, relieved of massive debt and personal guarantees to repay that debt. And who was rewarded with options and incentives. Who is also now, once again, the richest of all Icelanders.

Only two other Icelanders join him on *The Sunday Times*' 2018 list of the 200 richest persons in Britain.

Naturally, the two brothers.

YES, ICELAND CAN GROW

The opening scene of the global financial crisis movie, *Inside Job*, was shot in Reykjavik. The director chose empty offices in a new office tower, Höfðatorg Tower, as the location.

The tower lies next to the historic Höfði house. Here, the first radio communication between Iceland and the outside world was established, with a transmission to the UK. Here, Ronald Reagan and Mikhail Gorbachev met in 1986 to negotiate the Intermediate-Range Nuclear Forces Treaty to end the Cold War. Next door is the stylish headquarters of the old Kaupthing bank.

In November 2012, Iceland was still stuck in a cold war with the UK, Kaupthing had become Arion, and the top floor of the tower was still idle.

It seemed to be the perfect spot to present the McKinsey pro-bono report "Charting a Growth Path for Iceland", which I helped to write.

The report warned that Iceland risked remaining trapped in a vicious cycle of sustained capital controls, high capital cost, low investment and low economic growth.

"A necessary first step in breaking the vicious cycle is to agree on a credible agenda for real economic growth," it said.

The report found that Iceland's high per capita GDP is largely due to high labour force participation and long working hours. This masks a productivity problem in most sectors. Two stand out especially: the low productivity of labour in the domestic service sector and of capital in the energy sector.

The domestic service sector contributed 65% of GDP and employed 70% of the workforce, said the report. Hence, productivity gains here will allow for moving labour to more productive jobs.

Next, Iceland's natural resource sectors need to capture more value from their resource base.

Furthermore, the report stated, the international sector should be strengthened through renewal, increased availability of 'smart' risk capital, and by creating a globally competitive business environment.

Growth in this sector on the back of efficiency gains in the domestic service sector is key to strengthening Iceland's external balance, it continued.

The fishing industry, said the report, has both high labour and capital productivity. The productivity follows from sound regulation and exposure to competition. However, limited wild catch resources cap growth.

Value growth is still possible, by further improving the brand value of Icelandic seafood products and through fish farming. Later analysis shows a first aquaculture potential of 70,000 tonnes per year, while protecting the wild salmon rivers. Relative to the population, this exceeds Norway, where farmed fish is the second-largest export after oil and gas.

The Icelandic power industry has enabled large export-based heavy industries. The report notes that 25-30% of Iceland's capital stock is directly or indirectly invested in the energy sector. Furthermore, plans for developments and projects show a potential for growth, again when combined with environmental considerations.

Even in the period up to 2012, tourism grew substantially. Back then, the tourism industry accounted for 5% of the workforce and almost 20% of exports.

"It plays an important short- to medium-term role in maintaining employment and strengthening the trade balance," the report said.

"However, with its relatively low labour and capital productivity, stakeholders should focus on driving value as well as volume, for example by increasing capital investment, managing seasonality and targeting more high-revenue visitors."

"We also underline the importance of Icelandic stakeholders coming to an agreement on the nation's growth potential and ambitions, a strategy to realize them, and an economic policy to enable them," stated the report.

Some good news here. Since the report was presented, the uppermost floors in the tower have been filled. The top floor houses hotel suites, a testament to the growth in tourism. The next houses a law firm.

Two of the post-crisis growth industries in Iceland.

And, yes, Reykjavik and Iceland are unique. In the midst of the struggle in June 2009, a team from *60 Minutes*, a top news programme from US broadcaster CBS, came to Iceland. I was interviewed in my governor's office early on the Friday morning. I described the challenges, the pain and the struggle. I explained our plan and our aspirations.

After the long week and the long Friday, colleagues and I went for a dinner in the picturesque narrow main street in old Reykjavik, Laugavegur. As probably the only main street of any capital with this name, it means 'the wash road'. It used to be, and still is, the main route to the hot springs in Laugardalur. Here, in olden times, the women of Reykjavík took their laundry. It is also the name of one of the marvellous trekking routes in Iceland, a 34-mile route from the hot springs of Landmannalaugar, 63°59'28"N 19°03'37"W, to the glacial valley of Þórsmörk.

As we completed our dinner, we entered the street. It was packed with people. It was right after midnight. The sun was shining. The heavens were clear and light blue.

Lit by the midnight sun.

The CBS crew turned up. They were out filming. They recognized the governor. They asked for an after-midnight interview. Not the perfect spot and time for an interview, I thought, and rejected their request.

"Never, ever would we have seen Federal Governor Bob Bernanke strolling along a main street full of party goers, after midnight, under a shining sun," the lead journalist commented.

And she continued, "Reykjavik, even in crisis, surely beats New York."

YOU ARE LONG IN THE WRONG CURRENCY, MY FRIEND

The estates of the three fallen banks had three main categories of assets.

One was the international loan portfolio. The banks had outgrown Iceland and two thirds of their loans were to companies headquartered outside the country.

"There was almost no country where no loans had been given," says a creditor committee member. "Even to vineyards in Macedonia."

Hence, there was significant value that could be recovered. And, as the process dragged on, some positions became more valuable as the international markets recovered. These positions were mostly in FX.

The next category of assets was the estates' ownership of parts of the 'new' domestic banks, i.e. the estates' shares in Arion and Islandsbanki.

Here, the accounting value grew as the Icelandic economy started to recover, exceeding the initial very conservative estimates. The new banks counted as ISK assets. Their main earnings were in ISK. However, if owned by foreign creditors or sold to new foreign owners, these owners would most probably want their dividend converted into FX. In sum, the foreign ownership of the banks now became a risk to the ISK.

Haf and Holt, which BCL offered to Seðlabanki, explains the third category.

These were structures carved out pre-crisis from Glitnir and first offered to BCL as collateral. For some reason, Haf and Holt had been registered in Ireland. They had, therefore, been placed in the old bank as 'foreign' assets. It was gradually revealed, though, that they largely included loans to Icelandic companies.

It wasn't the only one. Loans had been placed in the old banks as they were thought to be international, but in many cases, the actual counterparties turned out to be Icelandic. In some cases, the international borrower was just a 'shell company'. When the banks collapsed, the real debtor turned out to be an Icelandic entity. Here, FX would be needed for debt service, both for the ISK and FX positions.

As an increasing part of the portfolio was monetized, the pile of cash and rights grew. In sum, this all added up to a mountain of FX and, to the surprise of many, also of ISK.

The latter grew to a point where the authorities began to see an unregulated outflow as a threat to the stability of the ISK and the economy. On top of the glacier bond positions.

"At first, there was limited movement on how to unwind the capital controls," says a decision maker at that time.

"A committee to establish a strategy was created in 2010. A first estimate showed an 'overhang' of ISK 150 billion. The IMF established a dialogue with several companies and accessed the best set of data."

However, at that time the IMF did not include the positions of the old banks. In the official statistics, there was a line that showed Icelandic currency, excluding the estates. This was what the authorities focused on. They simply believed the old estates held only FX, and hence posed no worry for the Icelandic economy.

"The next report came in March 2011. Now the all-inclusive ISK figure had reached 460 billion. It became clear that the bank estates, which were supposed to be non-Icelandic, held vast ISK positions."

Again, there were fears of an ISK collapse. A new crisis. What if impatient claimants were to sell all their ISK, take the ISK-value of the banks and turn it all to FX? And all run for the door at the same time?

The authorities were of the view that the shallow FX market would not be able to cope with such an outflow of ISK.

In March 2012, the Icelandic Parliament terminated the bank estates' exemption from the capital controls. Previously they had been able to exchange ISK for FX.

Not with the new law.

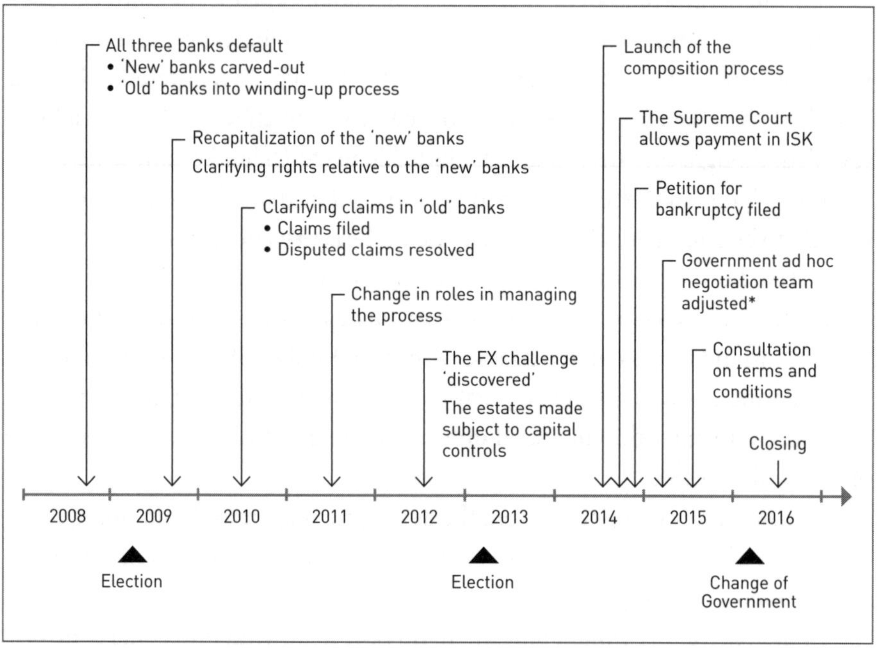

Timeline for the bank winding-up process.

* Final team established with Glenn V. Kim, Chairman; Benedikt Gíslason, Deputy Chairman; Sigurður Hannesson, Deputy Chairman; Ásgeir Reykfjörð Gylfason; Jón Þ.Sigurgeirsson; with the team in the early stages also including Eiríkur S. Svavarsson, Ingibjörg Guðbjartsdóttir and Freyr Hermannsson.

A legislative change was proposed to plug holes in the act governing the capital controls. Late in the evening, word spread that this would also include a lock-in of the old banks.

An army of lawyers invaded the parliament.

"I got a message," says a lead on the creditor side.

"Something is going on."

"All the winding-up boards had been called to Althing after markets closed. I got 99 emails asking what was going on."

The law was passed against the vote of the largest party and with another party abstaining.

"We had been promised a loosening of controls, not an out-of-context tightening," says the leader of the largest party.

"All the hedge funds were screaming," says the creditor representative.

"We must sue," he says of the creditors' first response.

The creditors' money was now placed on the 'wrong' side of the wall. And, worth noting, it could not be converted back to foreign currency and released to the creditors. The money was locked into ISK.

"We met the Central Bank Governor, Már Guðmundsson. It was important. Then we had something to report back. Things settled down," says Barry Russell, the creditors' spokesman.

While it was imprisoned in Iceland, the money filled up the new Icelandic banks in the form of deposits. Or, as stated by the IMF: "Funding is dominated by deposits with nowhere else to go, resulting in a rich margin."

Normally, one would expect a country in restructuring to be short of funds. In this case, the new banks were full, and they were running equity ratios triple the normal level.

"Our goals on economic development had been surpassed by 2012," now says Bjarni Benediktsson, the Minister of Finance of some later years. The question arose as to who should benefit from the upside.

"It was only fair that some would go to the creditors. In 2012, we saw a risk to the balance of payments, though," says Bjarni.

"The values were unknown at first. Then they got bigger. They grew and grew."

"With this, we thought, we will never be able to lift the controls."

BURNING THE CARRY

Hedge funds typically manage some of their administrators' money, but mainly they manage the money of others.

That money may belong to pension funds, companies, endowments, countries or wealthy individuals. The fund managers typically charge a fixed management fee. The largest part of their earnings, however, comes from what is called 'the carry'.

A fund manager may, as an example, get a fifth of the increase of the value of the invested funds that exceeds 8% per year.

Hence, the time to realization matters.

Most of the value of the bank estates was in foreign currency that was held in the international portfolios of the bank. Especially in Kaupthing. That was the part most funds were chasing.

"We just wanted to strike a deal and get the money," says one of the largest fund investors.

"It really got quite nasty," says a representative for the creditors. "It was quite aggressive. Yes, there was a lot of frustration."

"There were only two options: go completely hostile or work the process," says Barry Russell, the lead on the creditor side.

On 24 October 2012 an outline for a solution was finally filed.

Barry recalls: "When at lunch at Hotel Holt, we got hold of a newspaper. It had seven pages of coverage. While we had worked to find a solution, someone else had suggested that the estate should be split up and handed out to all the creditors in ISK. With the capital controls still in place.

"If so, we would be locked in indefinitely."

"Some Icelandic politicians just picked a fight that was not there," says a person working for the funds.

"Iceland would have benefited from a quicker solution."

As time passed, Iceland suffered from the capital controls and lack of clarity, while the fund administrators saw their carry burned.

"The largest danger we saw was the lack of engagement," says the person working for the funds. "The problem was not the deal that was concluded in the end, but the two and a half years of nonsense that preceded it, from October 2012 to March 2015.

"We could have struck a deal in 2012."

"The Icelandic state gained a larger share of the pie, but the pie didn't grow as it otherwise could have done."

But, on this, the Icelanders involved disagree. Time was needed to get the numbers right, to agree on the Icelandic position, to build leverage and to negotiate.

"We met with the trade finance committee," recalls a creditor. "We met some hostile politicians. One made a big fuss about the fabric of my new suit."

"He had a beautiful suit on," the representative had said.

That was his only comment. With that, apparently, all had been said.

"But on our side, there was huge reluctance toward creating distortions or destabilizing the situation," says a creditor representative.

He asks rhetorically, "Why?"

"It could have lowered the bonds' trading value."

THE GREEK TRAGEDY

"Money doesn't solve a deficit problem. Money buys time. If nothing is done, you are worse off. You can only solve a flow problem with a flow solution. A deficit doesn't disappear by taking on more debt. If you have excessive debt, you need to move. Ideally when times are good."
– Murilo Portugal, formerly of the IMF

Spending money a country or a state doesn't have can actually drive growth. For a while. But thereafter, one both has to adjust and repay.

Iceland's EEA/EU entry gave Icelandic banks access to vast amounts of money, which then partly was passed on to Icelanders. The euro inclusion opened similar opportunities for the previously restrained southern European governments. But here the private sector and the banks were less creditworthy. The state became the transfer mechanism. A fateful nuance.

Public spending in Greece escalated by almost 90% from 2004 to 2009, three times the increase in tax revenue.

The public deficit worsened, to 10% of GDP in 2008 and 15% in 2009. The public debt-to-GDP ratio rose from 109% in 2008 to 146% in 2010, with 200% in sight.

The current account deficit rose from below 5% of GDP in 1999 to a peak of about 15% in 2008 and 2009. Conspicuously like the fiscal deficit. No wonder. Both were financed by the same state borrowing. From abroad.

Overspending had become a driver of growth. Cost levels were excessive. Salaries rose. A pile of debt was the result.

After the global financial crisis, consumer and investment demand softened, access to new loans tightened and interest rates on the state debt rose. Reports of fiscal mismanagement and deception added to the interest expense. Leading brains in banks like Goldman Sachs had helped the Greek government come up with innovative structures to hide its debt.

"Remember only one thing," says Murilo Portugal from the IMF, then also overseeing Greece. "If you see a problem, never wait to resolve it.

"The Greek Minister of Finance under George Papandreu, Giorgos Papakonstantinou, called me in late 2009," he says. "On that day, the Greek interest rate was 500 basis points above the reference rate.

"Then five months passed by.

"When he called next, the spread was 1,300. It was a Thursday."

"We need money by Monday," Papakonstantinou told Murilo.

As a euro-state, Greece could not wipe out its high costs through a currency depreciation. What's more, in Greece, the state was the holder of the foreign debt. Private-sector restructuring, like the kind carried out in Iceland, was thus also not an option.

In Iceland, the debt had been 'private to private'. Private banks were lending to private banks. In Greece it was 'private to public'. European banks and others had provided loans to the Greek government. The government had thereafter spread the money out in Greece through public spending, insufficient taxation and government lending.

"Originally, private-sector lenders dominated the lending to Greece, foreign and domestic," says a then advisor. "While the ECB provided liquidity to the banks."

"Then many creditors sold out their loans, some at around 70 cents to a dollar of the original bond value."

"Tragically, Greek banks, pension funds and insurance companies bought."

They took the debt home.

"The crisis wasn't their fault. The banks were largely run as banks should be run," says an advisor to the Greek banks. "But they were dependent on the state. Now they saw a chance to support the government, a government they relied on. And to make some money. By stepping in to buy the state debt."

"The ECB tempted them by indicating that it would allow them to post the loans as collateral."

But that wasn't the way things turned out. Instead, they were confronted with the risk of a default of the Greek state, squeezed to write down the debt to about 50%.

Next, some familiar hedge funds stepped in and bought up some of that discounted government debt. Some of the funds refused to negotiate on repayment. They wanted full value and became known as the 'Holdout Creditors'. They threatened to sue. The ones that fought the longest indeed got 100% in a May 2012 settlement.

So it was that funds that had snapped up distressed Greek debt at steep discounts would now be paid in full. By Greek taxpayers.

Three funds were well known from Iceland. Marathon Asset Management, Och-Ziff and York Capital, part-owned by Swiss banking giant Credit Suisse, were among those who collectively might have built up sufficiently large positions to scupper the bailout deal, Reuters noted.

While active in Greece and Iceland, Och-Ziff Capital Management Group, OZ, later rebranded to Sculptor Asset Management, was also active in Africa. In September 2016, OZ agreed to pay $412 million to the US Department of Justice after the US government said OZ executives had paid more than $100 million in bribes to government officials in five African countries in return for natural resources investment opportunities.

In Greece, law firms known from Iceland, Bingham McCutchen and Brown Rudnick, supposedly campaigned for investor support to litigate and not to settle.

Possibly all were proud of forcing Greece to pay.

"And the ECB got difficult," recalls the advisor to the Greek banks. "What's more, even the 50% giant write-down didn't solve the problems of the Greek state."

In Greece, a range of EU and public institutions bought the debt at about 50% of face value.

The Greek debt was then 'public to public', turning everything into politics.

"In Iceland, the banks fell on the state. In Greece, the state fell on the banks," says Jón Sigurgeirsson.

In 2015, he got a call from the then Greek Minister of Finance, Yanis Varoufakis. Jón was asked to take a seat on the board of the Hellenic Financial Stability Fund, a position he retained as Euclid Tsakalotos became Minister of Finance. Now experiences of bank restructuring, value recovery and on battling the hedge funds could be taken to Greece.

"We looked for a measure like the Icelandic capital controls," says an IMF specialist. "Both in Greece and Cyprus. But with a common currency, such an option wouldn't have worked."

"Instead, restrictions with similar effects, limits on withdrawal of deposits, were pushed forward."

Cyprus implemented restrictions and a 'bail-in' system. In a 'bailout', the taxpayers carry the burden. In a 'bail-in', the creditors, and in Cyprus even the depositors, had to pay up. Suddenly, the EU had lost its passion for depositors. Who in Cyprus were largely Russian. The arrangement was dubbed by some a 'stability tax', a term later brought back to Iceland.

Cyprus also entered a programme of the troika, consisting of the EU, the ECB and the IMF in 2013. Cyprus could exit again as early as 2016. The draconian approach worked.

Soon after the crisis had hit Cyprus, the Cypriot Central Bank Governor visited Iceland. Now an Icelander returned the question to the friendly Cypriot; "How could you let this happen?"

The positive Cypriot burst out in laughter; "You never know your fate".

THE FINAL SHOWDOWN

In the European football championship in 2016, Iceland was up against England in the round of 16. The team was cheered by the entire nation. Despite meeting a mighty football nation, the homeland of football, the Icelanders were not inclined to give in. That's just not an Icelandic trait. And, yes, they won two to one.

Now, in the final showdown of the financial crisis, one side of the pitch was to feature 20 of the 50 largest US hedge funds. Some trained in Greece. The other side was to feature an ad hoc team made up of employees from Seðlabanki, from some ministries, a retired IMF director and some converted bankers.

In between were the IMF and the rating agencies, acting in mixed roles of observers and referees.

The Icelandic financial crisis wasn't just one crisis, but a string of crises. First the mini-crisis in 2006, the complete collapse in 2008, then the political battles in 2009, the years of fights over Icesave, household and corporate debt struggles, and court cases that with adverse rulings could have rocked the country and its banks all over again.

From 2012 onward, Seðlabanki and Icelandic policymakers saw yet another looming crisis.

They discovered that a mountain of ISK had ended up in the possession of foreigners. Unless the right measures were found, this ISK could at some point be converted into FX, once again knocking the still shaky Icelandic currency flat and again escalating household and corporate debt. And, worse, since Icelandic households, pension funds and companies themselves could also see such risks and had been locked out from investing abroad, even they might be inclined to join the stampede.

"We had our crisis in 2008 and 2009," says a former member of parliament. "We could not afford another crisis."

A mechanism was needed whereby a predictable conversion of ISK to FX could be ensured. And the sheer amount of ISK had to be reduced, to the point where an outflow would not cause problems.

Some wanted more than just the resolution to the ISK problem. Some on the government side also held the view that Iceland should be compensated for the cost of the crisis. The creditors, the bankers and the hedge funds should pay, they said.

The creditors, through the estates, didn't just sit on a pile of ISK. They had an even larger stash of FX, as the estates had turned their foreign loan books into hard cash.

Remember the rubble left behind?

Some felt the government should take the FX through taxation or other means to help pay the cost of debt relief for households, companies and the government.

"There were very different views in the state's first ad hoc group," says a person involved. The group had been formed to work on the issue.

Some wanted to chase the FX of the estates, not only solve the ISK challenge. Others considered such a position suicidal and fraught with legal risks. They feared a fight with claimants in 36 jurisdictions.

"We wanted a large tax on the estates," says a person active in InDefence, the grass-roots movement. "Imagine if an oil company had drilled outside Iceland and caused an oil spill. There is no way they would have been allowed to repay creditors and pay investors before they had paid for the damages. Especially if crimes had been committed.

"Why should banks be treated differently?"

"In 2012 and 2013, progress was limited," says a creditor. "The negotiations had stalled. The 2013 election left a gridlock. The authorities threatened to introduce a bank tax. We threatened to sue.

"Some creditors really dug into the trenches.

"Litigation could have taken three to five years. Bad for us. Bad for Iceland."

The prime minister from 2013, Prime Minister Sigmundur Davið, took a hardliner position. "He really favoured taxing the banks," says a state negotiator.

"I was made to read *Independent People* by Halldór Laxness," says Barry Russell, the lead creditor negotiator. "The main character never gives in. He rather sacrifices it all." A reflection of the Icelandic mentality, some will say.

On debt, the book from 1934 reads: "True, it had been quite usual in the old days for people to owe the merchant money and to be refused credit when the debt had grown too big. It had likewise been nothing uncommon for people thus denied sustenance to die of starvation, but such a fate, surely, was infinitely preferable to being ensnared by the banks, like people are nowadays, for at least they had lived like independent men, at least they had died of hunger like free people."

"In 2015, there was an opening," says a person on the government side.

"Some creditors wanted to leave. They realized that an agreement was needed. In 2015, they approached the authorities and said they were ready to negotiate."

"Something had to change. We needed a dialogue," says a creditor. "We could maybe get three to five bondholders engaged and get something done. Then we could cut a deal."

"Lee was now engaged by the government." says the creditor lead. "He now called and said a process could be launched."

THE DEBT NEGOTIATOR

"If I add it all up, I have worked on debt in well over 20 countries," says Lee Buchheit.

And, yes, his resume shows one-off, one-year work stints in Guyana, Peru, Panama, the Dominican Republic and Jamaica and three one-year efforts in Belize.

He worked for two years on Guatemala, Uruguay and with Kuwait after the first Gulf War. In Argentina he is still active.

He had three-year efforts in Mexico, Russia and Liberia.

The Nigeria effort lasted seven years, while Greece has kept him busy since 2011. And it still does. With the largest debt write-down in recorded history.

Four efforts exceeded ten years: in the Philippines, Ecuador, Tanzania and war-torn Iraq. Ever since the second Gulf War. Still listed as ongoing.

"Did any of these 20 other situations resemble Iceland?" I asked Lee.

First, he stressed, all the other situations were sovereign restructurings, which Iceland never was. One thing, though, is similar, he said. In some cases, creditors walked away with 10% of the face value and were happy. When they had bought at 5%.

He recites a French saying: "Sometimes one must accept an outcome for want of better and for fear of worse."

In Iceland, Lee had three appearances. First with Icesave in 2009, then in the ISK negotiations with the creditors, and last in the offshore króna negotiations in 2016.

"For me, it all started in Latin America in 1982," Lee says. "Most of the borrowing was in interest rates linked to US interest rates. Then the US raised its rates to solve a US problem. Inflation. Then many ended in distress. Similar situations hadn't really existed since the 1930s. There was no defined law. It was uncharted territory.

"A great first job.

"The debt culture varies. In Asia it is a disgrace and a sign of dishonesty if debts are not serviced. In some other countries, debt restructuring negotiations are as popular as soccer."

"The debt crisis of Latin America paid for the education of my children and two houses," says another negotiator.

"Earlier, the creditors used to be a small group of like-minded banks. It could take years to forget a write-off. It would blight your future," Lee says.

"Today, for some it takes a few hours to forget."

"In some cases, the new providers of funds are the ones most eager to push write-downs. Some lenders take the sword of the lord against old creditors."

And, the creditors are different; "It is much easier to put pressure on the commercial banks. The hedge funds are less susceptible to pressure."

In Iceland, a process started between the state and the creditor representatives. The state team was structured as an ad hoc group.The discussions went on and on and on. No solution was found and progress was limited.

A potential 39% tax on the equity of all banks was brought into play in case no orderly resolution could be found. A 'stability tax', a phrase inspired by the EU scheme in Cyprus.

Often taxes aren't popular, but few would question a country's right to impose them. Now Iceland got the upper hand. The threat of such a punitive tax provided a strong incentive to reach a deal. And, with the creditors hearing the protests in Reykjavik and the calls demanding that the creditors should pay, it was a credible threat.

And yes, the estates of the banks were registered as banks.

"Most understood the ISK challenge. Iceland had a legitimate concern about what would happen if all the ISK was converted to FX," Lee says. "But some on the government side wanted more."

"The ISK concern was legitimate," says a creditor representative. "Taking the FX wasn't. Any attempt on that could have stopped it all and caused litigation."

The funds in international accounts could have been blocked. The estates had recovered money in many countries. A lot was in legal units or accounts outside Iceland. A lot was at stake.

"There were some heated moments," Lee says.

A bit of mediation was needed.

"It was contentious. I had to use an illustration," he continues. "What if Barack Obama had wanted to send an airplane full of gold bullion to Ukraine during the crisis and it had been forced to land in Iceland because of an Icelandic volcanic eruption?

"To whom would it have belonged?"

Eventually, the ad hoc team, in agreement with the IMF, concluded that the ISK issue was the challenge to solve.

"So, you want to keep all the króna?" Lee had asked the ad hoc team in a discussion.

The team members nodded.

"Are you saying every ISK retained by the creditors is a lethal threat?" Lee asked sceptically.

"Yes," an Icelander replied.

"If so, let's try to make it happen," Lee concluded.

On a chilly, rainy New York day I headed off to meet his counterparties, the fund managers.

"We look for money displaced by events," says one manager who entered late and became one of the largest holders of defaulted Icelandic bank debt. "Call it transition capital. The old owners wanted to get out.

"We were there. It just helps to have a buyer. Like us.

"Imagine if we had been there in 2008 and 2009. By converting capital to equity and by injecting new funds, all the turmoil and the pain of the crisis could have been avoided. Really, very little value was created from 2009 to 2015.

"It is always a balance. In Argentina, the creditors pushed too hard.

"Iceland came within a hair's breadth of pushing too hard," says the fund manager.

A DEAD PERSON CAN'T SIGN

"Lee Buchheit told a story," says a person involved. "The story of farmer Joe and farmer Bob. It's a good analogy."

Joe and Bob lived next to each other on the plain. Farmer Bob had borrowed $10,000 from Joe. They were good friends. Bob got increasingly worried as the repayment day got closer. Bob had always honoured his debt and saw it as a moral obligation. But this time, he simply could not make the payment.

The night before the loan was due, Bob couldn't sleep. Hour after hour, he tossed back and forth in his bed.

Suddenly Bob's wife jumped out of bed, tore open the window and shouted toward Joe's house, "Farmer Joe, Bob owes you $10,000 and would like to pay. But he can't."

"Why did you do that?" Bob asked his wife.

"Well, now you can sleep while he can't," his wife answered.

She had just made the debt someone else's problem.

"Things were going nowhere," says Glenn Kim, one of the later heads of the Steering Committee on the Liberalization of Capital Controls. "The overhang could be removed through auctions, but that would take forever.

"Every day was one day less. The government wanted a solution. The creditors wanted a solution. Many were getting angry.

"There had to be a better way."

The challenge was to develop a plan that could actually be executed. To do so, it was necessary to understand the motivation of each party. The FX challenge had to be resolved. Litigation was to be avoided.

"The estates had claims in 36 countries, and the estates could be sued in all of them," says Glenn.

"If the Icelandic authorities went too far, they would be sued. In every meeting, the creditor spokesman brought a litigation lawyer. That was their 'Plan B'. That would have been ugly."

"Yes, the litigation lawyer was always there," confirms Barry Russell, the creditor lead. The litigator, Mark Dawkins, led a separate team that would move in if the discussions failed. His aim would then be to freeze the vast offshore assets of the banks and use the funds to repay the creditors.

But there were also large positions in Iceland.

"No one would recommend that foreign creditors take a case, the first of its kind, to a court in Iceland and risk a wave of rage," says a claimant.

"The creditors would say no, but not absolutely no," says Kim. "In the West, we believe a successful negotiation is completed when both parties shake hands and smile. In Korea, it is considered successful if both parties shake hands and cry."

Kim then turns to Iceland: "Time was the stick. A dead person can't sign.

"And, luckily after all, the funds holding the claims were economic organisms. They would not be rewarded for triggering a multi-year litigation process."

"Remember, the Icelanders are experts in not giving in. That's how the cod wars were won," says a political analyst. "They just kept their position, year after year. At some point, the other parties want to move on with their lives."

"The Minister of Finance, Bjarni Benediktsson, was clear," recalls the head negotiator. "'I will deal with this process,' Bjarni said."

The lead negotiator continues, "We needed to understand the drivers of the parties in each of the three estates. Typically, only four or five players were in the lead in each. They differed. Some were all in and needed a solution as soon as possible. Some were more patient. Some would only get paid the day all was paid out in FX.

"We had to understand how the funds calculated their returns, how they were paid by investors and how the fund managers were paid themselves."

"It was clear that the team from the government was well prepared," notes a hedge fund manager. "We were about to play a game of poker. They had worked to see our cards.

"They knew at what price we had bought and what we would consider a satisfactory outcome."

To prepare the negotiations, Lilja Alfreðsdóttir, Ingibjörg Guðbjartsdóttir, who headed the Currency Control unit, and Jón Sigurgeirsson went off to build alliances. First with the IMF technical expert. Then with the IMF legal department. Then, having received their thumbs-up, the three went to the rating agencies. Which were told that they surely could call the IMF.

"No big surprise. When the claimants received our proposal, they called the IMF and the rating agencies to complain," says Jón. "But all of them had been briefed."

"It was admirable how thorough a plan had been prepared to unwind the currency controls," says the IMF specialist.

THE GREY CAT

The Grey Cat, Grái Kötturinn, is a coffeeshop in downtown Reykjavik.

The Cat is a half-stair down, in the basement. Through the window, you see the boots of folks outside, passing by. The walls are covered with bookshelves, full of used books for guests to read. The tables and benches were likely modern when they were bought after the mackerel boom of the early 1960s. But the coffee is good and there is no sense of being hurried. A perfect place for me to meet with one of the state's negotiators to understand how it was all played out.

"We created the impression we could wait forever. And then we put the claimants under pressure by announcing a 39% tax on the holdings of the estates in half a year if no solution was found," says the negotiator.

"The preferred solution was a consensual solution, a Composition Agreement."

A Composition Agreement settles disputes between creditors and defines how funds are to be allocated. However, in Iceland, it became something more. It became the term for the solution to the ISK challenge.

"It was always going to be an extremely difficult transaction, but to have to do it and get everything approved by the courts in such a short period beggared belief," said the Kaupthing estate's lawyer, Rob Bennett.

"It wasn't a question of whether we could do it; we simply had to do it. For creditors to lose 39% before you even got to a recovery was a horrific prospect."

Especially because the new domestic banks would also have to pay the tax. The new banks that now were owned by the old banks.

"I have a carrot-and-stick approach," said an advisor to the state negotiating team at its first meeting.

"I take the carrot and I stick it up the a*# of the counterparties."

Did Iceland take half of the largest US hedge funds hostage? Yes, to some extent. It simply helps to have legislative power. And time.

But, the negotiators said, and IMF largely agreed, that the ISK could have crashed, again, if the ISK overhang wasn't neutralized.

If no agreement could be found, the estates would drift along and maybe one day go bankrupt. One local brought a claim and went to district court and filed for bankruptcy of the bank estates. If he won, the estate would be dissolved, and all value paid out to the creditors. In ISK, he hoped, in accordance with Icelandic bankruptcy laws. Subject to capital controls. But the creditors found another solution. They paid the local in full. Hence, now he had no claim. He had made a political point. And some money. Now he could buy some more claims.

But, in the end, the claimants could also always have argued for an extension. And they could have questioned the conversion of the claims to ISK, a view the Icelandic Supreme Court supported in a verdict. And the creditors could sue.

"Some in the state team preferred bankruptcy," says the advisor to the state. A conflict rose in the state ad hoc team, a controversy that is still alive, even now, many years later.

"Yes, I wanted to keep the option on the table," says the one who wanted to go the furthest. "We could have managed it. And, having it as a threat anyway gave us leverage."

Others disagree vehemently. "Any government intervention could have triggered a liability," says another member of the team. "The liability risk would have been massive if we had intervened in the court processes."

"In short, how do you get the most leverage and obtain your objectives while not getting exposed?" was the question to consider. The capital controls provided leverage. As did the possible tax. As did the unknowns posed by legislative changes that were needed to ease the process of handing out the funds to the creditors. While the rise in values due to the global boom helped.

"Without that, we might still have been fighting," says a fund manager.

"I was the first to join the task force," says Benedikt Gislason. "First, we calculated the net debt position of Iceland. We also calculated the ISKs in the estates that might leave Iceland if the capital controls were to be lifted."

The ambition, tactics and messages were prepared. The tax was the stick. An exit was the carrot. A deadline was the enforcer.

"We decided to start with the most fundamental position, namely neutralizing all ISK to FX outflows.

"Next was the tactics. We established rules hindering the estates from teaming up against the Republic. All had to sign confidentiality agreements. We got the five largest claimants in each bank to the table.

"We learned that the banks were different. Landsbanki had funds that in a consensual solution could be converted to FX and an upside from continued unwinding efforts. Kaupthing claimants saw the most value in foreign assets with further upside that could be accessed if an agreement was reached. They saw less value in Arion. Glitnir placed a lot of value on Islandsbanki and had limited further upside. Almost everything had already been monetized. Here, every ISK given would be a net loss."

"Glitnir was the problem," says a creditor representative. "The asset value would not match the bond values without including a part of Islandsbanki."

"Many had viewed the three banks as similar, but by now they were very different," says Lee Buchheit. "There was a curious asymmetry of positions. Some creditors had bought in at 2% of the original bond value, some at 20%. Some were ready to stay, some really wanted to get out."

"Some claimants sat in only one, some in many estates. Solus and Silverpoint in Glitnir, Davidson Kempner in Landsbanki. Taconic, Abrams and York in Kaupthing," says one.

"The base was laid to divide and conquer. Even to the possible disproportionate benefit of some."

"We first pushed for a conclusion with Kaupthing," says a member of the state ad hoc team. "They would gain most from an agreement, giving up their ISK while gaining a right to take the FX, as Kaupthing had the largest FX funds."

Glitnir was more of a challenge.

"Glitnir started by offering ISK 70 billion to the Republic. They then increased to 90, where they stayed for 90 days. Last, they offered ISK 230 billion, 30 hours before the deadline."

In return, Glitnir would get free access to the FX. And it would avoid the threatened tax.

"We negotiated all night, and by early morning Islandsbanki was gone," says a negotiator on the creditor side.

"The claimants threatened that even more aggressive funds would enter the negotiations, but we had phone access to the other funds even when they were out heli-skiing," says one from the state team. "The claimants were the competitors of the skiers. The skiers did not want the claimants to gain on their relative performance while they were out skiing."

"One fund famous for being among the most aggressive, Elliott, stayed away," says another. "They specialize in chasing governments and forcing them to pay, especially by using courts in the US. Iceland, however, never had a sovereign debt default and any conflict might have ended up in a Reykjavik court."

"The trick was to create incentives that did not go against the interests of the nation," says a member of the state's team.

"Actually, we were the ones in a hurry. The strength of the economy was undermining our arguments. The upside for the creditors was about to be taken out as the ISK gained value. We needed them to have an upside post-settlement."

The solution was announced late in the evening. The result would be a surprise for many. It had to be announced when no one was trading debt. The press officer set the alarm for 3am and pressed send at 4am.

The press conference was at 1pm. When the conference started, the chair did not know whether only two agreements, with Landsbanki and Kaupthing, had been signed or all three.

The Glitnir letter was signed at 1.02pm.

A member of the state team then gave a sign. With three fingers.

Some might say the balance of negotiating power had been a bit skewed. The state had patience and considered a firm solution critical. It had the authority to impose a tax on the other party. And it could decide if and when to terminate the prohibition against exchanging ISK into FX.

The creditors had no public spokesman and hardly even tried to build sympathy for their case. Many were impatient and some had already earned attractive returns, as they had bought the debt at a steep discount. Now they wanted a fast payout. They had no appetite for court cases.

"We had to take it on ourselves to get involved. We decided to restrict ourselves, to stop buying and selling bonds, and instead engage," says one of the hedge fund managers.

"Why did I, as an ex-banker, decide to work on the government side?" asks a member of the state team.

"As Icelanders, we again saw how bad it could get. We had to be on the right side. As a professional challenge it was rewarding.

"And yes, there was a bit of a feeling of guilt."

"In the end, we did agree on the concern of the authorities regarding the foreign currency balance," says a leading creditor. "They had a legitimate concern. After weeks and weeks of negotiations, a settlement was reached."

"In the end, it is a transaction we feel proud of. Without it, Iceland would have been stuck in a multi-year litigation," says a fund manager. "And commercially it worked out fine."

"What was best was that there were no outstanding legal issues," says a then minister.

"Both sides in the end played it well," says a creditor representative. "The danger had been the lack of engagement. That was finally resolved. I respect what they did. The risk to the króna was the last fundamental challenge."

"Almost existential," the creditor concurs.

In 2016, the magazine *The American Lawyer* picked the winners of their annual awards for legal work. Eighteen law firms representing four estates, the bondholders, the trustees and the Republic won the prize in the category 'Global Finance Private Restructuring'.

They had worked on a complex case.

The Icelandic bank restructuring.

BUY AT 4, SELL AT 24, ACTUALLY AT 40

Taking the average for the three banks, their bonds sold at 100, fell to 4 and then went to 24.

In Glitnir and Kaupthing, large gains were made by those who bought bonds early in the chaos of late 2008 and early 2009 and sold before late 2010. The Landsbanki bonds started even lower and continued rising until the final settlement in late 2015, as the Icesave debacle was sorted out.

By then, the Landsbanki bonds had climbed backup from 1.25% to 14% of their original value of 100, Glitnir from 3% to 30%, and Kaupthing from about 6% to 30%. On average from 4% to 24%.

"We entered on a small scale in late 2011 and ramped up in early 2012," says the manager of one of the fund structures that eventually became one of the largest holders of the bank debt.

"In 2012, we entered with our main fund. In 2013, we established a fund where investors could invest directly in the Glitnir and Kaupthing estates. In 2016, we added a direct fund that owned a part of the proceeds from the liquidation process. And in 2017, we added yet another fund, which held a portion of one of the new banks."

Quite a surprise, some may say. Even eight to nine years after the collapse, new funds were being established to invest in the defaulted banks.

All these structures, and many more in other countries, are managed out of the fund's offices in London and New York. The fund's administration occupies an entire floor, overlooking Park Avenue in midtown Manhattan.

"Actually, we made most of our money after the final agreement, the Composition Settlement. That was when we really started buying. We even bought in 2017. Since the agreement, value is up 65%," says the fund manager.

In New York, the return figures fill the investment analyst's screen as he hands me the numbers on what the fund paid and received.

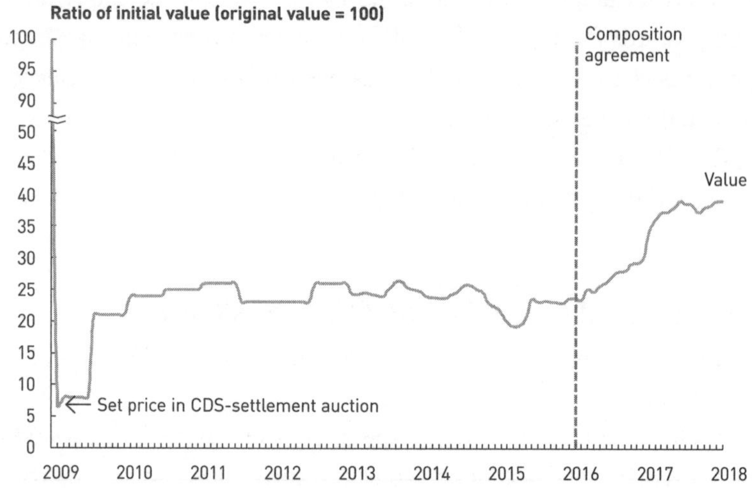

Return	2009	2010	2011	2012	2013	2014	2015	2016	2017	2018
%, last year	-93	264	8	-12	6	-2	-11	11	46	13
Absolute*	-93	17	2	-3	1	0	-3	2	11	4

↳ **Transaction value of Kaupthing-claims.**

* Indexed return on the entire stock of claims; Pre-collapse value =100.

Returns came from many sources. The bond value, the cash payments and the liquidation notes. On top came currency gains. Most numbers are outside the public domain, and even analysts following the process have missed out on the full picture.

The fund manager explains: "There was more value in the estates. The Composition Agreement gave us direct access to the assets. In early 2018, we held about 40% of one estate."

"Was it a strategy?" he asks and smiles. "Not really. It is the way we work, work and work. You really need to know the assets."

And what happened was quite predictable.

"Value normally spikes after a settlement," says a hedge fund director.

"It takes out an uncertainty and enables the creditors to access the assets. Also, investors who previously were restricted as insiders can now buy."

One of the managers of one of the first movers into Iceland in the fall of 2008 moved on to another situation shortly thereafter. He showed up in Rio de Janeiro.

The Brazilian economy was nosediving at the time, moving from positive GDP growth in 2013 to zero growth in 2014 and huge minuses in 2015 and 2016.

In sum, a reduction of 10% in GDP. Luckily, in Brazil the banks were resilient, and all major banks made it through the recession. One of the top energy companies, however, collapsed in one of Latin America's largest defaults ever.

I also moved to Brazil and had worked out of Rio de Janeiro since the fall of 2013. Over the years, I worked with multiple companies to improve their performance and to secure and strengthen their positions. Now I was brought in with colleagues to try to help bring the energy company back to life, to save jobs and values.

Here, I met the Iceland specialist of the hedge fund. This time he had teamed up with the old bondholders to provide a loan to the estate of the defaulted company. The loan carried interest, might be converted to equity and could even help save the company.

"In Iceland we earned a lot of money," he says.

"Not in Brazil."

I lived, in my childhood, for two-and-a-half years in Kenya, in Africa. Then and later we had numerous trips to the savannah.

And, yes, the vultures look ugly.

When eyeing a cadaver, they circle in the air above or sit in an adjacent tree waiting for the lions and hyenas to take their portions. Then the vultures move in and clean up the leftovers. They have no sense of smell, are far- but narrow-sighted. They have no feathers on their heads, allowing them to go deep into the mess while still staying clean. All the characteristics of a hedge fund, some may say.

A fund manager, some would say a vulture-fund manager, asks me rhetorically when we meet, naturally in a nice breakfast restaurant in Boston, "Are the funds less legitimate as creditors, especially if they have entered cheaply? Is it therefore justifiable to squeeze the funds?

"If so, the primary lenders might know that the funds will pay them less next time the funds move in. If so, the primary lenders will have to be more cautious when they consider the risks of the next loan. As they will get paid less if all goes sour.

"If so, they may in the first place be less willing to lend money to countries and companies in need," he continues, as he makes his case for the hedge funds. "Or, those in need may simply not get any loans."

It's well known that vultures play an important role in the ecosystem. He would say they also have a role to play in the world of finance.

He stays calm also when I ask whether they use what some may call dirty tricks. "Some use litigation, yes," he answers. "Especially if a case can be filed in the US.

"Sometimes we use private investigators, yes.

"Not in Iceland, though.

"Private eyes are mainly used to check out the management of companies where we are considering investing big money.

"Sometimes you find out some amazing things," he says, before he mentions some examples.

A COMPANY CALLED WINTRIS

"Have you or did you have connections yourself to an offshore company?"

This was the question asked of the then Icelandic Prime Minister, Sigmundur Davið, on 4 April 2016 in a TV interview. The two-minute interview sequence would effectively end his tenure as prime minister.

"Myself, no," he answered, before he stated that he always has put all his assets and the assets of his family up for taxation. "So there has never been any of my assets hidden anywhere."

"What can you tell me about a company called Wintris?" asked the reporter. The reporter had read the *Panama Papers,* and apparently found an offshore company associated with the Prime Minister. A company that, among other things, had invested in claims against the bankrupt Icelandic banks.

Actually, it turned out, the family of the Prime Minister, the proclaimed hardliner, had itself bought interests in the defaulted bonds. When and why they were acquired and who else knew of Wintris and its position as a bank creditor is unknown. At least some claim that some creditors knew.

On 7 April 2016, Sigurður Ingi Jóhannsson, also from the Progress Party, took on the position as prime minister.

FIRE EXTINGUISHERS MOUNTED TEN YEARS TOO LATE, OPERATED BY HEDGIES

"The Icelandic banking system hit the wall in 2008. Specific EU rules meant to help economies avoid or address such situations were put in place in 2014," says a Nordic FSA specialist.

"They were expanded to the non-EU EEA countries in 2016. Some countries plan to implement those rules in 2018."

Only ten years too late.

In 2008, the rules only required countries to create a deposit guarantee scheme. No state guarantee was required. And, interestingly, the new rules do not prescribe such guarantees either.

Instead, priority is, according to the new rules, to be given to depositor claims if a restructuring is required. The bank's owners and creditors will be obliged to 'bail-in'. They need to be ready to convert debt to equity or to inject new equity.

The new rules added yet another banking acronym to the lexicon, MREL. The Minimum Requirement for own funds and Eligible Liabilities defines how much capital banks' owners and creditors must provide and in what form. Crucially, it spells out which forms, for example subordinated debt, will be the last to see repayment if disaster strikes.

"The new rules aim to enable a continuation of the system-critical part of a bank's activity even if a crisis occurs," the specialist says. "Basically, to secure the deposits and the payment system." All very familiar.

"The banks are obliged to have emergency plans as to how a crisis is to be handled. They are obliged to have a structure that makes it possible to resolve a crisis. Similarly, the authorities are obliged to have a plan."

"As the final rules are to be implemented shortly, I now need to develop the emergency plans," he says.

The MREL will extend and define the 'buffers' of the bank. Hence, it is meant to reduce the risk of a new crisis happening. And it defines the rules and procedures in case a crisis does occur. Interestingly, if anything, the rules move the system closer to what was done in Iceland. Although with two differences: they require plans and rules set in advance.

"There is a but, though. Who will buy the MREL funds?" asks the regulator. "Pension funds and many institutional investors may find it hard to hold such assets, especially if there is a crisis looming."

"Maybe we are establishing a structure where the banks will be dependent on hedge funds."

Not only after a crash, that is.

FILLING THE RESERVOIR, CALMING THE WAVES

"We didn't have a situation that we with certainty knew would work. With the capital control in place, we could carefully manage the transition."
– Már Guðmundsson, Seðlabanki governor from August 2009 to August 2019

In Iceland, fewer and fewer interventions to support the ISK were needed from mid-2009 onward. The holes in the capital control system had been closed. Seðlabanki had engaged with the big companies to make them repatriate funds to Iceland. And even some smaller investors started to buy ISK again, some of them, maybe, at least a little bit, inspired by our speeches on the sound fundamentals of the economy.

Gradually, all of this started to have an impact. Market participants learned that the ISK could strengthen. It was no longer the case that everyone was on the sell side. More importantly, the impact of the strengthened trade balance started to work its magic. Most days, there were more participants that wanted to shift from FX to ISK, not as previously from ISK to FX.

Later this small trickle turned into a vast inflow, especially as imports stayed low and inbound tourism boomed. Now the Central Bank could be a net seller of ISK, and increasingly so.

The plan had been to use the borrowed money to boost the reserves, ahead of the removal of the capital controls. Now FX could be accessed in the market. The Central Bank could sell its own ISK for hard currency.

At one point, 60% of the net FX surplus was hoarded by the Central Bank. The reserves grew day by day, the ISK stayed weaker than it would have otherwise, and competitiveness was retained.

The strategy worked.

THE MONEY NOT REALLY NEEDED

"When it really works, the IMF is like a hospital," says Murilo Portugal of the IMF.

"The IMF should have all capabilities and competencies. But ideally, there should be no need for its money."

A bit like Iceland.

The Icelandic state had a reasonable pre-crisis balance. The post-crisis deficit could largely be covered by loan issuances in the domestic market. It's a paradox that the IMF insisted that Iceland should take its money and pay the full interest rate, even when the money really wasn't needed. Scarce Icelandic resources had to be used for interest payments, thanks to the IMF.

A system with a line of credit would had been better, as the IMF later established.

Still, having reserves came in handy, and their mere existence provided comfort.

In total, €3.5 billion was made available by the IMF and the Nordic countries. The first transfer had already been made by the IMF in the fall of 2008.

The Nordic loan agreement was signed in mid-2009. Some money could be drawn but, as for the IMF funds, the fight over Icesave hindered progress.

By the time of the IMF spring meeting in Washington in April 2010, the IMF was ready. Now Strauss-Kahn was ready to push it through the board. The situation was unlocked. The IMF provided the funds. The Nordics followed.

"Finally, now we are on safe ground," thought the Icelandic Minister of Finance.

"Now we had the reserves. But we drew the money as late as possible to save interest payments," says the Director of the Market and Treasury Department of Seðlabanki.

"The money was never needed to pay our bills.

"We had to draw before the end of 2011 or the drawdown rights would expire. Already in May 2012, a large part was repaid, as a ten-year dollar bond was issued. The rest was repaid when we issued a Eurobond in 2014.

"All was repaid well ahead of schedule."

The Nordic €1.775 billion loan carried an interest rate of 275 basis points over LIBOR, substantially above the 15-basis-point spread for the loan from the Faroes.

The 275 was below the risk premium the market was imposing on Iceland at the time, but way above the lending cost of the four countries.

In comparison, Sweden asked 1.08% and Denmark 1.07% flat from Ireland. Something I am often reminded of by my Icelandic friends.

"We were the toughest," says Anders Borg, the Swedish Minister of Finance at the time. "The Icelandic loan was the largest bilateral loan given out. Other countries, such as Spain and Greece, got no bilateral loans from anyone.

"But we had to protect the Swedish taxpayers."

And Latvia, right across the Baltic Sea from Sweden, was Sweden's main worry. It also had a crisis due to excessive debt.

"Latvia had its own crisis. The IMF was pushing for a depreciation of the Latvian currency. The local government disagreed. They had our support," says Borg.

"A depreciation would have reduced the international cost of Latvian properties.

"Latvia would have been all open for Russian money."

Seðlabanki asked to be allowed to pay only for the money it 'pulled' on the Nordic facility. The answer to this request was no. So, Iceland pulled all the available funds and repaid them in full. With interest. The other Nordic countries could now book a profit; for Norway alone, the guarantee provision was assumed to be about NOK 250 million, about $30 million. The gainers and losers from the Icelandic crisis can be found in the strangest places.

Lastly, maybe the fact that the money wasn't needed also made the IMF more tolerable.

The lack of a desperate need for money gave the IMF less leverage. Dialogue could steer the cooperation with us on the Icelandic side.

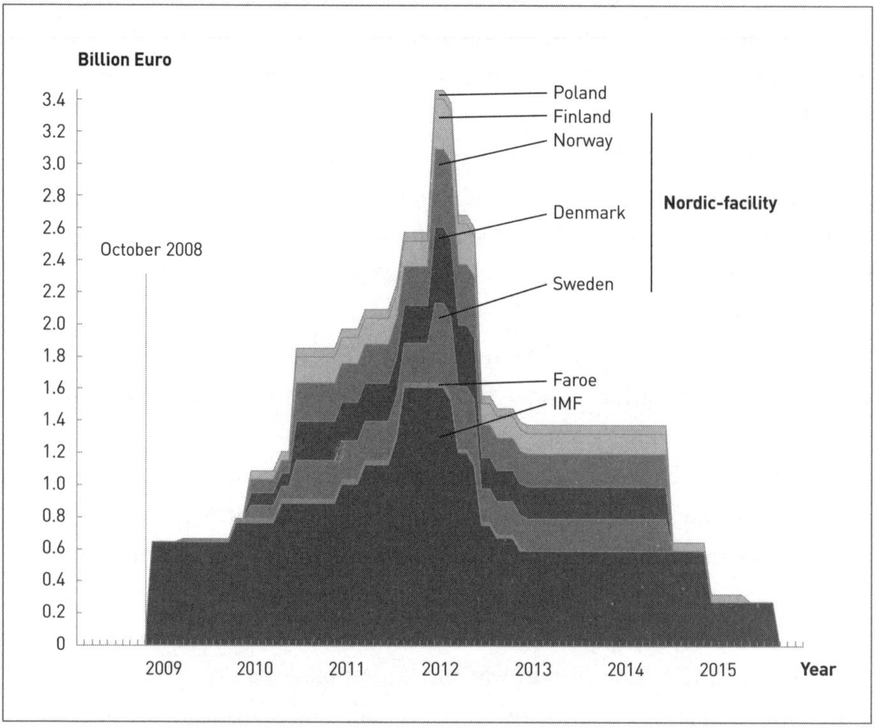

↳ **Amount borrowed on the lending facilities.**
Converted to euro based on average 2010 exchange rate.
Source: Seðlabanki

GEYSERS, VOLCANOES AND GLACIERS

In 2007, the number of foreign tourists going to Iceland was 490,000. Then it grew by a third in five years, to 673,000 in 2012. The next five years saw a tripling, to 2,195,000. By that time, the number of US tourists alone exceeded the total number of visitors in 2007.

This time the inflow helped Iceland.

"On a global basis, tourism is growing steadily year after year, on average by 4% annually. Some 500-600 million tourist trips are taken in Europe every year. Arctic tourism grows at an annual rate of 20%," I was informed by a specialist.

"Everything came together," says a tour operator. "The depreciation of the currency obviously helped. Iceland is viewed as a peaceful corner in a troublesome world. Many airlines promoted Iceland.

"We jumped over the hurdle, and many airlines got sufficient scale to launch Icelandic flights. Scale creates scale."

"Between 60% and 70% of tourists say they were inspired by social media. Now, everything can be bought online. We have overcome the scale challenge.

"Half of the tours we sell are day trips; of these, 60% target geysers, volcanoes and glaciers.

"*Game of Thrones* helped create an interest in Iceland. Eyjafjallajökull did a fantastic job. Iceland is the ideal place for selfies."

One joke was often told. The Brits and the Dutch put pressure on Iceland, demanding, "Pay us, send cash." the Icelanders never quite listened. "Pay us, send ash," was what they heard.

A STRONG BREW

Gudmundur Þór was impatient.

By 2014, he and Iceland were barely back at the level of 2006. It had been a rough journey, but now at least the ground had stabilized.

He could see a steady profit from his business, and he noted that the same was the case for Iceland. His discussions with the bank were settled. It was time to move on.

The lowered cost level due to the króna depreciation could still be felt and tourists swarmed his hotel, both in the summer and during what used to be the off season.

His hotel and his family could gear up their spending, and the planned hotel expansion could move forward. And now he was able to find builders to help, he could hire staff for his hotel, and even his former bankers were available to assist him.

To top it all off, as his business now made money, his bank had decided to let bygones be bygones and provide a new loan. The banks in his town were full of cash again.

With the capital controls still in place, investors' funds had been stuck in Iceland and the new banks had excess equity to back new loans.

Out on the open fields down south, the growth machine had started rumbling to life.

Exactly as for the Republic of Iceland.

In the period from 2015-2017, Iceland's GDP grew twice as fast as that of its trading partners, peaking at the end of 2016 at an annual rate of more than 10%.

Iceland's exports of goods and services grew at three times the pace of its trading partners' overall growth of imports. Iceland won market share.

Two thirds of the growth now came from tourism, some from metals and the remainder from other exports.

Post-crisis, some said that Iceland had already built whatever was needed for some decades, but now construction restarted. Half of all investments in 2017 were in transport and tourism.

The government balance had strengthened due to the boom. Now, government spending also escalated.

The exports served as an accelerator and a shield. They ensured that a positive external balance could be achieved, even as private consumption and investment grew.

Car dealerships boomed once more. Car sales for 2017 exceeded 2007. The Toyota Land Cruiser was again the top pick.

In 2017, Gudmundur Þór bought a new Toyota.

He was happy, but also a bit worried. The ISK had been strengthening ever since 2009 and was back on its 30-year trendline. Salaries had increased, first as a catch-up from past losses and then due to the tight labour market.

The earnings from his business had fallen by almost half.

283 BILLION BEHIND BARS GET A CHANCE AT THE LAST GET-OUT-OF-JAIL-FREE CARD

In total, the Icelandic banks sold ISK 687 billion worth of glacier bonds, or about €5.5 billion at the exchange rate of early 2018. Many had early maturities and were repaid ahead of the collapse.

About ISK 280 billion, or €2.2 billion, had an expiration date after markets closed on 3 October 2008. Capital controls were imposed. The money could no longer be changed from ISK to FX.

That was bad news for the three categories of bondholders. The first of these consisted of bond funds like Eaton Vance, Loomis Sayles and Pacific Life.

The next category were the so-called high-net-worth individuals, the rich, in private banking.

The third group was made up of investors like the Belgian dentist.

Some sold out along the way in the offshore market, accepting fewer euros for every ISK. Some exited through the auctions. But many were still locked in and contributing to a persistent ISK overhang.

The ISK holdings of the estates had been neutralized through the Composition Agreement. Still, the authorities again stated a fear of a risk of an abrupt depreciation of the ISK if the controls were to be removed in one go.

Three considerations were important.

One, the authorities wanted a 'good deal'. Some were of the view that also this group of foreign creditors should pay for their exit ticket and help fund the costs of the crisis.

Two, by now the authorities were increasingly eager to remove the capital controls.

Three, vast amounts of FX were entering the country due to the boom in tourism and increased confidence in the economy. The high interest rates in Iceland looked attractive again.

In 2016, Lee Buchheit was brought in once more.

The concept of the last get-out-of-jail-free card was developed. The Central Bank would run one last auction. Whoever did not bid for a card might stay locked in forever.

"They'll be offered the opportunity to participate in this auction. If they don't, it is their conscious decision to take a position in Iceland for the long term," said the then Prime Minister Sigurður Ingi Jóhannsson in a deep voice, trying to use the tone of Sigmundur Davið.

It is hard to think of a worse threat to make to a hedge fund.

But this time the creditors were reluctant. They saw the improved macro-trends and the krona strengthening. They still got high interest rates on their ISK. Why would they leave and accept an interest rate of only 0.5% from the European Central Bank of Mario Draghi?

All was set up by the government as it had been for the Composition Agreement. But now the leverage was modest and the investors reluctant.

The government had to sweeten their offer to investors by 25% more than envisaged originally. Now, investors could exit at a rate 20% less favourable to them than the official rate. Way better than the 38% haircut that many had expected, judging from their financial statements.

And yes. Some chose to stay locked in.

A short time passed, and then the controls on other outbound flows were removed. The ISK did not weaken. Once we had been laughed at when we said this was what we were shooting for. Now, it had come to pass. Even with a much stronger official rate.

Inbound flows matched the outbound flows. It all became a non-event, as hoped for. After eight long years, equilibrium was established.

Now with a bit of regulation on inbound flows.

THE LIONS RETURN TO THE CAGE

"I started laughing," says Glenn Kim.

"I was in a meeting where we discussed the concessions needed for the capital controls to be terminated," he says. "The large ISK holders fought to open the cage, allowing the locked-in ISK to be changed to FX.

"But what do the lions in the zoo do sometimes when their cages have been opened?

"They bump around a bit.

"Then they return to the cage.

"After all, the zoo provides shelter and free food. Like Iceland, after the removal of the controls.

"The interest rates were still way higher than European levels, with a Central Bank lending rate of 5%. And the currency was appreciating."

There is now such a big crowd trying to get into the zoo that an entry ticket has been introduced.

For the lions.

A new regulation has been imposed under the code term 'Capital Flow Management'. Its purpose is to hinder inflows or outflows of capital that could distort the economy. Remember the glacier bonds?

As of the rule of 2 November 2018, any investor putting funds into Iceland to buy government bonds must first place 20% of the funds in a zero-interest deposit account for one year. With this, the money will earn the right to enter.

What a paradox.

Especially as some money was still locked in, while other money was prevented from entering.

The day of 7 December 2018 became a noteworthy day. This day marked the removal of the last controls on the *outbound* flows of ISK. More than ten years after the crash.

Until 6 March 2019, only the entry fee requirement applied. For the lions. Then the rate, the ticket price, was set to zero. However, the rules were retained, and the limitations of derivative trading were kept.

Now only the entry ticket for the lions remains.

But the OECD and EU/EEA rules stipulated that capital flows are to be unrestricted. Therefore, in the long term, these controls, too, will have to be lifted. Whatever 'long term' means.

So far, neither the EU/EEA authorities, TD Securities nor any other international or Icelandic banks have, to my knowledge, stepped forward and demanded liberalization, as the rules require. But, who knows, maybe soon some carry traders, some previous creditors or some Icelandic bank will start to lobby for equal treatment and the freedom of movement for capital.

Allowing them to start all over again.

And, yes, on 13 March 2019, after the liberalization, a European financial house, Blue Bay Asset Management, recommended the purchase of Icelandic bonds. They expected high interest rates and a stronger ISK.

THE CENTRAL BANKS AND THE HELICOPTER MONEY

Since the pre-crisis world of 2008, the balance sheets of the world's five largest Central Banks have tripled. These five are the Bank of England, the Bank of Japan, the ECB, the People's Bank of China and the US Fed.

They have bought bonds in the market to increase liquidity, lower interest rates and increase inflation. They hope to strengthen demand and thus growth. Quantitative easing, QE, is the code that opens the vaults.

The balance sheets of the Fed, ECB and Bank of Japan are now about 23%, 40% and 95% of the respective economies' GDP.

'Helicopter money' is the expression for an imagined policy where a Central Bank flies over a country and makes drops of money to stimulate demand. QE is a modern and less transparent version of this.

The Eurosystem buys corporate bonds, covered bonds, asset-backed securities and, especially, public-sector debt. For the three first categories, possible losses are carried jointly by all ECB member banks. For the public-sector purchases, the risks are borne by the home country Central Bank. A fig leaf to silence critics claiming that the ECB finances governments.

As it does.

By the end of 2017, the ECB sat on about 20% of the euro countries' public-sector debt. Ever more frequently, it is constrained by the rule limiting its share of any issuance to 33%.

The programme restricts the purchase of new debt as it is issued, as the markets are supposed to set the price. This is a bit of a technicality, though, as the ECB sucks up a vast share of the debt in the days after.

Others may thus 'front run' the ECB by buying debt at issuance and then selling it on to the ECB.

As of July 2019, the programme included 1,200 positions in corporate bonds, worth a total of €177 billion. The 'covered bonds' programme constitutes €262 billion, and the public sector programme €2,089 billion.

One of the positions bought under the corporate programme was a part of Steinhoff Europe AG's bond. The parent company is South African, the bond was issued in the Austrian daughter company and bought by the Finnish Central Bank.

But the accounts of Steinhoff South Africa were allegedly misreported. Its investment grade was lost, and the bond value fell by 40% in a week.

The Iceland case, although extreme, illustrates three risks. First, how hard it is to reverse liquidity measures. Second, the extent to which even investment-grade assets may deteriorate and losses kick in. Third, the creativity some may show in tapping in to such programmes.

One may wonder if other structures as creative as the ones invented by the three banks exist somewhere today. Especially as the Central Banks now really have opened the taps.

One may wonder what the 2019 love letters may look like.

CRUSHED BY THE MIGHT OF THE STATE

"If you are to have a financial crisis, then make sure it is really big and all private."
– Icelandic economist

The US set an example with Washington Mutual. It protected the depositors and left the rest to the market to resolve.

In terms of sheer brutality, the case of WaMu exceeded what happened to the Icelandic banks. The bank owned by the holding company was carved out and sold to JPMorgan Chase in one go and at the depth of the crisis.

"We had positions both in Washington Mutual and in Glitnir," says one of my interviewees.

"We bought pre-crisis at full value and sat all the way through, not selling out.

"From Glitnir we got 38.6%. From WaMu 24.6%."

The lower recovery also reflects yet another paradox. In WaMu, the deposits represented a higher share of the bank's funding. Something that normally is considered a sign of robustness and resilience, as deposits are believed to be stickier. However, as deposits are fully guaranteed, the high deposit ratio also implies a lower recovery for others; in other words, a sign of danger.

A high deposit coverage ratio is great in life, but not in death or when death threatens.

Lehman went from its value in operations to its fire-sale value. In Iceland, in comparison, the creditors retained a part of the upside through their equity positions.

The US also set an example with Fannie Mae and Freddie Mac.

They were bailed out with the help of almost $200 billion of government money. Originally, the state was to receive a fixed 10% dividend. Investors took positions on that basis.

However, the earnings did not suffice to deliver an annual return of 10%.

A 'sweep' model was created. The state received all earnings beyond a bare minimum. That left nothing for investors ranking after the Treasury. By September 2018, $280 billion had been transferred back to the Treasury, almost 90 billion more than the cost of the bailout.

The US was the one to set the standards and references for splitting banks in distress and for resolution mechanisms after bailouts.

Not any ordinary banana republic.

THE BAILOUT THAT TURNED A PROFIT

"The authorities view the settlements as a resounding success. Painstaking efforts paid off, achieving the core goals of neutralizing the balance of payments threat and minimizing legal risks. Public support was overwhelming. Claimholders got a fair deal, in their view, with not one of the thousands of claimants challenging the process in district court."
– IMF, 2016, Article IV consultation summary

In Iceland, there was no state bailout of the banks.

Still, as a share of GDP, the Icelandic rescue operation was for some time the costliest of all comparable rescues required after the global financial crisis.

However, in the end, every dime of this cost was recovered. And more.

The initial costs to the Icelandic state were estimated at 34% of GDP, about three times the level in the Netherlands, five times the UK share and ten times the US share.

From 2009 to 2012, the government refinanced the banks. The cost was way less than initially envisioned, as the conversion of claims to equity replaced the bond structure. Still, a state capital injection equal to 15% of Iceland's GDP was needed. With the lion's share going to Landsbanki.

Seðlabanki also incurred huge losses on its 2008 liquidity support schemes. The collateral was insufficient. Therefore, in 2009 the government refinanced the Central Bank with an amount equal to 18% of GDP.

Then the tide turned. Funds adding up to 43% of GDP were recovered, 9 percentage points beyond the costs.

The recuperation had four parts.

First, in the 2009 bank recapitalization, the government received bank equity and bonds issued by the banks in return. These had a value of 15% of 2015 GDP, roughly equal to the injected value.

Second, while owning the banks, the government earned dividends, adding up to 3% of 2015 GDP.

Third, the Central Bank recovery unit, its asset management subsidiary, managed to capture some value from the collateral. This added up to about 8% of 2015 GDP, as compared to the cost of refinancing Seðlabanki of 18 percentage points. Contrary to the case for the ECB, here a large loss remained.

At this point, the government was still in the red.

The final agreements with the bank creditors, the Composition Agreements signed in mid-2016, yielded a value to the state that was equal to about 17%

of GDP. Islandsbanki, Iceland's third-largest bank, had a book value of 8% of GDP when handed back to the state. The Kaupthing estate committed, via bond contracts, to paying the equivalent of around 4.5% of GDP after its planned 2018 divestiture of Arion.

In addition, a range of further payments were to be made.

The estates agreed to distribute recoveries, counting the Central Bank itself as a creditor, amounting to 4%. A seven-year phasing of the estates' withdrawals of domestic foreign currency deposits will contribute another 4%. Lastly, transfers from the estates' external assets to refinance certain Central Bank and government claims on the banks will contribute 2.5%.

In addition, a prolongation of the estates' foreign currency deposits improves the currency balances of the banks.

In return, the estates could immediately distribute liquid foreign assets worth 35% of GDP to their largely foreign claimants, with more to follow over time. And the creditors gained control, allowing them to extract additional value.

Remember Deutsche Bank and the €500 million that ended up in its coffers in the spy versus spy arrangement? It took a few years, but Kaupthing eventually recovered $425 million. Which the creditors then got.

Even to Oslo, the creditors pursued their hunt. Even in 2017.

When Kaupthing Norway collapsed, the government appointed its winding-up board. It was led by respected Norwegian specialists. They were worried about the risks they undertook. They demanded that the state or an insurance company should cover their possible liability. First, the Ministry of Finance authorized a guarantee of up to NOK 500 million, about $60 million. After some back and forth, an insurance policy was signed instead.

But both schemes had an expiration date. The state guarantee was valid until the end of 2010. The insurance three years after the conclusion of the closure of the estate. Until 2013.

Along the way in the process, millions floated back and forth, claims were settled and collateral returned. In the midst of hundreds of transactions, shares were transferred to a Norwegian customer without the payment being made. The books showed $1,040,500 in deviations.

The customer and her advisor, her brother, former Head of Kaupthing Norway and member of the Kaupthing top team, maintained that they did not know of the case, and they requested documentation.

So instead, the creditors sued the three in the administration for Oslo Conciliation Court and demanded from them $1 million. Personally. Those who had undertaken a mission. A million dollars that they may have paid themselves, since both the state guarantee and their insurance had expired. But the settlement agreement was rejected and referred to the district court. There you have one year's deadline for taking out a summons. After that nothing has been heard, and a subpoena was not taken out.

So, then the case is obsolete. Maybe.

The gross external debt of Iceland was cut by more than 60% of GDP from about 190% to about 130% by the end of 2016 through the transactions, reflecting the transfers to the government and to the creditors.

The deal also turned the state into the controlling shareholder of two of the three main banks, Islandsbanki and Landsbanki.

Arion stayed partly private and was listed on the Stockholm stock exchange in 2018, still listing four hedge funds among its largest shareholders: Goldman Sachs, Taconic, Attestor and Och-Ziff.

In addition, the creditors committed to not suing the Icelandic state. While Norwegians could be sued.

For Iceland, the IMF summed it all up: "Iceland has ... fared remarkably well in terms of direct costs, with the state estimated to have made a net gain in excess of 9% of GDP. This compares favourably to many other crisis countries, a salutary feat given the enormity of Iceland's pre-crisis banking system relative to its economy. Taxes lost or gained are not part of this analysis. Nor is any attempt made to quantify the vast economic costs of the crisis."

FORTY BILLION EUROS BURNED

"How in the world can we Icelanders blame the creditors for what happened? Yes, many still blame them."

– Icelandic observer

All told, investors lost about €40 billion due to the collapse in Iceland, based on the banks' balance sheets and the recovery rates.

The chart on page 316 illustrates the split of the banks' liabilities. The light grey part shows the write-offs.

The shareholders of the three banks lost all the value of their equity. As did the providers of the loans that were treated as equity, the subordinated loans. In total, about €12 billion.

Next to lose were the lenders to the banks, with a loss of about €28 billion.

An equal amount of bank assets 'disappeared' as the value of the banks' loans was written off and some value was transferred to the state.

The banks' loans are, by definition, liabilities of the banks' borrowers. The borrowers owe money to the banks. Less so, though, after the write-downs. Hence, many who had owed money to the banks were released from their obligation to pay. Some for good reasons. Some less so.

Most extreme, the debt write-offs on the banks' loans to the holding companies were an astonishing 94%.

OFF TO KIRIBATI

The easy and convenient way of telling Iceland's story is to say that the banks' initial creditors left voluntarily and sold out. Thereafter, debt investors, often hedge funds, could enter at a low cost. Then the Icelandic government could play hardball with the funds and more than recover its direct costs and gain money to pay for household debt relief and other measures. Suddenly, we have a story with mainly winners.

But, as is usually the case, this story has at least two sides. A default on $180 billion of debt has its victims. Many victims.

The UK left Banaba a desolate quarry after exploiting its riches, leaving only shacks and discarded tanks behind, along with infertile soil and contaminated fresh water reservoirs.

The loss to the poor nation of Kiribati from the financial crisis was approximately at the same ratio to GDP as what the Republic of Iceland later would gain through its creditor agreements. One poor state lost, the other rich state gained.

When I told Gudmundur Þór of Kiribati, he was upset. This story did not fit well with the narrative he had heard and shared with his friends. That reckless bankers and vulture funds had to be fought and that the German banks had sold out voluntarily, an admission of their poor judgment.

"I never heard about Kiribati," says the lead creditor spokesman.

Apparently, making an effort to find the innocent victims that had suffered the largest losses hadn't been among the top priorities of the creditors. Strangely, as that would have allowed them to take the moral high ground.

Value of funding before failure (billion euros)		Recovery rates
Deposits in parent companies, incl. Icesave (~19)		100% recovery
Deposits in foreign subsidiaries (~15)		100% recovery
Other funding of foreign subsidiaries (10-20)		100% recovery
Other funding of parent companies, incl. borrowing, bonds, wholesale deposits (~53)		~30% recovery Corporate debt write-off
Subordinated loans (5)	Lost October 2008	Loss of value of equity in subsidiaries Restructuring cost and other leakages
Equity (~7)	Lost October 2008	Net proceeds to the Icelandic State Household debt write-off
Other liabilities (8)		~30% recovery

↳ **Flow of funds through the restructuring process.**
Source: "The Rise, Fall and Resurrection of Iceland".

Another illustration of how ineffective the creditors actually were: in the Icelandic and international press, they were pictured as savvy professionals with well-paid Icelandic and international advisors. But in reality, they played their game far from their home turf.

"I only came across it when we had to list all jurisdictions involved and needed to see where we could be sued," says a member of the government team.

Þór, like most Icelanders, is caring and has a strong sense of right and wrong. When I left him, he was thinking of Kiribati.

There is some good news, though. Kiribati has fared quite well since 2008. As it expanded its exclusive economic zone far into the Pacific, Kiribati found itself with the 12th largest economic zone of in the world. In size, it beats Iceland's four to one. Now it is making some gains on the value of its fisheries.

Furthermore, only part of its Reserve Fund was invested in the Icelandic banks.

On other investments, value has been gained.

In 2019, when the Republic will celebrate the 40th anniversary of regaining its independence after 87 years of British rule, the Fund is expected, for the first time, to top AUD $1 billion.

ICELAND, WELCOME AGAIN

As of mid-2008, the Icelandic state was effectively blocked from raising long-term debt in international markets. Among OECD countries, it was joined as an outcast by Greece and Ireland in 2010 and Portugal in early 2011.

However, markets reopened. Iceland was the first to return. It could go to the international market in June 2011.

"It was an important breakthrough," says the then Minister of Finance, Steingrímur Sigfússon.

"We tried to focus on the fundamentals. We were puzzled that the lenders lumped us together with countries with no resources, without fully funded pension funds and with no signs of recovery."

Some were surprised by the re-entry. Reykjavik had been warned that it would never be able to borrow again.

"Getting back to investment grade by 2011 was quite well done," said the Fitch analyst interviewed. Fitch was the only one of the three agencies to strip Iceland of its investment grade.

Iceland issued $1 billion of sovereign debt in June 2011 at an interest rate of around 5%. The issuance was twice oversubscribed by investors.

New issuances followed.

"This issue is a milestone for the Treasury, which has never borrowed funds on more favourable terms," the Minister of Finance commented after the late 2017 issuance.

This time, the interest rate was 0.56% per year for a five year €500 bond – €2 billion worth of orders were received within 90 minutes of announcing the sale. In the end, total demand ended at €3.9 billion. The investor group mainly comprised Central Banks and other institutional investors, primarily from Europe.

This time it was the Icelandic Republic that, albeit indirectly, could benefit from the ECB fountain of money.

THE 2019 GOAL LINE

"I thought of writing a book on my career," says a ratings analyst. "Fifty years of debt.

"I have seen many crises.

"Think about Korea."

"That was my message in meetings in Iceland in 2008," recalls the analyst. "That made the Icelanders really upset."

He believes Korea really stands out. Korea was rated AA- in 1996 and fell to B- by the end of 1997, in total 12 notches. But among countries that have fallen that many notches, it recovered the fastest.

"The Koreans were so embarrassed, they really wanted to come back fast," he says.

"In Korea, the sovereign was fine. But as troubles hit the banks and companies, Korea just ran out of FX. Now they have the largest foreign currency liquidity buffer relative to the size of the economy. It is gold-plated. Never again.

"It took them 13 years. Hence, counting from the first downtick of Iceland in 2006, that takes us to 2019. And now the restructuring in Iceland is done. It's smooth sailing from here."

HAPPILY EVER AFTER

"Iceland has never been as strong as we are today. That I never would have imagined in 2010 or 2011."

– Interview with former Icelandic Prime Minister and now Minister of Finance, Bjarni Benediktsson

In late 2018, the Icelandic economy was showing decent growth, about 3%. Measured from pre-crisis 2008, its GDP growth has clearly exceeded the growth of its main trading partners and the Euro countries.

Iceland has the world's highest rate of employment, higher than 85% for those aged 15-64. This compares to an average of less than 75% in the US and a Nordic average of about 80%. Unemployment is below 3%, the lowest of any western European country. In the years of crisis, about 4% of the population left Iceland, half Icelanders and half foreigners. Since then, on a net basis, new arrivals have added to the population by about 10%. Mostly foreigners, as the in- and outflow of Icelanders match.

The chart on Iceland's current account is, as a macroeconomist, the one I always find most spectacular. It again and again reminds one of the pre-2008 imbalances, as it shows a vast structural deficit. It demonstrates how dramatically far an economy sometimes may run over the edge of the cliff before financial markets and politicians realize that it is out there in thin air. It also, very clearly, shows the magnitude of the changes that occurred in 2009. And the steady trajectory thereafter. And, finally, how narrowly the economy balances in 2018.

The link between indicators of fundamental economic strength and the evolution of currency and share prices is often unclear. They may move in different directions and there may be delays. But, in the end, basic economic fundamentals matter. Hence, keep them on your radar screen.

The Icelandic government now once again runs a surplus, while the average OECD country runs a deficit. The general government gross financial liabilities of the Republic in 2018 are about 64%, beating the OECD average of 111%.

Inflation is modest. The sentiment, though, has changed. In mid-2017, market participants believed low inflation was here to stay. By late 2018, the expectation for long-term inflation doubled from about 2% per year to 4%. This raises a question of whether the recent five-year period in which inflation was contained to international levels was just a short-lived exception, and thus also the era of a continuously strengthening ISK. The ISK, on average, has weakened 2% per year against the euro for 20 years. In most of those years it was even weaker compared to the 20-year trend line.

Now, domestic private consumption is the main growth driver. Government consumption is also up, by as much as 4% per year. Export growth has ceased, as has the growth in tourism.

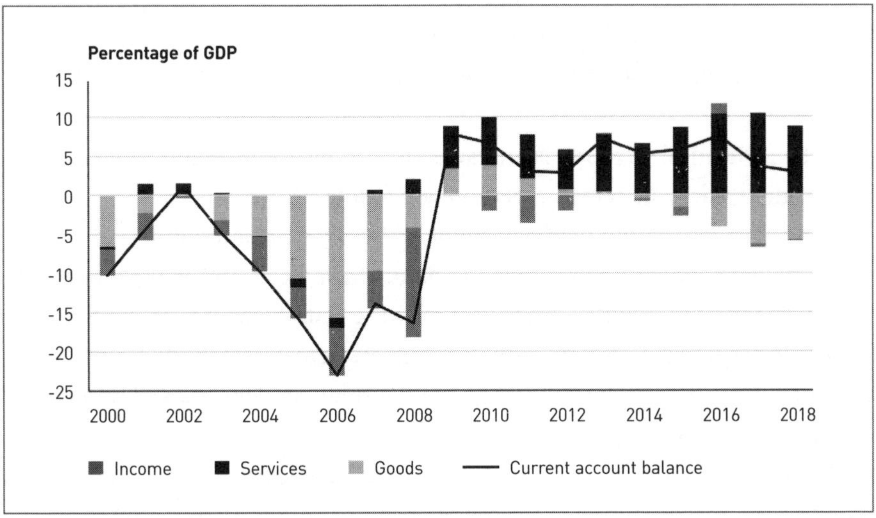

↳ **Iceland's current account balance, 2000-2018.**
Source: CBI

The debt-to-GDP level in the corporate sector and among households is declining.

This is a momentous change. The sum of the financial positions of all Icelanders, including households, companies, banks and the government yields what is called the Icelandic International Investment Position or IIP. Pre-crisis, it added up to more than a full year's GDP. To simplify, the country had 'borrowed' more than a full year's worth of all domestic production from abroad.

Today the IIP is zero. Iceland worked itself out of a crushing debt load as it worked its way through the crisis.

Recalling the cattle drive, apparently investors now expect the Icelandic herd to make it across the desert. Or rather the Arctic plain. The CDS spread on the foreign borrowing of the Republic is at its lowest in a decade, 0.6% as compared to Germany.

But the picture is not all bright. Exports are up, but so are imports. In sum, since 2013 the impact of changes in the balance of trade and services on domestic demand has been negative. The country is still running a surplus but has become dependent on a steady flow of millions of tourists.

And not only the geysers are giving off heat. While public consumption and investments were taken down during the recession years, both are now growing again. Spend is procyclical. Salary increases have been high over recent years. Unit labour costs have grown more than 5% per year. The exchange rate is back to its long-term trend. Business sector earnings have dropped.

"GDP growth is too short-term of an indicator," says an Icelandic Professor in Economics.

"The robustness of systems and structures is also important. We have seen double-digit salary increases. Inflation will follow.

"And then household debt will shoot up because loans are indexed."

Some have had the sense that the banks have been and will remain gold mines. A bank tax is still in place. But now the state owns two of the three big banks, and external investors with other investment possibilities are sitting on the third. Thus, the tax becomes a tax on the state, on deposits and on loans of households and businesses.

Work has been done to find a long-term sustainable pathway for salary levels, based on the approach used in the other Nordic countries. In these countries, the competitiveness of the sectors that export or compete with imports steers salaries. But the lack of large, labour-intensive externally competing sectors has made this a tricky exercise for Iceland. In Iceland, all three export sectors, fisheries, metals and tourism, are competitive, but with ebbs and flows in volume and value.

The elements for a model for stable and sustainable growth are known: industrial diversification, increased competitiveness, firm monetary policies, clearer income-policy norms and countercyclical government-sector fiscal policies, most likely topped up with a State Stabilization Fund.

Iceland needs it more than others.

"I wonder at what exchange rate the last tourist will stay home," says a tourist industry leader.

"Among the many beautiful places in Iceland, I find Öræfajökull to be the ultimate," says a friend of mine.

Öræfajökull is an ice-covered volcano in the southeast and is both the highest peak and the largest active volcano. But it may also be the most dangerous, with eruptions in 1362 and 1728, and with increased earthquake activity and tremors in 2017 and 2018.

An illustration of the vulnerability following from the dependency on tourism.

"Iceland's 2019 growth figures are remarkable," says an economic journalist. "Never before have I seen GDP figures drop due to a bankruptcy of one company." In March 2019, an Icelandic airline, WOW, went bankrupt. It had carried 30% of the tourists to Iceland. The GDP growth rate, previously 1.8%, was reduced to 0.4%.

WHEN THE POLITICAL CRISIS OUTLASTS THE ECONOMIC CRISIS

The Icelandic economy has largely recovered. But not the societal trust.

"No one died when the banks fell," says a former Seðlabanki employee. "But the trust in Iceland's institutions took a hit."

"The wounds are still open," says an employee in one of the three new banks.

"We collected a group of Icelanders in a room and ran a discussion. 'We were treated like fools,' said many in the group.

"'No one has taken any responsibility,' they said.

"Pre-crisis, many acted like they were geniuses. Then it all collapsed and now the geniuses said, actually, someone else made all the decisions."

A decade of loans to friends, debt write-offs for some, often based on discretion and individual assessments, capital controls, auctions and restrictions on inbound and outbound flows of money have also left their mark. It abounds with stories, rumours and assertions about hidden fortunes, about "the formation of small groups of operators working closely and strategically together" and secret owners.

Private economic conditions shook two of the prime ministers of the crisis years and led to the downfall of one, Sigmundur Davið.

This occurred while the Icelandic crisis left its scars. The ratio of families renting and not owning a house increased from about 14% to well above 20%.

"The growth of populism in Europe and the US after the financial crisis is partly linked to the lack of consequences," says Eva Joly, now a member of the European Parliament. "The lack of systematic investigations in countries like the US, the UK and Germany was a scandal. And yes, some banks went straight out and once again manipulated customers, markets and interest rates. As in the LIBOR case."

"We were contacted by some countries," reveals Jean-Michel Matt, the investigator. "They considered launching a systematic investigation as we did in Iceland. At least they wanted to say they were considering the possibility. But, in the end they didn't want to do it.

"It's a pity that more countries didn't do as Iceland."

CHAPTER 5

LESSONS FROM THE CRISIS

Remember the medical experiment and the need to understand where it all started and the relevance of the lessons on the cure and the outcome?

I summarize the lessons in the following, as I answer five questions:

1. What have we learned that can help us spot the warning signs that a crisis is imminent?
2. What parts of the journey to recovery ended up being most different from what was expected?
3. What lessons does Iceland provide on models for bank restructuring?
4. What are the lessons in the context of the broader European crisis?
5. Who is to blame?

MARKET AND POLICY FAILURES AND THE COST OF A COVER-UP

For some time, the growth of the Icelandic banks looked like an astounding success. For proponents of a free market and a small state, Iceland was the dream banking location. As intended.

The market was open. EU/EEA rules provided market access. Capital flows were unconstrained. Regulations were lax. The regulator was largely absent. Everyone put their trust in self-regulation of the banks and markets.

Even the regulations on deposit insurance, as shown by the ruling of the EFTA court, were primarily a mechanism designed to facilitate a free market.

The rating agencies were all there, with the Icelandic banks being frequent, well-paying customers. The ups and downs of the ratings, CDSs and share prices of the banks were closely monitored. Leading international auditing houses reviewed the accounts, never flagging any concerns.

And yet, it all came crashing down.

The institutions, banks and researchers gave mixed signals on their expectations all the way until the last day. By that time, the CDS costs had skyrocketed and the share prices had halved. Yes, the 'market' sensed that something was about to happen. Many experts didn't.

Proponents of free markets may say the problem was the ambiguity of terms. Some thought the Central Banks would step in. The Emergency Act was only enacted in the last moment.

Others may say self-regulated banking and markets will never work. The self-regulatory mechanisms are too weak, the booms and the virtuous and vicious circles are too strong and the collateral damage when things fall apart too big.

Before the crisis, the exaggerated growth of Iceland's three banks was visible to all. The absolute size of the banks as well as their huge size relative to the economy was apparent. If the banks themselves and the market could not spot the systemic issues this might cause, what then are market participants able to see?

In sum, the Iceland experience argues in favour of stricter regulations. Especially on growth and liquidity. But it also shows that terms and conditions must be clarified early if self-regulation is to work. That is the first lesson.

Growth is a sign of strength and a sign of danger. This is the second lesson.

This applies to countries and to banks. We are all trained to see growth as positive. But for banks, growth may mean stretched funding and a hunt for remote customers, in every sense of the word.

A Nordic Central Banker said in a discussion, "All banks growing beyond 10% per year should pay extra premiums to the deposit insurance funds. They are likely to become future takers."

Then comes the third lesson: making it through a storm does not make you invincible, it may just appear so for a short while.

The banks and the authorities should have taken the mini-crisis of the Icelandic banks in 2006 as a warning sign. Instead, as things improved, an illusion of invincibility spread, limiting and delaying the interventions.

After the first warning, the risks were multiplied through continued growth in lending, as the banks made more loans to the holding companies that owned them, by buying shares in the banks themselves, by attracting deposits through foreign branches, by making Central Banks a source of funding and by not relocating operations into structures supported by Central Banks of the necessary size.

Hence, take a close look when mini-crises occur and when the relative weighting of assets and liabilities shifts.

The next lesson is likely more controversial: one cannot conclude from the experience in Iceland that a country without a reserve currency cannot sustain a sizeable banking system in the long term.

The shock of the global financial crisis was extreme by most measures. And, naturally, there is a limit to everything. The Icelandic banks were oversized and the economy overheated. This does not mean that the system could not have worked, with prudent banking and prudent policies.

For such a system to succeed, the banks would have needed to be tightly governed by themselves and by their regulator. They would have needed to play by the rules and operate with robustness and integrity. Alliances and partnerships with banks, regulators and authorities in other countries would have been required to help support the system. Trust should have been built, not torn apart by deceit and broken promises.

The three banks should also have separated themselves with regard to funding, ownership and exposure. None of which happened in Iceland. Kaupthing paid a hefty premium for FIH, which mirrored all its weaknesses, beating out Landsbanki, its rival bidder. And worse, even as the storm was on its way, Kaupthing looked at buying NIBC.

The collapse of a system where all mistakes had been made and experience was seen as a liability doesn't prove that Iceland couldn't have stayed a relevant financial centre. Unless, of course, one claims that the mistakes were unavoidable and systemic.

On a country level, the macro indicators rarely look prettier than right before a bubble bursts. Inflation may serve as a warning sign, but not when it is mitigated by low-cost imports as the currency strengthens. A high current account deficit may act as a warning sign, but not if, as in Iceland, it can be explained away by high investment levels and foreign direct investments. Hence, watch and decode the fundamentals.

Debt is a growth enabler but can also turn poisonous. The Icelandic banks managed to attract immense amounts of capital. A portion of this was passed on to Icelandic companies and households. The holding companies went on an acquisition spree. They were perceived as holders of companies, but what they really held was debt.

Liquidity is what matters the most as a trigger of financial crisis. Many companies and countries churn their debt. Old debt is repaid by new. Even great companies would collapse if all current debt had to be repaid without access to new debt. This is even more true for banks. Banking is a business of churning debt – what banks owe to others and what others owe them. Solidity influences their ability to access liquidity, but fundamentally it is liquidity and the lack of it that matters the most.

Be aware of the debtor-creditor mix. Who has lent the money and who has borrowed the money?

This is an important differentiator when comparing Greece, Iceland, Ireland, Italy, Portugal and Spain. Restructuring, bankruptcies and renegotiations can all work when it's private-to-private, debtors to creditors. With public-to-public, it is all politics.

Markets running wild can cause havoc, but market mechanisms are great tools for solving problems. Markets set a price on equity and debt. This price may be right or it might be wrong, based on the underlying fundamentals. But at every moment, a price is set. A lack of confidence is translated into market prices. Transactions and restructuring can be executed.

It is the cover-ups and doubling down that really cause problems. The Icelandic banking system could have been saved by taking a different route back in 2006, said the SIC. Maybe even in 2007, I would add. Yes, a more thoughtful strategy based on a strong focus on soundness, liquidity, deleveraging, partial relocation, alliances, diversification and earnings could have taken the banks a long way. Instead, the banks doubled down. They continued their growth. Even in 2008, with a net increase in lending to foreign entities and holding companies, as measured in euros. More aggressive owners had by now taken control.

As is most often the case, the most severe financial and societal losses were risked and incurred due to actions in the cover-up phase. The lending from Glitnir to its owners doubled. Kaupthing started to manipulate its share price and the prices of its CDSs. Landsbanki began its deposit-taking activities in the UK. The ECB and the British and Icelandic Central Banks stretched themselves to provide liquidity. In the final days, the Icelandic government considered buying Glitnir.

As an investor, beware. The plunge from the peak erases years of upside. Countercyclical bets may pay off, but from a journey through a systemic collapse there is no full recovery.

BETTER, BUT WAY LATER

Looking back on Iceland's post-crisis journey, the impact of the capital controls deviated the most from what was expected in ways that were both helpful and harmful.

With capital controls in place, the rubble from the collapsed banking tower stayed in Iceland. It was then used to fill in holes and build new structures.

The controls, however, also delayed normalization, partly because slow-moving negotiations set the pace. Many regulations stayed in effect until 2017, yes, even until 2019. Only then could Iceland fully interact with international markets again.

The 2008 IMF LOI and the 2009 LOI-drafts were ambitious. Except for the missing section on growth, they covered most of the elements that turned out to be important.

The high interest rates, the rapid shrinkage of imports, the international loan arrangements and the capital controls solidified the currency. With a continued surplus in trade and services, the ISK strengthened after some time. And the Central Bank could build a vast war chest. Faster than expected.

Early in 2009, most expected the onshore and offshore rates to converge, and the eventual deregulation to occur at a rate somewhere in between the two. We were laughed at when we said the onshore rate would have the greater weight.

When the controls were finally lifted, the new rate ended up on a par with the onshore rate. Over the course of the recovery to that point, the ISK had strengthened from about ISK 160-120 per euro.

With support from the strengthening ISK, the salary freeze and the slack in the economy, the inflationary pressure ceased. As early as mid-2010, the 12-month rate of inflation fell to 2.5%.

The austerity measures were carried through as planned. The state debt rose, but the lower cost of the recapitalization process due to the choice of a better model, the improved macro-recovery, the fiscal tightening, and all the creative recovery measures lowered its peak and quickly brought it back down. The Icesave risk steadily decreased through recoveries and was finally completely removed by the ruling of the EFTA court.

The government debt peaked in 2011 at 95% of GDP, but the loan programmes provided comfort. Since then, the debt-to-GDP ratio has shrunk to 42% in 2017.

In December 2017, S&P Global Ratings affirmed its long- and short-term foreign and local currency sovereign credit ratings on the Republic of Iceland at 'A/A-1'.

S&P considered the outlook stable, with fiscal improvements being an upside and the risks of the economy overheating in the next two years being a downside.

The new domestic banks became fully operational in a matter of just weeks. With their strong capitalization, they even soon served as safe havens in the restructuring of the smaller banks.

A possible trade-off emerged in mid-2009. One option was to push for early removal of the capital controls as a way to gain earlier access to the markets. This might have sped up GDP growth. A set of auctions could have been conducted to manage the transition. Such an approach would have posed some risks, though; the outflow of capital might have increased again, exposing the economy. In August 2009, a strategy for a staged and tightly managed, yet rapid opening, was finalized.

However, in the end, a more tedious route was chosen. Maintaining the controls was, paradoxically, the smoother and lower-risk solution. Depreciation and inflation risks were contained and funding ensured. The IMF was a vocal proponent of this approach.

Keeping the controls, however, also necessitated a tightening of them. The capital controls had 'leakages', with breaches and circumventions.

With controls and tightening, huge funds were locked in. This meant there was a vast pool of money from which the state could borrow. The pool also ensured the new banks' liquidity. This again ensured access to capital for Icelandic companies. Last, but not least, the controls provided a framework within which later agreements could be tilted to the benefit of the state.

In Iceland, capital controls worked. Systems and regulations could be put in place. Most Icelanders did obey the rules, and Iceland's location in the middle of the North Atlantic limited the possibilities for circumvention and leakages.

The banks and the locked-in investors largely also stuck to the rule of law.

OPPOSITE STARTING POINTS, OPPOSITE SOLUTIONS

The specific structures chosen in the wake of a crisis must be tailored to the circumstances and fundamentals of the country. That is the main lesson from Iceland on the models for bank restructuring.

For many, quite erroneously, splitting banks into 'bad banks' and 'good banks' has become a synonym for bank-crisis resolution. Such a model was applied in Sweden's 1992 banking crisis and is sometimes referred to as the Swedish model.

In such a model, the 'bad' part, which holds all the losses, is split out into a new unit. Dedicated units are established to recover as much value as possible from the assets of the 'bad bank'. Then new capital is contributed by the state and the 'good' part re-established as the bank for the future.

The new bank can then continue, taking on the history, the brands, the systems, the customers and the staff of the old bank.

In Iceland, the starting point was the opposite. Most domestic companies were hit. With this came a paradox: here the 'bad bank' would largely have been Icelandic and the 'good bank' largely foreign. In Iceland, the 'bad banks', which became the 'new banks', had the most important societal role.

And luckily, despite all the losses, the value of the Icelandic banks' assets exceeded their liabilities as the domestic loan books vastly exceeded domestic deposits. The carve-out of the 'new banks' thereby brought with it a huge repository of value. This, as has been seen, created some challenges and many opportunities as the processes moved forward.

The Swedish model has a clear logic, but there was no direct way to apply it, given Iceland's circumstances. Its principle of asset transfer could apply, but tailoring was needed.

The Swedish model is speedy, simple, compelling and convenient for many. There is, however, no firm evidence that it maximizes value recovery. For good and bad, in the Swedish model, the recovery unit is split from the normal business. The bad bank has incentives to maximize recovery but is most often operating in a winding-up mode.

The Swedish model also carries the risk of just being a mechanism to offload problems from the banks, to inject new capital, and to shift attention away from the need to make more fundamental changes in the way the banks are run.

I have been in many countries with banking crises over the last ten years. In many, the bankers and authorities all point to the need for applying the Swedish model, in some countries again and again. Quite conveniently.

Instead, in many of these situations, a focus on the banks' rules and processes for providing credit and an end to connected-party or politically influenced lending is what is called for.

Hence listen, but be aware and be sceptical if anyone suggests the use of the 'bad-bank-good-bank' model. The Swedish model.

A paradox remains. Regulators can intervene with all their force to safeguard deposits, the argument for this being the need for system stability. But if all available tools are used to safeguard deposits, other contributors are left more exposed.

With the 2014 rules, the EU regulations describe a hierarchy of rights. Equity is most exposed. Then come the subordinated loans, followed by the unsecured loans. All of this is logical, but may hinder new capital contributions at a time of looming crisis. Most likely a structured mechanism for debt-to-equity conversion, if necessary enforceable by the FSAs, would have served us better. This would have provided the necessary buffers while also retaining upside value for the creditors.

And a modest conversion of debt, which is most often what that is needed, may be less frightening and harmful than a full-blown banking crisis.

KEEP PRIVATE, RESTRUCTURE, AND MOVE ON

"It is not only what we do, but also what we do not do, for which we are accountable."
– Molière

Countries differ with regard to how their debt accumulation drives growth, to what extent its end hurts demand, the position of the government, the composition of creditors and debtors, the dynamics of their economies and their currency and monetary systems.

Greece, Iceland, Ireland, Italy, Spain and Portugal all went into decline after the global financial crisis brought their debt-induced booms to an end.

In Iceland, the banking sector had brought money to the country, caused the currency to appreciate, and created a domestic boom and a whole new industry. The government had shown limited fiscal restraint but had at least run a budget surplus and reduced its debt.

In Ireland, the banks had brought money to the country in support of a vast construction boom.

In Spain and Portugal, all sectors had accumulated debt after the countries adopted the euro. Private companies in Spain and state-owned enterprises in Portugal were particularly aggressive, and the governments joined in. They did not restrain themselves in the boom and neglected to build buffers.

Italy and Greece went even further. Debt accumulation by the Greek government fuelled the economy. In Italy, borrowing enabled higher spending, lax taxation and ridiculous pension schemes. Money was provided to the government through lending, not through taxes.

Therefore, in Greece and Italy, the government finances were a mess on most dimensions. Spain and Portugal's state finances were reasonable and workable in normal scenarios. In Iceland and in Ireland, the government finances were in fairly good shape.

In Iceland, some sectors had benefited from the debt accumulation and associated appreciation of the currency. Others had not.

In Iceland, private-sector lenders had lent money to private-sector debtors. This was also the case in Ireland, until the state stepped in and took on the debt. In Greece, initially the state was the biggest borrower, with private lenders on the other side. The refinancing operations bailed out the lenders, with foreign state and state-sponsored agencies taking over their role.

Iceland had its own currency, which appreciated on the way up and collapsed on the way down. The banks in the five other countries operated in euro, in the Eurosystem and with backing from a European Central Bank.

In Iceland, labour force participation was and still is the highest in the world. In Ireland as well as in the southern European countries, female participation in the workforce is low. In combination with a low retirement age, Italy defines the western European low on both counts.

Some say Iceland can teach us the general lesson that governments should not bail out their banks. In Iceland, a bailout was not a viable option, but that is a weak argument for turning non-intervention into an ideal. In Ireland, refusing to bail out the banks could have been an option. Choosing that route might have eased the short-term financing pains of the government and moderated the need for austerity.

By now, however, the Irish government has recovered the cost of the rescue operation, and its intervention did stabilize the system. For the southern European countries, this discussion is of less relevance. Here, the challenges of the banks were a consequence of the crisis, not the cause.

Some say Iceland can teach us the value of a flexible exchange rate. This is partly correct. A broad-based depreciation achieves in one go cost adjustments that would otherwise require hundreds of decisions, political clout, negotiations and persistence. But remember: the flexible currency played a huge role in creating the problems in the first place. And the depreciation would have been of limited help if the employers and employees had not followed up with a price and wage freeze.

Some say Iceland can teach us that the government should moderate its austerity measures in a time of crisis. Yes, the Icelandic government tried to limit the adverse societal impact of the budget cuts and it looked with creativity to find stimulus measures. But the budgets were tightened significantly, albeit with some delay.

For these reasons, there are three other lessons that I view as more important.

One, it's important to put up a barricade when anyone seeks to socialize a debtor/creditor situation. In Iceland, the debt accumulation was all about loans from private creditors to private debtors. The same was the case in Ireland. The root cause of the problems in Italy was the private sector tapping the public sector. In Greece, the state had taken on loans for all sectors. Furthermore, Greece drifted from a private-private to a state-state situation, as the state borrowed for the private sector and the private debtors were bailed out. Restructuring, bankruptcies and renegotiations work when the restructuring is private-to-private. With public-to-public, it all turns into politics.

Second, a loss of demand or income of 10% or a need to reduce debt levels by 10% of income is challenging for any individual or enterprise, but usually manageable. For countries, it is typically way more difficult, but still doable. However, stakeholders will try to avoid taking the hit, with many seeking compensation, thus seeking to offset price and salary increases. In Iceland as in the Nordic countries, all the adjustments were made in one go, re-establishing a starting point for new growth. As always, a bill does not get smaller through a prolonged fight over who should pay.

And finally, what matters most in the end is the level of labour force participation, the productivity and the entrepreneurship in the country. On this, Iceland has long been world class.

A FOOL'S ERRAND

"It appears that both the parliament and the government lacked both the power and the courage to set reasonable limits to the financial system. All the energy seems to have been directed at keeping the financial system going. It had grown so large that it was impossible to risk that even one part of it would collapse."

– The SIC

Attempting to allocate guilt, responsibility and especially honour related to the Icelandic financial crisis may seem like a fool's errand, but it is called for in the end all the same.

The borrower is responsible for the loans he takes on and their repayment. If conditions have been set for the use of the funds, those obviously must be met. The borrower needs to have an idea of any adverse circumstances that could hit him and hinder his ability to repay. Companies and households often tend to take more risks in 'good' times and fewer in 'bad' ones; however, the opposite position may also serve just as well.

A 60% loss in value of the ISK in relation to the yen, as happened in a very compressed period between 2007-2010, was hardly to be expected. However, the ISK suffered a 75% drop in the period from 1981 to 1994. Drops of more than 30% also happened in 1991-1994 and again in 1998-2001, followed in both instances by a partial recovery. Given this history, FX loans in Iceland should have been restricted. As later court rulings said they had been all along.

A lender is responsible to himself and his funders for how he does the lending. The lender can say he relied on the accounting reports of the banks and the statements of the rating agencies, which are paid to assess risks. However, in the case of Iceland, the warning signals were there for all to see. Without a doubt, the lenders enabled the Icelandic boom and bust. Still, it is hard to see the basis for making them the main scapegoats.

In the pre-crisis phase, the rating agencies and the auditors compete for first place in the who-to-blame competition with the bankers, the authorities and the regulators.

The positions taken by the rating agencies in 2006 and 2007 were particularly odd. After the Norwegian banking crisis in the early 1990s, as well as after the Icelandic crisis, I remember being scrutinized by representatives from some agencies, who were all smart, professional and highly analytical. How one of them could miss the warning signs and give all three Icelandic banks straight triple-A ratings after the mini-crisis of 2006 remains a mystery.

But the rating agencies aren't the only ones who deserve a place on the podium.

"Nor did the auditors perform their duties adequately when auditing the financial statements of the financial corporations for 2007 and the semi-annual statements for 2008," said the SIC.

"This is particularly true of their investigation and assessment of the value of loans to the corporations' biggest clients, the treatment of staff-owned shares, and the facilities that the financial corporations provided for the purpose of buying their own shares," continued the SIC.

No criminal case was brought against the auditors. One of the estates, Landsbanki, sued PWC. Landsbanki asked for ISK 100 billion. The two parties settled out of court on 10 March 2017 but provided no details on their agreement.

For the pre-crisis years, the regulators also have a place on the podium. On no occasion did they try, in a decisive way, to make the banks reduce the size of their balance sheets. They imposed no requirements on the banks to move Icesave out of the Icelandic guarantee scheme.

Maybe it is just too much to ask of economic policymakers to be party poopers and end the festivities, as theory says they should.

If that is the case, this has profound implications for our ability to avoid future crises.

In Iceland, being a cheerleader brought accolades. Government spending increased as the cycle peaked, and there were no indications that regulators were increasing their scrutiny of the banks. When foreigners showed concern, it was viewed as a sign of envy and ignorance. The Financial Supervisory Authority, FME, the institution that bore the main responsibility for monitoring the activities of the banks, did not grow in proportion to the banks. Its practices and resources did not keep up.

The banks attracted capital and earned high ratings. Their lending growth was especially rapid during the latter part of 2007. Some analysts argue that Kaupthing and the others during and after the mini-crisis of 2006 chose an 'all or nothing' strategy. Bank managers who believe their bank to be insolvent may decide to conceal this from regulators and carry on, doubling down with even more risky bets, hoping for a good outcome.

Dubious business practices had been a part of the picture for a long time, for example, with owners taking control of bank A through loans from bank B, and vast lending to companies associated with the owners. In all banks, the principal owners were among the largest borrowers. In the last days of the banks' life this activity ramped up, with even more money tapped from the banks, the banks themselves buying equity and engaging in deliberate market manipulation and insider trading.

Hence, the system failed on the most basic level. The banks flouted even the most basic principles of prudent banking practices. The FME failed to spot the most basic systemic risks. The risks were either not flagged, or if they were, they were not acted upon by the authorities. Most wanted the banks to continue their excessive growth and did what was needed for that to happen.

As the SIC indicated, it was way too late to avert a collapse when the tower started to tumble in mid-2008. Iceland's failure to build trust and alliances over the previous years not only limited the measures available but led regulators and authorities in other countries to proactively cut funding, limit the transfer of funds and seize assets.

In hindsight, the emergency legislation of October 2008 with all its specifics stands out as an immensely important defence against a total collapse. The splitting of the banks, despite the problems it caused, eventually proved to be workable after a series of later modifications of the recapitalization plans and the operations of the bank. One may say it was a rare example of cleverness among all the events that unfolded in 2008.

Credit should also go to the IMF for the drafting of the crisis and recovery plan, and for becoming an ally in the end.

And even more credit should go to the Icelandic authorities in the period from 2009 onward, when they took on the unpleasant task of pushing through all the tough decisions needed to get the country back on its feet. And finally, to all of those in the government who drove the many initiatives forward and advanced in the art of planning, strategizing and coordination.

Simply put, before the collapse, everyone believed that all that could go well would go well. After the crash, they believed that all that could go badly would go badly. Before the collapse, no policy tools were used. After the crash, a huge range of tools were put into use.

But the most credit goes to Gudmundur Þór and his like for living through the years of challenge and for always acting on the opportunities offered.

Amid all of this, spare a thought for Kiribati.

LAST WORDS

APPLYING THE LESSONS TO TODAY'S WORLD

IT'S A PATTERN

"I arrived at my new job early in the morning. As a trainee. A special Monday. 19 October 1987," says Peter Hermanrud, for many years the highest-ranked equity market strategist in Norway.

"At Montgomery Securities in San Francisco, next to the Transamerica Tower. Then I was placed in a chair and asked to wait. Not to disturb anyone."

One, two, three hours passed by.

No one at Montgomery had time to talk to the young Norwegian. Peter thought he had lost his job on his first day.

It was 'Black Monday', the fateful day that marked one of the half-dozen stock market crashes in recent decades.

I was in a meeting in Stockholm that same day, in a meeting between the finance ministries of the Nordic countries. A Swedish attendee left the room every ten minutes. He wanted to get the latest news from Wall Street.

What happened there interested him the most, based on the possible impact on the economy. And on his own investments. Every time he returned, he had a more worried look. I followed with curiosity, as it was the first crash for me to observe as a professional. I, though, found the discussions to be speculative. On why the crash had occurred. And even more on how the crash, in return, would hit the economy.

The table below shows all stock market crashes beyond 15% in the US market, measured by the indicator of the largest US companies' market value, the S&P 500.

This chapter reviews their pre-warnings and the current situation. The book's lessons are put into perspective. What dangers threaten the world of finance in 2020 and where should we be on the watch? Can the 2019 figures enlighten us further on what happened in the Global Financial Crisis and on the precautions a 2020 citizen should take?

Lowest month, S&P	Occurrence	Drop	Months from peak to through and back		Main causes
			From prior peak	Back to prior peak	
November 1987	Change of market sentiment; 'expensive' markets	30%	3	20	Market sentiment
October 1990	Tighter monetary policy; increased oil prices; moderate downturn in the US; war in Iraq	16%	5	4	Macro; conflict
August 1998	Asian financial crisis; Russian crisis; oil price decline	16%	2	4	Debt; short-term financing
September 2001	Decline from a very 'expensive' market (internet); September 11	46%	13	68	Market sentiment; insufficient earnings
September 2002	Secondary impact from crash; often seen as the same recession		25	56	
February 2009	The Global Financial Crisis	53%	16	65	Debt; liquidity
September 2011	The euro crisis	17%	5	5	Debt

↳ **The largest US equity market crashes of the last 30 years.**
All drops beyond 15% over a three month period in the American index S&P 500.

The drop in the equity values in 1987 was triggered by a change in sentiment in the market. Nothing else. No wonder the economists in Stockholm were perplexed.

Next, in 1990, the US economy turned down, with weaker growth after a period of increased interest rates and tax changes. In the US, the construction industry had slowed down. The same was true of the housing sector. The first Iraq War increased oil prices. American consumers lost their confidence. In retrospect, many wondered why the market had not fallen before.

Before the fall of 1998, first the countries in Asia, such as Thailand and Korea, met markets that were shut. Then Russia. Investments, new buildings and expansion had been made possible by short-term international funding. But then the liquidity dried up. A familiar pattern by now. In retrospect, many wondered why the market had not fallen before.

Before the fall from 2000 to 2002, the equity values had been very high. The market had thought that the great news of the day, the internet, would enable eternal growth. Some companies were only valued based on the market's belief in their ability to grow. This ability was measured for some by how much money they used to grow. Their 'burn rate'. Their deficits, not their earnings, ruled their value.

The bigger the better. A classic stock market bubble. In retrospect, many wondered how the equity market could have risen so high.

Before or at the beginning of six of the last seven recessions since 1970 in the US, the housing market has weakened considerably. Not in 2001, though, when the macro impact only occurred as the companies cut their investments after the IT bubble burst. But even then, housing construction fell before the recession – the decline started in 1999 long before the recession.

The US housing market, however, played a key role in 2008. After an upturn hardly seen before, for house prices, housing construction and debt, the new construction began to fall late in 2005 and prices in early 2006. Later many wondered, again, why the stock market had not fallen before.

As of mid-2019, the increase in shareholder value as measured by S&P 500, assuming reinvestment of dividends, has been almost 11% nominal a year since the early 80s. Adjust for inflation and the figure is 8%.

An amazing number over such a long period. The gain from being in the market has been great. Strong arguments have been required for an investor to sell out. Each new peak has been higher than the previous one. The next bottom has also always been higher than the previous one.

At the same time, the valuation has fluctuated along a corridor, for example when measured by the ratio between the price of shares in companies and the companies' book values. Sometimes the ratio has been high. Sometimes low.

In total, all the major downturns in the stock market's value over the past four decades have started from the same starting point. On the top of the hill. With particularly high equity valuation. It is simply not possible to get an equally long descent from a lower starting point.

A simple decision rule for investors has thus emerged: if equity valuations are in the low range, always stay invested. If equity valuations are in the high range, stay invested if the broader economy remains on an upward trajectory and if the observed imbalances are modest. However, be on the alert if the business cycle is about to peak or if large imbalances can be seen.

In up to three quarters of the situations with large stock market drops, macroeconomic imbalances, due to high deficits or high debt, have played a role. Either in a leading role or in a supporting role.

Looking at specific cases in individual countries, they have played an even greater role.

THE FLASHING LIGHTS OF 2019

External deficits, a country's deficit toward foreign countries and the resulting debt, were among the lights that flashed the strongest in 2007. This, naturally, posed a definite risk. A country's policy makers can influence the access to domestic funding. Less so the funding from foreigners.

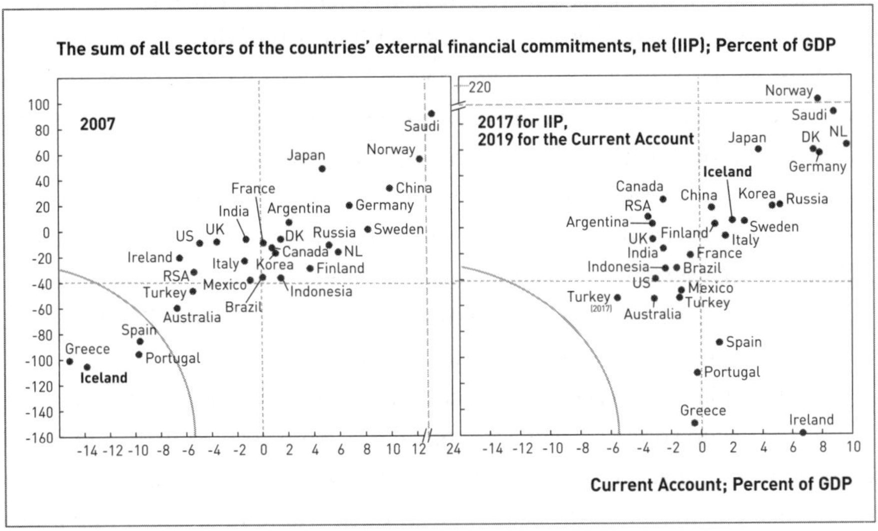

↳ **The countries' external financial balance.**
Saudi Arabia's current account surplus was just over 22% in 2007;
Norway's IIP was 220 in 2017.
2017 numbers included for Turkey.
Source: IMF

Then Iceland, Greece, Portugal and Spain had the greatest imbalances, as shown in the lower left part of the overview of the countries' financial balances. The overview includes all the Nordic countries and all the western European crisis countries, PIIGS, Portugal, Ireland, Italy, Greece and Spain. The chart also includes the Netherlands and all the major economies, the so-called G20 countries.

It shows the annual balance, the current account, in relation to the rest of the world. It also shows the country's international investment position, IIP, in simplified terms: the sum of the net external debt and foreign ownership rights, whether the debtor is the state, the companies, the households or the banks.

In 2007, the countries sat almost like pearls on a string, many with large deficits and large debts, others with a large surplus and a large reserve.

In 2019, the countries no longer lie along a straight line. Greece, Portugal and Spain are still struggling with their old debts and are dragged down to the bottom of the figure, but year by year they achieve a surplus. The lesson is clear: austerity can deliver a surplus but doesn't necessarily free you of your debt.

Iceland is the exception. The huge deficit is gone. The same goes for its foreign debt. The story of how this occurred has been told.

Ireland has become a socioeconomic rarity after, in particular, US technology companies have become wholly or partly Irish. Much of their licence revenue is now believed to come from the green island. Ireland's GDP has, therefore, on paper, increased dramatically. The same applies to its operating surplus, but also to the foreign ownership rights and the Irish corporate debt.

In 2007, Saudi Arabia was in front of another oil country, Norway. Saudi had a surplus of a formidable 22% of GDP and an IIP of nearly 90% of GDP. Norway followed with a surplus of 12% and an IIP of about 60%.

Now, Norway's IIP has risen to 220%, thanks to the rise of the oil fund's value, while the surplus has shrunk slightly due to lower oil prices.

Saudi Arabia's IIP and current account surplus are still among the largest, but so was the decline of its current account balance from 2007 to 2019. This trend must now be brought to a halt. No wonder the Kingdom has launched a wave of reforms. The impact of the Saudi reform work is among the most important trends to monitor, not least due to Saudi's role in the region and in the oil market

Turkey fell down into the left corner in 2017 and 2018, and in 2019 is now in the midst of its crisis, although with an expected improvement in this indicator. The Turkish equity market is among those that fell most in the last three years but is also among the ones that have improved the most into 2019.

The latest figures for this indicator in 2019 show few countries at risk, including none of the big ones. A big difference from the situation in 2007 and a confirmation for the world's optimists.

Among the rich countries, Australia is closest to the grey zone.

Japan and Germany continue as big exporters, also with large claims against other countries. Most noteworthy, and what alone accounts for half of the changes in the current account balances measured in US dollars among the countries shown, is China's journey. Exports as a share of GDP are down by as much as 16.5 percentage points from 2006 to 2018. More than half is offset by a 10% drop in the import share to GDP.

China no longer has any operating surplus. China has become more self-reliant, like the United States. The country has begun its move away from an export-led model such as in Japan, Germany and Korea, to an internally driven growth model. China doesn't have a lot to give before it finds itself in the red.

Dependence on foreign countries became particularly serious where it was combined with government deficits and debt, as for Greece. The next figure, which shows the balance in the public sector, illustrates this.

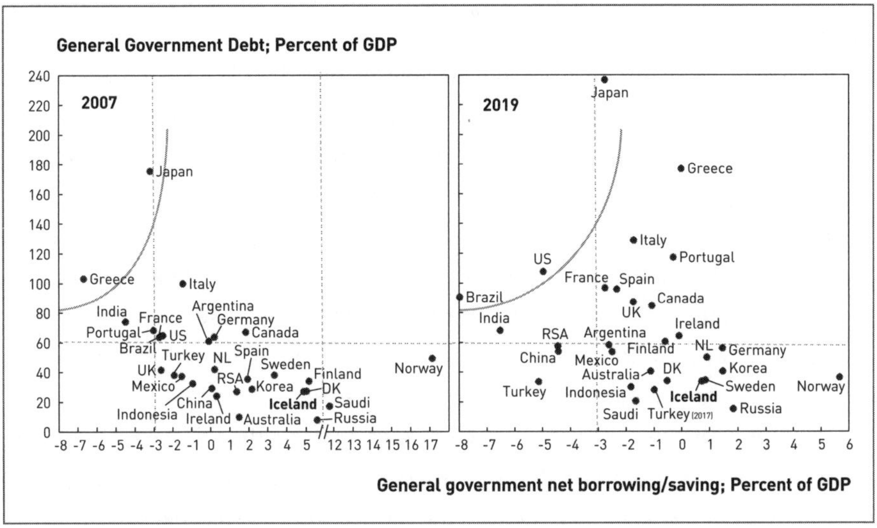

↳ **General Government Financial Balance.**
In 2007, the surpluses in Norway and Saudi Arabia exceeded 10%.
2017 numbers included for Turkey.
Source: IMF

Greece's journey from 2007 to 2017 was dramatic. The budgets were tightened and now show a surplus. However, the debt as a share of GDP has risen despite write-downs, because GDP has fallen and because further deficits along the way have been added to the debt.

Some debt was written off, but mostly the repayment periods were extended and the interest rate lowered. Creditors' debt relief may help a debtor survive, but not breath freely.

The programme negotiated in the summer of 2018 is valid for the years up to 2060! The then IMF Managing Director Christine Lagarde, though, said they were uncertain whether the programme provided adequate relief in the "really long term, when assessed until 2060."

A surplus is now required in Greece, as in Italy and Portugal. Budget surplus to service debt is achieved through austerity, which dampens growth.

Here, Iceland's starting point as the crisis hit was different, with budget surplus and low government debt, which Iceland again has.

Japan avoids attention to its government debt. Here, the Japanese themselves have loaned money to their own state. Japanese savers place money in the Japanese postal savings bank, the one with the largest deposits of any bank outside China. Then the state supplies itself.

For a national economist, this is a fascinating paradox. The Japanese who will soon retire puts money in the bank. Then her demand for goods and services is lowered. To compensate, the state runs a deficit and the Central Bank buys securities. It prints money. Demand is recreated.

The pensioner's own state now owes her a large portion of the money she has saved for her old age. It has to tax her or and the members of a shrinking workforce to pay her and the ever-increased number of elderly. Or the state can borrow more.

No one seems to doubt that this can continue. The market even rejoices, so far, when the deficit and money-printing increases.

Unemployment is at a record low. High exports strengthen the yen. Everything is compared at a strong yen rate. GDP appears to be high but has only increased 0.6% per year in yen since 2007. Scratch the surface and you see Japan's productivity problem. In the domestic sectors, productivity growth is low. The machine that will pay for the increased debt splutters. Nevertheless, the world relies on the persistent and loyal Japanese.

The pattern of Turkey's journey is by now familiar and is shown for Turkey in 2007, 2017 and 2019. The imbalance in 2017 gave an economic downturn.

The state footed a part of the bill. The deficit and debt are growing. Such are the situations that the state coffers must be able to withstand.

Most worrying in 2019 is the move of the major economies toward the grey zone: the United States, China, Japan, India and Brazil.

The first four are more or less in a boom, and their public accounts should now have been in balance with a deficit lower than their GDP growth. With this, their debt ratios would have been reduced.

However, the deficit in the United States has never before been as high as it is now, considering where the US is in its business cycle. The last time the United States had as low a vacancy as now, the country's state budget was in balance. Now, the US runs with a government deficit beyond 6%.

To simplify, the US government finances *before* a possible downturn are worse off than Turkey's *after* its downturn.

Brazil is in a recession, following a GDP drop of about 10%. In the past year, the Brazilian equity market was among the best, believing that the crisis had been overcome.

But, with every year without a real upturn, Brazil's need for budget reform is ever more urgent. The deficit is about 8% of GDP and the debt is rising rapidly. The fuse has soon burned out.

All the five counties mentioned have their own currency, and most of the loans are listed in this currency. For better or worse. Better short-term. Worse long term.

Increased interest rates and budgetary tightening could add up to one possible outcome: austerity and modest growth.

Inflation to eat up the debt is another.

Both outcomes are possible. Nothing is more significant, again, than what happens in the United States. Here the pessimist can find a good reason for his insomnia.

From mid-2016 to November 2018, the nominal yield on ten-year US government bonds rose from 1.37% to 3.24%, before falling again, in August 2019, to below 2%. The increase was due to inflation concerns. The drop was due to a fear of a cyclical downturn.

Corporate and household debts are also indicators that are worth observing. The overview of the positions in 2007 reaffirms the history of Iceland's crisis. The companies were heavily indebted, and the increase in the debt ratio was formidable. Of all the data points in the material, this is the most extreme. Yes, Iceland's crisis was not just an externally imposed banking crisis.

Spain followed suit, including the Spanish real estate developers. The correction in Spain was the single factor that contributed the most to the fall in aggregate European demand from 2007 to 2011. If all other demand components are netted out, this sector contributed two thirds of the total demand drop of the EU's 27 countries! Hence, even the specific balance of one sector in one country does matter. If the country is big and the imbalance vast, with it all being amplified through worries related to the banking system.

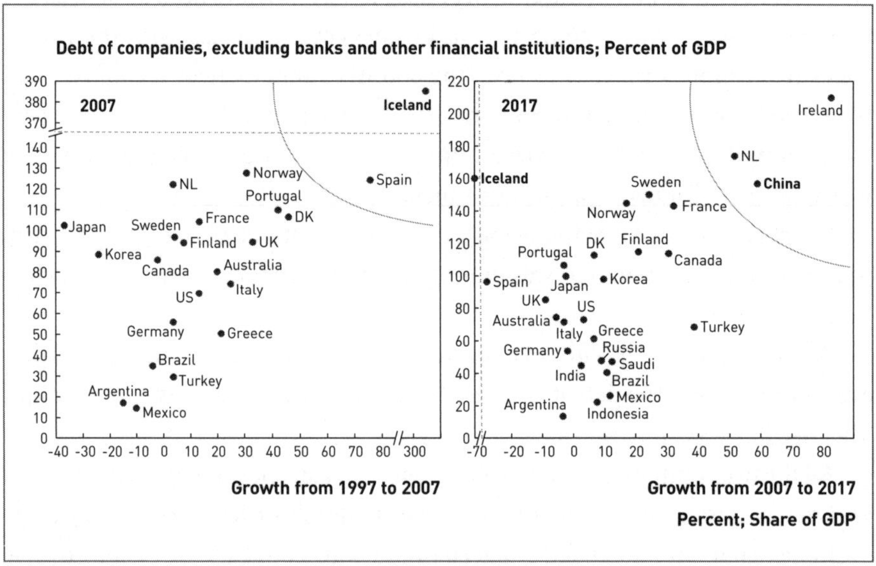

↳ **Debt level of the companies.** Source: BIS

The growth of Chinese corporate debt is on the list of worries of many.

Until recently, China distinguished itself by the fact that the share of corporate income used for wage payments, the wage share, was very low. Communist China was the country where wage earners' direct share of the value creation was the least!

And, not only that, the regular Chinese also saved a great deal of the little they received. What they saved, along with government contributions, went as loans to Chinese companies. And to buy US government bonds, since the world's richest country fails to or doesn't want to self-finance its own state. Here China, Japan, the UK and Brazil all made their contributions, just to name a few.

In China, with its low salaries, the Chinese companies also earned their profits. Much of this was held back in the companies, including in all the many state-owned enterprises, owned by the federation, the states or the municipalities.

This enabled the companies, and therefore China's, very high level of investment. With growth in exports, investments and other domestic demand, the Middle Kingdom became the world's definite growth winner.

But, the surpluses and loans also enabled unprofitable investments and a prioritization of large, rather than profitable, projects. In addition, businesses were continued, even those that delivered no pay-off.

Surprisingly, in many industries, in China one can find figures for the profitability of individual plants.

"Where did you find those numbers?" I was asked after I had held a presentation. It had shown that half of the factories we had looked at, 20 in all in two different industries, were unprofitable.

"In the West, all such figures would have been secret," the inquirer continued. But, on this the Chinese are more open. For those who know where to look.

Anyway, the figures show a rapid debt build-up among Chinese companies. Partly due to unprofitable projects.

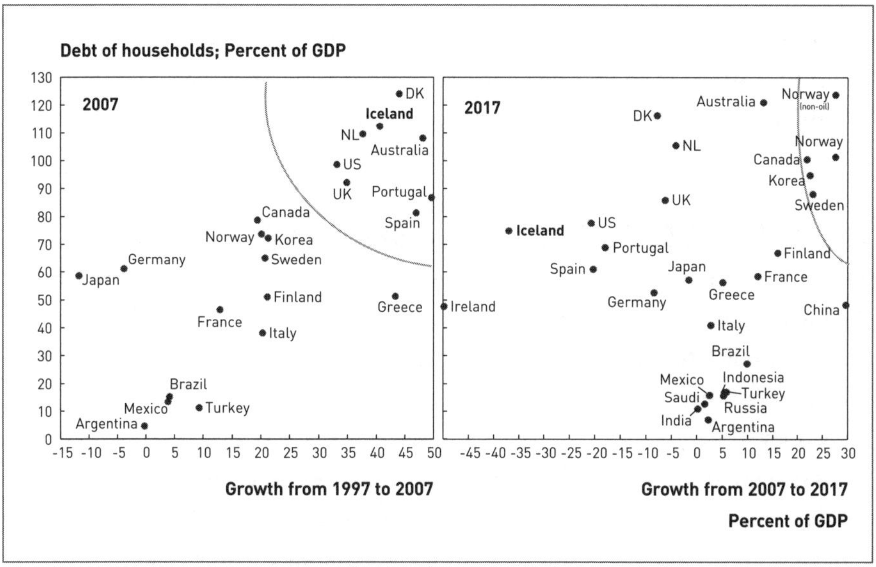

Debt level of the households. Source: BIS

In 1956, an economist, Robert Solow, described the economy's version of a treadmill. Large investments provide an ever-increasing capital base. If the return is low, an ever-larger share of the new investments will only compensate for the wear and tear. No added value is created. Ultimately, much of the resources, the income of the average citizen, are used for no other purpose than to stay on the treadmill. Then it is better to try to increase the returns, the companies' profitability, invest less and consume more. As China now does. For the world economy, little will be more important. Except China's work to solve its resource and environmental situation.

In 2007, a cluster of countries were in the grey zone in terms of household debt: United States, Spain, Portugal and Iceland, to name a few. About half of the eight countries ended up in serious problems. In Iceland, the debt fell most as a share of GDP, exempting the Irish special case.

Until 2017, households in many of the leading countries had paid off their debts. They were helped by, and not tempted by, the low nominal and real interest rates. Foremost among these is the United States. An argument for the optimist.

Five countries are now in the cluster in the grey zone: Australia, Canada, Korea, Norway and Sweden.

"Those who see us from outside see a bubble," said Harald Magnus Andreassen, Chief Economist at the Norwegian investment bank Sparebank 1 Markets.

"But bubbles are invisible when seen from within."

THE STRANGEST AMONG ALL SERVICES

Normally, the person who offers a service will think of himself as more affluent the higher the price he achieves for his service.

This applies to hairdressers, Über drivers and Airbnb landlords. But there is one exception.

Money.

When the price of lending out money, the interest rate, falls, securities with a fixed interest rate, like many bonds, become more expensive. As the interest rate is fixed, a higher price or value is required to generate a lower yield. A portfolio of long-term government bonds gets more valuable as rates drop. House prices also typically rise with falling interest rates. With lower interest rates, equities are also normally priced higher, everything else alike.

This raises multiple questions: has the last years' lowering of rates pushed valuations up, for equity, bonds and real estate? And what will happen if rates stay put or even increase? Can such a change in itself trigger a crash? And, by the way, can rates ever again increase?

Observing short-term data, the pattern is ambiguous.

In the past 20 years, interest rates have typically been reduced in 'bad times' and increased in 'good times'. Short-term *increased* interest rates have thus been accompanied by *higher* equity market valuations. And lower rates have been accompanied by lower share price indices. Not due to a cause-and-effect linkage though, but as 'good times' as such lead to two parallel consequences: higher rates and higher valuations.

The seemingly paradoxical interrelation between interest rates and valuations was enabled by yet another largely unrelated factor. For some years the Central Banks' primary task of controlling inflation has been ticked off.

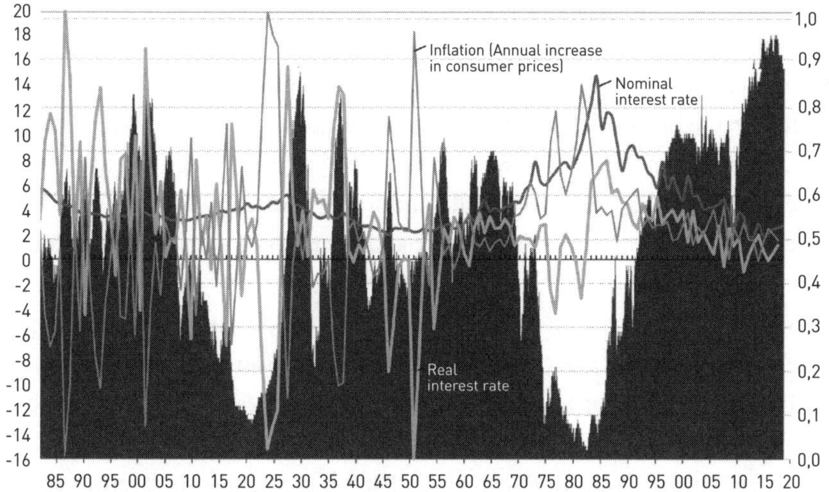

Interest rate, Inflation and value of a portfolio of securities.
Valuation of a US securities portfolio with 2/3 equity and 1/3 bonds. Peak value is equal to 1* (right side); Nominal and real interest rates on 10-year US government securities, % (left side); Annual increase in consumer prices, % (left side).
Source: Sparebank1 Markets (Pål Ringholm); FRED

* (0,67 x ((Equity 10 year P/E)/Peak 10 year P/E)) + (0,33 x (Bond value/Peak));
10 year Federal, nominal; USA

Thus, Central Banks have had the liberty to use the interest rates to help meet other policy objectives. They could lower rates to stimulate the economy, when needed.

More fundamental explanations for the share price appreciation can also be found.

"I do not think it is interest rates that have driven equity prices up or down, except in the high inflation period from 1970 to 2000," Peter Hermanrud says.

"Admittedly, equity valuations have risen steadily since the start of the fall in interest rates, but so has my age."

Peter continues: "The equity valuation has increased over time in line with the companies' profits. As always. Admittedly a little more, but I think the impact of the interest rate is limited."

"Last ten years' earnings are usually a good prediction on future earnings. For the past ten years, US companies' earnings have risen sharply relative to other countries'. The market believes this is a lasting adjustment. Thus, the price of US shares has been bid up, while it is lower for others."

"I think the market is right. In that case, the pricing in relation to the current earnings level, adjusted for business cycles, is a better metric."

However, when observing data through decades a pattern emerges. The next chart, with data starting in 1880, shows three lines: one each for the nominal interest rate, for the real interest rate and for the annual inflation. The latter is represented by a line showing the annual increase of the price of a consumer's basket of purchases.

The chart also shows the value of an equity and bond portfolio, here approximately made up with a two thirds-one third allocation.

The governors of the last few years can, with a certain right, with the figure in hand, raise their heads.

The enormous volatility seen until 1985 has apparently been overcome. The high real interest rates throughout the 1980s had their effect. Inflation was brought down and the system stabilized. Judged by the chart, we are back where we were in the 1960s, before the 1970s and 1980s climb over peaks and bottoms to ever-increasing inflation and interest rates. And to new bottoms for the value of stock and bonds.

Since about 1985, both the nominal interest rate and the real interest rate have fallen and fallen, in some countries with a nominal interest rate down to zero. In some countries even below zero. In July 2019, the Central Bank rate was lowest in Switzerland, set at -0.75. In Sweden it was -0.25 and in Japan -0.1. In the US, it was 2.25, up from 0.125 in 2014. In Iceland, it was 3,75. The other extreme was Turkey with 19,75%!

And, rightly so, over the year the value of the indicated portfolio has risen in value. To the highest level ever.

"In a hurricane even a turkey can fly," the Americans say. "At zero interest rates, most investments are profitable," is the economist's analogy.

We have been through nearly 35 years where the investors have had a tailwind, though with some whirlwinds.

If interest rates rise, valuations will be put under pressure.

INTEREST RATES AND INFLATION

"The debt load in the world is so high now that it can't withstand any historically normal size of interest-rate increases any more."
– Stephen Jen, CEO of Eurizon SLJ Capital
quoted by *Bloomberg*, April 22, 2019

Interest rates are partly determined by the Central Banks and partly in the 'market'. Most Central Banks in Western countries decide, in whole or in part, the policy rates on the basis of a target that states that inflation should be in the range of 2-3%. In the US, the rules provide some flexibility. For the ECB and in many other countries, the priorities are set in the Central Banks' instructions. As of today, about 30 currency areas encompassing about 60 countries are considered to be fully fledged inflation targeters.

They will typically lower interest rates if inflation is low. In addition, they can provide additional stimulants, for example buy securities to push the price up and thus the yield down.

Thus, multiple interest rates will be influenced: short-term and long-term, bank and market, both nominal interest rates and real interest rates.

In the mid-1980s most Western countries struggled with too high inflation, and interest rates were high. No one would then have thought that the Central Banks would ever have a goal of increasing inflation. As they now have, explaining the lowering of the interest rates and the purchases of securities.

Weak demand in many countries was for long believed to be the underlying cause of the lower inflation. We had the financial crisis and the euro crisis.

Households and companies have increased their savings. Most governments sought lower deficits. Those who were supposed to increase their demand, the companies through increased investments, have been reluctant. Some companies have almost ignored the Central Banks' interest rate cuts. They still require 15-20 annual returns on their investments.

Hence, after the crisis of 2008, unemployment was high in multiple countries. In some years the real wage even fell.

In 2019, however, unemployment is again at a record low, including in the US and in the UK. Still, inflation is in the 2% range. According to data and theory, a higher level of economic activity should yield higher salary increases and higher inflation. But the curve seems to have shifted. Now the same level of economic activity yields lower inflation.

Three possible reasons come to mind. One, inflation expectations are reduced, i.e. the automatic adjustment mechanisms are weaker after a decade with lower inflation.

Second, the enormous growth in exports from China and other countries in Asia has dampened inflation. Generally, Western-country-produced goods, and in particular services, have become more expensive. This is partly due to increased salaries, and partly to a lower productivity growth in service industries as compared to large-scale industrial production. However, the basket of imported goods has actually become ever cheaper. We can thank China for cheap goods and low interest rates, inflated equity values and rising prices on real estate.

Third, the way markets work may have changed. The negotiation clout of the workers may simply have been reduced. "Researchers are finding that low inflation is in part a consequence of globalization or automation or deunionization – or a combination of all three which undermine workers 'power to bargain for higher wages," *Bloomberg Businessweek* writes in its 22 April 2019 edition.

If so, a double dilemma, the labour's share of national income has fallen and as a result inflation is down, interest rates are down, and the fortunes of the wealthy have skyrocketed.

In their explanations some go even one step further, claiming it's incorrect that prices must rise with increased demand. Higher demand triggers higher capacity utilization, lower average costs, and possibly even lower costs as new investments brings lower cost capacity online. With ample investment funds, new technologies outsmarting resource constraints and agile investors, capacities aren't fixed. The supply curve is falling, in the economists' word. In short, no less than a new theorem.

Consensus in the fall of 2019 appears to be that inflation will "never again" reappear and high interest rates will "never again" be needed. Some policy rates have even been lowered. About $15 trillion of debt yields a negative interest rate, *Bloomberg* reports.

However, the traditionalists argue, the wage increase has accelerated; in the UK it surged to a 4% yearly rate in June 2019, leading to a three month average of 3.6%, the highest in more than ten years. UK productivity growth is very low, still well below 1%, way below the growth in salaries. Hence, unit labour cost inflation is running well above the inflation target. The US figures shows a similar pattern.

Furthermore, the profit share of the companies has fallen, finally some may say. Next, the China effect is due to dampen, partly as the macroeconomics of China change, as Chinese salaries increase and as the trade war, possibly, continues.

Not dramatic, but if a marked increase in inflation occurs then the tension between the objectives driving the interest rate will increase.

In any case, it is highly unlikely that falling interest rates over the next five to ten years will give investors a tailwind or even that there will be headwinds.

Most central bankers dislike the situation where they have become owners of huge portfolios of government debt and corporate loans. It is a priority to reverse these programmes.

Hence, in a world of inflation, an investor can no longer assume he will be rescued by the governors. If inflation again returns, the interest rate canon will again be set to hit the inflation target, regardless of whether the equity markets are strong or weak. Investors' interests will be of secondary importance.

The longer-term inflation outlook continues to be one factor that can change the trajectory of the 'corridor'.

CDOS IN A NEW COSTUME

Low policy rates aim to increase growth, within the constraint set by the inflation target. Increased investment is one 'channel', whereby this can be achieved. Still, in my experience, few traditional companies act as if the interest rate is low and access to funds ample. As mentioned, many still run with hurdle rates on their investments way north of 10%.

Others see this difference between low market rates and high 'internal rates' as an opportunity to borrow heavily, buy more expensively than others and sell on even more expensively – for example, to others with more debt.

One theme is thus the level of debt, in total and per country. Another is the distribution of debt and its quality. And more specifically on a macro level; are there accumulations of debt in countries and sectors that add up to a systemic risk?

The pattern is complex. Some companies act as if the interest rates are still high and appear cautious. They run with a high equity ratio.

Others use all possible opportunities to lower the equity, as the companies' earnings then can be divided into fewer equity dollars. The use of equity, for example when acquisitions are done, is fine-tuned by some. They take on debt, lease equipment and installations, sell their accounts receivable and divest support service companies.

Toys 'R' Us is one example. For years the company had carried a debt of about $1 billion. Then the chain was bought by two of the world's leading private equity funds. They loaded the company with debt, initially $5 billion in total. The company lost the ability to invest and renew itself. In 2018, the company collapsed with $6.9 billion of assets and $7.8 billion in debt.

High-yield bonds, so called junk bonds, were for long a preferred source of leveraged funding. It ran at a level of about $1.2 trillion in the US. More recently it has been supplemented, and in 2018 bypassed, by 'leveraged loans'.

This can be lending supported by limited or weak collateral, loans to businesses with low ratings or loans to companies or acquisition funds that are to buy other companies. Or Deutsche Bank's $2 billion loan to the Trump Organization.

The leveraged loans are bought by mutual funds, specialty funds and, mainly, sold as so-called CLOs. A CLO is a security that gives the right to an ownership interest in a portfolio of loans. It works largely as a familiar mechanism, the CDOs.

There was though, originally, one difference. The manager had to buy a significant part of the CLO it issued.

For a while, the magnitude of the CLO issuances was curbed by such rules introduced based on the lessons learned from the financial crisis. They demanded that the issuer itself purchase 5% of the value of the loans issued.

But in 2018, this limitation was abolished. Now all the faults of the past can again be repeated.

The figures are scary. Most of the borrowers have a high debt relative to earnings. In addition, as illustrated by surveys of loans, the earnings figures of a sample of borrowers were dressed up almost 50%. Lastly, most loan agreements are vague with few restrictions. Equally scary, in sum the market size is twice the size of the subprime segment as registered in 2006.

"The scope of collateralized loan bonds, CLO, is among what I follow," says Pål Ringholm, the highest-ranking credit analyst in Norway.

"The debt level is important," says Pål. "Of course, there will be no debt crisis without debt.

"And what's more, the access to debt drives the equity markets.

"The access to debt determines whether companies can be acquired. It determines whether companies can buy their own shares, whether they can buy others and the terms of the companies' own investments."

YOU WOULDN'T HAVE RECEIVED A BANK LOAN IF YOU HAD EQUITY AS A BANK

" ... what has not changed is a fundamental belief that it's okay to have banks bigger than the economy that they serve and that it's okay for banks to lend out much more capital than they have. Add to that a lack of contrition and an enduring sense of self-belief from the bankers themselves and you have a recipe for the next disaster."

– Philip Augar, British author and former equity broker in the *Big Issue*, August 2018

The system for assessing banks has changed in recent years.

The indicators that describe banks' liquidity and financing are given more weight.

After each crisis, we learn from some of our mistakes. Before we sow the seeds of some new ones.

One of the societal roles of a bank remains to be their role as a bridge between customers with deposits and those in need of long-term financing. A buffer is required to fulfil this mission, on solidity and liquidity. The solidity ensures resilience if borrowers default. The liquidity protects against mismatch of time and size.

But both have a cost. There is a cost of having an open liquidity line. There is a cost of having ample equity. The regulators and the banks therefore seek to optimize the trade-off between the risk and the cost of the buffers.

For banks, two measures are highlighted. One being the reserves relative to the banks' total assets. The other being the reserves relative to the so-called risk-weighted assets.

For example, loans to sovereigns in the EU do not require any specific support from equity. Loans to highly rated, investment grade, banks are weighted with 20% of their face value, which is what enabled the 'love letters'. Mortgages are typically weighted with 35% of their face value, assuming a loan to value ratio below 80%. The equity need related to derivative and trading positions is calculated based on the estimated risk related to the instruments and the counterparty.

If one believes the numbers, banks in the EU have become less risky since 2010. The ratio of risk-weighted assets to total assets has been reduced from 41% in 2010 to 38% in 2018. More remarkable, larger banks' assets are seen as less risky as compared to smaller, with a ratio of 34% and 57% respectively.

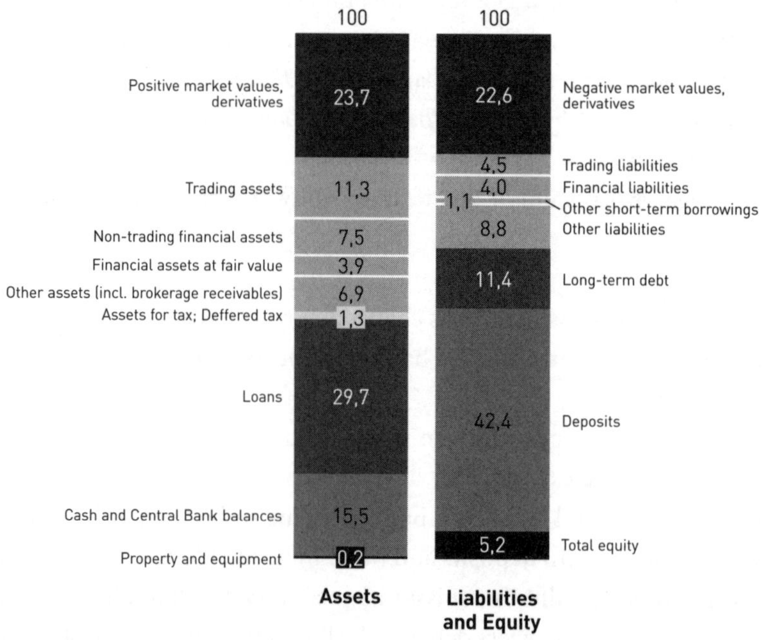

Example bank balance sheets.
Share of total assets and liabilities; %; 2018; Example European universal bank
Source: Annual report

"The large banks have more compelling risk model," says Pål. They are better at convincing the regulators.

The chart shows the build-up of the balance sheet of a large European bank.

Deposits and loans now represent about 40% and 30% of the liabilities and assets, respectively. Derivative positions are the largest part of what remains. Hence, the construct of the models matters.

Its total equity is about 5% of its total balance sheet at the end of 2018. End 2007 saw a ratio of the same bank of about 2%.

The bank's cash balance and long-term debt supports its liquidity, with the share of both vastly increased since 2007. The ratio of deposits and loans as a share of total asset values has more than doubled. The liquidity coverage, LCR, is systematically measured.

Hence, increased resilience appears to have been built, here as for many other leading banks. Within the EU's monetary union the banks' equity to to asset ratio increased from 4.7% August 2007 to 5.9% August 2019.

Across Europe, the CDSs of the large European banks have been running below 100 basis points for the last years. Deutsche Bank CDSs have, though, in periods traded up toward 250, and the CDSs on five leading Italian banks increased from about 50 early 2018 to about 200 early 2019, as doubts were raised on the government's economic plan.

A simultaneous beating of the leading banks in the main banking centres through a weakening of one or more of the main sectors will be needed for a full-blown financial crisis to be triggered in the years to come. A collapse in the CLO market due to higher interest rates or a weaker economy may be one possible trigger. A collapse of the confidence of the governments of some key countries another.

The rating agencies are now regulated. Authorization is required to provide a rating. Those who are not regulated can merely compile figures, not give their assessment and a 'rating'.

Unauthorized ratings based on qualitative reviews are prohibited, although experience shows that presence, experience and judgment were what was required to understand the weaknesses of Icelandic banks.

The numbers only told half the story, and barely that.

The three major agencies, Moody's, S&P and Fitch, who now have authorization, were barely met with sanctions nor fines after their errors in 2008.

On 23 July 2018, on the other hand, the European regulator, ESMA, fined five banks: Nordea, SEB, Swedbank, Handelsbanken and the 2006 whistle-blower, Danske Bank. Each with €495,000. They were convicted of having 'rated' banks, for having given shadow ratings. Without authorization.

SECTOR COLLAPSE, TECHNOLOGY AND CLIMATE

The S&P 500 index includes companies that contribute between 70% and 80% of the total equity value of listed US companies.

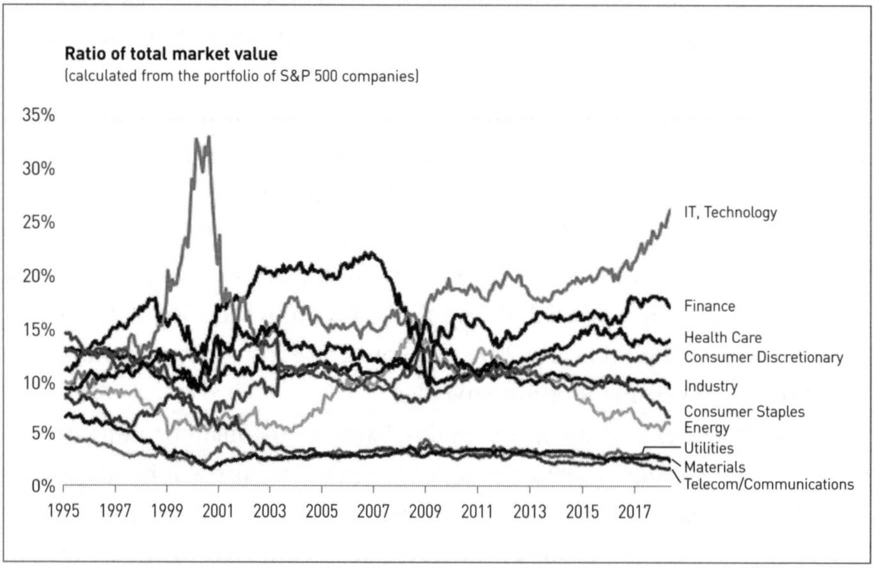

Sectoral split of the value of US equities.
Source: S&P 500; Datastream

Microsoft, Apple, Google, Facebook and Amazon compete for the position as the most valuable, each with a share of S&P of 2-3%. Even though half receive almost their entire income from only one product or service line.

A 30% decline in the value of one of these companies will hit their investors hard but will even out if one sees the market as a whole. However, shocks that hit the largest sectors, as in 2000, can bring the market down.

The split of the market value of all S&P 500 companies illustrates this.

The chart shows the extreme upturn in IT and technology up until the summer of 2000, and the collapse thereafter. At the top, the IT sector's share reached 35%, just over half of the banks' share in Iceland.

After the IT sector's crash of 2000, the financial sector became the most important. Until it collapsed in 2008. With high oil prices, the value of the oil companies also increased until 2009.

When everything else fell in 2009, as expected, utilities, companies in the health sector and producers of consumer goods became the investors' favourite pick.

Since 2010, IT and technology has returned as the big winner, with a share of total value approaching the share in 2000.

Health and consumer goods companies follow.

Energy, power and supply became the main losers. The energy sector's weight was 13.2% in early 2011, falling to 5.3% early 2019. The mining companies' share, including coal producers, is one tenth of their 1979 share.

The US capital market, at least the equity market, has already lived a large part of the burdensome part of the shift to a greener world.

MARKET FAILURE AND LOST OPPORTUNITIES

Dozens of companies conduct country risk analyses. For companies and banks about to lock in billions of dollars in a project, where ten-year operational stability is required to pay off the investment, country analyses are necessary. Knowing such analyses have been conducted gives comfort to external investors.

Those who assess country risks typically focus on political issues: political stability, the integrity of the institutions and the risk of conflict, of closures, tax increases or nationalization. These are important additions to the topics highlighted so far; deficit, debt, valuation levels and the attractivity of the industries as such.

The level of valuation of equities in different countries can be compared, for example, by looking at how the companies are valued in different countries in relation to their expected earnings.

In some situations, the valuation levels are obviously influenced by actual or assumed macroeconomic imbalances.

However, a positive sentiment, as in the case of Iceland pre-crisis, can drive the values upwards long after a correction should have taken place. Similarly, the values may stay down way after an economy has turned upwards.

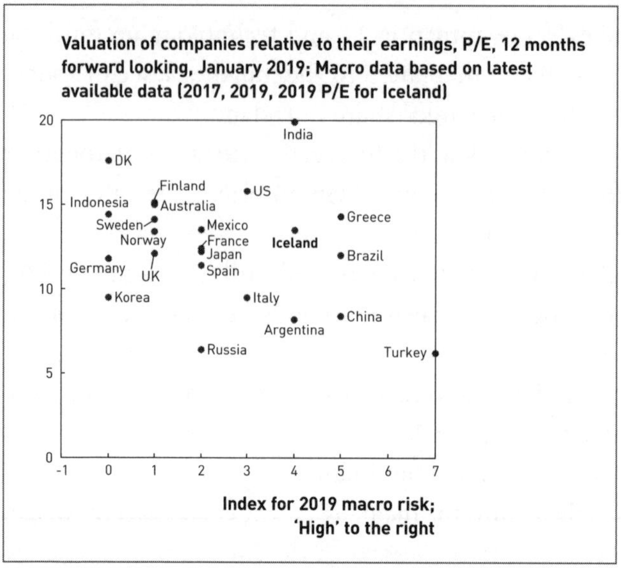

↳ **Country risk and company valuation.**
Price/Earnings, P/E, based on country index, typical of the 25-50 largest companies; P/E can be high/low due to fundamentally high/ low pricing or (temporary) decline/increase in earnings; the P/E comparison is most valid for sectors with the same debt ratio. The score for macro risk is an illustrative compilation of scores for debt level, debt growth and deviations in GDP growth from the trend for countries in the relevant GDP/population category, as well as for absolute GDP growth and transparency and integrity.
Source: BIS; IMF; Bloomberg

If one looks at the totality described above, summed up in a simple country indicator in the previous figure 'Country risk and company valuation', it may seem that history and sentiment, with some exceptions, still steer valuation levels way more than the future.

An understanding of risk governed by the past is today's greatest market failure.

Growth and returns are reduced because investment funds are biased toward the mature economies, the old technologies and toward producing yet another copy. But here the investment need is less, the risk of overcapacity more threatening and the return opportunities lower.

The market makes mistakes in the way it thinks about risk and returns, as illustrated in the electricity utility industry.

In fact, five times wrong. For investors, this is a threat and an opportunity.

The textbook states that an investor should be compensated for a devaluation risk, for example in developing countries where inflation is still often high. But, in many of the projects, the sales price is adjusted upwards with inflation. Then, indirectly, the inflation risk is often largely compensated.

Second, if the competition for new solar and wind power generation, as an example, is from dollar-based solutions, such as gas and diesel, the market price must, over time, move up toward international levels.

Third, it is far riskier to invest into markets with no demand growth, such as in western Europe, than in markets where new capacity is needed. Here, the price must be kept up so that new projects can be developed.

Fourth, there are single-country risks in, say, Africa, but across a portfolio this is leveled out. The new technologies enable this. Wind and sun, unlike coal, gas and partly hydropower, have the advantage that the projects can be developed in stages and in multiple locations. Anyway, the companies will also be less inclined toward deploying a large chunk of funds in one perceived high-risk country, they will stage their investments, and will seek all sorts of assurances and contracts.

Fifth, the real high-risk countries in the energy industry, and in most other industries, measured by the risk of loss of after-tax cash flow, are in western Europe and especially in the United States. Where else can companies implode due to 'just one' error or due to 'just one' litigation?

IT GOES UP, OR DOWN

If you plot the growth in world GDP and the increase of equity values over the last years, the you may see a correlation.

If you try hard enough.

A one percentage point stronger GDP growth coincides with 9% growth of corporate earnings and an equity value increase of 7%, says some research.

However, the picture is mixed.

In 1934, a Hungarian economist, Nicholas Kaldor, coined the name of an economic phenomenon, the pork cycle. Sometimes also called the hog cycle or the cattle cycle.

In good times with high prices, the farmers will offer more pork. Thus, the price falls. Then they will farm less pork. Then the price rises. The same mechanisms make their way in the global economy. As illustrated by the investment and debt figures.

"The market is unable to have stable expectations for the future," says Harald Magnus, the Chief Economist.

An investment cycle arises as businesses increase their investment to pursue attractive market opportunities. Demand is rising. The sentiment is positive. Banks provide more loans. Equity prices rise, especially for companies producing materials, energy and investment goods.

"Eventually the cycles are broken by their internal logic. The ups are often not sustainable. The debt becomes too high, some deficits too large, the investments excessive and the pricing aggressive," says Magnus.

"Pure equity bubbles are often not that serious for the economy. As illustrated by the 1987 case, the equity markets do often not create a crisis in the broader economy when they collapse. Unless they coincide with underlying imbalances, as in 2000 and especially in 2008. In the latter case there were signs of fatigue already in 2004 and 2005, but the journey continued.

"Before 2008, many countries had large imbalances and deficits. The downturn was long and fierce."

HALF THE WARNING LIGHTS FLASH

Mid-2019 the investment levels were high. Only twice since 1985 have they been as high relative to the trend; before the downturns in 1990 and 2008. Unemployment is low. In the US, it has fallen ever since 2010. It has not been as low since 1980. The US housing market is mixed.

In the US, the corporate debt to GDP ratio varies through the cycle by about seven percentage points. Companies invest in 'good times' and raise debt, actually taking the debt levels ever higher. As the cycle turns they slash investments and reduce their debt. As investments are slashed, the capacity for growth shrinks or even stalls. Shortages then occur, prices raise, and the new cycle starts.

Mid-2019 saw debt levels at an all-time high.

"We are at the end of the cycle," says Harald Magnus. "The market is expensive, and the economy is stretched."

"History has shown that if you are a long-term investor, you should always prioritize your equity investments," says Peter, the equity strategist. "If you have a three-year perspective then the answer has always been to sit in stocks when valuation is low."

So, yes, his audience on Wall Street should have listened to his presentation March 2009. That was when the global financial crisis hit its lowest level – eight months after Lehman.

However, when the valuation creeps up, it is time to sharpen the senses. No major fall in the last 30 years has occurred without the valuation first having been at peak levels.

In such situations, the assessments of the broader economy become crucial. Positive leading indicators and spare capacity can indicate further growth. If the leading indicators point downwards and there is little available capacity, then one should certainly be on the alert.

Risk appetite and capacity will vary from person to person. An alternative could be to turn the exposure more and more in a defensive direction the higher the market is priced; however, the valuation declines across most segments if a crisis hits.

The share allocation can be weighted between cyclical and defensive positions in accordance with market pricing and risk appetite and capacity. A high-risk, long-term investor may vary his equity allocation between 60% and 100% while another investor with a lower risk willingness and/or shorter horizon will be between 30% and 60%, depending on market pricing and macro risk.

When the markets have fallen a lot, one can argue that one should invest in the most geared and cyclical part of the market and take up the equity portion. This requires that one has the ability to distinguish the transient decreases from the permanent ones, the cycles from the systemic shifts. The ideal is to hit the bottom, but it may be more realistic to increase gradually as the market begins to tick up again.

Mid-2019, the leading indicators have turned from pointing up to pointing moderately downwards. Some had started to talk about inflation and hiked interest rates, but those voices went silent.

What still grows is the total pile of debt.

APPENDIX

SOURCES AND METHODOLOGY

I was fortunate to have a front-row seat as many of the events in this book unfolded. I have drawn on that experience. In addition, I conducted more than 90 interviews as part of my research.

Interviewees include former and current senior employees of financial market regulators, Ministries of Finance, Central Banks (governors, economists, market operations specialists, head legal counsel), Icelandic and international banks, members of government, business leaders, IMF employees, bank executives, credit and macro analysts, journalists, historians, investigators, members of grass-roots movements, lawyers, participants in the winding-up processes of the fallen banks and hedge fund managers. A list of the interviewees is included in the appendix. A handful requested anonymity.

There is no doubt that personalities, alliances and individual grievances have a bearing on policy decisions and the way policies unfold. Many are those that ideally should have been honoured, and some who could have been criticized by name. But this has not been the purpose of my book. Instead, my goal has been to describe the larger forces that converged on one small country in the first decade of this century, and the insights their impact provide on the world we live in and on what the future may bring. I believe that Iceland, in some sense, was a microcosm for much of what unfolded elsewhere and that its experience can help us to understand the strengths, vulnerabilities and policy options as we encounter new shocks.

With that goal in mind, I have deliberately omitted the names of most individuals involved and even those quoted, except in cases where the origin of the statements is of particular importance. The book does not attempt to describe the positions, decisions and actions of specific individuals, governments or parties. Similarly, descriptions of the goals and opinions of individuals has been kept to a minimum, reflecting the view that a government minister, an official or a business leader needs to stand behind the policies pursued and actions taken, or step down.

This book largely builds on the work of Iceland's Special Investigative Committee, or SIC, with regard to the period before mid-October 2008. The SIC was appointed by the Icelandic Parliament and charged with uncovering the root causes of the country's banking collapse. The SIC interrogated more than 120 people. It has not been my ambition to redo or question the report of the SIC and, for the most part, I did not re-interview SIC sources.

The mandate of the SIC, however, was largely focused on what happened in Iceland and less on the 'other side', i.e. the observations and views from abroad. I therefore made a deliberate effort to interview some of those who had key roles internationally. In addition, the SIC collected valuable perspectives from people close to the events immediately after they occurred. Many of the interviews for this book covered the same events, but obviously informed by a decade of hindsight.

As word started to circulate in Iceland that I was preparing a book, many have reached out to me with suggestions for areas of research and other ideas. I also received a wealth of documents and data, both on a solicited and unsolicited basis.

I'm grateful to all of those who shared their time, their ideas, and their research materials. They have made this book immeasurably richer. The author, however, bears full responsibility for all statements of fact and judgments made. No institutions or individuals have endorsed this book or any of its elements. I apologize for any errors made or credits omitted.

A dozen individuals, Icelandic and non-Icelandic, have read the text and suggested improvements. Some have spent a lot of time searching through their files to help with additional information and clarifications. Almost all the ones I wanted to interview made themselves available, they spoke openly, and they set almost no conditions. Joachim Huse has provided analytical support, including analysing the lists of creditors. For all this, I owe a lot of thanks.

DEFINITIONS AND CLARIFICATIONS

Up to 26 February 2009, the Central Bank had three governors. When the term 'governor' is used for the period up to 26 February, it refers to the chairman of the board, unless stated otherwise. The statements attributed to the special prosecutor are from the person who held the position from 2009 onward.

Technically a bank doesn't go bankrupt but will be placed in an administrative or winding-down process. These can be run by resolution committees, winding-down boards or other bodies. For simplicity, though, I use the words 'bankruptcy', 'default' and 'estates' to characterize what happened and how it was administered.

GENERAL SOURCES

Many descriptions are based on my own experiences. Wikipedia and other encyclopaedias have been used as a source for historical and contextual information. In particular, this applies to the chapters on Icelandic history, 'Some good years', and the chapters on Kiribati, on WaMu, on Pisa, Ireland and Greece.

All exchange rate figures are based on data from Iceland's Central Bank, Seðlabanki. Figures on unemployment and macroeconomic indicators, tourist traffic, etc., are derived from Statistics Iceland.

SOURCES BY CHAPTER

Only sections that build on specific sources are listed. Sources used in multiple sections are listed where the topics covered are discussed at greatest depth or where they first appear. Sources already specified in the main text are not listed in this appendix. The main text indicates which statements are based on interviews. Sources for data that are easily available in the public domain, for example, data on macroeconomic measures, inflation, interest rates and market indexes, have not been listed.

A UNIQUE OPPORTUNITY

The statements in this chapter are substantiated in the topic chapters.

IN THE YEAR 1262, THE CHIEFTAINS OF ICELAND MET

A historic summary can be found in the Central Bank's publication *Iceland, the Republic*, from 1996. The legislation passed on 26 February 2009 was an amendment of the Act No. 36/2001, on the Central Bank of Iceland. The provision allowing for an interim appointment was included in the Act 70/1996 on government employees.

PARACHUTED INTO THE EPICENTRE OF THE FINANCIAL CRISIS

The default ranking is from Moody's report from February 2009: *Corporate Default and Recovery Rates, 1920-2008*. It ranks the defaults based on 'default value', i.e. the value of the defaulted debt. The litigation of the 27 refers to a district court case related to SPRON.

A HIRED GUN OF FINANCE

The E24 article is from Sunday 29 March 2009 with reference to a speech at the Independence Party convention the same day. This again is based on a news report from RÚV, the Icelandic state broadcaster. The quote on the man from the mountain is from multiple blog entries of Hannes Hólmsteinn Gissuurarson.

THE FIVE STAGES OF A FINANCIAL CRISIS

William McChesney Martin Jr., US Fed governor, first used the punch bowl analogy in a statement in 1955.

LIKE BEES TO HONEY

This chapter largely builds on information from the report of the Special Investigation Commission (SIC), in particular the summary chapter in its English translation. The information on OMX composition is from calculations based on OMX monthly statistics for March 2007. The CDO figures derive from Reuters. A Citigroup report from 3 January 2007 provides information on Kaupthing's trading income, as Citigroup initiated coverage with a 'Buy – High Risk' recommendation. The FX debt figures are based on the Central Bank of Iceland Household Sector Database. The information on the banks' key ratios is from *Iceland's Failed Bank: A Post-Mortem*, prepared for the SIC by Mark J. Flannery.

WHEN REALITY DEVIATES FROM THEORY

The data on car loans in this chapter and on FX/indexed loans in this and later chapters are from the Central Bank of Iceland Household Sector Database.

NOT THAT UNFAMILIAR

Saga Íslandsbanka hf. og Útvegsbanka Íslands 1904-1980, issued in 1981 by Útvegsbanki Íslands, provided background on the history of old Islandsbanki and Útvegsbanki for the period 1904-1980. Ragnar Hafliðason, a former FME employee, provided invaluable background on Icelandic banking history. The Hauck & Aufhäuser description is partly based on an article on the website mbl.is dated 29 March 2017. The article "The Rise, Fall, and Resurrection of Iceland: A Postmortem Analysis of the 2008 Financial Crisis" by Sígríður Bendiktsdóttir, Gauti BerÞórusin Eggertson and Eggert Þórarinson, is recent and gives a good and comprehensive overview of the facts and figures related to the crisis. It provides the data on the debt financing of the purchase of the banks and is also used as a key source for the chapters 'The best buy', 'Something to celebrate' (including the statement on Switzerland), 'A spiderweb of linkages' and 'The phony equity'. The Hafskip case is summarized in the article "The Hafskip Affair" in *Ísland í aldanna rás 1900-2000.*

BOYS, DON'T YOU SEE THE PARTY?

A detailed and well-written overview of the sequence of events in the days of the crisis is provided in the book *Bringing Down the Banking System* by Gudrun Johnsen. This has been the source of the research and numbers on credit referenced in this chapter. The comparison to all crises since 1875 is from the Working Paper number 68: "The long history of financial boom-bust cycles in Iceland" from the Central Bank of Iceland. Here, the terms four, six and eight standard deviations are used, hence the text has been grossly simplified.

FIX UP YOUR HOUSE! WHY SHOULD I? YOURS IS WORSE

The quotes from a Kaupthing executive are from the book *Frozen Assets* by Armann Þorvaldsson, the UK CEO of Kaupthing Bank. The Glitnir statement was issued by Glitnir Research.

A COUNTRY THAT BUILT A FUND FROM SHIT

Unless otherwise stated, all information on claims in this and later chapters derive from the claim lists of the three banks from May 2012. The data on Kiribati's finances is derived from the IMF country reports and the economic plans of Kiribati. The Iceland exposure to GDP ratio shows the mid-2012 positions in May 2012 exchange rates divided by Kiribati's 2007 USD GDP.

BANKS THAT CHASE BORROWERS

The numbers on loan losses are from *Iceland's Failed Bank: A Post-Mortem*. This report also reviews the issues related to loan-loss accounting and the accounting principles applied.

13 REASONS FOR SUCCESS

The speech that is referenced is titled "How to succeed in modern business: Lessons from the Icelandic voyage," delivered at the Walbrook Club, London, and reproduced in full in *Reykjavik Grapevine*.

FINANCIAL WEAPONS OF MASS DESTRUCTION

Reuters quoted on 3 November 2008 the figures on open CDSs from Depository Trust & Clearing Corp. DTCC clears most of the trades in the credit derivative market. The quotes from Kaupthing executives are from *Frozen Assets* by Armann Þorvaldsson.

THE ALARM BELL GOES ON AND OFF, THEN ON AND ON AND ON

The description of the sequence of events and the funds made available is based on interviews with Fed employees.

A SPIDERWEB OF LINKAGES

The quote at the beginning of the chapter is from *The Icelandic Financial Crisis: A Study into the World's Smallest Currency* by Ásgeir Jónsson and Hersir Sigurgeirsson. This book provides a very good and comprehensive overview of the financial accounts and the post-crisis restructuring processes. The figures on connected party lending are from the SIC report. A large part of the data is presented in the article "The Rise, Fall, and Resurrection of Iceland." The illustration of the Icelandic ownership landscape was received from the files of a then Norwegian FSA employee. Its origin is unknown.

THE CASH MACHINE AND THE LETTERS OF ETERNAL LOVE

The Trichet quote is taken from the book *Iceland's Financial Crisis: The Politics of Blame, Protest and Reconstruction*, edited by Valur Ingimundarson, Philippe Urfalino and Irma Erlingsdóttir. The article "The Rise, Fall and Resurrection of Iceland" gives a good overview of the funding of the Icelandic banks.

PHONY EQUITY

An overview of the trading in shares is provided in *Bringing Down the Banking System*. The article, "Equity out of nothing," by Jón Þ. Hilmarsson and Stefán Svavarsson, both chartered accountants, was published in the online edition of *Viðskiptablaðið*, an Icelandic commercial newspaper, on 2 February 2018. The Landsbanki court case is summarized in an article in *Morgunbladid* on 12 March 2017. The settlement is announced in a press release from the estate 10 March 2017, referring to the court case E-3162/2012, which had been in process before the Reykjavík District Court.

THREE BANKS PREPARE THREE LIFEBOATS

The book references refer to *Frozen Assets*.

WORRIED NEIGHBOURS

The information on the Norwegian FSA report and supervision is from the book of then FSA General Director, Bjørn Skogstad Aamo, *Læring fra kriser*. The quote is from Professor Thore Johnsen's report "Island – Banker og Børsen" from January 2005.

A COUNTRY THAT HURTLED DOWN THE TRAIN TRACK

The data on FX loans is from the Central Bank of Iceland Household Sector Database.

THE 0.6% IMPACT OF A QUADRUPLE ECONOMIC SHOCK

This and the following Mervyn King quotes are from his speech on the BBC Today Programme Lecture on 2 May 2012. The information on the stress test is based on the FME press release dated 6 February 2008. The summary on the FME is based on a presentation by the SIC to the Norwegian FSA on 18 November 2009.

IT'S A CONSPIRACY

The quotes on Kaupthing are from *Frozen Assets.*

SPY VERSUS SPY

Deutsche Bank's information on the settlement can be found in "The third supplement dated 6 November 2017 to the base prospectus dated 22 June 2017". It referred to Kaupthing's claims that Kaupthing itself had funded the SPVs and that Kaupthing alleged that Deutsche Bank was or should have been aware that Kaupthing was economically exposed in the transactions. Kaupthing claimed that the transactions were voidable on a number of grounds, including that the transactions were improper because one of the alleged purposes of the transactions was to allow Kaupthing to influence the market in its own CDS spreads and thereby its listed bonds. Further information on the case is found in the records from multiple court hearings in Reykjavik and London. For an overview see article on *Icelog* of 3 November 2017 by Sígrún Daviðsdóttir.

THREE BANKS THAT ONLY PRETEND

The Kaupthing relocation plan and suggestion on a bond issuance is referred to in the book *Frozen Assets.* The quote of the Landsbanki owner is from the book *Billions to Bust – and Back* by Thor Björgólfsson. The speech of Trichet is titled "Remarks at the farewell event," dated 19 October 2011.

JUST FOUR DAYS AFTER LEHMAN

The then strictly confidential terms of the Nordic agreement are listed in *Bringing Down the Banking System*, page 186. This book also summarizes the contacts with central banks. The 19 September memo is titled "Follow-up information with reference to a strictly confidential memo to the governors of Sveriges Riksbank, Danmarks Nationalbank and Norges Bank," dated 16 April 2008.

JAZZ, FREDDIE, FANNIE, LEHMAN AND WAMU

The quotes come from *Gjennomslag*, a memoir by the then Minister of Finance of Norway, Kristin Halvorsen, and interviews with the Permanent Secretary. The data and comments on the swap lines are from the article "Central Bank Dollar Swap Lines and Overseas Dollar funding costs" by Linda S. Goldberg, Craig Kennedy and Jason Miu, all at the Federal Reserve Bank of New York. A participant has provided the quote from the European meeting among the FSAs.

The quotes related to Lehman are from the books *Stress Test* by Timothy Geithner and *On the Brink* by Henry M. Paulson.

WRONG NUMBER, CALL THE IMF

Further information on the position of the Fed can be found in the minutes from the meeting of the Federal Open Market Committee on 28 and 29 October 2008.

KEEP THE INFECTION AWAY

Information on the Glitnir transaction is available from the press releases from the Oslo stock exchange and financial news sites, for example, E24. The seller had one advisor, Arctic Securities. The buyer had two, First Securities and Sparebank1 SMN Markets.

THROWING PENSION FUND MONEY INTO THE FIRE

The report referred to was from a committee appointed by the Icelandic Pension Funds Association; see the report "Úttekt á fjárfestingarstefnu, ákvarðanatöku og lagalegu umhverfi lífeyrissjóðanna í aðdraganda bankahrunsins 2008", ref. chapter 2.1. "Summary of the Principal conclusions of the Review."

THE TOWER COMES DOWN

The data on the banks, their liquidity and the situation on Friday 3 October 2008 is from the article "Gambling for Resurrection in Iceland: the Rise and Fall of the Banks" by Fridrik Mar Baldursson, Reykjavik University, and Richard Portes, London Business School, September 2013. This article also provides a good overview of some of the specific triggers of the downfall of the banks. It is also the source of the statement on bank liquidity.

The data on the banks' ratios, adjusted and nonadjusted, are from the presentation "The Financial Crisis in Iceland: Reflections on Causes, Consequences and Lessons to be Learned" by Már Guðmundsson, May 2011.

The examples and wording are from research and articles of Fridrik Mar Baldursson and Richard Portes. A specific timeline of the events in the last days is provided in the book *Bringing Down the Banking System* by Gudrun Johnsen, which also includes the data on the banks' related parties' exposures. The example on the conditional credit lines is from *Iceland's Failed Bank: A Post-Mortem*. The old Central Bank Act of February 2001, its accompanying notes and a memo of understanding defined the split of roles between the FME and the Central Bank.

HEROES IN A TIME OF CRISIS

This chapter is based on interviews as listed and meeting summaries as presented in the book *Bringing Down the Banking System.*

GOD BLESS ICELAND

A full English translation of Geir Haarde's speech can be found in *Bringing Down the Banking System.*

WE ARE NOT TERRORISTS

The statements on the Russian loans can be found in the news archive of the press releases of the Central Bank.

A PACK OF WOLVES

The data on the claims are from the May 2012 list of creditors. Some creditors possibly passed on their positions ahead of this date. The quote from the Landsbanki owner is from *Billions to Bust – and Back.* The quote from the Minister of Finance is from the memoirs of Kristin Halvorsen. The statement on the views of some of the Norwegian government's legal advisors is based on my own observations. The wording of the Landsbanki freezing order can be found in *The Icesave Dispute: A Case Study into the Crisis of Diplomacy during the Credit Crunch*, by Eirikur Bergman. A comprehensive overview of Icesave matters can be found on Wikipedia.

50 BANKS, 20 COUNTRIES, ONE BIG CRASH

The overview of the positions of the three banks is from the material prepared for the 10 October teleconference among the European FSAs. The information on Kaupthing Norway is from the book *Læring fra kriser.*

THE FIGHT OVER HISTORY

The article "Lessons for Europe from the 2008 Icelandic Bank Collapse" by Hannes H. Gissurarson presents a perspective questioning the SIC conclusions. The quote on measures to support the banks is from the article "The Icelandic Banking Crisis and What to Do about It" from April 2008, written by the Professors Willem H. Buiter and Anne C. Sibert. The data on loans given in 2007-2008 is from a presentation by Tjörvi Ólafsson, "Lessons from the Icelandic households' risky ride on the credit carousel".

IN THE SMALL TOWN OF ÁLFTANES

This section is based on articles in *Icenews* on 18 June 2009 and 7 May 2011. For an overview of the impact on the municipalities, see the article "Weathering the Storm – Icelandic Municipalities' Handling of an Unprecedented Economic Crisis" by Magnús Árni Skjöld Magnússon.

ECB IS OFF THE HOOK. SEÐLABANKI TAKES A HIT

An overview of the rules on collateral lending of Seðlabanki can be found in its annual report for 2008. In a press release from 5 March 2009, the ECB provides information on its 2008 positions. The information on the outcome is based on information received from the Bank of Finland, dated 1 August 2018, following an interview with the Bank of Finland Governor, Errki Liikanen, on 11 June 2018.

EXPLAINING WHAT CAN'T BE EXPLAINED

A short summary of the glacier bond structures is provided in Appendix 1 of the IMF "Selected Issues" report on Iceland from August 2007. A more comprehensive overview can be found in the 3 June 2008 presentation by René Kallestrup, "The recent turmoil in the Icelandic foreign exchange market". Box 1 in the Monetary Bulletin number 4 from 2005 also seeks to explain the concept. Freyr Hermannsson also helped explain the glacier bond concept.

CLIMBING THE STAIRS OF THE PALACE OF JUSTICE

The ownership stakes are reviewed in the book *Bringing Down the Banking System.*

LOSING A QUARTER OF THE PENSION SAVINGS

This chapter is based on the report, "Evaluation of investment policy, decision making and the legal environment of the pension funds in anticipation of the banking crisis in 2008", prepared by a committee appointed by the pension funds. The figures on the discontinued businesses were calculated by the author and track the destiny of the companies that were listed on the Icelandic exchange in March 2007.

CALLS FROM ALL CORNERS OF THE WORLD

An article from Reuters on 3 November 2008 provides data on the results of the CDS auctions. Creditfixing.com lists the participants in the auctions.

48,580 POSSIBLE LOSERS

All the calculations referred to are based on the May 2012 list of creditor claims.

BARRICADES AT SEÐLABANKI

The poll referred is from the Icelandic newspaper *Fréttablaðið*, 2 March 2009.

STILL NOT AT THE BOTTOM

The data on Icebank are from the book *The Icelandic Financial Crisis*. The litigation of the 27 refers to a District Court case related to SPRON.

STEMMING THE JÖKULHLAUP

For a critical review of the capital control system and its supervision, see the book *Out of Control?* by Björn Jón Bragason.

MCDONALD'S CLOSES, LEAVES ICELAND AND BECOMES PART OF THE SOLUTION

The McDonald's story is based on an article in *The Telegraph* and on the BBC, dated 27 October 2009. The data on car sales, imports and exports is from Statistics Iceland.

A EURO ISLAND DOWN SOUTH

The currency impact on the fisheries companies can be seen in a review of their annual reports. Jan Ove Ekeberg, a Norwegian author, contributed the story of Harald III. The experience of Ecuador is based on interviews.

A DANGEROUS SPIRAL

The article "Financial Assistance Measures in the Euro Area from 2008 to 2013: Statistical Framework and Fiscal Impact" by Henri Maurer and Patrick Grussenmeyer is the source of the figures on the euro-area costs of the crisis.

A NIGHTMARE CALLED CDS, GOVERNMENT DEBT AND FISCAL AUSTERITY

All data on GDP, budgets, etc., are from the OECD Economic Outlook, IMF and the World Bank. The OECD provides data on the size of pension funds by country.

THE TRUCK DRIVER AND THE FLIGHT ATTENDANT

The UN report referred to is the End-of-Mission statement by Juan Pablo Bohoslavsky, United Nations independent expert on the effects of foreign debt and other related international financial obligations of states on the full enjoyment of all human rights, particularly economic, social and cultural rights, Mission to Iceland, 8-15 December 2014. The figures on the budget can be found in "Iceland – Fiscal Consolidation Plan", as presented by the Icelandic Ministry of Finance at the 33rd annual meeting of OECD senior budget officials.

LET'S SCRAP THE PLAN – IT DOESN'T WORK

The case referred to regarding the repatriation of funds is the effort of the estate of Anders Jahre. The FME comments on the valuation process are included in its 4 April 2009 statement "Summary of the Net Asset Valuation of the New Banks".

G4 MEETS IN SWITZERLAND

The description of the loan arrangements is based on the 2009 Annual Report of the Central Bank of Iceland. The statement on the IMF position is from a letter dated 13 November 2009 from the IMF Managing Director to "Open Civil Meetings."

MUAMMAR GADDAFI, THE NUCLEAR PLANT AND THE PACIFIC ISLAND

The summary of the court cases provided the information on the cases referenced. Further information on bank restructuring comes from the publication *Research Handbook on State Aid in the Banking Sector*, by François-Charles Laprévote, Joanna Gray and Francesco de Cecco.

WHEN SOCIALISTS TURN CAPITALIST AND CAPITALISTS TURN SOCIALIST

Law360 provides information on the Bank of Tokyo-Mitsubishi case against Kaupthing.

LIKE A PISTOL TO THE FOREHEAD

Parts of the section on FIH build on a comprehensive and well-written article from May 2016 in the Danish magazine *Finans*, titled "Den dag Lehman ramte Langelinie". An overview of the measures related to the banks can be found in the overview "Summary of Government Interventions in Financial Markets Iceland" by law firm Mayer Brown from 8 September 2009.

WE CAN'T PLAY GOD

The data on FX lending is from the article "Gambling for Resurrection in Iceland: the Rise and Fall of the Banks". Data on default rates and restructuring can be found in the presentation "Icelandic banks: Rebuilding a Financial System" on August 2012 by Yngvi Örn Kristinsson.

DOWN, DOWN, DOWN AND A THING CALLED AVENS

The article "Iceland's Failed Banks: A Post-Mortem" provides an overview of the collateralized lending and refers to the letter from BCL. The Seðlabanki press release of 31 May 2010 provides information on the Avens transaction.

THE EVEN LARGER CHALLENGE

The source of the data on household debt is "Working Paper number 59", dated June 2012 of the Central Bank of Iceland, "Households' position in the financial crisis in Iceland" by Þorvarður Tjörvi Ólafsson and Karen Áslaug Vignisdóttir. It was supplemented by material from Ólafsson's presentation "Households' Position in the Financial Crisis in Iceland: Analysis Based on a Nationwide Household-Level Database". The description of the debt measures and parts of the related text are from IMF Economic Outlook of April 2012.

TACKLED AND SUED BY NEIGHBOURS AND FRIENDS

The information on the Dutch figures is from a press release by DNB dated 27 August 2014. The summary of the EFTA Court judgment is based on the full text of the court from 28 January 2013. The quote related to Landsbanki is from the book *Billions to Bust – and Back.*

THE REYKJAVIK SYNDROME

The Seðlabanki 2009 Annual Report gives details on the interest rate conditions through 2009.

SMUGGLED IN BEHIND TINTED WINDOWS AND UP THE FREIGHT ELEVATOR

See also Jens Stoltenberg's book *Min historie.*

IN THE ECONOMIST'S MODEL

The description of the phases is based on data on the development of the GDP and its subcomponents 2007-2017 from Statistics Iceland and the Monetary Bulletins of Seðlabanki.

ONE JAILED BANKER IN THE US, 25 IN ICELAND

The article of the auditors referred is by Jón Þ. Hilmarsson og Stefán Svavarsson. The figures on jailed bankers is from an article in *Financial Times* on 20 September 2018. The list identifies the bank employees and directors that received jail sentences for issues directly linked to the crisis or the collapse of their institution. It should be noted that the sentences in some of the 47 cases may have been altered on appeal. The information on the one US banker and on US Saving and Loans is from an article in *The New York Times* on 30 April 2014 that also provides an excellent examination of US practices in investigation of wrongdoings in the financial sector.

IT WAS A CIRCUS

The list of hedge funds present is based on the 2012 list of claimants, the overview of funds in creditor committees and on interviews. The book *The Icelandic Financial Crisis* has also been used as a source. It includes comprehensive information and calculations on the positions of some funds. An overview of the positions of some of the funds can be found in the article "How Hedge Funds Hide" in *Institutional Investor*, April 2017. The count of funds is made by the author in comparison to the list of top 50 US funds in *The Hedge Fund Journal*, which is based on year-end 2011 figures. The figures on EU bailout costs are from the ECB Statistics Paper Series number 7 of April 2015.

THE ONES HAILED

The information on the Kaupthing borrowers is from *The Telegraph*, 4 August 2009. Articles in the same paper from 28 February 2015 and 10 and 11 October 2017 provide further information on Bakkavõr. Information on Bakkavõr is from its 2014-2018 annual reports. The reference to the debt restructuring involving Deutsche Bank relates to Actavis and the book *Billions to Bust – and Back*.

THE GREEK TRAGEDY

"The Greek Debt Restructuring: an Autopsy" by Jeromin Zettlemeyer, Christoph Trebesch and Mitu Gulati from 2013 gives an overview of the Greek debt restructuring. An article in *The New York Times* on 2 March 2012 names some of the engaged parties, as does an article in *Am Law Daily* on 22 March 2012.

A DEAD PERSON CAN'T SIGN

The information and quote on the litigation lawyer is from an article in *The American Lawyer* on 27 September 2016

THE GREY CAT

The quote of Rob Bennett is from an article in *The American Lawyer*, 27 September 2016.

BUY AT 4, SELL AT 24, ACTUALLY AT 40

The description of the profile of the value of the claims is based on the book *The Icelandic Financial Crisis*. The overview of the value of the Kaupthing position referred to in the chart is based on return figures received from one of the hedge funds.

THE MONEY NOT REALLY NEEDED

Seðlabanki has provided the data on the accumulated loan balances. The interest rate figures are from the press releases issued. The figures on booked guarantee premiums for Norway are from the Norwegian State Budget, St. prp. Nr. 1, while the interest rates paid by Ireland were quoted in *Irish Times*, 14 February 2015.

A STRONG BREW

The macroeconomic figures used are based on Monetary Bulletin nr. 2, 2018 from Seðlabanki.

283 BILLION BEHIND BARS GET A CHANCE AT THE LAST GET-OUT-OF-JAIL-FREE CARD

The book *The Icelandic Financial Crisis* by Ásgeir Jónsson and Hersir Sigurgeirsson provides an overview of the glacier bond positions. The calculations referred in this section are based on a spreadsheet overview of Eurobond positions as of 6 October 2008.

THE LIONS RETURN TO THE CAGE

The reserve requirement rules were on determined 4 June 2016, ref. 490/2016 from the Central Bank, with updates 7 on December 2018.

THE CENTRAL BANKS AND THE HELICOPTER MONEY

The data on ECB lending is from its webpage on the Asset Purchase programmes. QE monitor from Allianz Global Investors has provided the data on ECB's share of the holdings of government bonds.

CRUSHED BY THE MIGHT OF THE STATE

The Fannie Mae and Freddy Mac case is based on an article in the *Financial Times*, 22 February 2018.

THE BAILOUT THAT TURNED A PROFIT

The data on the cost of the crisis is from an IMF Staff report for the 2016 Article IV consultation. A comprehensive overview of the process and key figures is provided in the article "Iceland's Capital Control and the Resolution of its Problematic Bank Legacy" from July 2017 by Fridrik Mar Baldursson and Richard Portes.

FORTY BILLION EUROS BURNED

The aggregate cost estimate is from the article "The Rise, Fall, and Resurrection of Iceland: A Postmortem Analysis of the 2008 Financial Crisis." This data is also the basis for the illustrative chart.

OFF TO KIRIBATI

The IMF 2017 article IV consultation report of December 2017 on Kiribati gives a recent overview of its economic performance.

ICELAND WELCOME AGAIN

The information on the 2017 debt issuance is from the press release of the Ministry of Finance of Iceland of 13 December 2017.

HAPPILY EVER AFTER

The chart on Iceland's external balance is copied from "The Rise, Fall, and Resurrection of Iceland: A Postmortem Analysis of the 2008 Financial Crisis."

A FOOL'S ERRAND

This chapter largely builds on information from the Report of the Special Investigation Commission (SIC). The examples and wording come from research and articles of Fridrik Mar Baldursson and Richard Portes.

IT'S A PATTERN

The afterword has been prepared in collaboration with Peter Hermanrud, Pål Ringholm and Harald Magnus Andreassen, all in the Norwegian investment bank Sparebank 1 Markets. The author, however, bears responsibility for the final result and for the assessments. The comment on the US housing market is based on a comparison of the changes in average number of building permits and new home sales as compared to the timing of equity market 'crashes'.

THE FLASHING LIGHTS OF 2019

The figures are as far as possible drawn with the same scale for 2007 and 2017. In some cases with extreme observations, the scale is broken. This is then marked. All calculations are done by the author. The calculations of Spain's contribution to the demand reduction from 2007 to 2011 are based on an analysis of total demand falls in the 27 EU countries, by sector and country.

THE STRANGEST AMONG ALL SERVICES

The development of valuations since 1880 is based on analyses conducted by Pål Ringholm.

CDOS IN A NEW COSTUME

Statistics Norway published statistics for the equity ratio in Norwegian listed companies until 2016. The text refers to the equity ratio in 2016. *The New York Times* described Deutsche Bank's loans to the Trump Organization in an article on 18 March 2019. The information about the CLO regulations is from a *Reuters* article of 11 May 2018. The Toys 'R' Us data can be found in a case study from ACCID.

YOU WOULDN'T HAVE RECEIVED A BANK LOAN IF YOU HAD EQUITY AS A BANK

Capital requirements vary by regulatory region, most often defined based on the so-called Basel guidelines. The data on risk weighted assets compared to total assets can be found in the Statistical Data Warehouse of the Eurosystem. The balance sheet data is from a top ten European bank. The capital ratio figure is from the IMF's Global Financial Stability report. The bank capital to assets figure quoted is the ratio of bank capital and reserves to total assets. Capital and reserves include funds contributed by owners, retained earnings, general and special reserves, provisions and valuation adjustments.

MARKET FAILURE AND LOST OPPORTUNITIES

The discussion of the methods for land analysis is based on the author's interviews with companies in the energy sector. The index for the macro risk is indicative. Large imbalances in the form of deficits have given higher scores on each dimension than less. Risk deductions are given for stable high growth and IIP reserves and robust government finances.

The calculations are mechanically based on defined macro parameters and set a total score. Extreme values on single parameters can have as much effect on a country's vulnerability as a high average risk score.

APPENDIX

INTERVIEWEES

The persons listed below have all been interviewed in the preparation of this book. They carry no responsibility for the totality of the book or for the quotes selected and the context in which they have been placed. The listing of the interviewees' positions is not comprehensive and focuses on the person's position in the period about which they were interviewed.

About half a dozen people rejected requests for interviews, half a dozen did not answer and another half a dozen asked not to be named.

As customary in Iceland, all are listed alphabetically based on their first name.

Alexis Stenfors	Director, fixed income, currencies and commodities, Merrill Lynch, 2005-2009. Now Senior Lecturer, Economics and Finance, Portsmouth University. Author of *Barometer of Fear*
Anders Borg	Minister of Finance of Sweden from 2006 to 2014; head of the group of European Ministers of Finance, ECOFIN, first half of 2009
Anna Nordstrom	Head of Front Office Division, Directorate General Market Operations at ECB to 2008; Assistant Vice President, Federal Reserve Bank of New York from 2008 to 2012; Vice President since 2012
Annamaria Kokeny	Senior financial sector expert, Capital Control, IMF

Anne Krueger	Deputy Managing Director, IMF, from 2001 to 2006; Professor of International Economics at the Johns Hopkins School of Advanced International Studies; member of the ad hoc team working on the Composition Agreement
Árni Páll Árnason	Minister of Social Affairs and Social Security from May 2009 to September 2010; Minister of Economic Affairs from September 2010 to December 2011; MP from 2007 to 2016
Arnór Sighvatsson	Chief Economist, Central Bank of Iceland from 2004 to February 2009; Deputy Central Bank Governor, Seðlabanki Islands from 2009 to 2018
Ásgeir Jónsson	Chief Economist, Kaupthing to 2008; Chief Economist Arion Bank to early 2011; Associate Professor, Department of Economics, University of Iceland until August 2019, when he was appointed as Central Bank Governor of Iceland
Audun Grønn	Director, International Department, Central Bank of Norway until the end of 2010; alternate Executive Director at IMF to early 2012, then Executive Director
Baldvin Björn Haraldsson	Lawyer, BBA Legal, 1998 to present
Barry Russell	Lead creditor representative; partner, Akin Gump Strauss Hauer & Feld LLP
Beat Siegenthaler	Chief Strategist Emerging Markets, TD Securities (Toronto Dominion) from July 2005 to March 2010; Executive Director, FX Strategy in UBS Investment Bank from March 2010 to March 2015; now Global Macro Advisor at UBS Investment Bank

Benedikt Gíslason	Senior Advisor, Seðlabanki Islands; Vice Chairman of task force (the ad hoc team) for liberalization of Capital Controls from November 2013
Bjarne Borgersen	CEO of Fokus Bank to 1999; lawyer; Chairman of Kaupthing Norway winding-up board
Bjarni Benediktsson	Prime Minister of Iceland from January 2017 to November 2017; Minister of Finance and Economic Affairs from May 2013 to January 2017 and from November 2017; leader of the Independence Party from 2009
Bjørn Richard Johansen	Managing Director, Corporate Communication, Glitnir, September 2005 to December 2008; communication advisor since 2008
Bjørn Skogstad Aamo	Director, Norwegian FSA, from 1993 to 2011
Else Mundal	Professor in Philology, University of Bergen since 1994. Expertise in Norse philology
Erling Selvig	Chairman of the Board, Norwegian FSA from 1986 to 2002
Erkki Liikanen	Governor of Bank of Finland since 2004; member of the Governing Council of ECB since 2004
Eva Joly	Advisor to the special prosecutor; French magistrate and prosecutor; representative at the European Parliament; French presidential candidate
Frank Brosens	Principal and Cofounder, Taconic Capital, since 1999
Freyr Hermannsson	Senior Advisor, Seðlabanki Islands; member of ad hoc committee on the Composition Agreement; now Head of Reserves management

Geir Bergvoll	Head of Division, DnB from 2007 to 2014; Chairman of the Board of Eksportfinans from 2008 to 2014 and CEO since 2014
Glenn Kim	Employee at Lehman Brothers from 1987 to 2008; head of the Icelandic State negotiation team in the negotiations on the 'offshore kronas'; advisor to the Greek Ministry of Finance from 2015 to 2017
Guðmundur Kr. Tómasson	Payment system, Seðlabanki Islands; Director, financial infrastructure
Guðmundur Sigbergsson	Deputy Director, Capital Controls Surveillance Unit, Seðlabanki Islands
Gylfi Magnússon	Economist; Associate Professor at University of Reykjavik to February 2009; Minister of Business Affairs from February 2009 to October 2010; Chairman of Supervisory Board, Central Bank of Iceland
Gylfi Zoega	Professor in Economics, member of the Monetary Policy Committee, Seðlabanki Islands
Haukur C. Benediktsson	Advisor in Seðlabanki value recovery unit from 2008 to 2010; CEO of ESI, the Asset Holding Company of the Central Bank of Iceland since 2013
Helge Skogseth Berg	Lawyer, Lynx; part of the team of Eva Joly; advisor to the special prosecutor
Hulda Gunnlaugsdottir	CEO, Landspitali University Hospital, 2009 to 2010
Jean-Michel Matt	Investigator, Lynx; part of the team of Eva Joly; advisor to the special prosecutor

John Chambers	Head of sovereign ratings, S&P, from 2005 to 2017
Jon Gunnar Jørgensen	Professor in Norse Philology, University of Oslo
Jón Þ. Sigurgeirsson	Now alternate Director, IMF; Head of the Central Bank governor office, Seðlabanki Islands; advisor in the Greek restructuring processes; member of the ad hoc group; now Director of the International Relations and General Secretariat
Jon Thor Gunnarsson	Director, corporate loans, Landsbanki UK; Manager, international seafood financing and commodity financing Landsbanki from 2004 to 2009; owner and CEO, Arctic Adventure
Jónína Sígrún Lárusdóttir	Permanent Secretary of the Ministry of Economic Affairs and Commerce from 2007 to 2010; Managing Director of the Legal Division in Arion Bank since 2010
Kenneth Garbade	Vice President/Senior Vice President, money and payments studies function, New York Fed, from 2000
Klemens Hjartar	Senior Partner, McKinsey & Company
Knut Kjær	CEO of Norges Bank Investment Management (the Oil Fund) from 1997 to 2008; President of Risk Metrics Group from 2009 to 2010; President Trient Asset Management from 2011 to 2017
Lee C. Buchheit	Head negotiator for the Icesave process, the Composition Agreement and the overhang settlement, Cleary Gottlieb Steen & Hamilton LLP

Lilja Dögg Alfreðsdóttir	Deputy Director, International Affairs and Market Operations, Seðlabanki to 2010; advisor, IMF to 2013; Deputy Director, Seðlabanki to 2014; member of the ad hoc team; economic advisor to Prime Minister Sigmundur Davið to 2015; Deputy Director, Seðlabanki to 2017; Minister of Foreign Affairs; Minister of Culture and Education
Nils Christian Øyen	Financial analyst, First Securities from 2001 to 2011; since then financial analyst in Sparebank1 Markets
Már Guðmundsson	Deputy Head of the Monetary and Economics Department and member of Senior Management of the BIS from 2004 to 2009; Governor, Central Bank of Iceland, from August 2009 to August 2019
Michael Ridley	Vice Chairman, investment banking, JPMorgan from 1998 to 2015; advisor to the Minister and Ministry of Finance, Iceland since March 2018
Michael Walsh	Advisor in the Kiribati Ministry of Finance from 2001 to 2006; Honorary Consul of the Republic of Kiribati; writer of the history of Kiribati
Miguel Fidalgo	Managing Director, Baupost Group to 2015; now founder and portfolio manager of Triarii Capital, LP
Mímir Kristjánsson	Journalist, Klassekampen
Murilo Portugal	Deputy Managing Director from 2006 to January 2011, IMF; DMD responsibility for the Iceland programme
NN	Executive, one of the three banks

NN	Executive, one of the three banks
NN	Investment Director, US hedge fund
NN	Investment Director, US hedge fund
Oláf Eliasson	Member, InDefence
Ólafur Hauksson	Special Prosecutor since 2009; now District Prosecutor
Ole-Jørgen Karlsen	Head of Section, Management and Crisis Readiness, The Financial Supervisory Authority of Norway
Paul Rawkins	Senior Director, Fitch Ratings
Pedro Malo Rob	Head of Strategy, Structured Products, Fixed Income, Bank of America-Merrill Lynch from 2005 to 2010. CFO of Alicorp until 2018. Now Strategy and Digital Vice President at Alicorp
Petter Sandgren	Head of Trading, Emerging Markets, SEB, from 2006 to 2010; now Partner in Obero Partners AB
Pål Ringholm	Head of Credit Research, Swedbank Norway to 2017; now in same position in Sparebank1 Markets
Ragnar Hafliðason	Deputy Director General at the Icelandic Financial Supervisory Authority, FME, since 1999
Rannveig Júníusdóttir	Capital Controls Surveillance Unit, Seðlabanki Islands
René Kallestrup	Economist, Central Bank of Iceland from 2007 to 2009; PhD fellow and candidate; Partner, Capital Four Management since 2015

Sigríður Logadóttir	General Counsel, Seðlabanki Islands since 2004
Sigrún Davíðsdóttir	Journalist and author of *Icelog*, a blog covering the Icelandic financial crisis and its aftermath
Sigurgeir B. Kristgeirsson	Managing Director, VSV, Vinnslustöðin Hf since 1999
Stefan Ingves	Central Bank Governor, Central Bank of Sweden, since 2006
Stefán Svavarsson	Member of the board of the FME; Chief Auditor, Seðlabanki Islands
Steingrímur J. Sigfússon	Minister of Finance of Iceland from 2009 to 2013; Member of Parliament since 1983; now Speaker of the parliament
Sturla Pálsson	Director, Treasury and Market Operations, Seðlabanki Islands, from 2005 to today
Svein Gjedrem	Central Bank Governor, Central Bank of Norway from 1999 to 2011; Permanent Undersecretary of State of the Ministry of Finance of Norway from 2011 until 2015; now chair Economic and Development Review Committee of the OECD
Terrence Checki	Executive Vice President and Head of the Emerging Markets and International Affairs Group, EMIA, of the Federal Reserve Bank of New York to 2014
Þórarinn Gunnar Pétursson	Chief Economist, Seðlabanki Islands, since February 2009
Thorvaldur Gylfason	Professor of Economics, University of Iceland, from 1983 to today

Thomas Eitzen	High yield and convertibles analyst, SEB, from 2006 to 2012; now Chief Analyst, fixed income, SEB
Timothy Geithner	President of the Federal Reserve Bank of New York to January 2009; Secretary of the US Treasury from January 2009 to January 2013
Tom Grøndahl	Advisor, Glitnir Estate, from 2012; Deputy CEO and CFO, DNB, from 1998 to 2008; Chairman Norwegian Securities Dealers' Association from 2011 to today
Tore Eriksen	Permanent Secretary General of the Ministry of Finance of Norway to 2011
Tryggvi Pálsson	Director Financial Stability, Central Bank of Iceland, from April 2001 to September 2011; Chairman ISB Holding, from November 2011 to April 2013; Chairman of the Board, Landsbanki, from April 2013 to April 2016
Trygve Young	Chief risk officer, DnB, Den norske Bank, from 2001

ABOUT THE AUTHOR

Svein Harald Øygard was appointed interim Central Bank Governor of Iceland in the midst of the country's deepest crisis. He became the first non-national to head an independent Central Bank. Previously, he was Deputy Minister of Finance for Norway and he has worked at McKinsey & Company as a corporate strategist for 22 years.

Photo: Fartein Rudjord